BLACK SMOKE

BLACK SMOKE

AFRICAN AMERICANS AND THE UNITED STATES OF BARBECUE

ADRIAN MILLER

A Ferris and Ferris Book

THE UNIVERSITY OF NORTH CAROLINA PRESS

Chapel Hill

This book was published under the
MARCIE COHEN FERRIS AND WILLIAM R. FERRIS IMPRINT
of the University of North Carolina Press.

© 2021 Adrian Miller
All rights reserved
Manufactured in the United States of America
Designed by Richard Hendel
Set in Chaparral and Publicity Gothic
by Tseng Information Systems, Inc.

The University of North Carolina Press has been
a member of the Green Press Initiative since 2003.

Cover photograph courtesy of Andrew Thomas Lee,
www.andrewthomaslee.com.

Library of Congress Cataloging-in-Publication Data
Names: Miller, Adrian, author.
Title: Black smoke : African Americans and the United States of barbecue / Adrian Miller.
Description: Chapel Hill : The University of North Carolina Press, [2021] |
"A Ferris and Ferris book." | Includes bibliographical references and index.
Identifiers: LCCN 2020051252 | ISBN 9781469662800 (cloth) |
ISBN 9781469662817 (ebook)
Subjects: LCSH: Barbecuing—United States. | African American
cooking. | African American cooks.
Classification: LCC TX840.B3 M529 2021 | DDC 641.7/60973—dc23
LC record available at https://lccn.loc.gov/2020051252

The recipe for Spicy Grilled Kebabs (Dibi Hausa) © Pierre Thiam.
Reprinted by permission from *YOLELE! Recipes from the Heart of Senegal*
by Pierre Thiam © 2008 Lake Isle Press, Inc.

For celebrated,

underappreciated, and

undiscovered

Black barbecuers . . .

everywhere.

CONTENTS

ILLUSTRATIONS

FIGURES

RECIPES

SIDEBARS

BLACK SMOKE

INTRODUCTION
KINDLING MY BARBECUE PASSION

If Black people ever had a national flag, it would be the Black Power fist holding a rib!—As told to the late "Barbecue Poet" Jake Adam York by an anonymous African American man, circa 2012

Luke, you're going to find that many of the truths we cling to depend greatly on our own point of view.—As told to Luke Skywalker by Obi-Wan Kenobi, Jedi Master, in Star Wars: Return of the Jedi, 1983

"Dude! You smell like bacon. I mean, like, reeeeaallly bad." Those words greeted me when I returned from lunch to the oppressively small office in the Colorado State Capitol that I shared with Leslie Herod, a fellow policy staffer for Governor Bill Ritter Jr. Herod's rebuke dry-rubbed me the wrong way for several reasons. First, she was horribly imprecise. My perfumed state wasn't caused by bacon. It was from a barbecue meal that I had recently consumed at Boney's Smokehouse (known simply as Boney's)—a Black-owned barbecue restaurant in downtown Denver. Second, I figured, that particular smell should be welcome in most social situations. Why call me out so vociferously? Third, I had to admit that she had a point. Unbeknown to Leslie, within precisely three hours from her olfactory observation, I desperately needed to smell clean. Why? I had a blind date with Barbara. At least, I'll call her Barbara because I like how it sounds like "barbecue" and I want to protect her privacy.

I'm not going to lie. I panicked. All week long, I had anticipated my date with Barbara, and I felt that I was about to seriously mess things up. Given the nature of my job as a senior policy analyst for Governor Ritter, I didn't have enough time to go home, bathe, change clothes, return, and still get all of my work done. I also tried, to no avail, to find some Febreze or a similar deodorizer. All of those people in that big, old building, and I couldn't find one bottle. I felt that had no other choice. I called Barbara, made up an excuse, and asked if we could reschedule. I just didn't want her thinking that I had a hygiene problem. After all, it wasn't like we had been connected through www.bbqpeoplemeet.com. If, by chance, you think I should have gone ahead with the date, I'm guessing that you've been either married, or single, *for a very long time*.

Though I was looking for Barbara's love, my love for barbecue was responsible for the fateful chain of events that began to unwind that very day. That morning, a longtime friend visiting from Washington, D.C., had called me and asked if I was free for lunch. I immediately thought about taking him to Boney's. It was close to the state capitol, and they serve a nice spread of Memphis-style barbecue. Two years earlier, Boney's enjoyed a fleeting moment of international attention when then vice-presidential candidate Joe Biden stopped by its small kiosk on Denver's 16th Street Mall. Biden was in town for the 2008 Democratic National Convention, and with about a hundred admirers and press corps in tow, he ordered five pulled pork sandwiches and some lemonade. Presumably, the generous order was for his family back at the hotel.

In addition to the kiosk, Boney's owners ran a restaurant located several blocks south on the same pedestrian mall. That's where my friend and I chatted and blissfully munched on the Smokehouse Sampler — a quarter pound each of beef brisket, pulled pork, spicy beef hot link sausage, sliced chicken breast, three succulent pork spareribs, four hickory-smoked, then flash-fried chicken wings, baked beans, coleslaw, collard greens, and house-made cornbread. I recall thinking that they were doing something with the pit, as a thin haze of smoke ascended and clung to the ceiling as we ate, adding to the atmosphere. My friend and I parted ways, and soon after I learned from Herod that I was sublimely, but not subtly, hickory smoked.

When I finally fessed up to Barbara a week later, she responded, "Oh, I looooove the smell of bacon." Of course. Sounds like true love, right? Well, over the course of a few more dates, I noticed that I was doing most of the work to keep the relationship alive. I decided to pull back a little bit, just to see if she would reach out and let a brother know that she's thinking about him. I'm pretty sure that she's playing hard to get because I haven't heard from her in almost a decade. Now you see why I didn't begin this introduction by writing, "Barbecue Is Love." For me, amorous matters tend to be complicated.

Shall I count the ways that my love for barbecue is the real, true thing? Whether it's "pork shoulder with outside brown" from the Carolinas, rib tips, hot links, and fries from the South Side of Chicago, "burnt ends" and pork spareribs from Kansas City, pork steaks in Kentucky, coleslaw-topped pork sandwiches and barbecue spaghetti in Memphis, snoots (pig snouts) and turkey ribs in St. Louis, or brisket, boudain (a variant spelling of boudin, a Louisiana meat and rice sausage), chopped beef, and hot links in Texas, I'd eat some version of barbecue every day if weren't for some predictable health consequences. Looking back on it, I see that my barbecue life was shaped by a collection of pivotal moments, including that special blind date.

I pause now to share something that usually loses me all street cred on the subject of barbecue: I was born in Denver, Colorado, and raised in one of its suburbs. Wait! Let me win you back. My parents, Hyman and Johnetta Miller, are southerners, born respectively in Helena, Arkansas, and Chattanooga, Tennessee. They made barbecue for our family every Memorial Day, July Fourth, and Labor Day holiday. As a teenager, my first full-time job was at Luther's BBQ—a national chain that had a restaurant in Aurora, one of Denver's eastern suburbs. I was a busboy and dishwasher, so I was never involved in the barbecue side of the operation, but that didn't stop me from coming home smelling like smoke. Hmmm, I'm beginning to sense a pattern here. Unfortunately, Luther's burned down in the 1990s, a fate too common for such enterprises.

Still, my restaurant barbecue life was one of arrested development. Barbecue was home cooking or something served at church functions, extended family gatherings, and social functions with friends. Restaurant barbecue was rare for us. During summer, my deepest thoughts about barbecue were on the level of "Man, this is good!" I know, not that impressive. I didn't think deeply about barbecue much at all. I certainly didn't think about barbecue and race.

Things changed for me in 2002 after I learned about the Southern Foodways Alliance (SFA). Founded in 1999, the SFA "documents, studies, and explores the diverse food cultures of the changing American South." I had emailed the executive director, John T. Edge, inquiring about how to join the still-new organization. Promptly responding, he asked me why I was interested in the alliance. I told him that I was thinking about writing a book on the history of soul food, and as a person living outside of the South, I figured that joining the SFA was a good way to learn more. He assured me that it would be: the SFA's symposium and field trips were taking barbecue as their annual theme that year, and June's field trip was to central Texas, a place I had never visited. I needed to learn more about barbecue for my soul food research anyway, because so many Black-run barbecue joints serve soul food side dishes (black-eyed peas, greens, mac 'n' cheese, and so

3

on), and so many soul food restaurants have barbecue options on their menu (beef, chicken, or pork), even if the meat is baked. Plus, the idea of eating barbecue for three days straight in central Texas seemed like a phenomenal fairytale. I went.

I felt a little guilty about the circumstances surrounding my trip. That June, while I was in Texas eating high, and low, on the hog, forest fires ravaged parts of Colorado. My beautiful state actually smelled like barbecue, and I remember light showers of ashes dusting Denver a few days before I left. Nonetheless, I flew to Austin for what turned out to be, for me, a life-changing excursion called "A Taste of Texas Barbecue."

I gorged on fantastic barbecue made by Black, white, and Latino barbecuers. I listened to presentations by fascinating thinkers. Most important, for the first time in my life, barbecue fell into a larger culinary, historical, and sociological context. Barbecue now had meaning. I marveled at barbecue's complexity, the various ways it was defined, and how easily all these things could become fighting words.

The field trip also impressed on me the power of food to bring a diverse group of people together. There we were, academics, food writers, enthusiasts (like me at that time), professional chefs, and restaurateurs all grubbing on barbecue. I made enduring friendships that last to this day with people who loved food as much as I do. After the field trip, I immediately signed up for the SFA's fall symposium happening the following October in Oxford, Mississippi, and I looked forward to augmenting my barbecue knowledge. Once there, I felt as though I was at an intellectual all-you-can-eat buffet. After the symposium, my desire to learn more about barbecue went from smoldering to a full-fledged passion.

At that time, I was too broke to travel the nation to sample regional styles of barbecue. I wondered, could I still satisfy my barbecue appetite while in Denver? Believe it or not, the Mile High City, like many other urban areas in the United States, was, and still is, experiencing a barbecue renaissance. In Colorado, this renaissance wasn't confined solely to Denver. To this day, barbecue-related competitions, festivals, food trucks, pop-up experiences, and restaurants await discovery in all parts of the state, from the big cities to small resort towns in the mountains.

Nationally, barbecue continues to trend well. For several years, the National Restaurant Association included barbecue in its annual "What's Hot Culinary Forecast." Today, barbecue-evoking descriptors like "burnt," "charred," and "smoked" are prolific on fine dining and fast-food restaurant menus alike. Thanks to a boom in barbecue-related food media, there's been a sharp uptick in people barbecuing at home with a level of sophistication that goes beyond grilling hamburgers and hot dogs.

Like so many weekend warriors, I felt a lot of pressure to hone my skills by taking barbecuing classes. I can manage good ribs and chicken, but my game still isn't tight when it comes to beef brisket and pork shoulder. I also became a certified barbecue judge with the Kansas City Barbeque Society in 2004. By far, that has been the best conversation starter that I've ever had. More than one person has said to me, "You worked in the White House? Well, that's interesting, *but you're a barbecue judge? I want to talk to you about that!*" By then, I felt that my barbecue personality was rounding out.

A few years after that, I was intensely engaged in writing my soul food history book. For the sake of research, I dutifully ate my way across the country. Though I focused on soul food restaurants, I hit up a lot of barbecue joints, but sometimes the barbecue options served are baked and drenched in barbecue sauce.

And I noticed that, to varying degrees, African American–owned, brick-and-mortar barbecue joints that once dominated urban restaurant scenes were dwindling. This is probably the long-term result of a combination of factors—regular restaurant business attrition, a younger generation uninterested in carrying on the barbecue baton being passed by their parents, and gentrification driving Black businesses out of Black neighborhoods. Denver is no exception to these trends. The last Black-owned barbecue joint in Five Points, Denver's historically Black and rapidly gentrifying neighborhood, closed its doors in 2014. Boney's closed late in 2020 because of the pandemic.

With the sense of loss so palpable, I'm always eager to introduce and show off Denver's remaining and beloved Black-owned restaurants. Yet the situation is not dire. Fortunately, other aspects of this barbecue culture thrive. I see African Americans continuing to barbecue for their churches, family, friends, social networks, and workplaces, whether it be in a backyard, in a restaurant, in a parking lot, or on the roadside. Some are even doing their thing on the competition circuit. Black barbecuers continue to innovate with what meat they barbecue, how they barbecue (even a repurposed file cabinet isn't off-limits), and where they sell it (strip club parking lots are more common locations than you would think).

Why do I care about the ups and downs of Black barbecue? Because this goes much deeper than just loving barbecue. It's because I've been radicalized by something that I watched on television. Actually, it's more about what I didn't see than what I saw.

5

In May 2004, I was intrigued by a Food Network promotional commercial for a one-hour special titled *Paula's Southern BBQ*. At the time, I knew much more about barbecue than I did about the host, Paula Deen, and I hoped that Deen would be presenting more of an overview of southern barbecue culture rather than simply a cooking lesson or a cooking competition. I tuned in for the show. By the time the credits rolled, though, my mouth was hanging open—not from an appetite for barbecue but because I was stunned that not one single African American had been interviewed on camera. I saw shots of Black people in the background doing the actual work, but they were anonymous and voiceless. Today it may seem naive, but I recall thinking, as I turned off the television, "Is this what Black barbecuers have become? They're just B-roll footage now?" Maybe I had misread the ads for the show—perhaps it had been promoted as *Paula's Scandinavian Barbecue, Sponsored by Alabama White Sauce*?

It's easy to beat up on Deen, given the racism and improper appropriation allegations that surfaced against her five years later, but I think the show's production team shares the blame. They are the ones who scout the locations to film, decide who is going to be on camera, and write the scripts. If she'd had it in her, Deen could have leveraged her star power to create a more inclusive show, but this certainly wasn't a solo act. Apparently, no one had the vision. I admittedly haven't seen that show but the one time, so in writing about my impressions of it, I'm relying on my shocked memories alone.

That episode struck me hard. It showed me that amid all this barbecue abundance, something was missing. What was missing was public acknowledgment of, and appreciation for, African American barbecuers and what they've contributed to this hallowed culinary tradition. Imagine that you're barbecuing meat directly over a slow fire. A nice equilibrium exists as the meat slowly cooks while fat periodically drips down to fuel the fire and provide flavor. Then, after several hours of cooking, someone decides to move the fire gradually to the side of the grill, completely away from the meat, and continues to barbecue indirectly. Black barbecuers have similarly been pushed from the center to barbecue's margins.

How could and did this happen? *Black Smoke* answers that question. I will bring Black barbecuers back to the center of the fire. I will show you how, gradually, softly, and tenderly, some very influential food media platforms, traditional and digital, that decide who gets attention and what stories get told, have fallen deeply in love with four types of White Guys Who Barbecue. They are: the Urban Hipster, who sports interesting tattoos, facial hair, and stylish eyeglasses; the Rural Bubba, who is an overalls-and-ball-cap-wearing kind of guy that one might see on the television shows *Duck Dynasty* or the *Dukes of Hazzard* (1970s version); the fine dining chefs who have entered the barbecue game; and some guys who are a combination of the above.

The media coverage of these white guys is so intense, comprehensive, and constant that one could easily wonder whether Black people barbecue at all. Before Rodney Scott won a 2018 James Beard Award for Best Chef Southeast, the most high-profile African American barbecuer was arguably the fictional Freddy Hayes, who regularly served ribs to the diabolical president Frank Underwood on Netflix's smash hit political satire *House of Cards*. The entire situation is annoying enough to make a nice guy like me develop a "resting barbecue face."

This is all so weird because *before* the 1990s, food media regularly and overwhelmingly acknowledged Black barbecuers—so much so that, to this day, many people believe that African Americans invented barbecue.

Moreover, a general consensus emerged in the late nineteenth century that African American barbecuers made the best and most authentic barbecue. Even racist whites failed to pass up barbecue made by an African American. During the reign of Black barbecuers, barbecue was largely represented in media as hearty, messy, working-class food that was the delicious result of extensive, exhaustive, and specialized menial labor. And though what these Black barbecuers did often absolutely fit the definition of culinary craft, it was rarely presented that way to the larger public.

Think about the current conventional wisdom about what barbecue is. Your mental checklist probably includes poor or tough cuts of meat that must be cooked at a low temperature for a long time ("low and slow," in current parlance), served unsauced—and with an appearance that's social media friendly. Such thinking gained steam in the 1990s, and it has consequently, and unfairly, redefined barbecue away from long-standing African American barbecue traditions. That's where the opening quotation from Obi-Wan Kenobi comes into play. I know that he lived a long time ago, in a galaxy far, far away, but what Kenobi told Luke Skywalker readily applies to the current state of barbecue. So many are heavily invested in drawing partisan lines about what true barbecue is, yet they're unwilling to see how arbitrarily those lines are drawn. As *Black Smoke* will explain, defining barbecue, locally and globally, is highly dependent on time, place, class, race, and a fair amount of mythmaking.

Black Smoke matters because there's so much more at stake with barbecue than ever before. Barbecue's profile is much higher in terms of scope, cultural value, and potential profitability. Barbecue is now viewed as an urbanized, craft cuisine manufactured by so-called pitmasters with their own tribe of foodie followers. A barbecuer savvy in public relations and social media—or any personality with just enough barbecue expertise to exude authority—can now make a lot of money by selling high-priced barbecue, hosting special events, and hawking a line of accessories, cookbooks, and instructional videos. Barbecue circuit competitors have won up to a hundred thousand dollars in just one weekend.

Even barbecue writers may get in on this lucrative act. I was surprised to learn that Steven Raichlen, a prolific barbecue writer, has his own line of barbecuer gear. He's inspired me to develop a line of very stretchable barbecue clothing with elastic in strategic places. Look for it soon on the fashion runways of Milan and Paris.

As barbecue's cultural terrain has shifted and streams of revenue have flowed, the mainstream food media's lack of inclusive coverage has effectively told African American barbecuers: "We're just not that into you." That means Black barbecuers haven't prospered as much as their white colleagues even though they've made significant contributions to the culinary tradition.

The contemporary barbecue scene is déjà vu for me. Since the early 2000s, African American chefs—some by choice, others by circumstance or from a lack of resources—have missed opportunities to cash in on food traditions that they either created or raised to an art form. Think fried chicken (especially the Nashville hot version), shrimp and grits, and whole-animal cooking. The same need not happen with barbecue. I want African Americans to benefit in these barbecue boom times. *Black Smoke* changes the current narrative by informing readers about African American barbecue culture's glorious past, vibrant present, and expansive future.

Black Smoke is part celebration and part restoration. *Black Smoke* shows how African American barbecue culture unfolds and profiles the fascinating people who give it life and continue to push its boundaries. *Black Smoke* is a story of creativity and resilience in a time of tremendous economic, political, social, and racial challenges. *Black Smoke* shows that the only way to ignite a serious discussion about American barbecue is by including African Americans. *Black Smoke* is not intended to be a revival or some sort of fresh breath on the glowing embers of a dying culinary tradition. To the contrary, *Black Smoke* shows that African American barbecue traditions endure and that barbecue storytelling to the broader public should be more inclusive.

I've delved deeply into barbecue history via hundreds of books, cookbooks, newspapers, online resources, oral histories, and periodicals. I've interviewed people in the barbecue industry. I've talked to folks who are barbecue fans. I've consumed barbecue across the country (ok, that part wasn't hard) in more than two hundred restaurants. I've judged competition barbecue. I've even advocated for a Colorado regional barbecue style (not easy).

I now know why barbecue is an adjective, a noun, a verb, and a way of life . . . *my life*. In short, I've become an evangelist for African American barbecue—not one with the fervor to warn that the end times of African American barbecue are near but one who gleefully sees a universe of possibilities.

Black Smoke starts with the story of Native American meat cooking techniques before European contact, and it shows how those got mashed up with African and European ways of cooking and seasoning meat to become something different that we now call barbecue. We'll take a look at how enslaved African Americans took what they learned from Native Americans and eventually become barbecue's primary experts and ambassadors across the United States and, later, the world. We'll then examine how African American barbecue played out in subcultures including restaurants, competitions, and churches. We'll also explore what makes Black barbecue exceptional. We'll then look back across a couple of centuries of how the media covered Black barbecue brilliance and see why the current media exclusion is so bewildering. We'll end by opining on the future of African American barbecue.

Ultimately, *Black Smoke* presents an alternate history of barbecue, one centered in an African American perspective. This view sheds light on how barbecue performs within Black culture and how class, race, and power influence that performance. Periodically, I'll define what barbecue meant in a particular time to African Americans and how that was in tune with, ran parallel to, or completely differed from the mainstream definition—that is, how white people defined this particular food.

In looking at how race has shaped the development and enjoyment of barbecue, I recognize that neither the Black nor the white community is monolithic with respect to barbecue as a cuisine and the social, particularly racial, context that surrounds it. *Black Smoke* shows how the racial attitudes of whites toward Blacks in effect forced barbecue into the emerging foodways of enslaved African Americans. In a twist, racial attitudes objectified and even celebrated aspects of the Black barbecue aesthetic as it developed. But in the end, white racial attitudes have essentially managed to push the story of Black barbecue to the margins, off camera, off screen, and off the usual barbecue trail. So, in picking up this book you'll be introduced to a lot of people you've never heard of, people who shaped and invigorated a vital culinary tradition. Your sense of what barbecue is will be challenged. There'll be truth-telling, but it will be fair.

Let me extinguish some possible rhetorical flare-ups right now. By celebrating Black barbecuers, *Black Smoke* does not declare that people of other colors, especially white people, can't cook barbecue. Some of my best friends are articulate white people who voted for President Barack Obama and happen to make fantastic barbecue. This is about exclusion, not exclusivity. *Black Smoke* endeavors to reorient barbecue's future in the United States to be much more like its past: delicious, diverse, fun, and appreciative of African American contributions.

A quick word on ethnic descriptors. Even though they aren't always equivalent, I use the terms "Native American" and "Indigenous" interchangeably, as I do with the terms "African American" and "Black" and "European" and "white."

I'll define, and redefine, barbecue in later chapters, but for now, let's talk about *Black Smoke*'s recipes. They are primarily from African Americans, and they represent an expansive view of barbecue, embracing grilling, indirect smoking, and unconventional techniques. I know this is greatly unsatisfying for some, but I did this for two reasons. First, it's difficult these days to find traditional barbecue prepared entirely with wood smoke. As you'll see, lots of joints are being sneaky. Second, when I found such artists, they weren't giving up any information. Written accounts of traditional barbecue are so vague that it's very hard to reverse engineer recipes from those descriptions without having a research and development department at my beck and call, which I definitely don't have.

Please join me at this cookout. Fix a plate, play some bones (dominoes), bust some spades (a card game), tell stories, and do whatever you like to do when someone has a grill going. While you read *Black Smoke*, picture me waving with one hand that Black national barbecue flag that I mentioned in the epigraph while holding a bottle of Gates Bar-B-Q Sauce (my overall favorite commercial barbecue sauce) in the other. All the while, I'll sing, mostly on-key, that memorable refrain from the Ohio Players' classic song, "Fire": "Burnin', burnin', burnin', burnin'"!

PIT SMOKED
BARBECUE'S NATIVE AMERICAN FOUNDATION

In cooking outdoors sooner or later we have to acknowledge
our everlasting debt to the original American, the Indian.
— *The Browns in* Outdoor Cooking

Barbecue's history, or prehistory to be exact, begins with the Indigenous peoples in the Americas. Yet getting down to the bone of the cuisine's beginnings is much like the wonderfully messy endeavor of eating barbecue—you must get in there, bite down, and pull things apart. As we do so, let me first recognize the foundational presence of those who came before. I acknowledge that I wrote this book in Denver, Colorado, on the ancestral land of the Arapaho, Cheyenne, Sioux, and Ute peoples.

Since Native Americans had oral traditions, I'm relying on written accounts and illustrations by Europeans who encountered and observed barbecue in the Americas. In their descriptions, "barbecue" is spelled in a variety of ways and sloppily applied to a range of cooking methods and contexts. Consequently, the definition of "barbecue" frequently changed from the 1500s to the 1700s. Still, the meager sources available provide valuable information on how barbecue eventually formed a consistent identity with white people, acquired a terroir, diminished its Native American roots, and gained an African American vibe.

I usually get a double take when I tell someone that barbecue is rooted in Native American culinary traditions. "Black people invented barbecue, right?" is the usual sentiment. I understand why people think that way, given that African Americans have long been prominent barbecuers in so many communities. But let's face it: people were here, they knew the lands and the animals, and they were cooking meat over a fire before others arrived. Opinions differ on how Native practices influence the barbecue we make today. A wealth of accounts gives us clues, and two books that are very helpful in sorting out barbecue's early history are *Savage Barbecue* by Andrew Warnes and *Virginia Barbecue* by Joseph Haynes.

One of the earliest mentions relating to what we think of today as barbecue came in 1513, when, using source material from the ship's crew, Andrés Bernáldez published a recap of Christopher Columbus's second voyage to the Americas. In it, he shares the story of how Columbus sailed into what we now call Guantanamo Bay:

> In that harbour there was no settlement, and as they entered it, they saw to the right hand many fires close to the sea and a dog and two beds, but no people. They went on shore and found more than four quintals of fish cooking over the fire, and rabbits, and two serpents, and very near there in many places they were laid at the foot of the trees. In many places there were many serpents, the most disgusting and nauseating things which men ever saw, all with their mouths sewn up. And they were the colour of dry wood, and the skin of the whole body was very wrinkled, especially that of their heads, and it fell down over their eyes. . . . The admiral ordered the fish to be taken, and with it refreshed his men.[1]

Foreshadowing what Europeans would do with much of the Americas, Columbus and crew took and devoured everything they considered edible, without asking permission. Soon afterward, they met the Taino people, whose encampment they had raided. The Tainos communicated that they were preparing a feast. When Columbus explained what they had done, the Tainos "were greatly rejoiced when they knew that they had not taken the serpents, and replied that all was well, since they would fish again at night."[2] Historians later surmised that these "serpents" were iguanas.

Bernáldez's anecdote fueled the imaginations of European readers, and it established an early narrative about barbecue that often remains critically unchallenged. The basic story from a European-heritage perspective goes something like this: Europeans arrived in the West Indies, and they stumbled on strange people doing a strange type of slow cooking that involved small animals and plants laid on a wooden platform raised above a fire. Though unfamiliar, the food was delicious. In time, the Europeans, and enslaved Africans, traveled from the Caribbean to the colonies in British North America, applied those island cooking methods they'd observed to the European animals (cows, pigs, and sheep) that they had introduced in the colonies—and barbecue was born. Other narratives reach the same conclusion but greatly diminish or leave out entirely the Caribbean part of the story. And some storytellers insist that barbecue's only essential element is pork. From this viewpoint, barbecue doesn't begin before the Spanish explorer Hernando de Soto arrived in present-day Tampa, Florida, with thirteen pigs in 1539.[3] All of these origin theories treat the North American mainland as a blank slate and its original inhabitants as inconsequential.

Let's pause for a moment to look at what barbecue meant at this time. Andrew Warnes looked into the early etymology of the word "barbecue" and concluded, "It seems likely, then, that, throughout the Caribbean before Columbus, *barbacoa* was nothing more sinister than a framework of wood on which one might sleep, store maize, or suspend foods high enough above a fire that they could be left smoking with little risk of spoiling."[4] Joseph Haynes adds that "the words *barbacoa* and *barbecue* used in sixteenth- and seventeenth-century literature were nouns used to refer to platforms, tables, beds, bridges, houses, corncribs, and grills used for preparing foods."[5] Eventually, Spaniards used *barbacoa* as a generic term for the cooking apparatus, the cooking process, and the type of meat cooked this way. The English followed suit with this linguistic promiscuity, instead using their own word "barbecue."[6]

Now back to the cooking. At the time of sustained European contact, Indigenous peoples used multiple meat cooking techniques in the Americas. Our focus here is on what Europeans observed in the American South. These techniques may generally be categorized as:

1. Piercing sticks
2. A rotating spit over a fire
3. A raised platform
4. A vertical hole
5. A shallow pit

Each of these methods possessed the building blocks to become barbecue: wood, fire, meat, and skilled cooks. But how does each technique match up to what whites would call barbecue by the turn of the eighteenth century? Let's take a closer look at each.

PIERCING STICKS

With this method, the sticks were either stuck in the ground perpendicular to the fire, then angled toward the fire, or the weight of the meat morsel at the end of the stick bent it toward or over the fire. Sometimes multiple sticks were used to create a latticed frame. An Englishman named Mark Catesby observed this cooking method in the 1720s: "The manner of their roasting, is by thrusting sticks through pieces of meat, sticking them around the fire, and often turning them."[7] A Frenchman named Antoine-Simon Le Page du Pratz observed the practice while living among the Natchez in present-day Louisiana during the same time period. He wrote, "When the natives wish to roast meat in order to eat it at once, which seldom happens except during the hunting season, they cut off the portion of the bison which they wish to eat, which

Piercing sticks technique.
Illustration by Ben Dodd.

is usually the fillet. They put it on the end of a wooden spit planted in the earth and inclined towards the fire. They take care to turn this spit from time to time, which cooks the meat as well as a spit turned before the fire with much regularity."[8] For larger pieces of meat, several sticks would be used to create a vertical framework on which the meat rested. The cook's purpose for this method depended much on the intensity of the fire. If the fire was kept at very low, the food was being dried for preservation. If the fire was hotter, this method was more like grilling with the morsels intended for immediate consumption. Either way, the technique would not become what whites would call barbecue.

THE ROTATING SPIT

Colonial-era Europeans found this type of cooking most familiar. Instead of the metal rods that European cooks would have used, Indige-

Rotating spit technique.
Illustration by Ben Dodd.

nous people pierced chunks of meat with a large, sharpened piece of wood. That piece of wood in turn rested horizontally on two forked pieces of wood, spaced apart and planted vertically in the ground. The horizontal piece of wood through the meat was then turned by hand so that the meat roasted as it rotated over a fire and cooked evenly.

An Englishman named John Smith described spit cooking in the early 1600s while living among the Powhatans in present-day Virginia. "Their fish and flesh they boyle either very tenderly, or broyle it so long on hurdles over the fire; or else, after the Spanish fashion, putting it on a spit, they turne first the one side, then the other, til it be as drie as their jerkin beefe in the west Indies, that they may keepe it a month or more without putrifying."[9] He, and others, observed Indigenous peoples as far north as present-day Delaware, and as far west as the Great Plains, using the spit-cooking method, especially when they cooked bison.[10] Notably, Smith signals that this preparation was for later use versus immediate consumption. The closest analogue to a spit in contemporary meat cooking is a rotisserie. Getting closer, but still not what would become barbecue.

THE RAISED PLATFORM

In 1591, a Flemish engraver named Theodor de Bry created some of the earliest and most popular barbecue images for a western European audience. De Bry claimed that the engraving was based on a long-lost watercolor painting by Frenchman Jacques Le Moyne de Morgues, who accompanied an expedition to the area around present-day Jacksonville in the 1560s. That watercolor ostensibly depicts members of the Timucua tribe, whose ancestral homeland is northeastern Florida and

Raised platform technique.
Illustration by Ben Dodd.

southeastern Georgia, cooking small reptiles on a raised platform. De Bry's engraving created a highly profitable sensation in Europe. It also brought together so many elements for barbecue researchers like me: Native Americans, smoking whole animals on a raised platform, in the American South!

But the image, as well as many others of the Timucuas, is so riddled with errors and inconsistencies that Florida archaeologist Jerald T. Milanich asserts we've been "duped." Milanich "question[s] whether Jacques le Moyne actually did any paintings of Florida Indians," and he further concludes that the painting is likely based on images of Indigenous people barbecuing in South America.[11]

Putting aside de Bry's and Le Moyne's historical head fake, some Indigenous peoples in the American South did use this method during the 1700s. John Smith's experience with the Powhatans in Virginia was much like Catesby's observations of tribes in the Carolinas. "Besides roasting and boiling, they *barbecue* most of the flesh of the larger animals, such as buffalo's [*sic*], bear and deer; this is performed very gradually, over a slow clear fire, upon a large wooden gridiron, raised two feet above the fire."[12] According to du Pratz, the Natchez in Louisiana also cooked that way.

This cooking method didn't die out. In a 1990s cookbook about traditional Cherokee cooking, Lulu Gibbons gives a recipe for barbecued fish that a fifteenth-century Indigenous cook would immediately recognize: "Barbecued Fish—Build a rack with four corners of forked sticks driven into the ground, about 2½ feet high. Lay hickory sticks across rack. Clean fish and lay on hickory rack. Build fire of hickory wood—not too much fire; just so it will smoke good. Let fish cook half a day or until they are done. Fish may be eaten as is, or made into soup which is very good."[13] Most notably, Gibbons describes the fish as "barbecued." Sounds good in today's expanded definition of barbecue, but not in the narrower one that whites used in the eighteenth and nineteenth centuries.

THE VERTICAL HOLE

One finds the practice of cooking in a vertical hole, otherwise known as "earth ovens," in cultures around the world. It was common among Indigenous peoples across a broad swath of North America—from Mexico northward to the Great Plains and eastward to the American South. A 2014 article for *American Antiquity* magazine defined an earth oven as "a layered cooking of fire, heated rocks (usually), food, green-plant

Vertical hole technique.
Illustration by Ben Dodd.

packing materials, and sediment designed to bake food in moist heat at an even, relatively low temperature for periods of time ranging from a few hours to several days."[14] Typically someone dug a hole, started a fire at the bottom with some fuel source, and later added stones to retain heat. Alternatively, a separate fire was started above ground, stones were heated in the fire, and then the stones were dropped in the hole.

After the stones were sufficiently heated, meat, vegetables, and vegetation were added in alternating layers above the stones. Some cooks took the extra step of wrapping each chunk of meat with a protective layer of vegetation. Next, the hole was covered by either filling it back up with dirt or by adding a "lid" made from an animal hide. The vertical walls of dirt retained the heat. By the appointed time, usually the next morning, the meat was cooked and moist from the steamy environment created by the earth oven. If the meat was wrapped, it often lacked a smoky flavor.

Archaeological evidence of vertical-hole cooking, also called "pit cooking," exists in Maryland and Virginia. As author Jonathan Deutsch wrote in *Barbecue: A Global History*: "Atlantic Coast Native Americans appear also to have practised pit barbecuing. . . . Gerard Fowke, working on behalf of the U.S. Bureau of Ethnology, located 'more than 20 barbecue holes' in his investigations of the Potomac region. The holes had clearly been used for barbecue, as the bottoms were 'much burned' and 'in one was a quantity of burned stones.' The pits, which were circular in shape and twice as wide at the top as at the bottom, also contained charcoal, animal bones and mussel shells."[15] Earth ovens were not limited to the Atlantic Coast, and the method endured in other parts of the South well into the nineteenth century. During his Mississippi Valley journey in the years 1809–11, naturalist John Bradbury observed "barbique" events held by Indians in that region where meat was cooked "after the Indian method" in a covered pit filled with hot stones.[16]

In the late 1800s, well after barbecue had established a southern identity, large chunks of beef were cooked by digging holes and wrapping the meat in vegetation or moistened burlap or paper. This type of barbecue was more prevalent in the southwestern United States, especially in Arizona, California, Oklahoma, and western Texas during much of the twentieth century. Stripped of its Indigenous roots, this method would eventually be called "barbecue," but it was modified by the words "cowboy," "Spanish," or "western." Barbecuing this way is less common today, but it endures in the form *barbacoa* (a more specific use of an old term). Today, barbacoa is strongly associated with Latino people in South Texas and Mexico. Contemporary cooks make cows' heads (*cabeza*), goat (*cabrito*), and lamb (often called barbacoa on menus) by using vertical, metal pits instead of dirt-based earth ovens. Latinos considered this barbecue, but whites did not during the colonial period. That changed when barbecue's definitional tent expanded in the nineteenth century.

THE SHALLOW PIT

This shallow pit is similar to the vertical hole method, but the hole is not as deep, usually just deep enough to contain the fuel source (wood and possibly some stones) and the fire. Cooks either laid the meat directly on the coals or wrapped it in a protective bundle of vegetation or clay. Thus, food was cooked at ground level. This method gets us closest to the mainstream consensus of what barbecue was in the late eighteenth and nineteenth centuries.

John Clayton, a clergyman in Virginia circa 1687, wrote about "Vir-

Shallow pit technique.
Illustration by Ben Dodd.

ginia's Indians 'barbecueted' venison by wrapping it in leaves and roasting it in the embers."[17] Joseph Haynes surmises that Clayton probably described the use of an earth oven.[18] This type of cooking also extended northward to the Algonquian people living in present-day southern New England. In their informative book on New England foodways, Keith Stavely and Kathleen Fitzgerald note that "archaeological evidence indicates that clams and oysters were roasted or baked, sometimes in shallow round pits. . . . Lobsters were also 'roasted or dried in the smoak.'"[19] As the Powhatans' cooking method was a precursor to barbecue, so the Algonquian method inspired the modern-day oyster roasts and clambakes. As one who has been to both, I see the similarities.

Tribes farther inland also did shallow-pit cooking. In Oklahoma, Mrs. Lena Finley Barnard contributed a recipe for dried fish (*Kee-qus-no-swa Po-son-gee*) cooked in a shallow pit to the *Indian Woman's Club of Tulsa* cookbook printed in 1933.[20] Barnard was of Piankeshaw heritage, a tribe that lived in parts of present-day Indiana and Ohio. Revealing a culinary continuity well into the 1980s, Janie Hendrix added a similar recipe for cooking fish in her *Cherokee Cookbook*.[21] European colonists in the Americas melded shallow-pit cooking with their culinary traditions.

How did that happen? The roughly century-long (1600s to 1700s) transition from Indigenous meat cooking to barbecue isn't well documented, but we can infer some things by comparing the before and after. British colonists initially adopted Native food practices in order to stave off starvation. Once they were more food secure, the colonists either adopted, modified, or entirely rejected what they learned from Indigenous peoples. Simultaneously, they tried to transplant in the colonies the ways they knew how to produce, procure, process, preserve, and cook food as they did in their home country. Barbecue fell into a middle ground as a modified food because there wasn't anything quite like it back in Europe. The closest was the ox roast culinary tradition, which we'll later see was actually something entirely different. Let's look at how British colonists changed the critical elements of barbecue: the animals, the cooking process, and its social context.

Native Americans didn't domesticate animals, so they often barbecued the wild animals they caught.[22] Small animals were cooked whole, and larger animals such as bears, bison, and venison were first processed into small parts. Du Pratz, who observed Natchez people in Louisiana in the 1720s, wrote: "That the meat may keep during the time they are hunting and that it may serve as nourishment for their families for a certain time, the men during the chase have all the flesh of the thighs, shoulders, and most fleshy parts smoked, except the hump and the tongue, which they eat on the spot. All the meat that is smoked is cut into flat pieces to cook it well. . . . Thus they smoke their meat, which can be carried everywhere and preserved as long as it is desired."[23] Indigenous cooks took a long-term view indeed, and they often favored preservation over immediate feasting with the smoked meat used in a variety of future food preparations. The British colonists were certainly interested in preserved food, but they took the opposite view from Native Americans when it came to barbecue. Barbecue was party food.

By changing the purpose for barbecuing, the British colonists also changed the barbecuing process. When they preserved meat for later use, they salted or smoked meat as they did back in Europe. They did so in a contained building (usually called a smokehouse) where a slow fire burned on the building's floor and the rising smoke permeated meat suspended above, often tied to a rafter. Such smokehouses became an important part of small farms and the larger plantations in the antebellum South. Barbecue initially took form when British colonists, through experimentation, bent Indigenous meat cooking methods to their tastes by fusing it with their own quick meat cooking technique, something called carbonadoing.

In *Virginia Barbecue*, Joseph Haynes explains that "the verb *carbonadoing* comes from the English noun *carbonado*, just as the English verb *barbecuing* derives from the noun *barbecue*."[24]

> Carbonado goes back to at least the fifteenth century. An Italian cookbook of that year includes a recipe for meat cooked "in carbone" or on the coals. According to some scholars, this is the origin of the sixteenth- and seventeenth-century English carbonados. Most old English recipes for carbonado call for scoring or beating the meat with the back of a knife before grilling it on a gridiron without [Gervase] Markham's broiling iron or [Sir Hugh] Platt's paper pan. Scoring meat, as prescribed in carbonado recipes, increases its surface area, exposing more surface to high heat. This improves the flavor of the meat due to the increased area subject to caramelization and browning.[25]

During this era, if meat cooking were viewed as a spectrum, Indigenous smoking methods would be on one end and carbonadoing would be on the other. Barbecue, as we understand it today, falls somewhere in between because the meat is cooked at a higher temperature and faster than smoking but at a lower temperature and a longer amount of time than grilling and broiling. Importantly, carbonadoing changed barbecue's flavor profile. By cooking meat closer to the coals, the vaporizing fat distinctly and strongly flavored the meat, in contrast to the subtle smoke flavor that was infused in meat traditionally cooked by Indigenous peoples.[26]

Back in England, British cooks transplanted a modified form of barbecue by carbonadoing meat on a gridiron, a "cooking utensil" in use since the 1300s, "formed of parallel bars of iron or other metal in a frame, usually supported on short legs, and used for broiling flesh and fish over a fire."[27] One example of an early barbecue recipe for home use was "To Barbecue a Hog" in Nathan Bailey's *Dictionarium Domesticum: Being a New and Compleat Household Dictionary* (1726). After Bailey instructed his readers on how to butcher the hog, he added:

> Having a large iron frame or gridiron with two or three ribs, let it upon an iron stand about three foot and a half high, and upon that lay the hog, spread open with the belly sides downwards with a good charcoal fire underneath it, broil that side till it is enough at the same side, flouring the back often.
>
> This should be done in some out-house or yard with a tent over it.
>
> When the belly side is done enough and turn'd upwards so as to be steady upon the gridiron or barbecue, pour into the belly of the hog three or four quarts of water and half that quantity of wine.[28]

British-heritage cooks on both sides of the Atlantic Ocean used Bailey's cookbook. Those in the Virginia colony carbonadoed smaller cuts of meat instead of whole animals and imprecisely called it barbecue, which caused further confusion about the word.

This ersatz, make-it-indoors-kind-of-barbecue shows up later in some of the most iconic cookbooks of the American South, notably *The Virginia House-wife* (1824) and *The Kentucky Housewife* (1839). Ersatz barbecue continues to the present day. Far too many restaurants promise "pit-smoked barbecue" on their menus, but diners often get something boiled, steamed, baked, or heavily sauced.

Cooking on a gridiron was impractical for effectively fusing carbonadoing with large-scale, whole-animal barbecuing outdoors. Drawing on the various Indigenous meat-cooking practices, colonial cooks merged the spit and shallow pit methods. Cooks impaled smaller, whole animals (such as a young pig) through the mouth with a pole. Larger animals, typically hogs and sheep, were butterflied, and poles were thrust through the sides of the carcass. Cows were cut into quarters first and then given the treatment above. The poles were long enough to be laid across a trench (a couple of feet deep) that was filled with burning coals.

IN THE SMOKE WITH
HENRY "POPPA" MILLER

Henry "Poppa" Miller's influence on Kansas City barbecue might have been completely lost were it not for Dan Turner. Turner, a culinary arts instructor at the Johnson County College in Kansas, learned of this story, informed Doug Worgul, and connected him to Bob Miller, Poppa's grandson. Worgul was so impressed by Miller's story that he included a profile of him in his excellent book on Kansas City barbecue, *The Grand Barbecue*. Most of what we know about Poppa Miller is from an oral history provided by Bob Miller. I just have to warn you that things might get a little confusing because we've got several Millers involved (a good thing, I think), and Bob Miller and his great-great-grandfather share a first name. From now on, the former is "Bob the Younger," and the latter is "Bob the Elder."

Poppa Miller was born in Oklahoma in 1861 to an African American mother and a Cherokee father. As reported in a local newspaper, Bob the Elder had "learned the art from an Old Indian barbecuer on the Indian Reservation" and, in turn, passed it along to his grandson, Poppa Miller.[1] Bob the Elder taught him well. Poppa Miller eventually earned the title "The Barbecue King" after successfully barbecuing fifteen thousand pounds of beef, pork, and mutton for a group of Fort Arkansas businessmen in 1902.[2]

Poppa Miller had quite the culinary résumé, cooking at various restaurants and hotels in Arkansas, Colorado, Kansas, Missouri, and Oklahoma. According to Bob the Younger:

> Henry Miller was fluent in several Indian languages and was fluent in French and German. . . . He also sold barbecue behind the house where he lived in Kansas City, Mo. He was also a master stone mason and had built many barbecue pits throughout the Kansas City area. He cooked for several years in Kansas City restaurants and hotels. A few of these were the Old Savoy in 1903, the Coates House on Broadway and the old Wishbone Restaurant. My father told me he was the cook that made the original Wishbone salad dressing. He would make the dressing often in his restaurant. . . . Henry Miller moved to Leavenworth and got married to my mother [Clifton] and raised three sons.[3]

1. "Success of Miller in Barbecuing Due to Indian Recipe," *Leavenworth (Kans.) Post*, Aug. 22, 1922, 4.

2. "Success of Miller."

3. Worgul, *Grand Barbecue*, 19.

*Henry "Poppa" Miller,
Leavenworth, Kansas.
Illustration by Dion Harris.*

After getting married, Poppa Miller moved to Leavenworth, Kansas, and ran a restaurant renowned for its barbecue as well as its fruitcake. Poppa Miller attributed his fruitcake's popularity to a secret ingredient—whisky. The problem was that Poppa Miller sold those fruitcakes during Prohibition, which made them illegal. He got caught, and it cost him a hundred-dollar fine and thirty days in jail.[4]

Poppa Miller was unusual for his era in that local media took the time to interview him and treated him as a barbecue authority without trying to caricature or diminish him. From these interviews, readers gained rare insight into the mind of a turn-of-the-twentieth-century barbecue cook. One thing that is quite clear is that he held strong opinions about barbecue. In fact, if you know anything about Kansas City barbecue sauce, it may surprise you that he loathed one of its signature elements. In a 1922 newspaper interview, Poppa Miller emphatically said, "Many barbecuers use tomatoes, Spanish sauce, allspice, and cloves in making a seasoning for their meats. . . . This should not be done. Everyone knows that the flavor of barbecued meat comes from allowing the smoke of good old hickory wood to penetrate the meat, and not from any tomatoes or spice. I use a special sauce made by a secret recipe, which I have found to be the very best for use with barbecued meat. But it contains none of the ingredients which spoil the good old hickory smoke flavor."[5]

Some say that genetic traits can skip a generation, and this is certainly the case for this Miller clan's disdain of tomato-based sauces. Bob the Younger, certainly channeling Poppa Miller, told Worgul:

Now we all know how catsup, puree paste got into barbecue sauces. Today sauces aren't even cooked. Most sauces are mixed loaded with preservatives and put into about three styles of glass and shipped. I call these sauces Johnny-Come-Lately sauces. They come from everywhere. . . . Ever since tomato catsup was introduced into

4. "His Cakes Popular," *Council Grove (Kans.) Republican*, Jan. 31, 1929, 1.

5. "Success of Miller."

today's modern barbecue sauce, people have been misled about barbecue sauce. Catsup is thick and lays on top of the meat or food it's used on. Real old-fashioned barbecue sauce has no tomatoes in its contents. It is much thinner and is put on the meats for real barbecue taste. You don't get the two different items mixed up. Real barbecue is where "finger-lickin' good" originated.[6]

The Millers speak about BBQ sauce with a power that recalls Malcolm X's stern warning: "You've been had! You've been took! You've been hoodwinked! Bamboozled! Led astray! Run amok!"[7] News to all of us tomato-based barbecue sauce lovers, including me. What then provides the base instead? These Millers had a strong affinity for the vinegar-based barbecue sauces often tasted in the Carolinas and Virginia.

The pinnacle of Poppa Miller's barbecue career was also a glorious homecoming. In late 1922, the Oklahoma governor-elect John C. Walton inauguration committee contacted Poppa Miller, and they called on him to travel from Kansas to help prepare a mammoth barbecue. Poppa Miller's local newspaper announced: "Henry Miller ... the barbecue king ... has been called to Oklahoma City, Okla., to take over the preparations to be given at the inauguration of the governor of Oklahoma."[8] When it came to large-scale barbecues, nineteenth- and twentieth-century newspapers were notorious for their hyperbolic estimates of the number of attendees. If the estimated 150,000 attendees for this barbecue is accurate, it was arguably the largest barbecue in recorded world history.

Walton had pledged as a candidate that "when he got into office he would hold an old-fashioned barbecue and dance for everyone in the State."[9] It's unclear whether Miller actually made the trip and superintended the monstrous affair. Other media reports indicate that I. R. McCann, a white man from Pauls Valley, Oklahoma, was actually in charge.[10] If Miller ever elaborated on his role at that famous barbecue, it has not yet been found.

That inaugural barbecue cost a whopping $100,000 in 1923, roughly $1,549,285.71 in 2020 dollars.[11] Take a gander at the shopping list, and you'll see why: 100,000 buns, 100,000 loaves of bread, 5,000 chickens, 1,000 pounds of pepper, 1,000 rabbits, 1,000 squirrels, groundhogs, and frog legs, 1,000 turkeys, 500 beef cattle, 500 ducks and geese, 250 bushels of onions, 200 hogs, 200 possums (and "sweet taters" to go with them), 10 bison, 10 bears, 10 deer, 10 antelope, 5 tons of coffee, 5 tons of salt, and 5 tons of sugar.[12]

6. Worgul, *Grand Barbecue*, 20.

7. Smith, "Unlikely Echo."

8. "Oklahoma Calls 'Barbecue King,'" *Leavenworth (Kans.) Times*, Jan. 3, 1923, 3.

9. "World's Greatest Barbecue Closes," *Boston Globe*, Jan. 10, 1923, 13.

10. "Barbecue Pictures!" *Daily Oklahoman* (Oklahoma City), Jan. 10, 1923, 4.

11. Bureau of Labor Statistics, "CPI Inflation Calculator."

12. "World's Greatest Barbecue Closes."

After Governor Walton's inauguration, Poppa Miller spent the rest of his days in the city of Leavenworth running a barbecue restaurant near a bustling military base, operating a gas station, and traveling to several states to oversee barbecues for many prominent politicians. Worgul wrote: "Poppa Miller died in 1951 at age 90. Bob [the Younger] says that his father remained amazingly strong and active right up until the end. 'Even when he was 90 we would still go out together with our two-man saw to cut hickory, oak and apple wood or barbecue,' Bob says. 'He was cooking barbecue on the day he died.'"[13] I think that's a fitting end for the extraordinary life of a celebrated barbecue artist.

13. Worgul, *Grand Barbecue*, 2.

The far ends of the poles rested on the ground adjacent to the trench. To cook evenly, the smaller animals were rotated like on a rotisserie and the larger animals were flipped at regular intervals. Ultimately, the experimenters found a "sweet spot" for cooking meat at the right elevation (at ground level), duration, and temperature.

The last significant change the colonists made was turning barbecue into something more than a meal. Barbecue ultimately became a vital outdoor social entertainment. The closest thing that the British colonists had to an established outdoor and festive food tradition was the "ox roast." At that function, a giant ox carcass was roasted over a fire using a giant spit that cooks rotated. The earliest recorded ox roast happened in 1684, when a "frost fair" was held on the frozen Thames River in London.[29] The fair was a fundraiser organized by watermen who could not make a living during winter months. The event was so successful that copycat events proliferated during various parts of the year with festive elements added. A corollary event featuring lamb—called a "ram roast"—also emerged as a popular social event during the eighteenth century.[30]

The ox roast tradition lasted deep into the nineteenth century, as indicated by an Englishman named John L. Heaton, who waxed poetically about the history of ox roasts to American newspaper readers in the late 1800s. He wrote: "I have carved big slices from a seventy-pound haunch in an old English Inn kitchen, and there is nothing in America like it, except, perhaps, at a Virginia barbecue."[31] Before the nineteenth century, barbecues tended to be small and intimate, although some gatherings had as many as a few hundred people. Barbecues often took place in idyllic rural settings, and in addition to socializing and eating, the attendees drank alcoholic beverages, played games, and fired guns. Depending on who hosted, barbecues ranged from being genteel affairs to downright rowdy occasions. Put together the European domesticated animals, the modified cooking process and equipment, and the social atmosphere and you have the first historical transformation of the cuisine away from traditional Native American forms. Whatever terms Indigenous peoples and Europeans had previously used, Virginians now called this hybrid cooking method and the new form of social entertainment "barbecue."

Yet the food story wasn't the full story. Europe's colonial rulers saw the Americas as a tremendous untapped opportunity to augment their wealth and power. The main checks on a country's imperial designs were the capabilities of rival nations with similar ambitions, the influential power of religious institutions, and domestic public opinion. Domestic public opinion is critical and most relevant to this query. Again, we focus on England. Although the Spanish and French were in the American South during the sixteenth and seventeenth centuries, barbecue took shape in areas where British colonists lived. England experienced tumultuous political times while the Virginia colony was in its infancy. Though not quite a democracy, Britain had a limited representative government that enacted laws subject to final approval from the monarch.[32] During this era, Parliament spent a great deal of time building public support for marshaling the necessary resources to colonize and maintain overseas territorial possessions.[33]

After introducing barbecue to their readers as a culinary curiosity from the other side of the world, European writers used barbecue to implement a broader agenda: the successful colonization and conquering of the Americas. To facilitate those goals, a persuasive set of arguments had to be made for dispossessing millions of Indigenous peoples from their land.

As Brian W. Dippie writes of Native American imagery during the colonial period, "Traditionally, Indians were divided into two "'types'": noble and ignoble savages. The Indian woman was either a princess or a drudge, the Indian man an admirable brave or a fiendish warrior. . . . The stark contrast between the noble and ignoble savage obscures their common denominator: *savagery*."[34] Native Americans' supposed savagery justified European imperatives to invade, exploit, conquest, enslave, and implement genocide.

Could the supposed savagery of Indigenous peoples be cured? In addition to cultural, political, and scientific analysis, some thought that religion would help settle the issue, but proselytizing had mixed results. It really depended on which group of Christians were considering the questions of converting Native Americans, enslaving them, or leaving them alone. In Spanish-occupied areas, after doing considerable damage to Indigenous Americans' way of life and habit, as one religious scholar has noted, "the majority of the Catholic Church in Spain and the New World . . . early and successfully attacked the legality and practice of enslaving the Indians."[35] The question of enslaving Native Americans was resolved differently with the Episcopal Church and the Church of England (the "Anglican Church"), which were the dominant faith traditions of the English colonists in North America.

Administrative problems with how England-based Anglican leaders established local churches gave laypeople in the Americas more power, especially the power to choose their leaders, than would have happened otherwise.[36] With this change in the balance of power, clergy were less likely to tell people what to do about slavery because their job security rested on keeping slave-owning congregants happy.[37] Slavery developed and flourished in the Virginia colony because white clergy failed to exert clear and persuasive moral authority on the issue.

The Native Americans' supposed savagery often justified their enslavement. Though barbecue wasn't the only rhetorical device used to make this case, it proved useful. In numerous colonial period newspapers, the words written, and the images painted, about barbecue in the Americas ranged from depictions of banal scenes of everyday life to jaw-dropping accounts of grotesquely wild affairs. In the distorted narratives, human limbs replaced fish, small game, and vegetables on the barbacoa. Europeans falsely exaggerated their accounts of Native American cannibalism with profound consequences. Through this process of "othering" Native Americans, European elites not only mobilized popular support for their colonial ambitions but developed a workforce to realize those ambitions. Indentured white servants couldn't meet their outsized needs, so the colonists entered the prospect of enslaving Native Americans.

With such effective propaganda, the British colonists first enslaved Native Americans before transitioning to West Africans.[38] Enslaved Indigenous peoples thus cooked the earliest iterations of the redefined barbecue.[39] For a variety of reasons, Native American slavery didn't last long in the Virginia colony. The ease with which Native Americans escaped or succumbed to European disease soon led British colonists to transition to African chattel slavery.[40] The first enslaved West Africans arrived in late August 1619, only twelve years after Jamestown's founding, and from the 1670s on, the number of captives in the Virginia colony increased dramatically. By 1782, one authority indicates, "Virginia had 270,762 slaves and 296,852 free persons."[41] It was during this time that Native Americans passed their barbecue-making knowledge to enslaved African Americans. Since we lack documentation of this process, we surmise by looking at the end result. Did they barbecue side by side? Were there barbecue apprenticeships? No accounts of either exist at this time, but we know that by the late 1700s, African Americans emerged as barbecue's "go-to" cooks.

By the early eighteenth century, some European writers began lumping Africans, Native Americans, savagery, and cooking barbecue all together. A Brit named Ned Ward, whom one publication described as a "wit, hack writer, author of doggerel verses and scurrilous pamphlets," was one of these writers. His widely read pamphlet *The Barbacue Feast* describes the recreation in London of a Jamaican barbecue. Ward writes that properly cooked pig's flesh should resemble the "tawny belly of an Indian squaw." A later passage references sailors manhandling "negro wenches." As food writer Robb Walsh states, "We'll never know how accurately Ward described the behavior at London's early eighteenth-century barbecue recreations. But the disturbing account supports [Andrew] Warnes's contention that, for the English, barbecue conjured up images of sexual violence, savagery, racism, and cannibalism in the New World."[42] Notably, food historian Ken Albala, in a review of Warnes's book, feels that he read too much into Ward's writing and overstated the case.[43] Whether fact or fiction, in Britain, barbecue was certainly being used to reinforce dehumanizing perceptions of Native Americans and African Americans across the Atlantic.

The British colonists' intensifying desire for wealth fueled a westward expansion from Virginia, which devastated the Indigenous communities they encountered. Outside of the South, the same savage tropes used against tribes on the Atlantic Seaboard were applied to the Great Plains and western tribes. Tales of Native Americans scalping the heads of whites were just one example. This era also saw a pivot in the way the two most marginalized people were portrayed. While Native Americans were decimated by numerous conflicts with the U.S. military and private citizens, the country's slave regime simultaneously expanded and created a vast underclass of African Americans. Native Americans and African Americans become fellow travelers as American media marginalized them, but in differing ways and for differing purposes.

In his book *Indians Illustrated*, John Coward explains how this phenomenon played out in the nineteenth century. African Americans were routinely portrayed negatively in the press because they remained a threat to the white power structure. In the early years of the slave trade, Africans were depicted as savages, but that no longer held the same currency after generations of enslavement in North America. The new tactic was to emphasize the collective *inferiority* of African Americans, something we'll see more vividly in the next chapter. In contrast, by the late 1800s Native Americans were favorably depicted in popular media because they were no longer a threat to the white power structure. Too many had succumbed to European pathogens and violence against them for defending their homelands. Those left alive saw lawful peace treaties reneged upon by the U.S. government, and they were relocated to reservations.

"The Great Dying." That's one name given to the devastating impact that European contact and colonization had on Native Americans. Between 2.4 and 5.7 million Indigenous peoples lived in North America when Europeans began settling on its East Coast in the 1530s. By 1800, only 1 million remained. Across the Americas, the Indigenous population declined from 60 million to 6 million over roughly the same period.[44] African Americans, 4 million strong by the time of the Civil War, remained a threat to the status quo. Accordingly, African Americans continued to be ridiculed for being strange, uncivilized, and deserving of a permanent place in society's underclass.[45]

In the nineteenth century, the progeny of white European colonists, now U.S. citizens, weren't satisfied with pushing Native Americans to society's margins. They chose genocide instead. As a 2016 article in the *Atlantic* noted, "Many things contributed to the buffalo's demise. One factor was that for a long time, the country's highest generals, politicians, even then President Ulysses S. Grant saw the destruction of buffalo as a solution to the country's 'Indian Problem.'"[46] The bison population plummeted from an estimated thirty million to just a few hundred by 1900.[47] Barbecue—the way it was prepared, the cooks, and how it was eaten—reinforced Native American savagery. As part of his "Wild West" shows held in Erastina, New York, in 1888, the famed "Buffalo" Bill Cody once invited VIPs to dine on an "Indian rib roast" prepared by some "primitive sons of America." A *New York Times* article described them cooking buffalo ribs using the pierced stick method and referred to the Native Americans present as "noble chiefs" and their children as "young savages." Though the same article described the meal as "a la barbecue," it wasn't considered mainstream barbecue.[48]

Much like their physical presence in North America, Native Americans' role in barbecue history has greatly diminished in two ways. The whites' failed attempt to enslave Native Americans displaced them as barbecue's signature cooks, and whites disdained the way they barbecued. Yet one of the last times that Native Americans and barbecue were linked publicly occurred around the time of Oklahoma's statehood. During the 1890s and early 1900s, the U.S. government pressed statehood on the Native Americans who had been forcibly relocated to "Indian Territory" a generation before by way of the "Trail of Tears." The proposed state would be called "Oklahoma," and the Choctaw, Creek, Chickasaw, Seminole, and Cherokee Indian tribes living in that area would negotiate with a federal delegation commonly referred to as the Dawes Commission, after its chairman, Senator Henry Dawes of Massachusetts.[49]

One of the most crucial negotiation meetings took place in 1894, and the affected tribes hosted a barbecue. It's unclear whether or not bison was served, but newspaper readers got a heapin' helping of racism:

THE DAWES COMMISSION was treated to "an old-fashioned Indian barbecue" in the Indian Territory the other day. It is, perhaps, not a matter for sentimental regret, but old-fashioned Indian barbecue is no more. It consisted of a paleface copiously tomahawked and spitted, and roasted before a slow fire. This was also known in some parts of the country as an Indian pudding, we believe, but the progress of civilization has ended the vogue of this famous culinary specialty. The Indians, travellers tell us, no longer receive the white stranger warmly. Instead of roasting him, they play him a game of freezeout; and their utmost refinement of diabolism scarcely reaches the point of a civil service examination. As a cook the Indian is a copper-colored error.[50]

Even though Native Americans no longer posed a legitimate threat to the status quo, whites still felt an ongoing need to justify their track record of violence and broken treaties.

Tribal leadership contemplated statehood, but not quite in the way Congress intended. They petitioned Congress to create an independent state called "Sequoyah" that would be governed by Native peoples. That effort ultimately failed, and on November 16, 1907, Indian Territory was subsumed into the newly formed state of Oklahoma. That event, too, was commemorated with a big barbecue. The *New York Times* described the scene in a way that could only come from the perspective of the conquerors. "At the barbecue grounds portions of meats and other eatables were served to the thousands assembled on a semi-circular table from a huge pit in which thirty beeves had been cooked. Indians and whites mingled in picturesque fellowship."[51] Barbecue became a symbol of conquest, and whites frequently sought opportunities to remind Native Americans of that fact.

By the 1880s, Oklahoma was a place where the fellow travelers interacted in profound and complicated ways. Before the Civil War, numerous tribes were relocated to the area called Indian Territory. Slavery existed in the territory, with some Native Americans enslaving African Americans. After the Civil War, Indian Territory was increasingly seen as a place where African Americans had better opportunities. Along with a number of whites, thousands of African Americans arrived in the area.[52] Once again, the economic, social, and political status of Black Americans was in flux, highly dependent on the racial attitudes of the tribe that controlled a particular part of the territory.[53] Yet, there was a decent amount of social interaction and cultural exchange. As we'll see in a moment, some African Americans tout their Native American bloodlines as bona fides for their barbecue recipes and skill.

Oklahoma's statehood must have disappointed thousands of African Americans who had settled in Indian Territory hoping for a better life and a respite from white racism. Several Black migrants started all-Black communities like Boley, which was founded a few years before statehood. In an era of good feelings, the residents of Boley hosted a goodwill barbecue with their Native neighbors. After the dinner, one of the Native American guests said, "Indian always friend to Black man. Red man and Black man get well together. Red man he owns much land. Colored man he make big field make much cotton, much corn. Red man gets his share without law suit, no trouble with Black man. He good to work to pay lease. Red man has plenty of land, he want colored man to work his land. Indian man he wants to sell land. White man he wants to buy Indian land. Make big bargain take land away from Red man."[54]

With all that had happened, Native American barbecue traditions did not disappear. In addition to small gatherings, Native American barbecues continued to happen on a large scale. In October 1948, "six thousand members of the Cherokee, Chickasaw, Choctaw, Creek and Seminole tribes gathered in Muskogee, Oklahoma to commemorate the founding of the 'Five Civilized Tribes' pact created 100 years earlier. Those at the fairgrounds held a huge picnic on the second and final day. They feasted on elk, buffalo, and deer. Many of the young Indians never had tasted these foods. There were 14 whole elk barbecued in one pit, and savory odors permeated the entire city."[55] Readers weren't given much information on how the barbecue was prepared, but the choice of meats used show that the hosts embraced their own tradition rather than the invented one by British-heritage people.

Despite the modifications to the Indigenous peoples' cooking process and the subsequent erasure of their contribution, well into the twentieth century, African Americans remembered Native Americans as barbecue's originators. Black barbecuers gave a nod to Indigenous cooks by describing barbecuing as "cooking the Indian way," or some variation of that phrase. Take, for instance, this 1977 profile of Bill Dunham, a longtime African American pitmaster in Kingsland, Georgia:

> He attacks his job as pitman, caterer and chef unlike anyone has before or since. . . . "When I first started off barbecuing 47 years ago, it was to throw a party for my timber crew, to give them a big blow-out, don't you know. We did that maybe once every three months; there was 77 of them, and I couldn't afford to carry them

to no restaurant. So we'd buy a hog, and cook it here, the way the old Indian peoples did way back yonder. And then I kept going, kept going, until feeding became my business." The Indian method consisted of burning a large log—live oak or water oak or hickory (but no black gum or pine!)—on a grate until the coals fell through. These were shoveled into a deep hole in the ground, and the hog, which had been quartered, was laid on a rack above [the grate] to cook.[56]

Today, it's rare to hear barbecue described in such terms because so little of it is still cooked that way. Yet any close scrutiny of barbecue's history bares its Native American roots.

Despite all of the various applications, meanings, and spellings, what barbecue is seems to have coalesced into a mainstream consensus by the end of the eighteenth century. In 1791, the French traveler Ferdinand Bayard defined it as a gathering at a beautiful spot in the Virginia countryside where whole animals were cooked, with spits piercing the sides, directly over a trench filled with burning coals from hardwood.[57] The culinary revision became the template for the epic barbecues of the nineteenth century. When I see the way that Native American barbecue cooks were written out of the barbecue story, I see a playbook for what happened to African American barbecue and its cooks a century later.

Before that, Native Americans and African Americans interpreted and performed a new mode of barbecuing heavily influenced by British colonists. Though we don't have many eyewitness accounts of this partnership, one Corporal Bellaire, a white man who attended an 1878 barbecue in Indian Territory, gave us a glimpse of the possibilities: "I was at a barbecue where there were more than a thousand [Creek] Indians and colored folks. They were very friendly to us whites. They set a special table for us, supplied with an abundance of everything to eat, all free."[58] Aside from establishing that the hosts were good at hospitality, we get no information about the cooking or what was served. Fortunately, many people stood in the gap, like Henry "Poppa" Miller—an African American who learned the art of barbecue from Native Americans in his family—whom I profiled earlier. From their stories, we get a deeper sense of how Native Americans influenced African American and American notions of barbecue.

RECIPES

Dave Anderson's Legendary Pit Barbecue Ribs

Perhaps the highest-profile Native American barbecuer these days is "Famous" Dave Anderson, namesake of the Famous Dave's BBQ chain of restaurants. Anderson's ethnic heritage is that of the Lac Courte Oreilles Lake Superior Band of Ojibwe and the Choctaw Nation. While growing up in the Chicago area, Anderson's dad, a Native Oklahoman, took his family to the black barbecue joints on Chicago's South Side when he craved some "real deal" barbecue. Here's a recipe adapted from one that appeared in *Esquire*. Be mindful of the rub's high sugar content. If the ribs are placed over direct heat, those sugars may burn. *Note*: You'll use 1 cup of the rub for the recipe. The smoking process will take 6 hours.

Makes 6–8 servings

For the rib rub (makes 6 cups)
2 cups packed light brown sugar
1 cup kosher salt
¾ cup sugar
½ cup garlic powder
¼ cup chili powder
¼ cup lemon pepper
¼ cup onion salt
¼ cup celery salt
2 tablespoons coarsely ground black pepper
2 tablespoons whole celery seeds
1 tablespoon cayenne pepper
1 teaspoon crushed cloves
½ cup Mrs. Dash Original Seasoning Blend

For the ribs
2 (4–5-pound) racks pork spareribs
½ cup Italian salad dressing
½ teaspoon coarsely ground black pepper
½ cup packed dark brown sugar
1 cup minced dried onion
1 bottle of tomato-based barbecue sauce

For the grill
½ pound charcoal
3–4 pounds fresh-cut green hickory, or hickory chunks

TO MAKE THE RIB RUB

1. Thoroughly mix all rub ingredients and store in an airtight container.

TO PREPARE THE RIBS

1. The night before smoking, trim the ribs of excess fat. Place them in a large plastic bag and pour in the Italian dressing to coat. Seal the bag well, and refrigerate for 4 hours, turning occasionally.
2. Remove and wipe any excess dressing off the ribs. Sprinkle each rib rack with ¼ teaspoon of the black pepper, then with ¼ cup of the brown sugar and ½ cup of the minced dried onion.
3. Wrap each rib rack in plastic and refrigerate overnight.
4. The next morning, remove the ribs from the plastic wrap and wipe off the sludge from the ribs. Generously coat the front and back of the ribs with 1 cup of the rib rub, and using your hands, rub it into the meat. Set it aside. Reserve remaining rub for another time.

TO SMOKE THE RIBS

1. Using a chimney charcoal starter, get 15 briquettes red hot. Arrange the coals at one end of the grill, and place 1 pound of green hickory around the coals. Use water-soaked hickory chunks if you can't get fresh-cut hickory.
2. Keep the internal temperature of the grill at 200°–225°. Add more charcoal and hickory chunks every hour as needed.
3. Place the ribs bone side down but not directly over the hot coals.
4. After 3 hours, remove the ribs from the grill and wrap them in aluminum foil. Hold them in a covered grill at 180°–200° for 1½– 2 hours or until fork tender.
5. Next, build a really hot bed of coals over the entire bottom of the grill. Be careful because this next step goes quickly. Place the ribs back on the grill to add char flavor.
6. When the meat becomes bubbly, it is done. Make sure to char off the bone-side membrane until it becomes papery and disintegrates.
7. Slather the ribs with barbecue sauce.
8. Let the heat caramelize the sauce, and serve immediately.

The Sioux Chef's Grilled Bison Skewers with Wojape

This recipe is from *The Sioux Chef's Indigenous Kitchen*, a James Beard Award–winning cookbook by Chef Sean Sherman. Chef Sherman is a member of the Oglala Lakota tribe. Chef Sherman writes: "Everyone loves these kebobs, the recipe of Mikee Willard and his son Darius Willard, of the Northern Cheyenne tribe in Montana, and members of the Tatanka Truck team. They skewer chunks of fresh sweet corn (on the cob), turnips, summer squash, or partially roasted winter squash in between the bison. The skewers are then garnished with wojape or a sauce of stewed wild plums." Of wojape, Sherman recalls, "The scent of this traditional sauce simmering on the stove takes me back to my freewheeling six-year-old self. Our family relied on the local chokecherries that I gathered as a kid. We'd spread a blanket under the trees and gather buckets full. There's no need to pit them because the pits drop to the bottom of the pot as the sauce becomes thick and lush. We'd sweeten it for a dessert or serve it as a tangy sauce for meat and game and vegetables, and as a dressing."

Makes 4–6 servings

For the wojape
6 cups fresh berries (chokecherries or a mix of blueberries, raspberries, strawberries, elderberries, cranberries, or blackberries)
1 cup water
Honey or maple syrup, to taste

For the bison
1–1½ pounds bison sirloin, cut into 1–2-inch cubes
2 tablespoons sunflower oil, divided
Pinch of sumac, plus additional for seasoning
Pinch of smoked salt, plus additional for seasoning
2–3 ears sweet corn, shucked and cut into 2-inch chunks
2–4 young turnips, cut into 2-inch chunks
3 summer squash, cut into 2-inch chunks

TO MAKE THE WOJAPE

1. Put the berries and water into a saucepan and set over low heat.
2. Bring the mixture to a simmer and cook, stirring occasionally, until thick. Add more water if needed.
3. Taste and season with honey or maple syrup as desired.

TO PREPARE THE KEBABS

1. Heat coals or a gas grill for direct heat.
2. Brush the bison with 1 tablespoon of the sunflower oil, and sprinkle it with the sumac and smoked salt.
3. Brush the corn, turnips, and squash with the remaining sunflower oil.
4. Thread the meat, sweet corn, turnips, and squash, alternately, on 4–6 skewers.
5. Sprinkle the meat and vegetables with additional sumac and smoked salt.
6. Grill the skewers about 4–6 inches from the heat, turning frequently, until the bison is no longer pink in the center, about 15–20 minutes.
7. Drizzle with the wojape and serve.

Freddie Wheeler's Hot Honey Sauce

Freddie Wheeler, the late founder of Freddie's Southern Style Rib House in Cleveland, Ohio, inherited this family recipe from his grandmother, who belonged to the Blackfoot Nation and lived to be 107 years old. Wheeler remembers his grandmother barbecuing and making her own sauce. As Jim Auchmutey and Susan Puckett write in *The Ultimate Barbecue Sauce Cookbook*, "There's nothing particularly Native American about Freddie's sauce. A son of Troy, Ala., he's been making it since he was twelve and watched his grandmother pick her own vegetables and put up 10 gallons at a time. She'd cook it for hours. That's the secret to good barbecue, he said. 'You can't rush it.' Same goes for sauce."

Makes 7 cups

1 (29-ounce) can tomato sauce
¼ cup yellow mustard
2 cups water
1 cup cider vinegar
1 cup honey
⅓ cup packed light brown sugar
1 large onion, minced
Juice of 1 lemon
1 tablespoon coarsely ground black pepper
1 tablespoon chile powder
2–3 teaspoons red pepper flakes

1. In a large saucepan, whisk together the tomato sauce and mustard.
2. Stir in the remaining ingredients.
3. Bring to a boil.
4. Reduce the heat to low and simmer for 1 hour, stirring occasionally and tasting to adjust seasonings.
5. Serve warm. Store in jars in the refrigerator.

HOW DID "BARBEQUE" GET SO BLACK?

For while much in this history remains unquantifiable, it is certainly true that Black southerners were a good deal more than just smiling waiters, appointed only to ferry [barbecue] from its Native source out to the tables of white America. Both before and after Emancipation, on the plantation and beyond its disciplinary orbit, such known and unknown figures were instead the innovators, rejuvenators, and reinventors of the food.
—*Andrew Warnes,* Savage Barbecue, *2008*

They had barbecues. That's where the barbecues started from, I reckon, from the barbecues among the slaves.
—*Charles Graham, a formerly enslaved man, Clarksville, Tennessee, 1939*

I'll recycle a question raised in the last chapter: "Black people invented barbecue, right?" This is not a cool, dispassionate, objective thing to write, but I would love to prove that barbecue has an African origin while simultaneously forming an "X" with my arms across my chest and shouting, "Wakanda Forever!" Unfortunately, it's not that easy. Many West African societies have oral traditions, making it a challenge to find out what exactly happened with food several centuries ago. On top of that, people outside the region who wrote things down when they encountered West African people weren't always accurate and thorough in their writings. When it comes to West African history around the time of European contact, we've got a lot of folklore and "fakelore" to sift through.[1] Yet the prospect of finding African antecedents or influences on American barbecue is too tantalizing to ignore.

Most African-heritage people in the United States trace their roots to western Africa because that was the "Old World" focal point for the Atlantic Slave Trade. West Africa is a vast region (roughly five million square miles) that more than four hundred million people call home. The diverse and vibrant mix of cultures there makes the region one of the most fascinating places on Earth. From the rich mix, we'll ultimately focus our attention on two groups: the Senegambians of present-day Senegal and Gambia and the Igbo peoples of southeastern Nigeria. Why? Because, as slavery scholar Ira Berlin notes, "During the late seventeenth and early eighteenth centuries, captives from Senegambia and the Bight of Benin (present-day Nigeria) constituted about three-quarters of the slaves entering the Chesapeake. . . . Over the course of the eighteenth century, Igbo peoples constituted the majority of African slaves in Virginia and Maryland, so much so that some historians renamed colonial Virginia 'Igbo Land.'"[2] There were certainly enslaved people from other parts of West Africa, but these two groups had the numerical superiority to apply their culinary signatures to Virginia barbecue just as it took shape.

To investigate barbecue's possible African origin, I digested the work of leading writers on African American foodways and its connections to West Africa, namely James Beard Foundation Cookbook Hall of Fame recipient Jessica B. Harris, Frederick Douglass Opie, an author of several books on the subject, and James Beard Awardee and culinary historian Michael Twitty. To discern the presence of a West African culinary signature, it helps to understand what the region's meat-cooking and -preservation techniques and culinary traditions were prior to European contact.

What might the respective culinary signatures of Senegambians and Igbo peoples be? From a regional perspective, a typical West African meal consists of a "filling starchy carbohydrate such as rice, or a stiff porridge-like substance from corn or a grain such as millet or sorghum, or boiled and pounded root vegetables such as yam or cocoyam, accompanied by a thick soup, stew, or sauce."[3] Such meals tend to be mostly vegetarian, but when meat is added to a dish, it is usually as an ingredient in the soup, stew, or sauce rather than as an entrée.

Specifically, Senegambians have historically cultivated an indigenous rice, so we know what their standard starch would be. The Igbo have relied more on root crops such as yams. People living on the coast and in low-lying areas made fish, small domesticated animals, and bush meat their primary sources of protein. What about larger animals? The appropriate environmental conditions for cattle raising are found at higher elevations, for two reasons: it's easier there to cultivate grain to feed the cattle, and the dreaded tsetse fly is nowhere to be seen. The tsetse fly's blood-sucking, disease-transmitting capability would have devastated any attempt at animal husbandry in lower elevations. In modern times, humans have done much to manage the tsetse populations, but raising cattle remains a challenge.

Harris pioneered examining the culinary influences that West Africa had on foodways in the Americas. Her work shows that, in the realm of barbecue, West African cooks in Africa and the Americas shared the practices of "toasting" meat by a fire and the use of seasoning pastes to impart flavor and color to raw meat.[4] Opie has argued for an African provenance by examining how African women have cooked, seasoned, and sauced meat in a process akin to barbecue. Opie has also explored Zora Neale Hurston's writings on barbecue's African diasporic connections in Florida, Haiti, and maroon communities in the Caribbean.[5] Howard Conyers, a NASA rocket science engineer and South Carolina whole hog barbecue expert, is also exploring the maroon connection to barbecue. Also of note is the post on Twitty's *Afroculinaria* blog in which he admonishes, "We must cease and desist those efforts that would divorce barbecue from its African roots, connections and narratives rooted in slavery and the African Diaspora."[6] With that context, let's explore some possibilities and sort out fact and fiction by breaking down barbecue into its key elements: the meat used, the cooking process, the seasoning, and the sauce.

West Africans were already familiar with the domesticated animals (chickens, cows, goats, sheep, and sometimes pigs) that Europeans brought to the Americas. Either some species were native to their region or they were introduced during the colonial period. Today, beef, chicken, and seafood are popular with West Africans. As one travels away from the coast and farther inland, domesticated animals and bush meat, a generic term for wild animals, are eaten more often.

West Africans, past and present, preserve food through fermentation, frying, salting, sun drying, and smoking.[7] As we'll see in a moment, meat takes a more central and starring role for snacking and special occasion feasting. So, what in the ways did West Africans preserve or cook food that could lead to barbecue?

Last chapter, we saw that cooking at ground level over a shallow pit was the method that became synonymous with barbecue. At first blush, the argument for barbecue's West African provenance suffers for a lack of earth ovens in the region's archaeological record.[8] Did West Africans cook meat before European contact in the mid-1400s? Fortunately, we have substantial glimpses from the scholarship of Tadeusz Lewicki, an Africanist scholar. Lewicki compiled the references to West African food practices recorded by Arabs who encountered West Africans during the Middle Ages. Islam appeared in Africa south of the Sahara with Arab traders and scholars from about 1000 AD. It spread through the region with the growth of the trans-Saharan trade, with caravan routes

41

connecting much of West Africa to Arabs living in northern and eastern Africa. Over the centuries, Islam more or less merged with African cultures until, by 1500, it was widespread through the Sahel.

According to their travel documents, West Africans had a taste for a diverse number of animals: camels, cattle, dogs, donkeys, goats, pigs, poultry, reptiles, sheep, seafood, and wild game.[10] Though the mentions of these animals are numerous, the Arab chroniclers were less meticulous in describing how these animals were cooked.

In the few descriptions available, one sees commonalities in meat cooking methods with Native Americans and people living in the eastern part of West Africa. The Juddala Berbers cooked on a raised platform. As one observer noted: "The meat, cut into narrow strips, was hung on wooden sticks supported by four poles. The drying was watched by a slave who kept up a moderate fire below the meat, night and day. When dry, the meat was packed into leather bags. Prepared this way, it would keep for a long time without going bad."[11] The Sudanic Berbers ate mutton roasted on a spit, and the northern Tuaregs did the same with other meats. The Tuareg people also roasted meat (goat and sheep) directly in the ashes of a fire.[12]

Pit cooking was observed during the medieval period. The Zanaga of Mauritania roasted meat "in the ground in a deep ditch (pit) where fire had been kindled and covered with sand which had also been heated."[13] In addition, another observer wrote, "The Imraguen of the Mauritanian coast eat their fish roasted (in a hole dug in the sand)."[14] Most of the old observations occurred in the highland areas of the region, not from the low-lying areas where slave trading activity was at its heaviest. However, we do know that there was cultural exchange and contact in this area, so these techniques could have traveled with enslaved people across the Atlantic.

Some West Africans cooked meat in shallow pits, but it's unclear to what extent. Contemporary accounts of meat cooking in West Africa present a conflicting picture. In *The Art of West African Cooking* (1972), a cookbook that introduced the region's cuisines to American cooks, author Dinah Ameley Ayensu writes: "Lamb is usually grilled or barbecued whole, without the entrails, and served at buffet parties where each may help himself to his choice of the roasted animal."[15] Unfortunately, Ayensu doesn't provide a recipe or more context. In her 2005 survey of sub-Saharan food cultures, Fran Osseo-Asare writes: "Cooking is likely still done over wood or charcoal fires, often in a brazier placed on the ground. The most common traditional cooking arrangement involves three stones around a wood or charcoal fire on which a cooking pot or pots are balanced. . . . For roasting a larger animal, such as a goat, a pit may be used."[16] Again, we're still left guessing about what happened before European contact.

Ayensu and Osseo-Asare discuss and include recipes for a popular street food of pieces of meat grilled on a skewer. Though both authors speak to a contemporary cooking practice, this treatment of meat stretches back in time. West African cooks tend to butcher animals into smaller parts rather than cook the whole animal. An obvious advantage of this approach is to "stretch" its use. An exasperated white woman named Frances Anne Kemble, or Fanny Kemble, as she is often called, saw this up close and personal while she lived on a Georgia plantation in the late 1830s. In a letter to her friend Elizabeth, Kemble expressed her frustration with her enslaved African American cook Abraham's inability to prepare meat the way she wanted it:

> Dear E—— . . . I have often complained bitterly of this, and in vain implored Abraham the cook to send me some dish of mutton to which I might with safety apply the familiar name of leg, shoulder, or haunch. These remonstrances and expostulations have produced no result whatever, however, but an increase of eccentricity in the *chunks* of sheeps' flesh placed upon the table; the squares, diamonds, cubes, and rhomboids of mutton have been more ludicrously and hopelessly unlike anything we see in a Christian butcher's shop.[17]

Though Abraham was quite pleased with his presentation, he knew Kemble was not. Kemble noted, "Abraham, however, insisted and besought, extolled the fineness of his sheep, declared his misery at being unable to cut it as I wished, and his readiness to conform for the future to whatever *patterns* of mutton 'de missis would only please to give him.'"[18] From then on, Kemble instructed Abraham by sketching out how she wanted her meat cut.

Contemporary West Africans would laugh at Kemble's frustration and appreciate Abraham's presentation. Though Kemble's request for butchered, bone-in pieces required a specific skill set that Abraham lacked, his impulse was to butcher the meat the way a traditional West African cook would have done for a stew. It turns out that the same goes for the way that contemporary West African cooks grill meat.

West African barbecue, if it can be called that, is a wildly popular street food tradition that is called by different names throughout the region: *afra* (Gambia), *chichinga* (Ghana), *dibi* (Guinea Bissau, Senegal), and *tsire suya*, or sometimes just *suya* or *soya* (Nigeria). In this style, the meat (usually beef, mutton, and sometimes organ meat) is thinly sliced or cut into small pieces, seasoned with a spice rub, skewered, and then quickly grilled. Ghanaian cookbook authors Fran Osseo-Asare and Barbara Baëta remark, "*Chichinga* is usually made from a variety of protein sources, such as liver or beef (more traditional), chicken (more contemporary), lamb, or goat. . . . The distinctive taste comes from the rub, the *tankora/yaji/chichinga* powder, which includes roasted cornmeal, pulverized, fried, and then re-ground peanuts, dried ground ginger and red pepper, and salt, as well as other spices."[19]

James Beard Award–nominated chef Pierre Thiam, a native of Senegal, adds that this food "originates in Hausa land, located in northern Nigeria and southeast Niger, today's northern reaches of the domain of the nomadic Hausa people who travel throughout West Africa in search of pastureland for their cattle."[20] These glorious grilling traditions, however, remind me more of Middle East kebabs and Japanese yakitori than southern barbecue.

To the extent that there are large animal meat cooking traditions, we should consider Islamic feasting traditions, particularly those of the Fulani and Hausa peoples living in the northern portion of West Africa. All of the meat cooking examples that I cited from the medieval period are from people who lived in the areas where the Fulani and Hausa peoples now thrive. They've had centuries of sustained contact with Arabs. It's entirely possible that Senegambians and Igbo peoples, via the Fulani and Hausa peoples, were exposed to Arab meat cooking traditions like *mechoui*, where a whole goat or lamb is cooked on a spit or in a pit. I see a case for West African ways of cooking whole animals influencing the early development of barbecue, but I think more dots still need to be connected. We do know that West Africans had a taste for smoked meat, and enslaved Igbos and Senegambian peoples would have brought that flavor profile to the Americas. Enslaved Fulani and Hausa peoples would have brought a similar flavor profile and the know-how for cooking large, domesticated animals.

So much for the meat of the matter, but what about sauce? For West Africans, a typical meal is a savory sauce, soup, or stew (usually a mixture of meat and vegetables) served alongside, or on top of, a starch.[21] Sauce is usually completely integrated in a dish, but dipping sauces are common for grilled meats. When African-heritage cooks create a sauce, it tends to be quite spicy. As Harris notes, "The Creole cooking of the African Atlantic world is also known for salsas, *mojos*, marinades, sauces, *molhos*, rubs, seasonings, and pepper sauces—some of the most flavorful and the most piquant condiments in the world."[22] By many accounts,

African Americans prepared barbecue in the nineteenth century by seasoning it with a fiery sauce with red pepper as a key ingredient. This hints at an African culinary signature on barbecue since the Virginia-area tribes didn't season food with chiles. The rub here is that, at the time the earliest enslaved people were arriving in Virginia, chiles were not yet in widespread use in their ancestral homelands. They would have been accustomed to other "warming spices" like black pepper, cardamom, ginger, and "Grains of Paradise," or melegueta pepper.[23] Seasoning with chiles would be something they would learn first in the Americas.

In my final tally, traditional West African ways of preparing and cooking meat don't synchronize well with eighteenth-century barbecue in the American colonies. Enslaved West Africans had expertise with some meat smoking practices, but cooking large, whole animals in a pit would have seemed like something new or at least unusual to many enslaved people. The stronger arguments for West African influence on barbecue are the cooks' deftness with seasoning and saucing and cumulative years of honed expertise that were added to what they learned from their Native American teachers. Equipped with that knowledge, barbecue flourished thanks to the handiwork of Black barbecuers.

Back to British colonial North America, we now look at how enslaved West Africans encountered this likely unfamiliar way of cooking. Louis Hughes, who was once enslaved in Virginia, captured barbecue's nineteenth-century aesthetic: a barbecue "originally meant to dress and roast a hog whole, but has come to mean the cooking of a food animal in this manner for the feeding of a great company."[24] Previously, barbecue as a social event was marked by smaller gatherings punctuated by games, intoxicating drinks, and, evidently, gunfire.[25] Given the creative experimentation that happened during the 1600s and 1700s, cooks in the 1800s could barbecue large amounts of meat at one time to feed very large groups of people. The genius of the trench method was its complete scalability to cater to a crowd in ways that other cooking methods could not match. Want to feed hundreds, maybe even thousands, of people? Just dig a longer trench. The desire to turn barbecue into a more spectacular social event drove innovation in the cooking method. The hosts wanted a bigger, and better, party.

At this point in time in history, mainstream barbecue and African American barbecue were one and the same. Why? Because most times that barbecue was made, regardless of the context, African Americans were the ones barbecuing. Anything that deviated from what and how African Americans barbecued was not "real" barbecue. One thing that did change was barbecue's terroir.

45

IN THE SMOKE
WITH MARIE JEAN
A BARBECUE WOMAN WHO
BUILT A FREEDOM FUND

"An immense barbecue was prepared. Buck's Tavern cooking was represented in superior style. Col. James Scull owned cooks unequalled in the culinary art in this or any other land, who occupied the first position. MARY JOHN, the memory of whose splendid dinners at the Post of Arkansas, will never be forgotten by the few survivors of her day, was on the grounds, superintending."[1]

Let what you just read sink in for a moment. That part about "superintending" means that an enslaved African American woman named Marie Jean was in charge of a July Fourth, 1840, barbecue in Pine Bluff, Arkansas, when the town was a little more than a year old. Today, we would call this person a pitmaster. Just picture it: an enslaved African American woman telling a large, likely all-male, team of cooks and waiters, how to properly pursue one of the manliest of culinary pursuits . . . *in the South, two decades before the Civil War*. She shattered the forced invisibility of so many before and after her. Without the passage above from the memoir of Judge J. W. Bocage, one of Pine Bluff's city fathers, we may never have known of Jean's prowess as a pitmaster.

Marie Jean's story is so gratifying. Barbecue is presented as such a hypermasculinized, "for boys only" world that I'm surprised no one is currently marketing a barbecue sauce to, um, improve male performance. We know that women were, and continue to be, integral to fish smoking traditions in West Africa. We also know from Marie Jean's example, and that of so many others, that Black women have been in the barbecue game for a long time. Unfortunately, their stories remain hidden. I'm reminded of the lyrics from the James Brown song, "It's a Man's World": "It's a man's world. It's a man's world. But, it wouldn't be nothing, without a woman."

Marie Jean (spelled "Jeanne" in some sources) was a biracial woman who was born enslaved in Arkansas sometime during the 1780s when the French claimed that territory. On July 11, 1793, and quite

1. Core, "Mary John," 16.

46

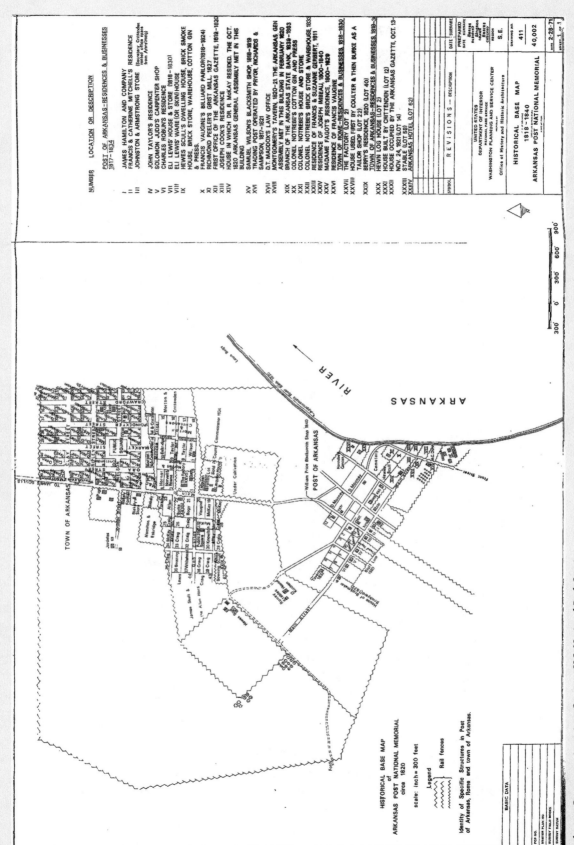

Arkansas Post map, circa 1820. Courtesy U.S. National Park Service.

possibly at a very young age, she married a white man named Michel Baune, who hunted as a profession. The marital notice indicates that the marriage "legitimized" their three children.[2] Her marriage didn't change her legal status as an enslaved Black woman, and it is unclear how long the union lasted. She was owned by different people before Colonel James Scull purchased her in 1811. Scull was a white Brit who resided at Arkansas Post, a bustling trading center and the first European settlement in that area. After the Louisiana Purchase of 1803, the influx of U.S. citizens necessarily changed the area's dominant cultural influence from French to Anglo-American. Marie Jean, well into adulthood at that point, had her name Anglicized, and from that point on, she was called Mary John.

A few months after the July Fourth Pine Bluff barbecue, Mary John had earned, and saved, enough money to do something that changed the course of her life.

> Know all men by these presents that I, James Scull Senr., of the County of Jefferson of the State of Arkansas, have for and in consideration of the sum of eight hundred dollars current money of the United States to me in hand paid before the ensealing and delivery of this bill of sale, the receipt whereof is hereby acknowledged, given and granted, and by these presents doth give and grant unto my slave Mary John her freedom, said Mary being a negro about fifty years old, to have and enjoy the same during life, free from the claim of all persons whomsoever, claiming by or through me or my heirs. In witness whereof I have hereunto set my hand and seal this 13th day of September 1840.[3]

So, how did John earn enough money to buy her freedom? Could it have possibly come from barbecue? In *A Savory History of Arkansas Delta Food*, Cindy Grisham suggests as much, noting that John "made her name catering large events at the plantation homes along the Arkansas River."[4] Whatever her financial source, the fact that John could even build a freedom fund is remarkable.

Once free, she stayed at Arkansas Post to be an entrepreneur, despite the risk of reenslavement by remaining in the antebellum South. An Arkansas county contemporary of Mary John named W. H. Halliburton wrote in his *History of Arkansas County*: "Arkansas Post, the seat of justice of the county (1845–50) was the only village or trading-post within the county limits. Twelve families, with the total of less than one hundred souls, comprised the population of this village. An old free negro named MARY JOHN kept here, the only

2. Clemons, "Marriages."

3. Core, "Mary John," 17–18.

4. Grisham, *Savory History*, 31.

48

hotel or public house in the county, which was, perhaps, the most celebrated in the State for the perfection of its cuisine."[5] Why Jean remained, we don't know. Perhaps she was so supremely confident in her public reputation that she didn't fear recapture.

Only scraps of information have survived to give us a window on Jean's life. The 1850 Arkansas county census lists "Mary Jean" as a sixty-two-year-old Black woman living at Arkansas Post with W. H. Hand, a thirty-three-year-old man and laborer from North Carolina. There is no indication of his race or what their relationship was.[6] Other than this, there are few official records of Jean's business affairs and her family.

Sadly, the most complete description of Jean's life came to public attention after her death. On May 30, 1857, the *Weekly Arkansas Gazette* ran this obituary using her Anglicized name:

MARY JOHN is dead—she died some weeks since at the Post of Arkansas. Reader, you may ask, who is Mary John? We will tell you. She was a free negress, as black as the ace of spades, some sixty-five years of age, and weighing smartly over two hundred pounds. She was the servant of the late James Scull, Esq., and in the early days of Arkansas, when he and his good lady kept an open house for every body, Mary John was the cook—and such a cook— Delmonico, if his were at stake could not get up such coffee and venison steaks as Mary John did. She was keeping a boarding house at the old Post, at the time of her death, having purchased her freedom some fifteen years ago. She was much respected, and her death is mourned by many, and among them, her old mistress and her master's children.[7]

Despite some racial condescension, this obituary is extraordinary for its time. It appeared in a majority newspaper with a white readership, Jean's full name is mentioned (a rare occurrence then for a Black person), and she's acknowledged as an accomplished professional. Her life was, and remains, testament to the fact that sisters have a long legacy of doin' it and grillin' it for themselves.

5. Core, "Mary John," 16.

6. Cover, "Arkansas County Census 1850," 49.

7. "Mary John Is Dead," *Weekly Arkansas Gazette* (Little Rock), May 30, 1857, 5.

The westward expansion of the United States and the development of a robust domestic slave trade fueled an insatiable appetite for enslaved African American labor to develop land for agriculture and other profitable uses. In this time, slavery's epicenter, as well as barbecue's, moved away from Virginia. Historian Ira Berlin notes how dramatic this shift was. "In 1790, nearly half of all enslaved African Americans resided in Virginia; on the eve of the Civil War that figure had shrunk to 12 percent."[26] Wherever Virginians went, they took barbecue with them, and that was made possible by relocating enslaved people as well.

Barbecue, as introduced by resettling Virginians, was embraced in new communities. This was certainly the case for a July 4, 1838, barbecue that took place outside of Louisville, Kentucky. A description of the event pointed out "the free, single hearted Kentuckian, bold, erect, and proud of his Virginian descent, had, as usual, made arrangements for the day of his country's Independence." The article also noted that the host was assisted by "many servants," which was code for enslaved Black people.[27] Despite its distinctive elements, a Virginia-style barbecue was increasingly tied to place. In time, it was just as common to see "Georgia barbecue," "Kentucky barbecue," and "Texas barbecue" in media as it was to see Virginia barbecue. As more locales and states across the South embraced this style of cooking, barbecue was also viewed as a regional cuisine. Barbecue was part of southern cooking, and it was called "southern barbecue."

Barbecue became a regular feature of antebellum social life. In 1860, according to, the South Carolina *Edgefield Advertiser*, the most prominent were social barbecues, political barbecues, and plantation barbecues.[28] To this list, I'd add Independence Day barbecues, which often doubled as political barbecues. For enslaved people, the opportunities for barbecue were numerous: New Year's Day, the Fourth of July, Christmas, an enslaved wedding, a reward for finishing a laborious task or any good deed done, a use for excess meat after a hog killing, saying a good word about Jefferson Davis, or simply that the weekend had come. Enslaved people in the North experienced a similar dynamic since "[barbecue] was the main dish at all Pinkster, Election Day, Camp Meeting, and Christmas holiday feasts."[29] Wherever enslaved people lived, barbecue was a special occasion food that sharply contrasted with the monotonous and meager food rations they ate the rest of the time. At this point in our story, let's focus on the plantation barbecue.

The "plantation barbecue" held special meaning in the antebellum South. Rather than the smaller scale, mundane, impromptu barbecues that could take place, the plantation barbecue was a highly anticipated feast held to celebrate the final work of cultivating a crop during the summer months before the fall harvest.[30] The timing of the barbecue depended on the crop, but this usually happened in midsummer. Whenever a barbecue took place, enslaved people did most, or all, of the work to prepare the feast. Putting on a barbecue, especially a large one, was a logistical challenge. As Mary Ross Banks recalled of a plantation barbecue from her enslaved childhood:

> After an hour or two spent hanging on, as the preparations progress in the kitchen, I grow tired of the stirring and mixing, so wander out to the yard, where I soon become greatly interested to know how Daddy Smart will proceed to cook meat in "that grave" he has dug. He has thrown fat lightwood splinters and torches, with great sticks of wood into the pit, and now there is a bed of red hickory coals, from which a stream of hot air arises. He next lays poles across the opening, from each of which he proceeds to suspend, by a strong twine, a side of pork or kid. Near the pit stands a large tin bucket containing a mixture of butter, salt, vinegar, black and red pepper, which, together with the drippings from the browning meats, he constantly applies with a mop, that all may be thoroughly seasoned when ready to serve. After watching and questioning him until I am pretty well initiated into the mysteries of barbequing, and receiving, in good faith, old daddy's assurance, "Dat's de bes' way ter cook human vittles in de worl', missy."[31]

Scenes like that played out thousands of times on plantations, and the work was labor intensive: the barbecue grounds had to be cleared; animals slaughtered and prepped; new trenches dug or an old trench cleaned out (usually by hand); wood chopped and burned down to coals; the appropriate sticks found, or made, for piercing carcasses; cooking equipment prepped; meat barbecued; sauces, side dishes, and drinks prepared in mind-boggling amounts; and, finally, the feasting.

Because of its prominence, plantation barbecue got caught up in slavery politics. Abolitionists frequently pointed out that the constant food insecurity of enslaved people was inhumane. The enslaved were malnourished, the abolitionists argued, and even when fed, the enslavers provided rotten food. Slavery's defenders countered with the annual plantation barbecue as proof of their generosity. Here's a typical "defense" using a barbecue that Mrs. Shorter hosted on her Alabama plantation in the late 1850s. In addition to copious amounts of food being served to seventy enslaved people, an advocate smugly asserted:

If those who are at all skeptical about it could attend a barbecue on one of our Cowikee plantations, which are given annually to the negroes, they would soon be convinced that the Southern negro needs no sympathy from Northern philanthropists, and that his condition would not easily be bettered. . . . No one who will look at [slavery] right, and divest himself of prejudice, can help admitting that instead of its being a moral and social evil, it is a blessing to all concerned, and will recognize in it the hand of Providence, directing it for the amelioration of the condition of a degraded race.[32]

Such disinformation campaigns tried to demonstrate that the enslaved workers were ultimately happy, treated well (far better than poor whites in the North, they often argued), and wouldn't want it any other way. The abolitionists didn't buy it one bit.

The enslaved fought against food insecurity in other ways. One was getting food outside of the controlled parameters set by slaveholders. When a pig was acquired, a barbecue commonly followed, but there was an element of danger here. Because of the work involved, the smoke, and the aromas, barbecuing could be detected. The enslaved thus waited until nighttime, or for other opportune moments, with the hope of minimizing detection. Martha Jones remembered from her enslaved childhood in Virginia one time when they barbecued while their enslaver was away from the plantation:

Yes'm I 'members some stories my granny tells when we wuz jes little chilluns. Ole Massa went way, so we n—— celebrated by killin' de fattest pig an' having a barbecue an' dance. . . . All of a sudden some one whispered, hist! who dat man sittin' ober in de corner all ragged and dirty? Sister Mollie say, its ole Massa foolin' us, ole Massa all blacked up an' was dere all de time an' knew jes' where de pig come from. Roun' and roun' he marched us as he cracked his whip at us to fin' out who stole his pig but we'alls so skeered dat he cant tell which one 'twas, so he let us go when dey gives de barbecue an' dat broke up de party.[33]

If the barbecuers were caught, the planter's punishment could be severe. Though the plantation master laid a trap and tried to mete out punishment, the enslaved barbecuer managed to escape that predicament on this occasion. Enslaved testimony shows that many other attempted barbecues ended with enslaved people being badly beaten.

How white hosts felt about race dictated how much interracial social interaction occurred at a barbecue. Sometimes it was a smoothly integrated experience. Lois Osburn, who was enslaved as a child in Louisiana, remembered: "When de work slight, us Black folks sho used to have de balls and dinners and suppers and sech. We git all day to barbecue meat down on de bayou and de white folks come right down and eat long side de cullud."[34] Most of the time, though, barbecues were strictly segregated.

At plantation barbecues, a color-conscious choreography for barbecues ensued where the enslavers and the enslaved knew their roles and the proper sequence of events. Dr. John Breward Alexander captured the essence of this racial etiquette of the antebellum barbecues in North Carolina when he wrote:

> Every gala day the white people who held the slaves were permitted to look on. All the traveling circuses were well patronized by the negroes. In the olden times every Presidential election called for big public speaking, and barbecues to draw out the crowd: long trenches were dug where the fires were kept to roast the meats, beef, pigs, and muttons, until all were well cooked. This work was all done by negroes, under the direction of an expert. . . . In the fall of 1840, when Gen. Wm. Henry Harrison was the Whig candidate for President . . . I was fortunate enough to attend one of the big meetings twelve miles from Charlotte. . . . The negroes were busy all morning keeping up fires, carrying water, settling tables, etc. After the white people were served, the negroes helped themselves, bountifully of the abundant repast.[35]

Alexander's observation shows that even a generation after slavery's demise, Black people were still considered the best to make and serve barbecue to whites. African Americans' own enjoyment of barbecue at these social events was secondary.

As images and descriptions of the plantation barbecue proliferated in popular media, several important things happened. The first is that so-called authentic barbecue became a pan-southern institution tied to any place where slavery existed. Southern barbecue, like slavery, was part of the cultural mix that distinguished southern life. The second is that authentic southern barbecue was inextricably linked to enslaved Blacks in terms of who was best at making it for, and serving it to, whites. Slavery was the African American barbecuers' training ground, and these specialized cooks gained elevated status on plantations. As southern food authority Martha McCulloch-Williams wrote, "The plantation barbecuer was a person of consequence—moreover, few plantations could show a master of the art. Such an [sic] one could give himself lordly airs—the loan of him was an act of special friendship—profitable always to the personage lent. Then as now there were free barbecuers, mostly white—but somehow their handiwork lacked a little of perfection."[36]

The link between Blackness and barbecuing was so strong that media reports of barbecue made African American expertise an essential part of the cooking process. Such thinking was not an automatic conclusion. Up north, the ox roast tradition thrived and had special meaning in communities where enslaved and free Black people lived, but excellence in its preparation was never tied to African Americans.

Barbecue had a nefarious and disturbing side as well. Cruel enslavers used heat and smoke to punish enslaved people, a practice that wasn't limited to the South. After a 1712 enslaved rebellion in New York City, a newspaper reported that "thirteen slaves were hanged, one left to die in chains without substance, three burned, one burned over slow fire for eight to ten hours, and one left broken on the wheel."[37] Ella Pittman remembered one Arkansas slaveholder who took barbecue to a horrific extreme: "I know they was a white man they called Old Man Ford. He dug a pit just like a barbecue pit, and he would burn coals just like you was goin' to barbecue. Then he put sticks across the top and when any of his n——s didn't do right, he laid 'em across that pit. I member they called it Old Ford's Hell."[38]

Such sadism was not limited to one plantation, and it was part of a larger problem. In 1830, an enslaved man was burned alive for "an assault upon his mistress." A Boston newspaper reported the event and, not sure what to make of it, drew its readers' attention to a response editorial by the *Charleston City Gazette*. "We have burnt negroes and sometimes whitemen [*sic*], by the dozen, and weekly, time out of mind. For the last fifty or hundred years not a week has passed without witnessing some five or ten of these exhibitions in some part of the State; and nobody ever thought to say any thing 'til now. A spectacle of this kind is nothing out of the way with us." The *Gazette* went on to describe a person being "invited to a barbecue of two negroes and one ox."[39] Thus, we add "negro barbecue" to a growing list of euphemisms for violence that will rear its ugly head in the postbellum South. The Boston newspaper's editorial staff couldn't tell if the *Gazette*'s writers were exaggerating, but even one such death is deeply disturbing.

With much of barbecue's recorded history being told from a white perspective, it's easy to miss its backstories and underappreciated elements concerning Blacks. More needs to be known about how African Americans used barbecue to resist the slave regime. This resistance gives us some clues why whites policed even the simple act of cooking. Whether motivated by interracial goodwill, hunger, or the need to reassure one's racial status, southern whites had another practical reason to attend Black barbecues: surveillance. Any Black gathering generated suspicion from local whites that the gatherers were up to no good. With larger gatherings, suspicion turned into fear. Though much time had passed, perhaps it was due to lingering nightmares of the nearly successful slave rebellions led by Gabriel Prosser (near Richmond, Virginia, in 1800), Denmark Vesey (near Charleston, South Carolina, in 1822), and Nat Turner (in Southampton County, Virginia, in 1831).

Nat Turner's case is probably the most noteworthy example of barbecue as protest. According to a recounting published in the *Atlantic Monthly*, after a church service on August 21, 1831, "in the woods of the plantation of Joseph Travis, upon the Sunday just named, six slaves met at noon for what is called in Northern states a pic-nic and in the Southern a barbecue. The bill of fare was to be simple, one brought a pig, and another some brandy, giving to the meeting an aspect so cheaply convivial that no one would have imagined it to be the final consummation of a conspiracy which had been six months in preparation."[40] The first to arrive were "Henry, Hark or Hercules, Nelson and Sam. Two others were novices, Will and Jack by name."[41] After they were gathered for three hours, Nat Turner joined them.

The next day, the men initiated an insurrection that played out over a couple of months until Turner was finally captured. In between, an estimated fifty-five whites and two hundred Blacks were killed in the violence. Turner was hanged on November 11, but some of his alleged associates were executed by means of a "negro barbecue."[42] A southern newspaper floated the idea of "barbecuing" the editor of the *Liberator*, an antislavery newspaper that widely reported the insurrection.[43] Turner's limited success shocked the slave regime's stakeholders in Virginia and other states. It is widely believed that the Prosser rebellion was planned at African American–only barbecue as well.

A slave revolt was an omnipresent fear for many whites in the antebellum South. In response to previous rebellions, some communities formed so-called committees of public safety to regulate Black liberty, especially gatherings. In 1856, the committee in Clarksville, Tennessee, passed a resolution that specifically mentioned barbecues: "We further think that Slaveholders are guilty of gross folly when they permit their negroes to go to barbecues and other public gatherings, where public speakers, of the one party or the other, discuss those delicate subjects of negro Slavery, the true bearing of which they do not comprehend, and where they may imbibe crude and disjointed notions of freedom, which only imperil the safety of the white, and the certain destruction of the Black race."[44] Despite the dangers, Black barbecue culture thrived. Apart from barbecues involving "borrowed" pigs, Blacks agreed with whites on what real barbecue was and how it should be prepared. Then came the Civil War.

The Civil War disrupted many aspects of the South's foodways and social life, and barbecue was no exception. The large-scale barbecues happened less frequently during the unrest, and the host planter always ran the risk of getting surprised by unwelcome guests. The arrival of Union soldiers at a plantation was momentous, for the enslaved often interpreted it as a sign that they were free, and joyous celebrations erupted spontaneously. The enslaved often extended their gratitude through food. Barbecue happened if the troops could stay awhile. The planter had to assess the troops' motives: were the troops there to pillage or free the enslaved? The recorded testimony from the enslaved suggests that such visits were much more mundane in purpose. The troops merely wanted something to eat. Laura Montgomery shared this incident that she witnessed during the Civil War:

> I must tell you 'bout de Yankees when dey cum. Dat was one time old Marster 'peered lak he was scared. Me an' my mammy was standin' by de china-berry tree when dey come ridin' up on fine hosses. Dey was all dressed in blue coats an' all had guns. I thought dey was comin' to sot us free. Dey jus' ask Old Marster iffen he had anything to eat, an' old Marster said "nuffin cooked." Well dey tol' me an' mammy an' Cindy to go to cookin' bread, an' dey went down to de fiel' and kilt our fattes' cow, an dug a hol' out'n front of de stump an' puts green hick'ry logs over dat hoe an' put a fire in dat hole and baked dat meat right dere, an' we cooked de bread. Den dey tuk old Dan, Marse Bill's fines' hoss, an' did Mistiss cry? But dey didn' bother nuffin' else much, an' when dey lef' Old Marse Bill was mighty mad an' said, "iffen de rebels had bin dar dey sho' would kilt dem Yankees."[45]

"Old Marse Bill" may have been strong in his convictions about how much bravery the rebel soldiers would have shown, but this memory from an enslaved man named Levi Shelby Alabama puts Bill's assumption to the test: "I 'member one day Mr. Tom was havin' a big barbecue for de Rebel soldiers in our yard. Come a big roarin' down de military road, an' three men in blue coats rode up to de gate an' come in. Jes' as soon as de Rebels saw 'em dey all run to de woods. In 'bout five minutes de yard was full of blue coats. Dey et up all de grub what de Rebels had been eatin'. Tom White had to run 'way to keep de Yankees from gittin' him."[46] Unfortunately for Marse Bill, those rebels were runnin'.

The Civil War raised the consciousness of African American barbecuers, who realized that they could help the Union Army's war effort by feeding their troops as they advanced in the South. Some enslaved cooks escaped for the sole purpose of offering their services in exchange for their freedom. An enslaved man named "Uncle Joe" enlisted his barbecue in service of the Army of the Republic. "'So you didn't fight in the Civil War?' was asked Uncle Joe. 'Of course I did, when I got old enough I entered the service and barbecued meat until the war closed.' Barbecuing had been Uncle Joe's specialty during slavery days and he followed the same profession during his service with the federal army."[47] Thank you for your service, Uncle Joe!

"After Freedom," or "After Surrender," as some African Americans called the time following Emancipation, Blacks barbecued on their own terms in plain view and and no longer in secret, as they so often had to do before. The most popular occasions involving large gatherings were Emancipation celebrations, church socials, and political barbecues.

Technically speaking, Emancipation barbecues hosted by African Americans predate the Civil War. However, most of those antebellum celebrations happened outside of the South. They were organized by free Blacks, some who had recently escaped slavery, and white abolitionists. Because millions of African Americans remained enslaved on their home soil, antebellum barbecue hosts celebrated Emancipation milestones for previously enslaved African-heritage peoples in the Americas. The dates picked for the barbecues coincided with the anniversaries of significant milestones in the international antislavery movement, such as Great Britain banning the slave trade in 1807. For example, in 1852, the *National Era* newspaper ran this story: "A CELEBRATION. — The First Colored Independent Philanthropic Grand Lodge of Free and Accepted Masons of the State of New York, in connection with a committee of colored citizens in Newark, New Jersey, intend having a great celebration there next Monday, in commemoration of the emancipation of 800,000 slaves in the British West India Islands, August 1st, 1834. There is to be a procession, and an ox roasted, with all the most approved proceedings on barbecue occasions."[48] Note that this northern celebration featured the ox roast rather than traditional southern barbecue.

Once Emancipation happened in the United States, there wasn't one agreed upon date to celebrate. In fact, a patchwork of regional Emancipation celebrations emerged. Some celebrations were tied to specific legal events associated with the process of emancipation. Others marked the days when enslaved people got the word, often late, that they were free. Historian William H. Wiggins categorized these celebrations:

> January 1st celebrations, which are traditionally held in a church, are primarily sacred celebrations that feature prayers, sermons, dramatic readings of the Emancipation Proclamation, and the singing of "Lift Every Voice and Sing," the Afro-American national anthem. August 8th celebrations, which are normally held in a community park or on church lawns are secular celebrations, characterized by baseball games, barbecues, excessive alcohol-drinking, and dancing. And some June 19th, August 1st, and September 22nd celebrations, whose multiple rituals are observed in community auditoriums and open fields, are a part of a third variety of celebration that combines elements from both sacred and secular.[49]

These celebrations were hyperlocal at first but then spread as African Americans migrated to other parts of the United States. At the turn of the twentieth century, one could often tell from whence people migrated by the date that they held an Emancipation celebration.

One of the earliest recorded Emancipation celebrations in the South was arguably the most joyous. Roughly eighty miles south from where the Civil War's opening shots were fired at Fort Sumter, South Carolina, thousands of recently freed African Americans gathered in Port Royal, South Carolina. A local newspaper reported:

> The first day of the New Year was spent in great glee by the negroes in this department. Speeches, flag presentations, barbecues, dancing, and prayer-meetings, were the order of the day and night. The grand affair was celebrated at Smith's plantation with great enthusiasm. The following address of Gen. Saxton issued some days since, attracted to the beautiful grounds of Camp Saxton a crowd of nearly three thousand people . . . and the crowd then adjourned to the eating ground, where a barbecue, consisting of twelve roasted oxen and numerous barrels of molasses and water, was soon disposed of. At four o'clock, the negroes re-embarked for their homes, having participated in the celebration of the happiest New Year's day that has ever dawned upon them.[50]

Interestingly, this barbecue featured beef rather than pork—another indication of the diverse ways that African Americans made barbecue.

As the first freed people's generation passed, Emancipation became more of a collective, but fading, cultural memory than a memory of direct experience. By the turn of the twentieth century, various local Emancipation celebrations had either coalesced around one anniversary or completely fallen by the wayside. "Juneteenth" has proven to be one of the few Emancipation celebrations with staying power. Juneteenth celebrates the day June 19, 1865, when the Union army's Major General Gordon Granger, commanding officer, District of Texas, read "General Order No. 3" stating: "The people of Texas are informed that, in accordance with a proclamation from the executive of the United States, all slaves are free."[51] This happened two and a half years after the Emancipation Proclamation went into effect.

Originally, it was called "the 19th of June" or the "June 19th" celebration. By the 1910s, people inside, and outside, of Texas called it "Juneteenth." After years of lobbying, the State of Texas recognized Juneteenth as an official state holiday in 1980.[52] Though Juneteenth started out in Texas, migrating Texans have transplanted the celebration all across the nation. Surprisingly, Juneteenth has now supplanted the local and traditional Emancipation celebrations of most communities—even celebrations that had a deep and rich history. It's the most popular and widely celebrated Emancipation celebration in the country, and it shows you the power that Texas cheerleaders have for their expanding their culture and food traditions.

"Barbecue and baseball" had long been Juneteenth's unofficial motto. Black communities would come together on church grounds or in public recreational spaces to celebrate with food, music, and games, especially baseball. Given its declined popularity among Black youth, the "baseball" part no longer applies. That's not the case with barbecue. "Barbecue is the most popular down-home dish served at these celebrations. Mr. Paul Darby, a Juneteenth celebrant, noted the special cultural significance ascribed to barbecue: 'They really set aside that day for special cooking—you didn't eat the same thing, you know, like everyday—that day you had special food, barbecue beef, mutton, pork, everything is 'specially set aside for that day.'"[53] Juneteenth is also marked by eating "red foods." In addition to barbecue (red because of the sauce), the Juneteenth "trinity" includes a red drink, preferably Big Red soda from Waco, Texas, and a ripe watermelon.

Emancipation barbecues certainly had their place, but political barbecue was the genre's biggest attraction in the nineteenth century. The whole point was to put on a good show so that people would vote for a particular candidate. Barbecue and politics went hand in hand, and white politicians used political barbecues with staggering success, sometimes drawing crowds with tens of thousands of people. As the *Macon Weekly Telegraph and Messenger* editorialized in the 1870s, "It has long been known and admitted in this section [the South], that a barbecue is the quickest and safest thing to infuse life and action into a drooping campaign. . . . There can be no barbecue until there is a Southern campaign."[54] White politicians used barbecue to great effect, garnering huge crowds of thousands of people, as compared to perhaps a few hundred attendees that one might get at an eighteenth-century barbecue. The ethos of the time was that barbecues should be hosted by sponsors and that the food should be given away for free. In most media accounts of political barbecues, the cooks were often unnoticed. Readers typically got a list of who spoke at the event, the food served, and the event sponsored. By the 1840s, more commentators mentioned the race of the cooks, and African Americans were strongly represented.

Just like their white counterparts, African Americans held barbecues to rally others in their community for politicking, registering voters, and getting out the vote on Election Day. During the Reconstruction era, though Blacks possessed newly minted political rights, these barbecuing endeavors were fraught with peril. Southern whites reacted in three primary ways to increased African American political power created by the Thirteenth (abolishing slavery), Fourteenth (granting citizenship), and Fifteenth (granting the right to vote) Amendments to the U.S. Constitution and the federal civil rights legislation enacted in the 1870s. The first was outright, violent, and extralegal hostility, notably from the Ku Klux Klan and other hate groups. They made sure that African Americans got the message that their political ascendancy was not appreciated, and their violent acts seldom led to prosecution and punishment. Second, public officials at all levels of government constrained and suppressed African American political power by restricting their voting eligibility through the use of literacy tests, poll taxes, and property-owning requirements. A third option that some whites chose was to accept Blacks' political power and thus court them as they would any other voters. For the latter, political barbecue was extremely useful.

White Democrats and Republicans hosted barbecues for Black voters. The simple political calculus was that the best way to secure a vote was to feed potential voters a great barbecue meal. The *Daily Phoenix* newspaper in Columbia, South Carolina, quipped in 1869, "Giving negro barbecues in Alabama is called 'stuffing the ballot.'"[55] Even further, the *Atlanta Constitution* editorialized in 1888, "If the northern republicans really want the negroes to vote, they should make a campaign in the south, organize the colored brother, and stir his soul with brass bands, barbecues, red lemonade and speeches. But this is just what our republican friends are striving to avoid."[56] Taking a page from the eighteenth-century playbooks of politicians like George Washington, hosts made sure that something stronger than red lemonade—liquor—flowed freely at these events. As with the plantation barbecues, even though these political barbecues were ostensibly for African Americans' benefit, Black people did the cooking. The big difference now was that the cooks were paid for their work.

The potential political power of an active, Black electorate was palpable, and newspaper editors, in the North and the South, had no qualms about raising alarms with respect to this phenomenon. In 1868, an article in *Brownlow's Knoxville Whig* titled "Colored Conservatism" openly called for the Ku Klux Klan to shoot Blacks before they had a chance to cast votes against the interest of the white status quo.[57] Around the same time, the *Chicago Tribune* warned that Black voting power meant that an "African Democracy" would affect something as vitally important as the election of a U.S. president.[58] Sadly, many editors at northern newspapers and southern newspapers shared the same perspective about growing Black political power.

For decades, political barbecues were quite effective at generating goodwill with African American voters. However, the strategy didn't always work. In 1879, a budget debt relief measure was put on the ballot for Virginia voters to consider. The *New York Times* reported, "There has been one continued succession of barbecues and discussions for 60 days. Every county and district has been closely canvassed. The speakers have done much to enlighten the masses, but the press has done vastly more." Yet "the vote in [Richmond] is the smallest ever polled. . . . But few negroes voted."[59] Many other newspaper reports suggested that Blacks were gaming the system, telling candidates and political operatives whatever they wanted to hear in order to get some barbecue and booze. Even if true, candidates didn't want to take any risks, and these white-hosted, Black-attended political barbecues continued until the end of the nineteenth century.

African Americans also hosted political barbecues, but typically on a smaller scale than their white counterparts. White newspaper editors who were hostile to Black progress called the gatherings "colored barbecues" or "negro barbecues" (different from the violent connotation that we learned earlier)," and they took every opportunity to bad-mouth them. If any barbecue involved drunkenness or violence, especially a

IN THE SMOKE WITH "OLD" ARTHUR WATTS
SHOWING THAT BARBECUING NEVER GETS OLD

(as told by Eudell Watts IV, Arthur Watts's great-great-grandson)

Arthur was born enslaved in spring 1837 in Randolph County, Missouri, just outside of Kansas City, Missouri. He was one of the seven or eight slaves held on the Watts farm, and it became clear shortly after his birth that Arthur did not have the brown eyes of his mother, Sylvie, or his father, Reuben. Instead, he had the same distinctively blue eyes of his enslaver, James Watts. Watts's wife took notice and quickly deduced who fathered him. That marked Arthur as a frequent target of Mrs. Watts's humiliation and rage, especially when Master Watts left the plantation, sometimes for several weeks at a time.

For reasons we can only speculate, Mr. Watts kept Arthur's chores close to the house, with tasks like keeping the kitchen and the outdoor hearth and open pit stocked with firewood. This made him an easy target for Mrs. Watts. The lady of the house would lay in wait for any opportunity to beat him "within an inch of his life" whenever Mr. Watts left the farm on business. Arthur quickly learned to avoid her ire by disappearing into the nearby woods upon his master's departure.

Arthur would often carry the equivalent of a meal or two with him when he slipped off to hide in the woods to escape the plantation mistress's wrath, though the food would not last when his master left for a week or more. That forced Arthur to learn to live off the land. He came to know intimately what foods were edible and how they tasted.

As a teenager, Arthur was assigned cooking tasks, especially the time-consuming ones such as roasting meat over an open pit. With little instruction, he grew more adept through trial and error at open-pit cooking, and he became obsessed with making the meat taste better. From his time spent foraging in the woods for food, he

"Old" Arthur Watts as a young man.
Photograph courtesy of Eudell Watts IV.

developed an uncanny knowledge of the natural flavors of the plants growing around him. He started to experiment with herbs and any other spices he could get his hands on to complement the meat he prepared. His curiosity quickly began to pay off, earning him praise for his flavorful creations. Arthur began to take pride in his cooking, and, for the next decade or so, he obsessed daily over improving his culinary skills.

Upon being freed at age twenty-eight, Arthur immediately set out on foot to seek employment. Hearing that other freed slaves had found paid work in Central Illinois, Arthur hopped a train "hobo-like" and rode about 150 miles to Kewanee, Illinois—a thriving hog-raising hub and the manufacturing home of the newly patented and popular Kewanee Boiler. He got a job at a local tavern, but on his first day, he got in a fight with three local white men who felt he had taken their work opportunities away from them.

After the men beat him senseless, Arthur was arrested. He was surprised twice later that day, first by the bar owner who willingly testified on his behalf with exculpatory evidence and, second, by the judge who sentenced him with a simple order: "From this date forward Arthur Watts may strike no man with a closed hand." So shocked was Arthur with this outcome that he knew he had found his home. Indeed, he never moved away from Kewanee.

While working a number of physically demanding odd jobs around town, Arthur resumed his passion for open-pit barbecuing, with a plan to share it with his newfound community. He knew that the flavor and quality of his barbecue was unequalled and that anyone who tasted it would love it. Exercising some business savvy, Arthur volunteered to barbecue for church and social events in Kewanee, and his reputation grew. Over time, cities, towns, and counties as far away as fifty miles from his home sent for him to cook at major festivals, sometimes feeding tens of thousands of people over the course of a weekend or more. When Arthur cooked large-scale barbecues, he preferred to cook pork shoulder. When he cooked for himself, however, his favorite alternated between a shoat, a young pig—especially one that was newly weaned—or a kid, a newly weaned goat. Arthur was also meticulous in his specifications for building an open-pit barbecue.

When asked to oversee a large barbecue, he stipulated that those hiring him must supply the manpower and resources to build and staff a "proper pit." For Arthur, that meant supplying the men and equipment to dig a trench forty feet long, six feet wide, and four feet deep. The men would then throw untreated oak railroad ties into the bottom of the pit, top the wood with metal pipes at four-foot intervals, and then cover the entire pit with cattle wire. The timber at the bottom of the pit would be set afire in the early evening so that by midnight the logs would be reduced to embers. At that point, Arthur's team would place pork shoulders atop the cattle wire to cook. Arthur would space men at five-to-six-foot intervals on both sides of the trench. Armed with pitchforks, the men would turn the shoulders through the night, and by lunchtime the shoulders would be ready to eat. Arthur insisted that pork shoulder be sliced, not pulled. His method ensured that every sandwich got a portion of that flavorful bark that came from the application of his delicious dry rub prior to cooking.

Arthur went to great lengths to guard the secrets of his craft from others. When commissioned to do big events, he often enlisted the help of his extended family, but he kept his methods secret even from them. To supply sauce for a citywide festival, for example, Arthur would have to make as much as 100 gallons of sauce, not to mention blending and applying dry rub to one or more tons of pork shoulder. For the sauce prep, in order to keep the recipe secret, he would have family in one nearby town combine the ingredients in the first half of the recipe, then have family in another location combine the ingredients to create the second half. The families would then haul their respective batches to Kewanee, where Arthur would bring them together and blend them into the finished product, what he called his red sauce. In an age without telephones, this method lessened the chance that anyone could discover the full recipe. Only he could put the two halves of his recipe together. No one ever got the complete recipe unless he wanted someone to have it—and these cases were few and far between over the years!

As a result of many years of hard work, Arthur and his sons saved enough money to purchase a small amount of land on the edge of town. From this homestead, Arthur raised a variety of typical midwestern crops. He also kept a fully functional open-pit barbecue on which he constantly practiced his craft and refined his recipes. Over the decades, Arthur's celebrity grew more and more, and demand for his skills and product came from an ever-increasing distance.

Arthur stayed active and vibrant for more than a century. Local newspapers carried articles describing him supervising the annual Hog Festival Barbecue in Kewanee when he has 101 years old. He outlived his wife, Laura, by a little more than seven years. He lived alone and continued to farm until the age of 107. At that age, a freak train accident involving his wagon put Arthur in the hospital for the first time in his life. He was not pleased. No one can say with certainty why—perhaps due to confusion caused by his pain medication, or from delirium from the fever brought on by the sepsis that had set into his wound, or maybe just because of his cantankerous nature—but Arthur got up in the middle of the night determined to head home. In his haste, Arthur tripped down a flight of stairs as he exited the back of the hospital. The fall broke his hip. Now immobile, Arthur lingered several months in his sickbed. He died shortly after his 108th birthday.

His passing was acknowledged as a loss by Central Illinois communities far and wide. Municipalities from as far as one hundred miles away sent flower arrangements in recognition of the large community barbecues Arthur had conducted over the years on their behalf.

Fortunately, Arthur left behind a tremendous gift. Arthur was not literate, so he passed along his complex and unique recipes by dictating them to his children. Written in their hand, Arthur's recipes have made it possible for his descendants to create a company to produce "Old Arthur's Barbecue Sauce & Dry Rubs" that are true to the flavors he created some 160 years ago.

death, that was often front-page news, even when white interlopers instigated the violence.

Election night in 1876 marked the tragic end of Reconstruction—a grand experiment to treat African Americans in the South as political equals. In order to have their candidate, Rutherford B. Hayes, prevail in that year's hotly disputed presidential election, the Republican Party agreed to retreat from its ambitious efforts to reconstruct and build a multiracial democracy in the South.[60] This capitulation led to the public erosion of the political gains that African Americans had briefly experienced. This public retreat also ushered in a time when the negative connections between Blackness and barbecue intensified.

Freed from federal oversight, racist whites tried to resurrect, as much as they could, the racial caste system that existed during slavery. The "Cause" was lost but not abandoned, kept alive through lengthy, violent campaigns against African Americans to intimidate any effort to participate fully in American society.[61]

One ghastly and highly effective means of intimidation was through lynching. Researchers at the Equal Justice Initiative "documented 4075 racial terror lynchings of African Americans in Alabama, Arkansas, Florida, Georgia, Kentucky, Louisiana, Mississippi, North Carolina, South Carolina, Tennessee, Texas, and Virginia between 1877 and 1950—at least 800 more lynchings of Black people in these states than previously reported in the most comprehensive work done on lynching to date."[61] Anything could justify lynching an African American, and common reasons were the alleged rape of a white woman, not showing adequate deference to a white person, or white envy of a Black person's success.

If fire was involved, the lynchings were often called "negro barbecues," reviving the same term used for the grotesque murders of enslaved people in the antebellum period. Many of these negro barbecues were impromptu murders, but on occasion, a lynching was premediated and designed to send a message to the Black community. In one of the sickest manifestations of a sick society, many whites showed up dressed in their finest clothes and with little children in tow to witness a lynching. Afterward, they'd surrounded the grotesquely disfigured and still-smoldering corpse to take a picture with no hint of disgust or remorse on their faces. The horror didn't end there. Pictures of the lynching were turned into postcards. The burned corpse would be cut into pieces as mementos that attendees could carry with them. Sometimes the charred remains were displayed in the storefronts of local merchants.[63]

Racist and complicit whites coupled their physical terrorism with racist propaganda. Denigrating, food-related tropes were long fodder for humorous portrayals of African Americans, particularly with the minstrel shows that emerged in the 1820s.[64] Barbecue, alongside fried catfish, fried chicken, and watermelon, was frequent fodder for caricaturists. As a tactic, this one's a real head-scratcher since whites loved the same foods. The cultural propaganda was effective and widespread because whites controlled most media platforms to flood our culture with negative imagery. Black media certainly tried to counteract the messaging, but they were no match for the hegemonic soft power flexed by white media. By casting African Americans as childlike simpletons, or as less than human, the media bolstered the argument that rights afforded to Blacks should be eliminated or sharply curtailed. After all, African Americans were inferior. About two decades after Reconstruction ended, Jim Crow segregation became the law of the land when the U.S. Supreme Court decided *Plessy v. Ferguson* in 1896. Though much of this culture war originated in the South, media creators and content providers outside of the region were happy to disseminate the information.

In this context, one of the most remarkable developments of this era is something that didn't happen. Despite the dominance of African American barbecuers and their close association with that style of cooking, white business interests didn't create on a widescale basis a fictional character akin to the recently retired Aunt Jemima, Rastus (the Cream of Wheat man), or Uncle Ben to hawk some barbecue-related product and reinforce racial stereotypes. As Toni Tipton-Martin explains in her groundbreaking and James Beard Award–winning book, *The Jemima Code*: "Historically, the Jemima code was an arrangement of words and images synchronized to classify the character and life's work of our nation's Black cooks as insignificant. The encoded message assumes that Black chefs, cooks, and cookbook authors—by virtue of their race and gender—are simply born with good kitchen instincts. It diminishes the knowledge, skills, and abilities involved in their work and portrays them as passive and ignorant laborers incapable of creative culinary artistry."[65] It may be because barbecue was viewed differently—a culinary process requiring so much more expertise than southern cuisine—that it could not simply be reduced to something based on natural ability. Barbecue was associated with virtuosity.

The commercial caricature almost arose when the "Georgia Barbecue Sauce Company" debuted the United States' first commercially available, bottled barbecue sauce in 1909. The bottle's label assures that the sauce perfects the taste of a wide variety of meats, vegetables, and a soup called "Brunswick stew." The label depicts an elderly Black man kneeling on one knee with a bottle (presumably of the named sauce)

Georgia Barbecue Sauce Company newspaper advertisement, Atlanta Journal Constitution, *Feb. 3, 1909.*

in one hand and a long, pitched fork in the other to tend to the meat laid out over a gridiron-type pit. In sharp contrast to many depictions of that era, the anonymous man looks professional, as if working in his natural element. He does so free of caricatured facial features and exaggerated dialect. The product didn't last long, but apparently, the company's owners avoided using racist tropes to boost sales.

In sharp contrast, racist stereotypes thrived in restaurant advertising and material culture as southern barbecue spread across the country. Sadly, southern barbecue carried with it preconceived notions about the South. Numerous restaurants, even ones outside of the region, created an atmosphere that made diners feel as if they were on a plantation, complete with Black servants at their beck and call. Even immigrants got in on the act. In the late 1920s, Sam Todorofsky from Montreal, Canada, operated a restaurant in the Chicago area called "Sam's Pickaninny Barbecue."[66] The barbecue restaurant's advertising in Chicago-area newspapers would have whetted the appetite of any Ku Klux Klansman visiting the Windy City. During the same time period, "Mammy's Pit Barbecue" opened on Wilshire Boulevard in Beverly Hills, California, showing that the toxic pairing of barbecue and race extended far beyond the American South.[67]

Matters got worse in the late 1930s with the immense popularity of *Gone with the Wind* and the cresting wave of antebellum southern nostalgia that it rode. Such media added an entertainment element that typified southern barbecue during the Reconstruction era. Southern barbecue was packaged as an "experience" for locals and tourists alike. *Vogue* described this scene in 1947, "At a typical [Texas] barbecue, guests sit at a long table, under the trees, and eat the meats that have been roasting over the deep barbecues since the night before. There are chickens, pigs, and baby goats, burning with pepper, sweet with herbs. After lunch, there is a semi-religious 'sing,' with Negro spirituals and often a benediction by the plantation preacher."[68] It's hard for me to read such accounts without imagining a Disneylike chorus singing, "There's a Black World After All," instead of spirituals. Cast as mere entertainment, barbecue reminded the attendees of why they inwardly feared a multicultural world where Black people had opportunities beyond making their food, serving it, and entertaining them. These types of barbecue events reassured them of their place in the social order.

Through the 1880s, for better or for worse, public representations of barbecue and Blackness were inextricably linked in terms of the labor involved, the expertise required, the recipes used, how it was served, and the entertainment provided afterward. The collective thrust of these social messages was that African Americans had a certain place in society—at the bottom. As media had pounded the drumbeat of "Indian savagery," the same techniques were used to convey African American inferiority. Mainstream barbecue and African American barbecue still remained one and the same in terms of menu and technique. On the flip side, Emancipation gave U.S. barbecue culture something that had never existed before: a new class of barbecue entrepreneurs who were all about making money on their own terms. Marie Jean and "Old" Arthur Watts are excellent examples of barbecuers who successfully transitioned from enslavement to entrepreneurship.

RECIPES

Chef Pierre Thiam's Spicy Grilled Kebabs (Dibi Hausa)

This recipe is adapted from Chef Pierre Thiam. A Senegal native, Thiam is doing much to educate Americans about the food of his native country. This is a great way to get a taste of West African barbecue in a short amount of time. Though this recipe calls for beef, you many use any meat or vegetable to achieve delicious results. If using wooden skewers, soak them in water for an hour before using.

Makes 4–6 servings

For the hausa spice mix (tankora powder)
1 cup roasted, unsalted peanuts, crushed into a fine powder
½ teaspoon cayenne pepper
1 teaspoon ground ginger
1 teaspoon salt
1 teaspoon freshly ground white pepper

For the kebabs
1-pound round steak, cut into strips about 1½ inches wide by
    2 inches long and ⅜ inch thick
¼ teaspoon finely grated fresh ginger
½ teaspoon minced fresh garlic
2½ tablespoons finely grated onion
1 tablespoon tomato paste
1 chicken bouillon cube, crumbled (optional)
1 tablespoon peanut oil
½ teaspoon salt
½ teaspoon cayenne pepper
1 teaspoon freshly ground white pepper
8 (6-inch) skewers

TO MAKE THE HAUSA SPICE MIX
1. Combine all the ingredients and set aside. *Note*: If you aren't using it right away, the mix will last up to 2 months in an airtight container.

TO PREPARE THE KEBABS
1. Preheat an outdoor grill over high heat.
2. In a large bowl, combine the meat, ginger, garlic, onion, tomato paste, and bouillon cube, if using.

3. Add the oil, salt, cayenne, and white pepper. Stir well to blend.
4. Allow to marinate for 10–15 minutes.
5. Thread a few slices of meat onto each skewer.
6. Pour the tankora powder spice mix onto a plate and roll each skewer in it, evenly coating all sides.
7. Shake off any excess powder.
8. With a pastry brush, brush about 1 teaspoon of marinade over each skewer.
9. Place the skewers on the grill, and cook 5 minutes on each side.
10. Keep brushing with marinade during the first part of the grilling to prevent them from drying out. Serve hot.

Old Arthur's Pork Belly Burnt Ends

I thank Eudell Watts IV, Old Arthur's great-great-grandson, for this recipe. Pork belly burnt ends are a riff off the traditional burnt ends made from beef brisket. This recipe calls for a three-step process that candies the pork belly by smoking, then rendering, and adding barbecue sauce at the end of the smoking process. You may substitute your favorite dry rub and sweet, tomato-based barbecue sauce.

Makes 6 servings

6 pounds pork belly, cut into 1-inch cubes
½ cup Old Arthur's Smokestack Dry Rub, or your favorite dry rub, divided
1 stick butter, sliced into pats
1 cup packed dark brown sugar
1 cup honey
½ cup apple juice
½ cup apple or fig jam
20 ounces Old Arthur's Barbecue Sauce, or your favorite barbecue sauce, divided

1. Place the pork belly into a large mixing bowl.
2. Sprinkle ¼ cup of the dry rub into the bowl and then toss vigorously with your hands to coat each piece thoroughly.
3. Bring the smoker to an internal temperature of approximately 235°. Use your favorite fruitwood or hardwood to create the desired smoke once the smoker has reached the correct temperature.
4. Arrange the seasoned pork belly pieces evenly on a wire cooling

rack. Take care to space the pork belly pieces so that they do not touch one another. Place the rack in the smoker.

5. Smoke the pork belly pieces for 3½ hours at 235°–250°. If you have not already done so, add your wood pieces to the fire so that you are now producing smoke.

6. Remove the rack from the smoker. Using your hands (gloved), carefully transfer each cube from the tray to an aluminum foil pan. Arrange the pieces so that they are uniformly level in the pan.

7. Distribute the butter, brown sugar, honey, apple juice, jam, the remaining ¼ cup of the dry rub, and ½ cup of barbecue sauce over the pork cubes.

8. Cover and seal the pan with aluminum foil. Return the pan to the heat of the smoker. Allow it to stay inside for 2 more hours at a target temperature of 250°.

9. Remove the pan from the smoker. Remove the foil lid, and carefully transfer the individual pieces from this braising liquid into a new, clean foil pan. Discard the old pan and liquid.

10. Drizzle the remaining barbecue sauce over the pork cubes.

11. Place the cubes in the new pan (no lid) back into the smoker for 15–20 minutes more to let the sauce get a little tacky, but don't leave the pan in too long, or you will sacrifice that rendered texture that you have worked so hard to achieve!

12. Remove from the smoker and enjoy!

BURNT OFFERINGS
BARBECUE IN AFRICAN
AMERICAN CHURCH CULTURE

This method of serving meat is descended from the sacrificial altars during the time of Moses, when the priests of the temple got their fingers greasy and dared not wipe them on their Sunday clothes. They discovered then the rare, sweet taste of meat flavored with the smoke of its own juices.
—*Columbus B. Hill, 1902*

Before exploring other aspects of African American barbecue culture, it's important to consider its connection to religion. Barbecue is about building community, and the Black church was arguably the first autonomous institution shaped by African Americans in the United States. As we'll see, barbecue was useful in creating a multitude of believers.

I begin by confessing, which seems entirely appropriate for a discussion of how barbecue and spirituality intersect. As a Christian and lifelong member of the African Methodist Episcopal Church, I bare my soul and share with you that barbecue has been quite distracting to my spiritual life. When I think about the book of Exodus from the Hebrew Bible, in which Moses encounters the burning bush, I wonder if it smelled like hickory, mesquite, or oak wood. Do you also wonder, as I do, if, when the Prophet Ezekiel had a vision about a "valley full of dry bones," they looked like a pile of spareribs? Does your mind wander whenever you read the words "burnt offering" in passages like this one from the prophet Micah in the Hebrew Bible:

> With what shall I come before the LORD
> and bow down before the exalted God?
> Shall I come before him with burnt offerings,
> with calves a year old?
> Will the LORD be pleased with thousands of rams,
> with ten thousand rivers of olive oil?[1]

With that scripture, clearly the prophet Micah wrote of beef barbecue with a sauce, right? I know. I have problems, and I need spiritual—and probably other forms of—counseling.

Despite my foibles, it's undeniable that more than any other cuisine in the United States, barbecue is often served with a side of religious fervor. The atmosphere and language that surround barbecue, the words and phrases that food critics and aficionados use to describe it, are often rooted in things spiritual and holy. Even among the most secular, barbecue and religious imagery seem to go hand in hand. Food writers, for example, gush about "the scales falling from [their] eyes" after eating superlative barbecue nowhere near Damascus (at least not the one in Syria—although maybe the one in Georgia). Pitmasters are likened to preachers, and their barbecue pits, pulpits from which the holy "word" is served.

A barbecue joint in Denver once proudly claimed to serve "nondenominational barbecue." Rather than taking sides in the sectarian divisions of the barbecue world and committing to a particular style—Kansas City, Memphis, North Carolina, South Carolina, or Texas—this restaurant took an ecumenical approach, drawing from each to create something new, something "quintessentially Coloradan." This ecumenical approach, the word "eclectic" is more apt, didn't work well for this particular restaurant (it closed a few months later), but it's far from heresy. Newer barbecue restaurants often take the approach of an itinerant elder: the owners have traveled the country, sampled the best barbecue, got trained in the proper techniques, and compiled an eclectic menu that they now serve to you—and you should feel blessed by their hard work.

The religious vibe of many African American–owned barbecue restaurants is unmistakable. There's religious iconography everywhere. Faith-based inspirational sayings and scriptures are commonplace decorations. Gospel music is piped through the sound system, a sharp contrast to the baby-making music of Barry White and Marvin Gaye that is often played at soul food establishments. Depending on the age of the restaurant, portraits of Jesus Christ and the Reverend Dr. Martin Luther King Jr. hang on the wall. Abraham Lincoln, John F. Kennedy, and Barack Obama might have an honored place, too, as a short canon of secular, presidential saints. The staff tells you how they are blessed, and they wish God's blessings upon you. Even sales receipts offer a benediction. Also, not a drop of alcohol is sold, antithetical to the idea that good barbecue must be paired with beer. To drive the connection home, some restaurants have religious names. In Anne Arundel County, Maryland, one longtime joint was known as "Homer Hall's Dixie Pig, the King Is Here, and Church of God, the Gate of Heaven Church." Hall supposedly grilled on converted jailhouse doors. When you dine in one of these restaurants, it's not like you're going into a temple. It's more like being welcomed into a religious person's home.

Barbecue restaurants are gathering places that also have the power to bring wandering souls closer to God. Pauline J. Coffee "had a glamourous career. A former movie actress and dance hall singer, she was once a partner of the well-known comic actor Stepin Fetchit, both on stage and in the movies."[2] After a religious conversion to Christianity in 1929 at Doc Hamilton's Barbecue Pit in Seattle, Washington, she became known as "the Converted Actress." Based on what we'll find out about Doc Hamilton in chapter 5, maybe it was because of all that sin that she witnessed up close in his restaurant. Anyway, "She started preaching seven months after conversion and was ordained by Aimee Semple McPherson and was known as the colored evangelist of Angeles Temple." Coffee's career lasted into the 1970s and was marked with success as well as some controversies, including a nervous breakdown and a mysterious disappearance.[3] At least one Cleveland pastor lost his job for allowing Coffee to preach from the pulpit in 1939—something that some conservative Christians won't allow women to do.[4]

Black barbecue restaurateurs looked to divine texts and Black church culture for inspiration. I don't know when the words "church" and "barbecue" were first joined, but the "church barbecue" has a rich and long history in the United States. For African Americans, it began with the spiritual lives of the enslaved.

Enslaved West Africans didn't arrive in the Americas as blank slates in terms of spiritual belief and practice. Many brought their traditional West African spiritual beliefs with them, and others brought Islam. Yet Christianity is the dominant faith tradition in the United States, and so I focus on its influence on Black barbecue traditions. During slavery, Christianity and barbecue were connected via Christmas.

In the antebellum South, the Christmastime barbecue was highly anticipated. As Easter Reed, who grew up on a Georgia plantation, remembered: "On Christmas and the Fourth of July big celebrations were held for the slaves. They either visited other plantations or had guests of their own on those days. Games and dances lasted all day. One of the most interesting events of the day was the feast served about one o'clock. Generally, on the Fourth of July, they enjoyed a fish fry. At Christmas time a pig was barbecued."[5] Reed's memories indicate that regional and seasonal differences existed toward July Fourth barbecues but the Christmas barbecue was a uniform practice.

For whites, Christmas barbecues had deeper cultural meaning than other barbecues because of its long ties to European tradition, dating as far back as 1170 CE. In Great Britain, Germany, and some countries in the Balkans and Scandinavia, a boar's or pig's head was served on Christmas Eve or Christmas Day. One historian of this tradition notes, "It is difficult to trace how the eating of Boar's Head came to be connected with the Christmas Feast.... We may possibly find the right reason why ... in the 80th Psalm, in which Satan is called 'the wild boar of the woods.' In carrying the Boar's Head in procession and eating it, we show the final defeat of man's greatest enemy, and what better day to show this than on Christmas Day?"[6] Whites passed this custom along to enslaved African Americans who embraced it and morphed it into a Christmas barbecue tradition that lasted long after Emancipation.

An elderly resident of New Jersey reflecting on her Virginia childhood during the 1950s said in an interview, "That Christmas was wonderful to me.... We had 'tato pies, coconut pies and chocolate. All different kinds of cakes too. Daddy would kill a pig and he would bar-b-que him in the yard. And we would cook up a whole lot of collard greens."[7] Don't think for a moment that Christmas barbecue was solely limited to the South. Barbecue was also a featured dish at antebellum enslaved festivities in the North: "Barbecue was also consumed in great quantities at some Saturday night parties; it was the main dish at all Pinkster [Pentecost Day], Election Day, Camp Meeting, and Christmas holiday feasts."[8] Enslaved people infused Christmas barbecues with religious meaning as they gradually adopted Christianity.

An enslaved person's conversion to Christianity was highly shaped by the racial and spiritual attitudes of enslavers who often had differing opinions. Some slaveholders discouraged proselytizing Christianity because it conferred a level of humanity on enslaved people, thus undermining one of the strongest rationales for slavery. In these situations, the enslaved had to worship in secret. There were also slaveholders who allowed their enslaved to become Christians: some because they genuinely believed it would be of personal benefit, others because they thought religion would make the enslaved easier to control. Either way, Christianity was typically presented to the enslaved in an unattractive way. When white preachers preached to the enslaved, their "sermons" emphasized the scriptures that supported slavery and obeying one's master. During the long period of chattel slavery in the antebellum South, proselytizing was scattershot, church buildings were scarce, and many of the enslaved were unchurched. Barbecue gradually became associated with three distinct expressions of Black worship.

One is the "invisible church" which was the coined term for surreptitious worship by enslaved people. They would sneak into the woods at night to avoid detection by the enslaver or the overseer. Barbecue, as an after-worship meal, heightened the anticipation for the worship experience, if the enslaved could "lay hands" on a pig and successfully "liberate" it from the enslaver. Barbecue was well suited for secret meals because it could be made in a variety of locations, required little equipment, and was cooked in a way that lessened the chance of detection. In terms of cooking location, any open space with a nice patch of diggable ground and plenty of wood nearby did the trick. In terms of equipment, trenches could be dug by hand, and the cooks needed only something sharp enough to butcher and process the pig. With fried chicken or fish, one would have to lug around iron cooking equipment and oil. Plus, who knows how long it would take to catch a fish. Thus, barbecue could be easier to make.

Last, there's the question of detection. A scholar on Black religion surmises: "To avoid detection, [a pig] was placed in a hole dug in the ground and cooked with coals from aromatic firewood, hence the hickory and oak flavors. The pig was wrapped in leaves to prevent the skin from burning and packed with herbs found in the nearby woods. The smoke could not be seen from the big house in the night and there was no flame to give the worshippers away."[9] The fact that this method required glowing coals instead of a raging fire was key. After the worship and meal were over, the enslaved slipped back to their plantation cabins.

Most religious enslaved people experienced a second type of church the way Jasper Battle did, confined and segregated in an indoor building:

Slaves went to de white folks' church and listened to de white preachers. Dere warn't no colored preacher 'lowed to preach in dem churches. Dey preached to de white folks fust and den dey let de colored folks come inside and hear some preachin' atter dey was through wid de white folks. But on de big 'vival meetin' days dey 'lowed de N——s to com in and set in de gallery and listen at de same time dey preached to de white folks. When de sermon was over dey had a big dinner spread out on de grounds and dey had jus' evvything good t' eat lak chickens, barbecued hogs and lambs, pies, and lots of watermelons. Us kept de watermelons in de crick 'til dey was ready to cut 'em. A white gentleman, what they called Mr. Kilpatrick, done most of de preachin'. He was from de White Plains neighborhood. He sho' did try mighty hard to git evvybody to 'bey de Good Lord and keep his commandments.[10]

IN THE SMOKE WITH
CHARLES W. ALLEN
THE BARBECUE MISSIONARY

In the mid-1890s, Father John F. Cummins had a vision. Actually, it was more like a directive to build a church in Roslindale, a southern suburb of Boston, Massachusetts. He needed to raise a lot of money to fund the construction, and for whatever reason, the Charlestown, Massachusetts, native thought "southern barbecue." When the local press got wind of Father Cummins's plans, they were understandably intrigued. The *Boston Herald* noted, "New England barbecue in the past may be reckoned on the fingers of one hand."[1] In fact, the newspaper had to explain at length to its readers what a barbecue was and how it operated. In 1894, in order to make his dream a reality, Father Cummins summoned from Lexington, Virginia, a veteran barbecuer named Charles W. Allen.

Allen arrived at Boston with an impressive barbecue resume. He reportedly had "barbecued oxen and hogs for some of the best-known men of the South. Among his hirers were [U.S. Senator and] Gen. Mahone, [Congressman] John S. Wise, and Randolph Tucker, from all of whom he was written recommendations. He is about 50 years of age, a mulatto, and has helped in days past prepare barbecues IN HONOR OF STONEWALL JACKSON and Gen. [Robert E.] Lee." For the feast, a thousand-pound ox was "roasted whole, the interior being stuffed with sweet corn, sweet potatoes, and other vegetables."[2]

Apropos of the times, Father Cummins was not content with having an impressive barbecue spectacle. He had to go full antebellum plantation. In addition to the meal, a newspaper article announced, "A troupe of genuine colored minstrels and comedians will enact features of plantation existence, sing and play negro melodies, and perhaps give an exhibition of a real cake walk."[3] In 1895, "Rogers's Mississippi Colored Troubadours, 50 black Americans [sang] special barbecue songs" in addition to the cake walk.[4]

One transplanted southerner, writing for a local newspaper, waxed nostalgically, "It seems singular to me to find all the accompaniments of a gathering like this, to which during more than 20 years of my life

1. "It Will Be a Royal Feast," *Boston Herald*, Aug. 27, 1894, 5.

2. "Royal Feast," 5.

3. "Royal Feast," 5.

4. "Another Big Barbecue," *Boston Journal*, Aug. 30, 1895, 9.

CHARLES W. ALLEN OF LEXINGTON, VA.,
WHO WILL "BARBECUE" THE OX.

*Charles W. Allen, Lexington, Va.
Boston Herald, Aug. 27, 1894.*

I was so accustomed. The presence of the negroes themselves; that weird, peculiar southern melody; those strange songs which had their birth and have found their permanent home in plantation life in the South—these I have heard here among the leafy foliage of the suburbs of Boston; and your games and sports, and all that surrounds me, recall the events of my earlier life. Nothing could inspire me more."[5]

The barbecue feast was a huge success, with fifteen thousand attendees and more than five thousand dollars raised.[6] It is thought to be the first southern barbecue in Boston, though not the first barbecue. On January 24, 1793, an ox was roasted on the city's Copp's Hill in honor of the French Revolution.[7] Father Cummins was so impressed that he invited Allen back the next year. That year's barbecue was another tremendous success. Cummins ended up making the barbecue an annual tradition that was relocated to a larger venue, the Apollo Grounds. In 1897, a staggering sixty thousand people attended the feast in support of the Church of the Sacred Heart.

In a newspaper recap of the 1896 barbecue, readers got some tantalizing tidbits about Allen's backstory and how he cooked. First, the newspaper observed that "He *and his wife* know all that is to be known about conducting a barbecue, for they have had long experience in the south, and are in much demand in this part of the country too."[8] This may be the first time a husband-and-wife barbecue team was reported. As for the cooking, one article speaks more of technique. "Before the beef is placed over the fire a knife is thrust into it in a dozen or more places to a depth of 10 or 12 inches. In the cavities thus made salt, pepper, and other condiments are placed. The cook finds that this keeps all the rich juices in the meat, and only fat drops out in the pan under the beef. Every now and then the meat

5. "Barbecue Comes to Stay," *Boston Herald*, Sept. 8, 1895, 9.

6. "That Barbecue," *Boston Post*, Sept. 1, 1895, 5.

7. "That Barbecue," 5.

8. "Cooking an Ox Whole," *Pittsburgh Press*, Sept. 25, 1896, 5, emphasis added.

is basted with a savory sauce. This sauce is made from the recipe of a famous old French cook, and the secret of its composition is carefully guarded by Mr. Allen."[9]

Because of the large crowds, the Allens cooked additional items because one ox could go only so far. Chicken, mutton, and pork were added to the menu. In the 1897 barbecue, a reporter took note that Allen prepared an interesting side dish: "Sweet potatoes in large quantities were baked, to be served with the meats. Mr. Allen was disappointed in not being able to serve roasted corn. He has a special way of preparing this vegetable which makes it most toothsome. For a genuine southern barbecue . . . the chef serves what he calls a 'gumbo barbecue,' including a broth of chicken, with gumbo and tomatoes; also corn, turnips and potatoes."[10] The "gumbo" here is okra, and given the rest of the recipe, it looks as if Allen put his own spin on Brunswick stew.

The Allens' run with Father Cummins came to an end, but not their barbecue excursions to the North. In 1904, the Allens were brought to Montpelier, Vermont, to do a barbecue for the Barre Granite Manufacturers' Association and the Quincy Granite Manufacturers' Association.[11] Though they did secular barbecues, their experience with Father Cummins made them one of barbecue's earliest missionaries to the North. In a way, they were a mirror image of all those evangelists who brought Christianity to the South.

9. "Cooking an Ox Whole," 5.

10. "Notable Barbecue," *Boston Journal*, Aug. 22, 1897, 7.

11. "Quincy Men Coming," *Montpelier (Vt.) Evening Argus*, July 27, 1904, 4.

Battle's recollection puts us on the road toward a theology of barbecue, and it's all due to the stark contrast between the ways enslaved African Americans were treated in the confined, indoor church and the expansive experience of the outdoor camp meeting.

Even for those who weren't religious, church barbecue was part of plantation social life. Walter Leggett said of his enslaved experience on a plantation near Whitesville, North Carolina: "I ain't no church man and I don't hold nothing with them but when I was little chap the n———s used to have big doings at they church on Sundays. We had a church at Captain Burn's place and in the yard they had long tables and they'd nuf vittles for a hog killin'; pork, barbecue, fried chicken, molasses cake, big as a wash tub and spongy, then sweet 'taters puddin'."[11] Though tenuous, unchurched people like Leggett still associated barbecue with some aspect of church life.

The third type of worship experience occurred outdoors with a large crowd. Known variously as "big meetings," "bush meetings," "camp meetings," "protracted meetings," and revivals, these worship services were often massive, multiday outdoor events designed to win converts. White Baptist, Episcopal, Methodist, and Presbyterian clergy saw tremendous opportunities to grow their denomination's presence in the South via camp meetings, and the competition for converts was fierce. It's unclear whether they were inspired divinely or by politicians, but many camp meeting organizers figured out that barbecue was an excellent recruiting tool. The whole animal cooking, the wafting scents, and the sounds of sizzling meat demanded and attracted a crowd.

Many, but not all, camp meeting organizers took a "y'all come" approach to both their faith and their food, inviting the general public to partake, free of charge, and the invitees were happy to oblige. It certainly made an impact on Robert Shepherd, who was enslaved in Georgia and remembered, "When de craps was laid by and most of de hardest wuk of de year done up, den was camp-meetin' time, 'long in de last of July and sometimes in August. Dat was when us had de biggest times of all. Dey had great big long tables and jus' evvything good t'eat. Marster would kill five or six hogs and have 'em carried dar to be barbecued, and he carried his own cooks along."[12] As with Shepherd's experience, the camp meetings connected to plantations were segregated affairs following a prescribed social order.

In time, the camp meetings held farther away from plantations were open in all senses of the word. The Reverend Jermain W. Loguen, a formerly enslaved man, described one of these gatherings in a book he wrote in 1859:

81

The Methodists largely prevailed in this portion of Tennessee; and in the neighborhood of Manasseth's plantation was a notable camp ground for their great gatherings. At those annual gatherings, the inhabitants of the surrounding country assembled in great numbers, in their best costumes. As a general thing, the slaves also were there, as servants of their masters and mistresses, or to enjoy a holiday of personal relaxation and pleasure, or to sell the fruits some of them were allowed to raise on their little patches of ground. The free Blacks and poor whites were there also, with meats, fruits, and liquors of various kinds, to sell to the white aristocrats, who, from pride, or fashion, or religion, were attracted to the place. The camp was the universal resort of lovers and rowdies, politicians and pleasure seekers of every kind, as well as religionists, who gathered about the preachers, or promenaded in the woods, or refreshed at the booths, where the poor whites and Blacks exposed their provisions for sale. For years the old distillery monopolized the entire wholesale liquor trade on those occasions. The poor people aforesaid purchased it of Manasseth at a whole sale price, and retailed it at a large profit, to the world's people and christians [sic] who attended the meetings.[13]

This type of camp meeting gave both free and enslaved African Americans (at least those who got the master's permission or managed to "steal away") the opportunity to enjoy so many things that make us human: equal access to the divine, unfettered worship, the freedom to associate on equal terms with people of a different race, and an adequate, even abundant, amount of food and drink. In the racial caste system of the antebellum South, African Americans too often lacked all these and more. The freewheeling atmosphere of camp meetings was a stark contrast to the confining and rigidly segregated spaces that marked indoor church services of that time, where worship style, social interaction, and feasting were far more regulated.

So, we come to the meat of the matter: a theology of barbecue. Barbecue brings people together, creating a space where we can recognize the divine in each other, reaffirm our individual and collective humanity, and live the good life—*here, now*, not waiting until the afterlife. Today, we call this "radical hospitality," which "means finding ways to welcome the marginalized, forgotten, and misunderstood among us."[14] Radical hospitality transformed individual and collective mindsets because it gave the enslaved a window on a possible, alternate reality: a reality where they are seen, accepted, and loved as human beings.

Camp meetings drew large crowds; they were, by nature, temporary events. Yet the evangelists channeled the religious fervor they unleashed into the more enduring work of church planting. As congregations were formed and buildings built, the creation of worship spaces had tremendous religious and social implications for African Americans in the post-Emancipation South. Historian W. E. B. Du Bois noted in 1903, "The Negro Church [was] the first distinctively Negro American social institution. . . . The Church became the center of amusements, of what little spontaneous economic activity remained, of education, and of all social intercourse."[15]

Preachers, especially the great ones, operate as leaders of a particular flock and of an entire community. As Anthea Butler, an expert in religious studies, explained in a 2007 National Public Radio interview, there are historical reasons why African Americans look to preachers as community leaders. "In the slave community, the preacher arose as someone who could join the slave community with God and stand in the gap against the master in a certain sort of way. Post-slavery, we see the preacher as being the figure that's the one way in which an uneducated or an educated African-American man can rise to power."[16] Skillful preachers often used barbecue in their rhetoric to show "the common touch," display humor, explore theological concepts, and build a sacred community.

Community building was certainly the story with Henry Evans, a free African American cobbler and a Methodist preacher. Evans traveled from Virginia to Charleston, South Carolina, in the mid-1770s, and while passing through Fayetteville, North Carolina, he witnessed so much moral depravity that he felt compelled to stay awhile and preach the Gospel to African Americans in that area. He was so successful that city officials banned proselytizing in the city and he was forced to conduct secret worship services in the nearby woods. According to local legend, he used barbecue to recruit congregants to his invisible church. His barbecue was so good that it even converted local whites who were previously antagonistic to his evangelizing. Bob Garner writes in his history of North Carolina barbecue: "Local tradition maintains that this change of heart occurred just after white citizens searching the sandhills discovered—and ate—a hastily abandoned pig barbecued at the site of one of Evans's meetings."[17] Evans died in 1810 at the age of fifty, and the church that was built in his honor still stands in Fayetteville. I wanted to worship there in November 2019 but was unable to because the building was closed due to severe damage caused by 2018's Hurricane Florence.

Preachers understood that barbecue was extremely useful for building community. C. B. "Stubb" Stubblefield, a legendary Texas barbecue man and American Royal Barbecue Hall of Fame inductee, remembered his father's success as a "brush arbor preacher . . . in Navasota, a small town on the Brazos River, in the East Texas cotton belt."[18] Stubb told his biographer: "Preacher Stubblefield had a knack for bringing folks together with uplifting music, inspirational stories, and plates of barbecue. . . . He preached under trees or tents, fueling his congregation on potluck dinners of beef, pork, and even raccoon and possum."[19]

Socially and culturally, across the South, the rural church event was one of the few gatherings available to geographically isolated people. Even so, pastors knew that they faced competition for their congregants' attention against worldly distractions, and religious events with superlative food gave them an edge. Although a variety of foods was served at these church-hosted meals — sometimes called "dinner on the ground" if held outdoors — the holy trinity was fried chicken, fried fish, and barbecue. Fried chicken has a hallowed place on the Black church menu, but barbecue has certainly held its own. As more and more rural churches hosted barbecues, these faith-filled events reinforced to congregants that they weren't alone, that they belonged to something greater than themselves.

Later, when rural African Americans migrated to urban areas, they felt a new form of isolation, more social than geographic. Longtime African American urbanites snubbed the newcomers as unsophisticated country bumpkins and often refused to accept them. Once again, the Black church came to the rescue, replicating familiar and welcoming social customs, adapting them to an urban setting. A hand-dug barbecue pit in a country field was exchanged for a church's yard, a basement with a modern kitchen, or the sidewalk. The tools and techniques changed, but the theological goals remained the same.

As African Americans moved to urban areas across the country, they happily brought barbecue with them. In the urban context, the cultural expressions of "theological barbecue" varied. For an overwhelming number of churches, regardless of location and the demographics of their congregation, barbecue has built community through fellowship. As the *New York Times* reported of one Harlem congregation: "The Rev. Simon P. Boule, who comes from Columbia, S.C., is the pastor of Metropolitan A.M.E. Church. He describes what Sunday dinner means to his parishioners: 'Ninety percent of the people may not remember the exact theme of the sermon, but they will remember who they saw and who they talked with. They will remember the fellowship.'"[20] The food is certainly important, but it's the act of coming together and getting to know one another that brings meaning.

On par with, or even outstripping, the social aspects of church barbecue is its fundraising potential to support the church's work. Many churches took a page from medieval monks and tapped the talent of the artisans in their midst. I like the spiritual underpinning for this monastic fundraising concept explained on the Monastery of Christ in the Desert's website: "If there are artisans in the monastery, they are to practice their craft with all humility, but only with the abbot's permission. If one of them becomes puffed up by his skillfulness in his craft, and feels that he is conferring something on the monastery, he is to be removed from practicing his craft and not allowed to resume it unless, after manifesting his humility, he is so ordered by the abbot. Whenever products of these artisans are sold, those responsible for the sale must not dare to practice any fraud."[21] Black churches sold all types of food, but few passed up the opportunity to tap the expertise of barbecue artisans in their congregations. The increased competition could create resentment. In 1959, one barbecue business owner told his local newspaper, "If some churches don't stop selling so many barbecue plates, he's going to have to start holding some revival meetings and passing the hat."[22]

The frequency of church-hosted barbecue fundraisers often depended upon the barbecue talent in the congregation. If the talent was there, the sky was the limit. In the early 1980s, Thompson Memorial Church in Auburn, New York, Harriet Tubman's home church, hoped that a barbecue fundraiser would raise enough money to meet an existential threat and keep its doors open.[23] More typically, the proceeds from barbecues helped pay a church's bills. That was certainly the case at my church, where every July until recently the men organized a barbecued rib sale to celebrate "Men's Day." During my childhood, a group of volunteers spent hours under the tutelage of our congregation's leading barbecue men: Frank Garth and Willie Shinault. Garth and Shinault were rivals, friendly for the most part, and we would snicker as they gave us conflicting instructions on what to do to skin the ribs and season the meat before putting it on the grill. It was common for each to comment on how the other "doesn't do it right." The other men in the kitchen would silently laugh.

Garth made a highly regarded barbecue sauce that dates back to the 1940s. Garth was wounded in World War II, and while recuperating in a Veterans Administration hospital, his roommate gave him the recipe for the sauce. I couldn't get many specifics on the circumstances surrounding such a gift, but Garth ended up giving me the recipe. I had just graduated from law school, and Garth had hoped that I could bring his sauce to the commercial market. He also had enough faith in me that I could sell his sauce for $250,000. After researching the bottled barbecue sauce market, I realized that Garth would need a lot more charity to have that happen. Unfortunately, Garth died in the mid-1990s before we could capitalize on his idea. Talk about a crowded field! For the record, the sauce is blissful, and Garth's kids and grandkids make the sauce and sell it to people around the country.

There are also preachers who relied on church barbecue revenue to pay their salary. In the early 1990s, New Beginning Missionary Baptist Church in the Watts neighborhood of Los Angeles, California, did that very thing for its pastor, the Reverend Donald Clay:

> On the preceding Saturday, the kitchen at Minnie Dooley's house was taken over by the "By the Grace of God" barbecue team: [Daisy] Pearson at the stove over the baked beans and the sauce, Deacon Anthony Spears at the back-yard grills—chickens on one, ribs on the other. The team sold meals to go—$5 for chicken, $5.50 for ribs—to raise funds for Pastor Clay's third anniversary gift. By close of business, they had boxed 100 meals. "We don't give him a salary," Spears explains. "This is the only way we have of paying him back. Only he winds up giving it all back."[24]

Pastors and congregations certainly know that it is as much a blessing to give as it is to receive, and they endeavor to share their barbecue gifts with the world.

Many African American clergy are bivocational because they serve low-income sacred communities that are unable to compensate them for full-time work. To fill the gap, a remarkable number of Black clergy have made barbecue their second profession, or at least a profitable side gig. I have wondered why so many African American clergy feel called to preach the word of God and smoke meat. Could it be as simple as what Brother Hill said in the epigraph to this chapter? Several pastors have functioned as a pitmaster for their church barbecue, following the scriptural dictates to be a "servant leader." Others choose to run barbecue restaurants.

Good examples of the former are legion. In 1899 the Reverend A. W. Davis and Henry Elgin supervised an all-night barbecue with proceeds to benefit the building of a new church in Hopkinsville, Kentucky.[25] The year before, the Reverend Jay N. Taft upped the bar for all pastors by not only supervising the barbecue for his Long Island, New York, congregation but going to Maine and hunting the venison that was cooked.[26]

The Reverend J. B. Payton of St. James's African Methodist Episcopal Church in Newark, New Jersey, was so good at barbecuing oxen—and making money from it—that the Reverend R. H. Goden of Bethel African Methodist Episcopal Church in Jersey City hired Payton for his own church barbecue fundraiser in 1896. The *New York Times* reported that Reverend Payton "has been wondering for a good many years whether he is as good a preacher as he is a barbecue cook. He makes as much money doing the one thing as he has gathered in doing the other, but he is not willing to call the contest a draw."[27]

Barbecue restaurants were also a magnet for holy purposes like the civil rights movement. Civil rights leaders like the Reverend Dr. Martin Luther King Jr. often met at barbecue restaurants to strategize while getting good grub. One of King's favorite spots in his hometown of Atlanta, Georgia, was Aleck's Barbecue Heaven run by Ernest Alexander. Alexander opened his restaurant in the 1950s. Sometimes King and others stopped at Aleck's just to get a needed break. "King, [the Reverend Ralph David] Abernathy, and their followers would gather in a corner booth at the eatery during the heat of the civil rights movement. There, tired after campaigning, they would wolf down plates of ribs, coleslaw, pound cake and iced tea instead of plotting strategy."[28] Andrew Young, a King contemporary and civil rights legend in his own right, added, "This was one of Martin's favorite stopping places. . . . He only lived six blocks away, and many nights we'd stop at Aleck's to get ribs. If he was in a mood to read or write he'd take a slab of ribs home. If he felt like swapping stories with old man Alexander, we'd stay."[29] Aleck's kept that corner as a King memorial until the restaurant closed in the 1990s.

A barbecue restaurant can also be a form of ministry by showing kindness to others. This makes me think of the Reverend Jim Davis of Davis Grocery and Bar-B-Q (DGBBQ) in Taylor, Texas. Reverend Davis leads Rising Star Baptist Church in Rockdale, and he was working the front counter the day I visited his restaurant. As I was deciding what to order, he handed me a piece of mutton and said, "This is what you want. Do you remember your first kiss?" The good reverend had no way of knowing this, but his comparing something to my first kiss was not a good move for me, since the first girl I kissed immediately responded with "Yuck!" Fortunately, this time, the results were much more positive for all involved. The mutton, something that I don't normally get to eat, was a smoky, greasy delight. Though he ministered personally to my stomach, Davis also demonstrated empathy for his elderly customers via an off-the-menu item that he calls a "fat sandwich."

Some of DGBBQ's faithful customers are elderly folks with few or

IN THE SMOKE WITH "DADDY" BRUCE RANDOLPH SR. (1900–1994)
A GRACIOUS PLENTY OF BARBECUE

Most stories of "Daddy" Bruce Randolph's barbecuing life begin at age nineteen. After "walking away" from his home in Pastoria, Arkansas, Randolph returned to work for his uncle, Dr. M. M. McBeth. McBeth, whom Randolph called "Doc," was a strong influence, and Doc really believed in Randolph. He put him to work collecting bills for his medical practice. It turned out that he was a highly effective collector, probably because of his charm. For some reason, he had a yearning to get into the barbecue business. "'A man up the river had 200 to 300 head of hogs settin' on his place,' Randolph says. 'I'd buy one, butcher it, barbecue it, cut a piece of meat off and put it twixt two slices of bread, then sell it for 10 cents a sandwich.'"[1]

What's missing from the multiple accounts that I read are how he learned to barbecue in the first place. Unlike his uncle, who stayed in one community for years, Randolph had a peripatetic practice. After flirting with dance hall businesses, he headed west. "A restless Bruce, closed the dance hall and moved to other areas of the country. He finally found himself in Pampa, Texas, where he opened a restaurant and sold barbecue. The restaurant was a resounding success. He ran two restaurants there. One was in the black area. The other was in what was called 'Whitetown.' Bruce was the first black person to have a restaurant in the White area of Pampa. In addition to that he had a hotel and taxicab business."[2] Randolph prospered, but he was financially drained after a bad divorce. "'I just went and married the wrong woman,' Randolph says in his soft Arkansas drawl. 'When her lawyers got through with me, I was just about busted again.'"[3] He ventured to Tucson, Arizona, and started another barbecue business, but the seasonal nature of being in a college town wasn't profitable enough. He arrived in Denver in 1960, and he did a series of odd jobs to feed his family. Yet that barbecue yearning hit him again.

Then something unusual happened. "Randolph convinced an Englewood bank to loan him $1,000 on his signature. He used the

1. Mullen, "Daddy Bruce," 10.
2. Grant, *Daddy Bruce Randolph*, 23.
3. Mullen, "Daddy Bruce," 11.

money for a down-payment on a portable barbecue oven and he and
his son towed the 'barbecue pit on wheels' to company picnics and
parties all over Denver."[4] From that, he earned enough money to get
a permanent restaurant. As word of his barbecue skills spread, people
flocked to his restaurant. Randolph later became the official caterer of
the Denver Broncos football team.

He once told the *Los Angeles Times* that "his passions are the Lord,
people, and the Denver Broncos, in that order."[5] The *Times* added,
"When the Broncos went to the Super Bowl [in 1978], Bruce flew down
after them with a 'bunch of ribs, four hams, and five big briskets.'
[Broncos assistant public relations director Dave] Frei had a hotel
room and a bottle waiting for him, then Daddy Bruce was escorted to
the kitchen where employees were told 'fix everything like I wanted it.
My biggest job was keeping them cats in the kitchen from eating it all
up.'"[6] Randolph would smoke wild game by customer request.

His generosity is what stands out. He gave everything of himself.
He mentored Football Hall of Fame nominee Winston Hill—a former
offensive lineman for the New York Jets and Los Angeles Rams who
went on to run his own successful restaurant in Denver. "Even the
'street people' and the gamblers who haunt Five Points shine parlors
and taverns know that Randolph will serve up a plate of ribs, beans
and 'slaw on credit with no questions asked."[7] It's the free meals that
we remember most.

A deeply spiritual man, Randolph figured that he could follow

4. Mullen, 11.

5. Bill Curry,
"Daddy Bruce Says
His Thanks by
Giving," *Los Angeles
Times*, Nov. 25,
1982, 1.

6. Carol Krek,
"Daddy Loves His
Barbecue," *Denver
Post*, Sept. 20, 1978,
AA10.

7. Mullen, "Daddy
Bruce," 11.

Jesus's example with the biblical story of feeding five thousand people. Instead of fish and bread, he used ribs. Any holiday was an opportunity to help someone. He hosted an Easter egg hunt, Fourth of July barbecues, and Thanksgiving dinners. "He has devised a secret way to feed the multitude and he has his mother's secret formula for his barbecue sauce."[8]

It was truly a secret to most because Randolph adamantly denied getting any donations, at least in the early 1980s. No one knows when the tradition started, but Randolph took it up a notch in 1980 with a goal to feed five thousand people "turkey, ribs, potatoes, beans, bread, and assorted other treats."[9] After that, the amount of meals served grew exponentially to eight thousand the next year, then fifteen thousand the year after that. Some claim that the number got as high as fifty thousand. During several Februarys, he would travel back to Pine Bluff, Arkansas, to feed thousands of people *on his birthday!*[10]

As for that sauce, Randolph always credited his grandmother, whom he deeply loved, for his barbecue sauce. Though I grew up in Denver, I never ate at Daddy Bruce's, so I have no personal memories of the sauce. Most accounts described it as "pungent," and many have told me that it was very vinegary. When asked about the sauce's secret ingredient, Ron Mitchell, one of Randolph's first cousins and a longtime manager at the restaurant, said, "Just a lot of tender loving care. You could put all the ingredients in it, but without that, it wouldn't taste the same."[11] Bruce was a little more forthcoming when he was asked a decade earlier. A reporter noted, "His Grandmother's sauce recipe has served him well for six decades. Pungent with catsup, Worcestershire, Tabasco, vinegar, garlic, sugar and salt, it's the sauce that makes the difference, he said, not the wood smoke."[12]

Randolph's legacy endures. The street where his restaurant once stood was officially named after him in 1985. There's a book about him, a video documentary of him, and he even once got a shout-out in a rap song. Most important, I think, is that a score of faith leaders, volunteers, and corporate sponsors come together every Thanksgiving to feed needy families in Denver. I've volunteered in the massive assembly line myself on a crisp Thanksgiving morning, and everything except my back felt great about the experience. Randolph had a saying that adorned a billboard on his truck and was also right smack in the middle of his menu. He also thought it was the secret to his success. "Just say, God loves you and so does Daddy Bruce."[13]

8. Grant, *Daddy Bruce Randolph*, 49.

9. Curry, "Daddy Bruce Says," 1.

10. Marion Fulk, "It's His Birthday, but Daddy Bruce Does the Giving at a Barbecue for Thousands," *Arkansas Gazette* (Little Rock), Feb. 13, 1984, 1B.

11. Fulk, 1B.

12. Kreck, "Daddy Loves His Barbecue," AA10.

13. Grant, *Daddy Bruce Randolph*, 52.

no teeth. Understanding that even the tenderest smoked meat may be hard to handle, Reverend Davis created something that would be easier for his customers to eat. A fat sandwich consists of white bread, a slice of the fat cap that's been removed from the smoked brisket (making sure that there are a few shards of smoked meat needling the fat), and some of DGBBQ's famous "comeback" juice. As we'll see in chapter 7, this is a nickname for a popular barbecue sauce that has deep roots in African American barbecue culture. I know that this sounds kind of nasty, but I took a bite from a modified version of the sandwich using saltines instead of white bread. The taste was a revelation. The unctuous fat, the smoky meat, the salty cracker, and the spicy sauce melded together quite nicely. Perhaps God had intended the fat sandwich to include white bread, but the saltines really set it off.

If there is a promised land for Black church barbecue restaurants, most praise reports would mention Texas. I encountered more pastor-run barbecue restaurants there than in any other state. Yet they did exist elsewhere, and sometimes these operations became so ingrained in a city's barbecue culture that they were subject to full-blown restaurant reviews. In the late 1980s, Charles Perry, of the *Los Angeles Times*, reviewed Mt. Hermon Baptist Church in Santa Monica, California:

Mt. Hermon is not exactly a restaurant, though. It doesn't have — well, there isn't much point spelling out all the things the usual restaurant has that Mt. Hermon lacks, starting with walls and a roof. It's actually just the parking lot of a Baptist church. However, you can get some very good Southern barbecue there. The barbecue operation is a fund-raiser for the church, which is why there's a list titled "Donations" instead of a price list. It's undoubtedly why the people serving you are so sociable because they're clearly volunteering parishioners rather than restaurant professionals.[30]

Perry accepted the church barbecue for the earnest, no-frills operation that it is. He gave Mt. Hermon a favorable review and also noted in terms of ambience: "Eating here is always a social occasion, once in a while spiced up by a genial argument about the correctness of someone's views on barbecue (having been brought up in Texas and always having had it such and such a way regularly seems to be a decisive argument)."[31]

New Zion Missionary Baptist Church in Huntsville, Texas, was by far the most famous Black church–affiliated restaurant. May Archie, a church employee and restaurant staffer, shared in an interview that this barbecue business began with Sister Annie Mae Ward just doing a good deed for some church workers in the late 1970s.

[Sister Ward] was making barbecue for the pastor and her husband underneath an umbrella with a little barbecue pit and a table. Men were driving by, and they smelled the barbecue, and they started coming back, asking her if they could buy a sandwich. And she first said no because "I'm just cooking for my husband and the pastor." So many people stopped that the pastor finally told her, "Well, you know, maybe you should start selling. That will be money for us, so maybe you should start selling them sandwiches. So they started getting enough for her to cook and started selling sandwiches. The business got so big that they had to put her up a little building. It went from that to what you see there now. And as far as how many years it's been here, I'm pretty sure it's well over twenty-five.[32]

Word spread, and the flow of barbecue-seeking customers became so constant, that the church built a separate building from which the barbecue business operated. The barebones restaurant expanded its menu beyond chopped pork sandwiches to sell brisket, sausage, and sliced pork. It was so profitable that barbecue revenues financed all the small church's budget. The business lasted forty years until it quietly closed in November 2019.

Though we've dealt with Christianity extensively in this chapter, it was not sole expression of Black spirituality. The fastest growing religious identification among African Americans is Islam. There are several currents within Islam, but they all prohibit pork. So, other meats are in play, most typically beef. Halal barbecue restaurants are opening up, with some of the better ones in Detroit, Michigan, and different parts of Texas, namely Houston. If there are African American–run halal barbecue joints, I have not found them. Additionally, the Nation of Islam–backed Salaam restaurants featured meatless ribs on their menus in the 1990s, made from a closely guarded, secret recipe.[33]

Because barbecue is so engrained in African American church culture, it created multiple opportunities for people to learn and display their craft. Much as singing in gospel choirs proves a thriving training ground for many influential Black singers, so Black church barbecues provided the same opportunities for Black barbecuers who would later transition to commercial operations. Charles Allen, a man who was regularly summoned to cook at a famous annual church barbecue in the North, did so at the turn of the twentieth century. Though "Daddy" Bruce Randolph Sr. didn't learn to smoke meat at a church, he was a barbecue man who lived out his faith. Let the church, even if it's a meat church, say, "Amen!"

RECIPES

Mashed Potato Salad

In his book *Legends of Texas Barbecue Cookbook*, Robb Walsh credits this recipe to the cooks at New Zion Missionary Baptist Church. There it's served with an ice cream scoop. I hadn't really experienced this type of potato salad before I started eating my way through Texas. Walsh notes that this "soft and fluffy" style of potato salad is common in East Texas. I add some mustard to make it slightly tangy.

Makes 4 servings

1½ pounds russet potatoes
½ cup mayonnaise
3 teaspoons prepared yellow mustard (optional)
2 green onions, sliced
1 tablespoon pickle relish
4 teaspoons pickle juice
4 teaspoons hot pepper sauce
Salt, to taste

1. Peel the potatoes and cut them into 1-inch chunks.
2. Place the potatoes and enough water to cover in a 4-quart saucepan.
3. Bring the water to a boil over high heat.
4. Cover and simmer 15 minutes, or until the potatoes are tender.
5. Drain.
6. In a large bowl, coarsely mash the potatoes.
7. Stir in the remaining ingredients.
8. Serve at room temperature.

Jason Pough's Smoked Cabbage

I discovered righteous 'cue on a military base, of all places. Jason Pough runs Le'Pough's Barbecue out of Fort Lee, Virginia. His place caters to those on base, so the hours can be limited. Call before you visit, but it's worth the drive for his ethereal pork spareribs and chopped pork sandwich doused with a mustard sauce. This is a nice riff on braised cabbage, which is a popular side dish in soul food restaurants. Pough suggests using "Slap Yo' Mama" brand seasoning, but any spicy seasoning mix will do the trick.

Makes 8 servings

½ cup butter
1½ tablespoons garlic salt
1½ tablespoons cup sugar
1 head of green or red cabbage
Salt and pepper, to taste
Chopped parsley, to taste

1. In a small saucepan over low heat, melt the butter, and add the garlic salt and sugar. Set aside.
2. Bring a smoker to an internal temperature of 275°, adding wood chips to create the desired smoke once the smoker has reached the correct temperature.
3. Slice the cabbage head in half.
4. Season the cut sides of the cabbage with salt and pepper.
5. Wrap the cabbage in aluminum foil and place it in or on the smoker for approximately 2 hours.
6. Once the cabbage is sufficiently soft, remove the foil, cut the cabbage to serving-size pieces. Rewarm the sauce and spoon on top of the cabbage. Sprinkle with the chopped parsley. Serve immediately.

RISING SMOKE
THE ASCENDANCY OF THE AFRICAN AMERICAN BARBECUE SPECIALIST

Some things have always been typical of a Tennessee welcome. Some you will get, and some you will not get. A barbecue was one of them. I do not know whether altogether we have lost the art or not. So many of the old negro barbecue cooks are dead that a barbecue is a rather difficult matter to bring up to the old-fashioned standard. The negro barbecue cook, like the old cook who made biscuits that you gentleman from the East have heard of, and have eaten imitations of, has pretty nearly passed away. . . . Most of the experts in that line are dead and what we have now is rather a cheap imitation of the old type and style.
—*John Bell Keeble, 1919*

When Keeble sounded the alarm about the passing of a generation of Black barbecuers, it's hard to know if his national, geographically diverse audience of white architects in Nashville truly appreciated his concern. Keeble had clearly witnessed a generation of African American barbecuers who were of tremendous value in plantation culture. Yet in the media accounts of barbecue, these cooks typically remained anonymous. During the nineteenth century, these anonymous cooks saw barbecue transition from being reasonably sized private events that punctuated plantation life to something engrained in multiple aspects of southern society. Major life events such as a child's birth, a graduation, a wedding, or a funeral could involve barbecue. White tourists on fishing and hunting trips in the South often hired an African American cook to join, and barbecue could be on the menu depending on what was caught. Private barbecue clubs formed, and southern college fraternities and sororities started barbecue traditions that survive to this day. Any civic occasion—completing a public works project or celebrating a holiday—could lead to what was typically called a "monster barbecue" because of its huge size. In the vast majority of these situations,

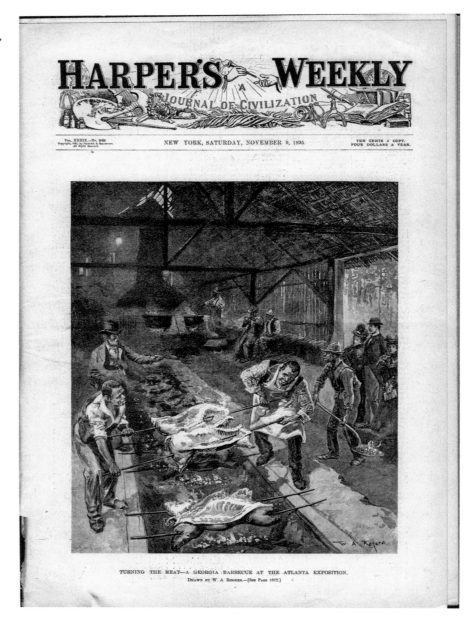

TURNING THE MEAT—A GEORGIA BARBECUE AT THE ATLANTA EXPOSITION.
Drawn by W. A. Rogers.—[See Page 1072.]

from the mundane to the monstrous, African Americans barbecuers were hired.

The mainstream barbecue of the nineteenth century, heavily influenced by Virginia barbecue, had these core elements: a certain way of cooking, Black cooks, Black servants, and Black entertainment. This pattern still held true at the turn of the twentieth century. What differed was the rise of a class of independent Black barbecue experts who could make barbecue on their own terms and get decently compensated for it. In this chapter, we'll look at how Black barbecuers were conferred expertise, what a typical job would be for them, and the challenges they faced in practicing their trade.

In the nineteenth century, when most people thought of "authentic" barbecue, they thought about southern barbecue. In time, local barbecue traditions popped up inside and outside of the American South. A communal pride emerged as people living in certain places were happy to cheerlead for the way barbecue was made in their area. Despite the attempts to create and celebrate these differences, the type of meat (beef, mutton, and pork) and the way it was barbecued was remarkably consistent across the South. Operationally, there was little difference, aesthetically and logistically, between, say, a "Virginia barbecue" and a "Kentucky barbecue." They all used some variation of the trench method that was developed in Virginia in the 1700s. As we'll see, the more discernible regional differences in terms of preferred meats, side dishes, desserts, and beverages appeared by the late 1890s and early 1900s.

Regional barbecue cooks could showcase their skills with a particular meat, but usually a wide variety of meats were cooked for barbecue events. For example, food media has distilled Kentucky's diverse barbecue traditions to one city and one type of meat—mutton served in Owensboro. In reality, the city boasted many different barbecue traditions during much of the 1800s. In 1868, the *Cincinnati Daily Gazette* reported on a barbecue held in Falmouth, Kentucky. The menu featured "shoulders of mutton, hams and ribs of pork and beef." The article also described how a "chief colored cook, in his uniform of white apron and paper cap, passed briskly around with his badge of office, a large butcher knife in hand, attending to the roasting, and giving directions to his help."[1] In 1896, the *Louisville Journal Courier* indicated that in Kentucky, "the fine beeves, mutton, and pork all serve to make this form of open-air entertainment a most attractive one."[2] Keeping with the pattern of showing regional distinction, numerous articles on Kentucky barbecue described the local side dish of "burgoo," a thick meat (usually lamb and chicken) and vegetable stew, and how to make it.

Newly freed Blacks marketed their barbecue skills to an enthusiastic and hungry public. Well into the twentieth century, African Americans enjoyed a competitive advantage in barbecue because of a widespread belief among southern whites that Black people made the best barbecue. Slavery's shadow loomed large in such thinking. The bona fides of a Black barbecue cook were inextricably linked to bondage. In 1909, nearly six decades after Emancipation, President William Howard Taft traveled to Augusta, Georgia, and devoured some barbecue prepared by a man named John Hays. A local newspaper reported, "The old darkey, John Hays, made the 'cue' just exactly the same as he has been doing every month 'since long befo' de war.'"[3] Black barbecuers of that era were similarly described in media.

Many barbecuers earned their reputation based on patron testimonials and word-of-mouth advertising. Newspapers gave barbecuers another platform to tout their skills. Some left it to reporters to tell of their culinary exploits, but such articles rarely gave details about the cooks. There was usually a fuller description of what brought about the occasion, the barbecue's program, the number of attendees, and generally what food and drink was served. Even with the richest depictions, the Black cooks were just a part of the scene's background.

In 1843 the Reverend Hamilton W. Pierson, a well-accomplished itinerant Presbyterian minister, wrote a remarkably complete description of a Kentucky barbecue in the 1880s called *In the Brush*. He commented on the Black barbecuers' "excitable natures . . . being [that] they were supremely happy" and how they "cheerfully plied their task, . . . frequently [singing] those strange, wild African songs that they are accustomed to improvise while at work and upon all kinds of occasions, and as they echoed among the forest-trees and floated out upon the night-air, the soft sweet melody was most enchanting."[4] Pierson's readers would have been familiar with the "happy slave or worker" trope. After all, how can servitude or low status in a racial caste system be all that bad if Black folks are happy and singing while doing the work?

Pierson's readers outside of the South were probably unfamiliar with his references to the African Americans singing work songs. Given how labor intensive it is to make southern barbecue, I suspect that they sang to coordinate their activity and make the job easier. Folklorist and music scholars note that work songs have a deep history in African American life that connects back to Africa. The context for many of the work songs that have been written down or recorded tends to be agricultural work or prison labor. I have yet to find a work song that explicitly refers to barbecue, and I can only wonder what Pierson experienced. Given the time period, he might have heard an early version of the blues.[5]

By the 1870s and 1880s, descriptions of barbecue in the media got more detailed, particularly when it was presented to readers as a curiosity. In addition to the spectacle aspect of a barbecue, reporters scrutinized the Black people who made the barbecue possible. From even the briefest interviews, the general public learned the names of Black barbecuers and gleaned insight into their barbecuing methods. Here's one such interview from a report on a Virginia barbecue in the late 1880s.

Down among the Chincapin bushes, at the base of the hill behind the house, a dozen colored men were engaged in preparing the barbecue. Long trenches had been dug and the carcasses of divers steers and sheep were spitted and placed over the coals in the pits. "How are you getting along, Uncle Henry!" asked Maj. Stofer of the boss roaster, a strapping big colored man. "O, pretty well, Massa Al," was the reply. "We's been a cookin' all night. I's jist a puttin' de finishin' touches on de sheep and beef dat wasn't done quite 'nough."[6]

Consistent with the racial etiquette of the time, Henry wasn't respected enough by the publication to have his full name listed. Far too many other Black men and women who barbecued in this era were identified as "Uncle" or "Aunt," respectively. Fortunately, in the 1880s and 1890s, racial attitudes shifted enough that white reporters began identifying Black barbecuers by their full names.

Some writers really didn't know what to do with empowered Black barbecuers. The way they presented barbecue cooks to readers revealed their own biased agenda. For example, barbecuer Columbus B. Hill, who is profiled in this chapter, was described in completely different ways when interviewed by two separate writers on the same day of a momentous barbecue event happening in Denver, Colorado, in 1898. The *Denver Post* depicted Hill as a knowledgeable and dignified expert who spoke standard English, and the image of him was drawn as any white person would have been at that time. In *The Rocky Mountain News*, Hill was portrayed as knowledgeable, but he spoke in a barely discernible plantation dialect, and he was caricatured with exaggerated features as if he had just stepped out of a minstrel show.[7]

Despite such racist depictions, white culinary experts consistently promoted African Americans as the essential barbecue cooks well into the twentieth century. In 1928, *Chicago Tribune* food columnist Jane Eddington wrote about barbecue's popularity and emphasized, "It is said that the colored man revels in this type of cooking, and many pretty things have been written of his work."[8] In 1952, famed Texas folklorist J. Frank Dobie expressed a similar sentiment when he informed his readers that barbecue's "expert cooks [are] usually Negroes."[9] These stamps of approval propelled Black barbecuers to local, regional, and even national repute.

With firmly established reputations as barbecue's "go-to" cooks, freelance barbecuers must have enjoyed boundless economic opportunities. Undoubtedly, there were some constraints. White racism and envy presented Black barbecuers with a commercial conundrum when practicing their trade in the South: They had to find the sweet spot between making enough money to eke out a living but not so much that would generate white resentment, and likely violence, against them.

Before refrigeration was widely available, barbecue was a seasonal business, beginning in May and usually ending by late fall, with the fall months being the busiest in order to avoid excessive heat, humidity, discomfort, and meat spoilage. Hot weather also brought pests. I experienced this firsthand during a family reunion that I attended in Helena, Arkansas, in July 2002. We had a barbecue picnic one afternoon, and even though the food we laid out was completely covered, flies descended on the scene like a biblical plague.

Since barbecuing wasn't a year-round business, freelance barbecuers pursued as many opportunities as they could during the peak season. Such opportunities were plentiful during Georgia's 1888 political season when five or more barbecues were held *every week* for a couple of months. Local cooks were usually tapped for such work. The dearth of newspaper advertisements during that time period suggests that recruiting was done largely by word of mouth. Don't get it twisted and think that barbecuers weren't good at self-promotion. Quite the opposite is true.

Today, barbecue experts are apt to call themselves "pitmasters," but back then, "barbecue king" was the preferred appellation. These royal figures were usually self-appointed and as numerous as today's proclaimed princes in Saudi Arabia, Nigeria, and Bel-Air, California. I'm not mad at them; I did the same thing when I appointed myself "the soul food scholar." Fortunately, I backed up my claim. If not "barbecue king," the person overseeing a barbecue was most commonly called the "superintendent," "barbecue artist," or "barbecue man." According to Texas barbecue expert Daniel Vaughn, the term "pitmaster" wasn't regularly applied to barbecue cooks until the late 1930s.[10]

At times, freelance barbecuing could be fraught with peril, especially when racist whites believed that someone was barbecuing to support a "pro-Black" cause. Thomas M. Drennon of Atlanta, Georgia, found himself in that situation in the early 1870s when Ku Klux Klan members tried to intimidate him from doing a barbecue for a Black political rally. This is going to sound like a fairy tale, but congressional leaders were so concerned about this that they held hearings. On October 21, 1871, Drennon traveled from Atlanta to testify before a congressional committee at the U.S. Capitol. At the time of his testimony, Drennon was a blacksmith and wagonmaker who cooked barbecue as a side vocation.

Drennon testified about a harrowing, late-night visit he'd had earlier that year when he was roused from his sleep late at night. Though the pretext for the visit was cooking barbecue, the Klan was much more concerned about how he exercised his political power. Drennon successfully dispersed the Klansmen by telling them that he voted a "white ticket," which they must have interpreted as him voting for white supremacist candidates. Drennon elaborated to the congressional committee in further testimony:

> Question. You told them you voted a white ticket?
> Answer. I said that I voted a white ticket; that was the answer
> I gave them.
> Question. What did they understand by that?
> Answer. I do not know.
> Question. You meant it to be somewhat equivocal?
> Answer. I just meant that I voted a piece of white paper; that is,
> that my ticket was on white paper.

It's hard to tell if Drennon was intentionally or accidentally brilliant, but the net effect is the same.[11]

Yet the very same kind of racists who intimidated Black barbecuers could turn right around and hire them for their own barbecues. African American barbecuers were a common sight at Confederate veteran reunions and Klan barbecues.[12] Sometimes, the Black barbecuers were depicted as supportive of the Lost Cause. One such example is Shackleford Pounds, who was profiled in a 1906 *Richmond Times Dispatch* article. The story is told of how Pounds became a Confederate army cook, joined the fighting, was armed with a musket in order to defend himself, and treated the wounded. To emphasize his pro-Confederacy sentiment, Pounds was observed to have been at Lee's surrender: "At Appomattox Shackleford Pounds walked up in line with the white men and surrendered his musket and wept over the necessity just as the white soldiers did."[13] After the Civil War, Pounds reportedly was a truly "independent voter" because he consistently voted for Confederate army veterans regardless of their political affiliation. Pounds, and others who were so portrayed, were useful foils to the independent-minded, freelance barbecuers who cooked for whomever they wanted.

Black barbecuers also ventured outside of the South and capitalized on plentiful opportunities to take and display their talent in other parts of the country. Many left the South during the Great Migration (1910s to 1970s) and settled in areas where southern barbecue was unknown. Freelance barbecuers were recruited, hired, and put on boats, trains, and stagecoaches to locales around the country to supervise events where the local hosts wanted a demonstration of "real southern barbecue":

101

IN THE SMOKE WITH COLUMBUS B. HILL
LEGENDARY BARBECUE MAN IN THE WEST

According to accounts from Denver, Hill is the real thing when it comes to barbecues and can put up a meal that would entice the average man away from home. For thirty years Hill has been the chef at all barbecues worthy of mention at Denver.
— *"Decorators Are Hampered by Delays,"*
Seattle Times, May 15, 1908

In 1888, Denver, Colorado, was a bustling town with a promising future. In a moment of pure self-congratulation, a group of prominent businessmen decided to throw a giant public barbecue, much like the one they hosted in 1882. For this barbecue, they hired a man named Columbus B. Hill to cook the meal of "barbecued beef, 'possum, bread, cheese, pickles, and other tempting delicacies."[1] A local newspaper described Hill as a "corpulent" man who is "active and spry for his years. He is a good cook and a good manager in the kitchen. To him more than anyone else is due the honor of the savory roasts enjoyed by 2,500 or more people yesterday."[2]

We don't know much about his early life, but Hill grew up in west Tennessee and moved to the Denver area in the 1870s. He was no doubt brought to the merchants' attention by Mohican Hill, his older brother, who was a noted Denver-area chef. Hill is listed in the *1887 Denver Directory* as a cook at Walker & Bailey restaurant at 1449 South Twelfth Street, and he lived at 1447 Stout Street, in the heart of what would later become downtown Denver.[3] The 1888 merchants' barbecue was tremendously successful, and it burnished Hill's reputation as a barbecue expert.

Hill went on to superintend several high-profile barbecues in Colorado, including one to celebrate the laying of the state capitol's cornerstone on July 4, 1890. The *Denver Republican* newspaper described the astonishing Independence Day scene:

1. "Banquet and Barbecue," *Rocky Mountain News* (Denver), Apr. 1, 1888, 3.
2. "Banquet and Barbecue," 3.
3. *1887 Denver Directory.*

Chef Hill, the Biggest Man in Denver This Day.

Columbus B. Hill, Denver, Colorado.
Denver Post, Jan. 27, 1898.

There were 30,000 pounds and over of beef, mutton, and veal, to be sure, but the [host barbecue] committee had also provided small-items in the shape of four tons of cheese and 5,000 loaves of bread, as well as 30,000 cucumber pickles. The three hundred waiters who attended to the wants of the guests were kept busy bringing bucketsful of ice-cold lemonade — and it was not circus lemonade, either — with which the barbecuers might assuage their thirst. In manufacturing the beverage, eighty-five boxes of lemons were used, and it required the major portion of 5,000 pounds of sugar to make it sufficiently saccharine for the taste of the multitude. Eight thousand tin cups were agents by which the refreshing liquid was transferred to thirsty lips. In a word, everything was on a scale which immensity alone can describe. . . . It was a study both in a picturesque as well as gastronomical sense.[4]

The number of cups provided gives one a good idea of how many people the organizers expected to attend. They were way off. Thirty thousand people showed up for the barbecue, and many went hungry. In the late edition of the paper, the very same *Denver Republican* editorialized: "There is no disguising the fact that yesterday's celebration in this city was disappointing to the people. The barbecue was a stupendous mistake, and the chorus of 1,000 voices a flat failure. It would have been far better to have provided a fine display of fireworks and a striking street illumination. We have no doubt that the managers meant to do what was best, but the general verdict is that they did not succeed."[5]

Despite the apparent disappointment, Hill's illustrious barbecue

4. "Ate and Were Merry," *Denver Republican*, July 5, 1890, 9.

5. *Denver Republican*, July 4, 1890, 9.

career continued. In early October 1894, he roasted an ox served with potatoes, bread, butter, and coffee for Greeley, Colorado's Potato Day harvest celebration. The *Greeley Tribune* noted that "C. B. Hill is a colored man and has a great reputation as a barbecue cook. He has officiated at more barbecues the past twelve years than any other man in the Union. From Missouri to the Lone Star state he has baked meats for hungry thousands and he thoroughly understands his business."[6] Once again, far more people showed up than expected, and a riot of the famished ensued.

This unfortunate turn of events still wasn't enough to kill Hill's career. Hill was given another big barbecue stage at what was called the Last Buffalo Barbecue, held in Denver on January 27, 1898. A group of Denver's prominent citizens wanted the city to be the permanent home of the National Stock Growers Convention— an annual gathering of prosperous cattlemen who bought, traded, and talked all things livestock. The ongoing economic benefit to Denver was not taken for granted. The concerned citizens figured that seducing the convention organizers and VIPs with a lot of Hill's barbecue would do the trick. On the gargantuan menu for the five thousand expected guests were 2 buffalo, 10 cows, 4 elk, 30 sheep, 2 bears, 15 antelope, and 200 possums. The side dishes included 35 barrels of yams, 10,000 pickles, 3,000 loaves of bread, a half-ton of cheese, 300 kegs of beer, and 200 gallons of coffee.[7]

This barbecue was well publicized, and the run-up to the event, especially the barbecuing, was heavily reported on by the local press. Unusual for that time period, Hill was extensively interviewed by a few of the local newspapers. He was highly respected by all for his cooking ability. Illustrations were made of the entire cooking set-up, the interracial team of barbecue cooks, waiters, and assistants, and all of the ancillary preparations. The local community was so fascinated by the event that some took the time to photograph it, though Hill is not identifiable in any of the pictures.

Sensing a theme to Hill's career, you probably already know what I'm writing next. Due to the great anticipation for the event—and the aroma that wafted all through town—an estimated thirty to fifty thousand people showed up for barbecue. That was far more than the five thousand expected VIPs, and they were all hungry. Someone had the bright idea to serve the beer first, hoping to mollify the throng. Predictably, a riot soon followed, causing Colorado's governor and Denver's mayor to run for shelter. The newspapers reported that many, especially women, children, and the cooks, were reduced to

6. "Greeley's Potato Day," *Greeley (Colo.) Tribune*, Oct. 18, 1894, 7.

7. Schlichting and Noel, "Ill Smelling Bones," 37–38.

tears. With some hyperbole, the *Littleton Independent* editorialized, "It was probably the last time that buffalo meat, bears' meat, opossum, antelope steaks, and venison will be served in barbecue style on the American continent."[8]

Unfairly, Hill was assigned much of the blame for the failed spectacle. It took a few years for his reputation to recover, but once again, like a phoenix, he rose from the career-killing ashes. He did a number of barbecues for African American churches (including my very own Campbell Chapel AME Church) and civic groups in the Denver area. His last reported big barbecue hoorah came on May 25, 1908, when Hill traveled to Seattle, Washington, to supervise a barbecue for the Atlantic battleship fleet, which had come to port after an extended tour of duty. In Hill's last-known newspaper statement, he said of the upcoming feast, "The sailors will sholy [surely] have a feast when they come to Seattle ef [if] I know anything about it. They've been having a good time all right down South, but when they get here they'll have a barbecue that is a barbecue."[9]

Hill died in Denver in 1923, leaving behind a wife and no children. Hill's body lies in an unmarked grave at Denver's Riverside Cemetery. Given the ups and downs that he experienced, I could have begun this chapter by calling him barbecue's comeback kid. The glimpses of his achievement that I share here shows that Hill was truly one of the greatest men that the world of barbecue has ever seen. He deserves more recognition for his barbecue legacy.

8. *Littleton (Colo.) Independent*, Jan. 28, 1898, 4.

9. "Decorators Are Hampered by Delays," *Seattle Times*, May 15, 1908, 10.

a taste that in some places has lasted to the present day. It was during a century spanning from the 1870s to the 1970s that African Americans were southern barbecue's most prolific, prominent, and effective ambassadors. Some stayed in an area just long enough to complete their appointed task, people like Henry "Poppa" Miller, Columbus B. Hill, and Charles W. Allen, all of whom were profiled earlier. Others decided to stay and live in new communities, starting barbecue enterprises there, as we'll see in the next chapter.

By the turn of the twentieth century, several things were in motion that fundamentally changed the nature of southern barbecue, with varying consequences for Black barbecuers. First, the days of "barbecue as a gargantuan public spectacle" declined, especially the political barbecues. Some candidates felt exploited by freelance barbecuers. In that era, political barbecues were free for attendees, and the candidates were expected to cover all costs. They were already in deep for other expenses, and they didn't appreciate barbecuers charging a premium for their services. In 1912, A. C. Kinard expressed this sentiment when he bitterly complained in a letter to the editor of the *Columbia Record*: "Candidates are not usually made of gold. (If they were we would not want them in office). And it is an outrage to impose them with this systemic robbery. . . . There is quite some profit in this, and yet the great majority of the candidates get nothing in return for it. And more than that, it has a bad moral effect on the people. It implies that a man will sell his vote for a 'cue dinner."[14] Kinard was as upset with the political system as he was with the barbecuers for hire.

One example of a dramatic intervention happened in the 1930s when political party officials coordinated in a way that limited the number of rallies and imposed price controls for the food provided. As the *New York Times* reported in 1934:

> Almost from the beginning of time, the open pit barbecue has
> been the lodestone that assured a crowd. It is an ancient Southern
> custom. A shallow pit, a sufficient supply of green hickory wood,
> a pot of hot sauce made of vinegar, salt and plenty of two colors
> of pepper; some rags on long sticks on which to baste the broiling
> shote and yearling; some Negro citizens to do the sopping of the
> sauce for the privilege of licking up the leftovers; and two-cent
> beef and three-cent pork on the hoof, soon became dollar-a-pound
> provender for the political aspirant. The office seeker was expected
> to bear the expense of the feast for the privilege of haranguing the
> multitude.[15]

Rather than be "rallied to death," the party officials believed that coordination "guarantees the personal appearance of all candidates, inspires them to supreme effort through increased attendance, and makes of the expense a tithe of its former self."[16] Rather than pay the high cost of barbecue, some candidates passed along the costs by charging attendees, or they shifted to serving a different type of food altogether. In 1882, "Instead of the old-fashioned barbecue and ox-roasting the political clubs of Baltimore County are introducing picnics and potato roastings."[17] The net effect was a dwindling number of opportunities in this field.

Another change during the 1890s was that more white men delved into the business of barbecue. White men had always been in the barbecue game to some degree, but now they started getting significant press on par with, and at times, exceeding what Black barbecuers got. Two such freelancing barbecue men were Sheriff John W. Calloway and Gus Jaubert.

Sheriff Calloway of Wilkes County, Georgia, is one of the earliest and most prominent examples of the celebrated white barbecuers. Perhaps no other barbecue was reported on more extensively than the barbecue Calloway supervised at the Cotton States and International Exposition in Atlanta in 1895. Vivid descriptions of the barbecue appeared in syndicated newspapers across the country. I opened this chapter with an unforgettable image of the scene, which made the November 9, 1895, cover of *Harper's Weekly*—a highly influential and popular magazine. The image is remarkable because all the action is centered on what the Black men are doing, and Calloway seems to do very little. This work dynamic is supported by print descriptions of what happened that day. I can see why some called it "superintending."

A decade later, Calloway was extensively interviewed in Charleston, South Carolina, ahead of a barbecue event, and he shed light on his barbecue past. "'But how did you learn this art of preparing a barbecue?' Mr. Calloway was asked. 'That was thirty years ago. I learned it from the ordinary [a local religious leader] of Wilkes County. He was an expert at it and he said that I was an apt scholar.'"[18] Later in the interview, Calloway spoke of his African American assistant, Henry Pettus: "Mr. Calloway is quite sure that no one could 'touch him' in Georgia in the way of preparing a barbecue. He says he has thirty years' experience, and he has brought to Charleston a negro who has been helping him for twenty years. 'But Henry hasn't the courage to do it alone,' said Mr. Calloway with a good-natured smile. . . . 'My man is afraid to attempt it by himself, but he is a fine cook, and next to myself knows more about preparing a barbecue than anyone in Georgia.'"[19] In a recap of an 1890 barbecue at Stone Mountain, Georgia, Calloway was described as the "presiding genius at the pits and pots. The right-hand man was Henry Pettus."[20] For Calloway, Pettus seemed truly indispensable, and I hope we can learn more about him as more source material from the past becomes available to researchers.

Monsieur Gus Jaubert of Lexington, Kentucky, also gained national prominence. Barbecue historian Robert F. Moss wrote of Jaubert: "If John W. Calloway was the barbecue king of Georgia, Gus Jaubert played the same role for Kentucky. At the age of 14, he was hired to help turn the spits at a political rally in Hopkinsville and was hooked. After learning the art from the local experts, he emerged after the Civil War as Kentucky's top barbecue cook. In 1866, he first served barbecue and burgoo (Kentucky's now-famous slow-simmered stew) together at the same event, and he helped make burgoo a staple part of the state's political rallies."[21] Jaubert was certainly one for self-promotion. He told a Louisville newspaper: "'The largest barbecue ever attempted in the United States,' said he, 'was the one I got up in Louisville for the G.A.R. [Grand Army of the Republic] veterans in 1896. There we prepared to feed 100,000 people, and over-estimated. I took sixty negro cooks and 170 waiters with me from Lexington, and these were reinforced by Louisville cooks and waiters.'"[22]

Though he came on the scene decades after Calloway and Jaubert, Walter Jetton was another great freelance barbecue man and one of the last of such stature. Jetton gained a national reputation as the favorite barbecuer for fellow Texan President Lyndon Johnson. Jetton was profiled in the influential magazine the *Saturday Evening Post*. As big a media splash as that was, the writer fortunately acknowledged one of Jetton's longtime assistants. "Jetton's barbecue expert is Ethan Boyer, a dignified, sixty-year-old Negro who has been with him for thirty years. Boyer presides over an enormous brick oven with three separate grills, in which as much as 20,000 pounds of meat can be smoked daily."[23] This raises the question of how one separates the superintending from doing the actual work. Was the product of this interracial team of barbecuers truly a joint effort?

Calloway, Jaubert, and Jetton had one important thing in common: they all relied heavily on Black labor and expertise, and they weren't the only white men to do so. As we saw in the last chapter, most barbecuers, Black or white, needed a corps of assistant cooks and waitstaff to pull off the event. Black staffers were overwhelmingly called upon for such work. We may never know the dividing line between what the white barbecue men knew, where they learned it, and how much work they did at these barbecues as compared to the Black barbecuers.

As mentioned earlier, Calloway and Jaubert, in particular, earned a national barbecue spotlight, but they reigned at a time when their type of barbecuing, and the large events associated with such barbecuing, were in decline. The 1880s and 1890s saw barbecue change in significant ways. The "monster" barbecues were downsizing. The notion of a free barbecue was fading away. During much of the nineteenth century, it was understood that a barbecue host committee would supply every need. Now notices for barbecues were charging a nominal fee or asking attendees to bring their own food as they would for a potluck meal. Just because big barbecues were less frequent and more economical doesn't mean that the reputations of African American barbecue specialists waned. They maintained their status as the masters of all schools of slow-cooked barbecue and were sought-after cooks in any setting: public or private, indoors or outdoors.[24]

Barbecue was also transformed a second time to emphasize cooking smaller cuts of meat in contained cooking apparatuses rather than whole animals in open-air pits. This new type of barbecue suited barbecue stand operators and restaurateurs who wanted to commercialize barbecue further. This shift from the al fresco, whole animal barbecue to urbanized, indoor cooking featuring smaller cuts of meat was the most consequential redefinition of barbecue since it had been invented by fusing Native American smoking traditions with carbonadoing. In fits and spurts, African American barbecuers gradually lost their dominant advantage over their upstart competitors.

Previously, for much of the nineteenth century, barbecue was something that few white people did as a profession. That dramatically changed by the century's end. I wondered why, and a conversation with legendary North Carolina pitmaster Ed Mitchell, provocatively, provided some insight. He explained that many people simply lack the skills to do whole animal barbecuing properly, but they saw how much money these Black barbecuers were making. If you can't cook the whole animals yourself, or you can't hire a Black person to do it for you, what do you do? You make it easier to cook by breaking it down into more manageable parts. If that became an acceptable form of barbecue, more people could enter the field.

What Mitchell said made sense intuitively, but I wondered what historical evidence supported his theory if I broke it down into manageable parts. As for the cooking expertise required with whole animal cooking, Sam Jones, another whole hog barbecue legend, and a white

IN THE SMOKE WITH WOODY SMITH AND HIS BARBECUE TREE

Being chosen as helper by the appointed barbecue cook was also considered to be extremely advantageous. The helper was usually younger and could assume that if he learned from his experiences that the job of cook may some day pass on to him. There were also smaller functions in the area, usually associated with church picnics, which afforded experience for the cooks and their helpers, but these were not considered as important as other celebrations.
—*John Marshall, circa 1983*

If you looked up "barbecue tree" in the dictionary, it would probably be defined something like this:

> **barbecue tree** *n* 1) any tree that is chopped down and used for fuel to prepare a barbecue, as in apple, cherry, hickory, mesquite, oak, peach, or pecan; 2) *plural*: **barbecue trees** a nickname for two circular groves on the east side of the U.S. Capitol building, planted during the presidential administration of Andrew Jackson, where the Democrats and Whigs held partisan barbecues.

I'm adding a third definition, one pertinent to an African American man named Woody Smith and analogous to a "coaching tree" in professional sports. Sports media uses "coaching tree" to colloquially describe the influence of a successful coach whose staff members go on to demonstrate coaching success on their own. A "barbecue tree" in this sense means "the influence of a barbecuer who trains or mentors others to become highly regarded, successful pitmasters and/or restaurateurs." Henry Perry, who is discussed in the next chapter, lays claim to the most famous barbecue tree. He's credited with not only kickstarting Kansas City's barbecue scene but training Arthur and Charlie Bryant, George Gates, and Arthur Pinkard, men whose culinary prowess further defined Kansas City barbecue. Many other barbecue trees took root all over the country, but they remain unacknowledged. It's time we recognize Woody Smith, who put an enduring stamp on barbecue in Hickman County, Kentucky.

Woody Smith, Arlington, Kentucky.
Photograph by John Marshall.

Woody Smith arrived in tow as a one-year old when his parents, Willie and Effie Smith, moved from Obion, Tennessee, to Hickman County in 1909.[1] Willie Smith was a great barbecue man himself, having learned the art from a man named "Uncle" Ben Hayes. Hayes "has an established reputation as a barbecue cook in the district, and when called on several times a year to cook for social functions or political gatherings, Uncle Ben would enlist the aid of Will Smith. The experience not only increased the reputation of Will Smith, but it also enabled him to develop the necessary expertise to cook for himself and for others when the time came."[2] By learning from his father, Will Smith, Woody Smith became a part of the Ben Hayes barbecue tree.

Smith got his crack at the pit when he was "'about twelve or thirteen,' when he was asked to help his father cook for a function at Vaughan's Grove near Spring Hill in Hickman County. Since he was five or six years old, Woody had been going with his father to sit up at night while his father was barbecuing with and for others, however, his first experience as his father's only helper, and one from which he made his first barbecue money, was at a function at Vaughan's Grove."[3] It was an important time for Smith not only to learn this specific culinary art but to bond with his father. He told folklorist John Marshall that "for fifteen or sixteen hours the Smiths sat through the night and early morning watching the sheep cook, tending the fire, putting glowing hot coals into the pit and scattering them around under the animal, talking and laughing."[4]

Thanks to *The Kentucky Barbecue Book*, a definitive work by Western Kentucky University literature and writing professor Wes Berry, we have a strong sense of how influential Smith was in creating a hyperlocal style. "Hickman County barbecue, as passed down by local legend Woody Smith, who got it from his father, one of the oldest pit

1. Lillian Marshall, "Where There's Hickory Smoke, There's Barbecue," *Louisville Courier Journal Magazine*, May 6, 1973, 93.

2. Marshall, 93.

3. Marshall, "Traditional Barbecue Methodology."

4. Berry Craig, "Barbecue: For Scholar, It's Food for Thought," *Paducah Sun*, Jan. 1, 1982, 1.

masters in these parts, is defined by whole pork shoulders cooked over hickory coals for a full day in covered cinderblock pits. The local sauce, served at all three barbecue places, is mostly white vinegar with a heavy cayenne pepper kick."[5] Smith trained on barbecuing sheep, and Smith's expertise extended to cows, pigs, and wild game. "In addition to their regular work, pit-barbecue places do a great deal of 'custom cooking.' . . . Woody Smith of Clinton, who used to cook for the famous Fancy Farm barbecue before he started his own business, reports a brisk demand for cooking groundhog, beaver, raccoon, opossum and venison."[6] Though Smith began barbecuing in the 1920s, he was rather unheralded in the press until the later years of his professional career.

Smith's career was peripatetic. "For many years, Smith cooked at the Spring Hill Y, at the intersection of U.S. 51 and Ky. 809 in Hickman County, just over the line from Arlington in Carlisle County. . . . Smith cooked in Arlington before moving on to a pit near Wingo."[7] A 1973 roundup of Kentucky barbecue by the *Louisville Courier Journal* pointed out another location. "You'll have no trouble finding good pit barbecue, whether you're on U.S. 51 that goes past Woody Smith's place near Clinton."[8] Though he had several cooking stints in various locations, Smith left a mark wherever he worked.

In July 1977, a *Washington Post* columnist had the nerve to write about southern barbecue without mentioning Kentucky. The defenders of Bluegrass State barbecue invoked Woody Smith without explicitly mentioning his name or the place where he barbecued. Congressman Carroll Hubbard also chimed in by listing several notable places that he felt should have been included: "Then, there's this place (Nicky's) on Highway 51 between Clinton and Arlington in Hickman County."[9] Though not specifically mentioned, locals knew Hubbard was talking about Woody Smith.

In 1975, a reporter for the *Louisville Courier Journal* lamented: "The first generation of barbecue-shop proprietors are disappearing. Woody Smith, whose reputation as a master barbecue was widespread, retired last year and passed on his skills to young Nicky McClanahan, who runs a shop at the same location in Clinton."[10] Nicky McClanahan, longtime owner of Nicky's B-B-Q in Clinton, Kentucky, confirmed when interviewed by Berry:

I was in manufacturing for twenty years before this, and I didn't know anything about cooking, I hadn't even boiled water. But there was a man here, a Black man named Woody Smith, that had been

5. Berry, *Kentucky Barbecue*, 35.

6. Marshall, "Where There's Hickory Smoke," 93.

7. Craig, "Barbecue," 1.

8. Marshall, "Where There's Hickory Smoke," 93.

9. Ed Ryan, "Spitting Mad," *Louisville Courier Journal*, July 15, 1977, B3.

10. Irene Nolan, "Pit Barbecue Is a Regional Art," *Louisville Courier Journal*, Mar. 2, 1975, G1, G3.

here several years, and he was retiring, and Harper's Hams owns the building. So, Mr. Harper called me and said he wanted me to run it. I told him I didn't know anything about cooking, barbecuing, or anything. It took me about two months to make up my mind. Finally, I called him and told him, I said, "I'll take it under one condition—that if Woody will work with me a year." So he did and we cooked everything while he was here that year that he'd ever cooked. Then he retired and I'm still here. Barely.[11]

I appreciate how transparent McClanahan is about how he got his barbecue training.

The same goes for Red Grogan, of an eponymous barbecue joint in Hickman County, who added, "Woody was king. . . . When I was ten years old we didn't have a lot of food around the house, and I'd go sit up all night with Woody [while he tended the pits] and he'd feed me. I didn't think I was learning, but I did that until I was sixteen, and I guess I learned something."[12] Even Gordon Samples of Ruby Faye's Bar-B-Que said, "My first memory of barbecue was that cooked by Woody Smith at the Springhill 'Y.' I loved the smell when we would go to pick up barbecued pork shoulder from hogs that we had raised on our farm. The taste was equally satisfying. We are honored to continue the tradition and add to this legacy from our past."[13]

Smith was a humble man who once said, "I was never a hand to brag on myself."[14] That leaves others, like me, to do it for him. Smith was the greatest barbecuer in the Ben Hayes barbecue tree in terms of productivity, longevity, and legacy. It makes one wonder why Kentucky barbecue is always confined to the city limits of Owensboro, when other subregional cuisines thrive within the state. Woody Smith's example shows that, occasionally, it's okay to lose sight of the forest by focusing on the venerable barbecue trees in our midst.

11. Berry, *Kentucky Barbecue*, 37.
12. Berry, 38.
13. Berry, 41.
14. Craig, "Barbecue," 1.

dude, agrees with Mitchell. "In eastern North Carolina, more so than anywhere else in the country, the definition of barbecue has historically been pretty simple: a whole animal cooked over wood, or coals. . . . It was done that way out of expediency when the slaughter was part of the barbecue event, and meat didn't arrive in a refrigerated truck. . . . I personally don't believe you can re-create what happens when you cook a whole animal when you start with an individual cut."[25]

Before you completely brush off their comments as North Carolina barbecue partisans, note that the emerging urban barbecue scenes of that era featured smaller cuts of meat. John Shelton Reed and Dale Volberg Reed write, "The first barbecue stands in Lexington and Salisbury [North Carolina] were just cooking parts of the hog-loins, hams, and especially shoulders" by people who shared a common German ancestry.[26] Texas folklorist Frank X. Tolbert writes similarly of the early barbecue proprietors in central Texas: "In fact, in these towns where there are many folk of German, Polish, or Czech ancestry, the best places to eat are often in the smoky back rooms of meat markets. . . . Part of the back room will likely be taken up by a small sausage factory. There will always be a big brick barbecue pit over which beef, mutton, goat meat, and sausages will cook for hours, very slowly, from smoke as much as heat radiation."[27]

The "skills envy" part of Mitchell's theory is harder to prove, but there is circumstantial evidence. Though people of all types opened barbecue restaurants, it was common for a place to be owned and operated by a white person while African Americans were the main barbecuers. The examples are too numerous to recount here, but I offer one. In 1930, the Cozy Corner restaurant in Roswell, New Mexico, beckoned customers by advertising in the newspaper that this restaurant was "where will you find your Southern Barbecue cooked by a [sic] old southern colored cook, Uncle Sam."[28]

The 1890s were a tremendous time for the business of barbecue. The growing emphasis on smaller cuts of meat paved the way for an urbanized barbecue featuring some of today's most distinctive styles. In addition to the above examples from eastern North Carolina and central Texas, by the 1920s, a vibrant mix of native Blacks, whites, and immigrants created their own traditions with smaller cuts of meat in places like Kansas City, Missouri (brisket, sausage, and spareribs) and Memphis, Tennessee (pork shoulder and spareribs).

The takeaway here is that Black barbecuers began to face intense commercial competition from whites in a field that they once dominated. White entrepreneurs started opening restaurants featuring this new and expanded version of barbecue. The earliest iterations of these restaurants were rudimentary barbecue stands, but they eventually evolved into sit-down, brick-and-mortar locations that would help define a region's barbecue style.

African American barbecuers adjusted to the shifting barbecue terrain and the increased competition. Any significant competitive disadvantage to white barbecuers didn't last long, as Black barbecuers gradually started their barbecue-related businesses. They had a firm foundation to do so, thanks to freelance barbecuers like Columbus B. Hill of Shelby County, Tennessee, and Woody Smith of Hickman County, Kentucky, whose barbecue excellence paved the way for others.

RECIPES

Henrietta Dull's Whole Hog Barbecue

This recipe for Georgia barbecue is excerpted from *Southern Cooking* by Henrietta Dull, which was first published in 1928. Barbecuers like Columbus B. Hill, Marie Jean, Woody Smith, and Arthur Watts probably used a similar old-school method. It assumes that you already know how to build a pit. Should you choose to update this recipe, you may easily find information online about how to build a cinderblock or metal pit to the right specifications.

First, select first-class meat, weighing from 35 to 50 pounds. Remove head near shoulders and feet just above the first joint. Cut or saw smoothly, longitudinally through the center of backbone so the pig will open perfectly flat. Cut out the thin flanks on each side of carcass in circular cut and throw away. Now it is ready for the pit. Run sharpened iron rods (or oak sticks) longitudinally through [the] hams and shoulders, allowing extensions of both sides to catch the banks of the pit. This makes it convenient to hold carcass up and furnishes hand holds to turn.

These rods should be inserted near the skin and under the ribs in order that the neck, shoulders and hams may go down lower into the pit for better cooking, and the rods under the ribs prevent their falling out when tender.

Laterally insert three or four small rods (iron or oak) which must be stuck through at proper intervals at sides extending through the carcass. This prevents meat from dropping off when done. The rods are strapped in place by using hay wire.

The pit is sixteen inches deep and as long as needed. Small green oak wood is best to use for making the red coals. The heat must not be too great when the cooking is first begun. When the meat is warm, baste with a strong solution of warm salt water containing a little cayenne pepper. This is continued at intervals until meat is nearly done. The moisture from the water prevents the meat from scorching. As often as the meat becomes dry, turn meat side up and baste with this salt solution. Never salt before cooking. About one quart of salt made into strong solution will be necessary for basting a 50 pound pig.

As the meat cooks, more heat may be applied. Keep the coals bunched under the shoulders and hams, allowing the thin part of the pig to have less heat. When meat is nearly done, baste two or three times with plain warm water. This drives the salt in and washes off the outside salt. Always use warm water, never cold. Place carcass over pit, meat side down and cook this way, only turning long enough to baste the inside and allowing the skin to become hot from time to time. Meat must not burn and should be watched carefully.

When nearly done, place skin side down and begin basting with the butter sauce. When done and very tender, remove some of the coals from pit, turn skin down to brown and crisp. At this time it should be watched closely. The skin should be brown and crisp, not gummy. During this last cooking the meat side is up and the basting done frequently.

The sauce, as well as the salt water, must be kept warm. Remember the cooking is slow and takes a long time, so it will require a good deal of salt water. Again let me say during the first cooking when the salt water is used the meat side is kept turned to the coals.

When ready to serve, cut up, putting skin in one pan, meat into another. Baste meat frequently with the butter sauce. Do not put any sauce over the skin, this will make skin soft and gummy. To be good it must be crisp and brittle.

Butter Sauce

This barbecue sauce is the "butter sauce" that Henrietta Dull references in the above recipe. Butter-based barbecue sauces are fairly common in old-school Georgia barbecue circles. This is definitely a recipe for a crowd. I have retained most of her original language.

2½ pounds of butter
2 quarts of apple cider vinegar
1 pint of water
1 tablespoon dry mustard
½ cup minced onion
1 bottle of Worcestershire sauce
1 pint of tomato catsup
1 pint chili sauce (medium size)
2 lemons, juice only
½ lemon, put in whole (seeds removed)
3 cloves garlic chopped fine and tied in a cheesecloth bag
2 teaspoons of sugar
Salt and pepper, to taste

1. Mix all together in a large saucepan.
2. Cook until heated and well blended and season well with salt and pepper.
3. With a mop baste meat. This sauce is used when meat is about three-fourths done.
4. The sauce must be kept warm.
5. This is for a large quantity. It can be reduced to the quantity desired.

BARBECUE IS MY BUSINESS
THE EMERGENCE OF AFRICAN AMERICAN BARBECUE ENTREPRENEURS

5

It's been less than a week
And almost out of meat
All except for those pig feet
Lord time is so hard
I just ran out of lard
This is no good for my heart
Junior clean up the yard
Money is what I need
To make ends meet
So, I think I'll sell some Bar-B-Que pigs feet.
—The Reverend Charleszetta "Mother" Waddles, 1970

Mother Waddles (1912–2001) was a legendary figure in Detroit, Michigan, for decades. An impressive combination of community activist, entrepreneur, philanthropist, and preacher, Waddles aided thousands who grappled with the harsh realities of inner-city life and living at the bottom rung of a racial caste system. To supplement what she got from government assistance programs, Waddles sold barbecue from a tub in front of her house. Her barbecue was so good that she turned a one-time customer into a husband. A lot of Black folks sold barbecue to make ends meet, and Black entrepreneurs found many ways to do so. Based on how the last chapter ended, you might expect me to pick up the story in the 1890s, but Black entrepreneurship with barbecue goes way back in the day.

I am not sure what Ophelia Settle Egypt expected to hear about barbecue entrepreneurship history when she interviewed Cornelia in the late 1930s under the auspices of the Social Science Institute at Fisk University, but that's what she got. As Cornelia drew on memories of her enslaved childhood near Spring Hill, Tennessee, she shared history and an incredible tale:

Master Jennings allowed his slaves to earn any money they could for their own use. . . . Every Sunday, Master Jennings would let Pa take the wagon to carry watermelons, cider, and ginger cookies to Spring Hill, where the Baptist church was located. The Jennings were Baptists. The white folks would buy from him as well as the free Negroes of Trenton, Tennessee. Sometimes these free Negroes would steal to our cabin at a specified time to buy a chicken or barbecue dinner. Mr. Dodge's slaves always had money and came to buy from us. Pa was allowed to keep the money he made at Spring Hill, and of course Master Jennings didn't know about the little restaurant we had in our cabin.[1]

Cornelia's unnamed father ran what possibly was the first underground takeout barbecue business from his slave cabin that served an interracial, economically diverse clientele: more proof that African Americans, even under horrific circumstances, have been hustling from Day One. Cornelia's father is one of barbecue's earliest reported entrepreneurs, keeping company with John Stavely, a white man who served barbecue at his Alexandria, Virginia, restaurant in 1798, and possibly Marie Jean, who is profiled in chapter 2.[2] If you're thinking about Skilton Dennis and his barbecue wagon near Ayden, North Carolina, as the earliest barbecue business, get that out of your mind. One of Dennis's descendants, Sam Jones, dispelled that myth in his book *Whole Hog BBQ*.[3]

Cornelia's story is hard to verify, and it does raise questions. Unfortunately, we know neither Cornelia's last name nor her father's full name. It's also hard to believe that Jennings was clueless about the operation. One gleans from Cornelia's interview that Jennings probably operated a small farm with a limited number of enslaved people rather than a sprawling plantation. How could he have not smelled the barbecue or seen the flow of customers? Most likely, Jennings knew about it and considered it an extension of the money-making activities that he already allowed. If true, this one of the earliest recorded Black-owned barbecue businesses.

The story of the African American barbecue entrepreneur is one of challenge, triumph, a fair amount of racial irony, and resiliency. Though freelancing, hired-out cooks remain an important aspect of Black barbecue business culture, I'm focusing this chapter on restaurateurs in brick-and-mortar locations. Here, we'll see the roots of barbecue restaurants in rural areas, how they adapted to an urban context, the challenges urban barbecuers face, and how they are adapting to a more competitive environment.

Marie Jean and Cornelia's father show us that Black entrepreneurship predated Emancipation. During the antebellum period, free and enslaved African Americans worked in a variety of enterprises, many of them using specialized skills that they developed in bondage.[4] Though sometimes surreptitious, this activity was often sanctioned by the enslaver. After the Civil War, the emancipated African Americans' expertise in food service transferred into successful catering, restaurant, and street vending businesses. As just one measurement of growth, the 1910 U.S. census indicates that during the previous decade, African American restaurant keepers grew from 3,995 to 6,369 (a 59 percent increase). The 1910 census also listed 3,434 Black hucksters and peddlers. Although we don't know how many barbecue-related businesses were included in these statistics, they are a clear indication that restaurant activity boomed. Monroe N. Work, a researcher at the Tuskegee Institute, concluded from 1910 census data that "in the ten years, 1900–1910, the Negro had made about as much progress as he had made in the previous thirty-five years."[5] Specific statistics are hard to come by, but newspaper advertisements and business directories indicate that Black food entrepreneurs often specialized in barbecue, fried fish, and fried chicken. The ease of starting a barbecue business at the turn of the twentieth century shows why. All one needed was a place to dig a pit, a reliable fuel source, an animal to cook, and the requisite skills to cook it.

In rural areas, barbecuers dug a pit on their property, at a secluded area in the woods, or along a roadside to take advantage of passing traffic. These were the kind of places where one often had to get "country directions" to find them: "You go down that road until you see a stump. Then turn right, and follow it to Old Man Johnson's place, the one with the broken fence, then make a left." These operations ran then pretty much the same way they do now: "The vast majority of truly rural pits are open for business on only two or three days a week (Thursday, Friday, and Saturday), though most cater special events on other days. These places commonly sell more food as carryout than is/was consumed on the premises."[6]

Few rural barbecuers generated enough money to sell barbecue full-time, so their barbecue business was a side hustle. As sales improved, they could be open more days of the week. As they prospered, some entrepreneurs improved the physical plant of their business by adding walls and a roof and perhaps seating. Given the barebones setup, these places weren't called restaurants but were usually named "shacks" or "stands." For Blacks and whites in rural communities, these eating places were part business, part community center—a rare place to gather in sparsely populated areas. As one observer noted in the 1940s, "A Texas contribution to Negro folkways is the barbecue stand, with its outgrowth of customs. Business deals are often closed and social engagements made at a barbecue stand, where meats cooked in open pits by Texas Negroes have a flavor which they claim is distinctive."[7] I've witnessed this myself on numerous occasions. The staff and customers interact in a way that demonstrates the enduring community-building and power-reinforcing of the Black barbecue restaurant, even if the place is primarily takeout.

As barbecue businesses gradually appeared in urban settings, some Black barbecuers like Harry S. Green (1855–1922) of Owensboro, Kentucky, followed the example of their rural counterparts. It was written of Green that "although his barbecue pit was 'simply a hole dug in the ground,' his decision to sell the product established his business as the first barbecue stand in the city. . . . He was successful, selling as much as 1,000 pounds of barbecue during each year's county fair. . . . Historians of Owensboro have mentioned the small business he ran out of his home as initiating a long tradition of barbecue businesses in the city."[8] Green dug his barbecue hole in the 1890s at his home on the corner of Ninth and Hall Streets in Owensboro. In time, he became famous for his mutton, which remains the city's signature contribution to the national barbecue canon. He never transitioned from his home-based business to a brick-and-mortar location, but he kept busy for over three decades by catering for local events, most notably the annual Daviess County Fair.[9]

Other urban barbecue entrepreneurs, especially those without enough money to operate in a building, set up shop in urban common spaces such as alleys or sidewalks. That was certainly the case with Henry Perry, generally credited as the "father of Kansas City barbecue". He preferred calling himself, no surprise, the "King of Barbecue." Perry was born in 1875 in Shelby County, Tennessee (where Memphis is located), and, after a nearly two decades of itinerant employment, made his way to Kansas City in 1907. He first worked as a porter at a saloon, but soon afterward, he was selling barbecue in a Banks Street alley near downtown Kansas City, Missouri. Barbecue had certainly existed in the Kansas City area since the mid-1850s, but Perry is regarded as the first person to sell it commercially as a regular business.[10] In the two decades after opening for business, Perry changed locations several times, along the way showing his versatility at adopting new cooking technologies and his virtuosity. Sometimes he operated from a pushcart, a streetcar, a pit he dug in the ground, or a brick pit.[11]

In a hilarious 1911 interview for the *Kansas City Star*, Perry shared how he stepped up from a simple trench to a brick pit:

> "Now, here's where I barbecue," and Henery [*sic*] showed the caller a brick-lined pit some three feet deep, three feet wide, and ten feet long, over the top of which was an iron grating. "I build a charcoal fire in that pit a day before the barbecuing begins and get all this ground around good and hot. Then I roll the beef or pork on that grill and start the real barbecuing. Sometimes it takes twenty-four hours to cook it. I've never seen a meat yet that I couldn't barbecue. That goes for sheep, hogs, geese, chickens, fish, rabbits, squirrels, 'possums, oysters and most everything [*sic*] you've heard of. And this barbecue system is getting popular with the white folks, too."[12]

Perry's business was little more than a tent and the barbecue pit. He was interviewed during the dead of winter, so he must have been making enough money to operate year-round. Business was slow that day, and he did tell the interviewer, "This is the dull season. Just come around here when it gets warm weather and you'll see King Henery [*sic*] browning the meat and smell that sage gravy."[13]

Perry's experience spotlights how technology played an important role in the early barbecue restaurant business and the cuisine's spread. The inventions of brick, glass, and metal barbecue pits allowed entrepreneurs to replicate the horizontal trench in a variety of locations, all year long, and with predictable results. In 1897, Ellsworth B. A. Zwoyer patented a design for charcoal briquettes, though Edward G. Kingsford and automobile manufacturing magnate Henry Ford far more successfully popularized their own version in the 1920s.[14] Cooks no longer needed access to wood, and they could still give meat a distinctive flavor. Barbecue was now a movable feast that could expand throughout the South and be transplanted outside of the region.

As mentioned in chapter 4, millions of African Americans decided, like Perry, to leave the South for better opportunities elsewhere. This gradual and massive movement of an estimated six million African Americans has been coined the "Great Migration."[15] Some of the longest-running Black barbecue restaurants fired up their pits during the early years of this migration. Circa 1910, Walter Jones opened the Hole in a Wall in downtown Marianna, Arkansas. Jones's grandson, James, now runs the business as Jones Bar-B-Q Diner out of his Marianna home.[16] In 2012, the restaurant received the James Beard Foundation "America's Classics" Award, and the sandwich of sauce-doused, chopped pork between two slices of white bread is barbecue simplicity

at its best. In 1912, Jack Patillo opened a restaurant in Beaumont, Texas, that is now run by his grandson, Robert. It's one of the oldest barbecue restaurants in Texas, and we'll learn more about this amazing restaurant and its history in chapter 6.

When they arrived in cities outside of the South, the Black migrants were awestruck. As one Smithsonian Institution publication describes it: "Excited by the size of the buildings, the bright signs and lights, and the bustle of the streets, they were also impressed by the absence of obvious signs of segregation. They noted that Blacks and whites mingled on the sidewalks and sat together on streetcars. They noted that there were no (or almost no) 'Colored [only]' or 'Whites Only' signs on drinking fountains or in restaurant windows."[17] In some places, the sense of wonder was fleeting. Whites viewed the migrants as unwelcome competitors for their jobs and disruptors of their way of life. Even if segregation didn't officially exist with some public accommodations, whites still drew the color line against Blacks in schools and residential housing.[18]

The migrants also got another reality check, one they probably didn't expect—a frosty reception from Blacks who had already lived in communities in migrant destination cities for a long time:

> The newcomers also met with a less than open armed welcome
> from those Blacks who were already established in the North,

sometimes for generations. This group had at first encouraged the migration. But as the number of newcomers grew, the "Old Settlers" realized that they were fast becoming a minority within the Black community. Until this influx, their numbers had been small enough so that African-Americans were not particularly conspicuous as a group. In most places in the North, they had lived scattered throughout the city. Most newcomers had country ways. Many wore headscarves and overalls. They spoke differently, were often more boisterous, and they tended to be less educated than their northern counterparts. Many Old Settlers viewed these newcomers as a threat to the gains that the previously established African Americans had made. And in fact, for a variety of reasons, it was true that discrimination was on the rise in the period after World War I.[19]

Initially, at least, the Old Settlers divided their transforming Black communities by drawing class and cultural lines against their new neighbors. Rather than criticize, some segments of the Black community, namely churches, media, and social agencies, tried to help Black southerners make the transition to urban life with all its complexities.[20]

Food became a focal point in some of the social clashes, and barbecue operators were sometimes the targets. A good number of the early barbecue entrepreneurs improvised and operated from flexible locations. They were street vendors or pit diggers; some had basic set-ups where they barbecued out of an oil barrel or, if really desperate, a used mattress spring. Once the meat, seasoning, and other inventory were procured, all one had to do was start a fire and let the aroma announce to potential customers that the business was "Now Open." That "Hot Light" at Krispy Kreme has nothing on the unmistakable and irresistible wafting scents from the early barbecue stands.

African American newspaper editorial boards were some of the harshest critics of the urban barbecue entrepreneurs. In the 1920s, the *Baltimore Afro-American* described barbecue's arrival in hostile and pessimistic terms: "Barbecue, that juicy, succulent and fragrant meat which has won almost as many elections in the South as the Democrats has invaded Pennsylvania Avenue. . . . Only occasionally does a former resident of Nashville, Tenn., Beale Street in Memphis or parts west come in to try the savory pork ribs, shoulder or beef shortribs."[21] The article went on to argue that barbecue's failure to catch fire "may be due to the superior tastes developed by Maryland cuisine, or the inborn hatred of all things southern by the most southern of the northern ports."[22]

Though the newspaper predicted failure, barbecue eventually gained in popularity.

In 1922, the *Chicago Defender* was no less kind when one of its headlines screamed "Germ Dealers Imperil Health on South Side." The unappetizing editorial elaborated:

> Not satisfied to plaster their house fronts and fences with the ridiculously misspelt and dizzy-looking "cue" signs, these burnt meat merchants are erecting open-air grease joints and fly traps on every vacant lot in the district covered by the Second and Third Wards. . . . There is no place for this sort of thing in this great community. "Open air kitchens," as some of the operators of these places please to call them, may be O.K. in the sunny South, but Chicago and other northern cities should not and will not stand for them.[23]

This was certainly harsh, but the editors were building on things they had previously written.

A large number of these barbecue entrepreneurs had a horrible reputation for selling burnt, spoiled, undercooked, or unappetizing meat. "Thank heaven for the winter time!" the *Chicago Defender* editors exclaimed in late October 1921. "It is to be hoped that the same chilly blasts that kill the germs in the alleys and in the air will so stiffen the dirty barbecue hucksters that they will pass away like the last summer, never to return again."[24] The *Chicago Defender* drove the point home even harder again in that 1922 editorial by describing the bedspring grills as infected with bedbugs and the hucksters masking spoiled meat by drowning it in barbecue sauce. The editorial concluded, "Can you beat it? Is there any wonder that the ordinary barbecue joint has an odor like a soap factory?"[25]

Mainstream barbecuers in this era also faced ridicule, but mainly for making barbecue so poorly. Roadside barbecue stands drew the most ire. In 1935, a *New York Times* writer plaintively asked, "Where, the tourist may ask, are the famous barbecues that started with the frontier and flourished for years on the Lincoln Highway as far as Allentown, Pa.? Compared to that hearty Indian cookery of the lusty past, the minced meat in a flat roll with tomato sauce, now sold at roadside stands, is scarcely recognizable as a 'barbecued' viand."[26] By 1949, a writer for the *Saturday Evening Post* bitterly bemoaned to readers that what he ate at many of the "cutely named Bar-B-Q or Bar-Bee-Cue places" was "apt to not be barbecue at all, but half-done pork, slices of which are lathered with a hot sauce." The article then explained the way to make barbecue properly, promising that "it rests on the stomach like a benediction and may be fed to suckling babes."[27]

Despite these critiques from minority and mainstream press, barbecue's popularity grew, and barbecuers proved to be some of the most colorful characters in a city's dining scene. As African Americans prospered, dining out increasingly became an option. In a national survey of African American food habits done in the 1940s, Natalie Joffe noted: "From region to region, the restaurants patronized by Negroes differ in character and quality. In the rural South they are few and in Southern cities they are small and none too numerous. Barbecue parlors, cafes, and diners are usually found in the Negro business districts. Since many people in the South go home to eat, there is not much demand for regular restaurants."[28] Joffe went on to state that restaurant options for Blacks, and the demand by Black customers for such restaurants, varied outside of the South, and that when African Americans dined out, "barbecued ribs are a popular dish."[29] That love for ribs, as well as other barbecue dishes, inspired many entrepreneurial dreams, but such dreams frequently got a rude awakening.

It's often said that running a business is a marathon, not a sprint. Imagine a marathon where some runners have to clear hurdles periodically along the route, when others don't. That's what it's like for Black entrepreneurs, who face a host of race-based obstacles in addition to the regular ups and downs of running a barbecue business. I lump these race-based obstacles together into a category that I call "ill will." Ill will is the exact opposite of "goodwill," which is an accounting term used in valuing a business. Here's a good working definition of "goodwill": "To put it simply, commercial goodwill is the various advantages and benefits associated with having a strong name, reputation and connection with other companies and organizations operating within your industry. It is something which, over time, pulls in new customers and helps you remain competitive—it enables you to distinguish yourself as an established and trusted firm, something which new companies struggle with in the beginning. Any intangible attribute which contributes in the long-term to a company's earning potential can be described as goodwill."[30] For a barbecue restaurant, goodwill can mean the individual and collective reputation of staff members in their community, the restaurant's name recognition, patrons' perception of customer service, social media influence, and, most critically, intellectual property such as recipes and cooking processes.

Ill will, then, is the culmination of tangible and intangible race-based factors that give African American barbecue entrepreneurs businesses

IN THE SMOKE WITH JOHN HENRY "DOC" HAMILTON
BLACK BARBECUE'S BAD BOY

Doc Hamilton has always seemed about as genial and harmless an old sinner as anyone could wish for. He really is an essential figure in Seattle's position as a "big city"; certainly he has led the most consistent fight for night life here, in the face of tremendous odds, that has ever graced the records. Doc's majestic stature, his beaming smile, and his fried spring chicken (even at $1.50 a shot) would lend prestige to a community. — *"Doc Hamilton Seeks to Keep Half His Pit," Seattle Times, July 1, 1932*

John Henry "Doc" Hamilton was a larger-than-life figure in Seattle, Washington. He moved from West Point, Mississippi, to Seattle around 1915, possibly for military service. By the 1920s, he was already known in the community as a World War I veteran (serving a stint in France), a serial entrepreneur, an accomplished cook (particularly barbecue and fried chicken), and a notorious gambler. Legend has it that he laid down a thousand dollars on a roll of the dice.[1] Hamilton's first enterprise was running a high-class speakeasy out of his apartment at 1017½ East Union Avenue during Prohibition. While he was vacationing at the Hood Canal, the police raided his home by axing down the door and seizing the liquor and cocktail-making paraphernalia.[2] Hamilton actually petitioned the court to return the seized "Champagne, gin, Scotch and Irish whiskey, Bacardi rum, Crème de Coco, Sparkling Muscatel, Curaco and Cascade beer."[3]

Down but not out, Hamilton opened Doc Hamilton's Barbecue Pit a month later with fifteen thousand dollars from his own funds and some financing provided by his brother.[4] Get any idea of a run-down place out of your mind. This was an upscale club that rivaled Harlem's famed Cotton Club in décor and service. Business was bustling, and Hamilton earned quite the reputation for his barbecue beef sandwiches, fried chicken, Virginia ham, and biscuits. Terry Pettus, a longtime African American resident of Seattle, reminisced in 1984: "Doc was a real character, and his place was very high class. The food

1. Ralph Matthews, "In Seattle," *Baltimore Afro-American*, April 7, 1934, 5.

2. "Batter Down Three Doors, Seize Whiskey and Cocktail Shakers," *Seattle Times*, July 28, 1924, 13.

3. "Asks Court to Return Seized Liquor," *Seattle Times*, Nov. 28, 1924, 4.

4. "Incorporations," *Seattle Times*, Aug. 22, 1924, 21.

John Henry "Doc" Hamilton, Seattle, Washington. Seattle Times, Feb. 21, 1926.

there was just terrific. He ran a high-rolling craps game in the basement, but most of us went for the food." Pettus added that Hamilton was fascinated with cookbooks and that he might have gotten some restaurant experience in New Orleans.[5]

Hamilton's love for intoxicating drinks was well known, and law enforcement repeatedly raided his restaurant in search of liquor. Even when caught with the goods, Hamilton frequently escaped severe penalties because he had friends in high places—many of them customers. In 1926, Hamilton was one of several codefendants in a sensational public trial that alleged a conspiracy of law enforcement officials, politicians, and private citizens to smuggle booze from Canada to Seattle. The public's fascination with Hamilton grew as local press commented on his outlandish outfits, charming smile, witticisms, and habit of sleeping during the trial. The last item could be a mix of confidence about the trial's probable outcome or the fact that he still ran his barbecue business at night to make ends meet.

Despite the stress of being on trial, Hamilton had his mind on his barbecue. As the proceedings dragged on, one particular day Hamilton was supposedly "aroused to a state of nervousness for fear that he won't get up to his 'Barbecue Pit' in time to see that the roast beef is done just right for the sandwiches."[6] Hamilton even once gave out free barbecue sandwiches to court employees—not to the judge or the jury—as a kind gesture. He was ultimately acquitted.

Yet Hamilton's legal troubles persisted. The police raids continued (despite his payoffs), and he was sued multiple times for failing to pay his bills. For a time, the cycle of restaurant raid, arrest, and exoneration (at the very worst, light punishment) seemed endless. After one arrest, Hamilton promised the judge that he would be on the up-and-up by obtaining "a trained police dog with ears so

5. Emmet Watson, "Old Time Radical Reminds Us Human Nature Is Nothing New," *Seattle Times*, Jan. 24, 1984, 9.

6. *Seattle Times*, Feb. 2, 1926, 7.

sensitive that he will set up a ferocious barking if he ever hears ivory tickling against ivory." He named the dog Ham, and police officers later verified that it worked. The dog seemed to keep Hamilton from playing old tricks.[7]

Eventually Hamilton crossed an unforgivable line. It wasn't because of a vice but likely because he wanted to buy a nice house in a white neighborhood. Sensing that he was breaking an unwritten rule, he fronted the purchase with a white man. Of course, the true tenant was discovered, and after that, his legal problems got more serious.[8] On November 16, 1931, Hamilton was "arrested in the rear part of his pit at the height of what the state contended was a brisk dice game."[9] To escape this predicament, Hamilton pleaded with the state to let him keep the barbecue half of the business open while everything else was shut down.[10] There was no reprieve.

The summer of 1932, Hamilton was sentenced to serve one to five years in the state penitentiary located in Walla Walla.[11] Legend has it that he traveled to jail in style via a limousine.[12] Media reports say it was by train. In December 1933, the state parole board released Hamilton. As a free man, as always, Hamilton pursued his dreams. Before prison, he had dreamed of running a massive dude ranch that would include a possum farm. He kept eight opossums in a pen at his barbecue joint, and someone stole three of them. "Reporting the theft to police . . . Hamilton had to tell about his dude ranch enterprise—how the eight 'possum were to be the progenitors of generations of thousands of real old Southern 'possum dinners, and how there will be turtles and horses as the rest of the ranch's livestock—horses for the paying guests to ride and turtles to make rich green soup as a first course for the hungry riders."[13]

He operated the dude ranch in Berrydale (five miles south of Kent) and debuted the property by placing a newspaper advertisement inviting "his friends and former patrons" to a free barbecue.[14] The dude ranch wasn't as successful as he hoped, so he returned to his old spot at 908 Twelfth Avenue to run a place called the Bagdad, which specialized in southern food.[15] Hamilton's last act literally involved comeback sauce. This is commonly known as a sauce so good that it makes one come back for more. Here, Hamilton hoped that selling his barbecue sauce door to door would fuel his comeback to prosperity, but that dream never came true.[16] He died on September 9, 1942, in poverty and living in a hotel. He was 51 years old.[17]

7. "Doc's Dice Hound Is on Job," *Seattle Times*, May 27, 1927, 17.

8. Watson, "Old Time Radical."

9. "Doc Hamilton Seeks to Keep Half His Pit," *Seattle Times*, July 1, 1932, 3.

10. "Doc Hamilton," 3.

11. David Suffia, "The Saga of Doc Hamilton," *Seattle Times*, April 1, 1974, 13.

12. Armbruster, *Before Seattle Rocked*, 137.

13. "Somebody Played 'Possum on Doc; Ranch Secret Out," *Seattle Times*, February 29, 1932, 7.

14. *Seattle Times*, July 19, 1935, 3.

15. *Seattle Times*, Jan. 3, 1937, 13.

16. John J. Reddin, "John J. Reddin Remembers," *Seattle Times Magazine*, Aug. 24, 1969, 2.

17. Suffia, "Saga of Doc Hamilton."

a competitive disadvantage. The main ingredients of ill will that I focus on are the racial attitudes of whites toward Blacks, government regulation, a lack of access to capital, and the theft of intellectual property. Let's take a closer look at each factor.

The racial attitudes of whites toward Blacks generate the most ill will. Before we go further, I must note that white racial attitudes are not monolithic. How whites have felt about, and treated, Blacks varied greatly in intensity across time and place. With barbecue, these racial attitudes could cut either way, and as a result, Black-run barbecue joints often find themselves located at the intersection of food, race, and absurdity. As a 1947 study of Black businesses observed, "In nearly every southern city, however, there is a Negro-operated barbecue stand which draws considerable general trade either because the Negro cook has an established reputation or because community legends hold that only Negroes can cook 'real' barbecue."[31] The interesting legacy of this specific expectation from whites gave Black barbecuers a competitive advantage for decades.

Because of the ways that Blackness and barbecue were wedded in the eighteenth century, many whites sought out barbecue made by Blacks, regardless of how they felt about the cooks. Though most whites would carry out their barbecue, some sat down and dined in Black establishments. Depending on the owner, the dining would be "come one, come all" or segregated. Black barbecuers were often lauded in the Black press for their ability to attract white customers. A 1919 article in the *Topeka Plaindealer* applauded: "In Oklahoma City, Okla., you will find Mr. John G. Gholston, located at 18 California Avenue. He is known as the 'Barbecue King' of the world. Here you will find people of all nationalities wending their way to his establishment. Here you will find delicious barbecued meats of all kinds. Even the prejudice of the white people cannot keep them away from his place, and his kind, courteous manner retains them as customers."[32]

Such hospitality was not always reciprocated. In a common practice in white-run restaurants in the South, but certainly not exclusive to that region, Blacks could only carry out their food from a restaurant's side window or back door. Remarkably, some African American barbecuers themselves drew the color line by operating whites-only dining rooms. Such practices were protested in the 1940s, 1950s, and 1960s, and both Black and white establishments were the targets of such direct-action techniques as sit-ins. In 1962, Daisy Bates of "the Little Rock Nine" fame picketed a barbecue joint in that city, alleging that the owner, a Black woman, had a segregated dining room; half of it was air-conditioned for white diners.[33]

Government action is a big component of ill will. It's one thing for individuals or groups of people to have racial animus toward African Americans. It's another if the state discriminates, and, by action or inaction, aids and abets private discrimination. A critical means of control is access to prime real estate, or as they say, "location, location, location." Jim Crow segregation and anti-Black sentiment limited where Black entrepreneurs could set up shop. The lack of access to storefronts in downtown areas, business districts, or wealthy sections of town required a change in business strategy. Instead of operating in a stand-alone building in an urban center, many started their barbecue businesses at their homes, improvised in available public spaces, or operated from remote locations outside of town.

City planners confined Black businesses to the "run-down" parts of town, which limited their access to customers and potential profits to grow their business. As one study of residential segregation observed:

> It is not uncommon in these small towns to find a block in the older and less desirable part of the main street, or on a side street, turned over entirely to Negroes for their small businesses and service establishments. The restaurant or barbecue stand . . . are located here. In a few of the cities of the South there is a concentration of the Negro population which approaches complete segregation. The separation may be marked by a railroad track, stream, or other fixed barrier. . . . Generally considered, the core residential sites of Negroes will almost certainly be found near centers of cities in the oldest residence areas, where buildings are out of date, depreciated, difficult to keep in repair, and practically impossible to purchase because the area has only a limited residence value.[34]

Home-based and stand-alone restaurants didn't fare much better in the North, where Blacks tended to settle in "sites abandoned by early white residents, along with or in close succession to other racial groups of similar or slightly higher economic status."[35]

When operating home-based restaurants, many Black barbecuers typically did so in racially segregated neighborhoods. One barrier to residential integration was racially restrictive covenants in neighborhoods where white residents agreed that they would never sell or lease their home to Blacks. Another barrier was a Depression-era federal government program. "The establishment of the Home Owners Loan Corporation in 1933 helped save the collapsing housing market, but it largely excluded Black neighborhoods from government-insured loans. Those neighborhoods were deemed 'hazardous' and colored in with red on maps, a practice that came to be known as 'redlining.'"[36] Though this practice was banned more than fifty years ago, the resulting "racial discrimination in mortgage lending in the 1930s shaped the demographic and wealth patterns of American communities today, a new study shows, with 3 out of 4 neighborhoods 'redlined' on government maps 80 years ago continuing to struggle economically."[37] Redlining affected these businesses in two profound ways. These businesses operated in areas where the local customer base tended to be low income and thus price sensitive. Second, depressed home values limited entrepreneurs' use of home equity as a financing option for their businesses.

Those who could open brick-and-mortar barbecue joints frequently operated in dilapidated buildings in an area with poor public amenities. This situation was so pervasive that it has become essential to the Black barbecue aesthetic. Black customers often expect a "legit" Black barbecue restaurant to look run-down. I'm reminded of a conversation I had with Mary Gatlin, who helps her son Greg run the fantastic Gatlin's BBQ in Houston, Texas. She told me, "Customers tell me all the time how clean our restaurant is."[38] In many economically distressed, high crime areas, customers must negotiate looking through bulletproof glass, interacting through a loudspeaker, receiving one's barbecue through a turnstile, and eating it elsewhere because there's little to no seating. The mix of the poor physical condition and a high number of Black people in the surrounding neighborhood are enough to keep an appreciable number of white potential customers and influential restaurant reviewers away. As such, Black barbecue restaurants get less business and attention than they should.

The dynamic between Black business owners and their white customers wasn't always permeated with fear. Between Emancipation and the widespread enactment of Jim Crow segregation laws in the 1890s, Black businesses catered to both Black and white clientele, and they were conveniently located in vital sections of the city where it was easier to attract customers. Jim Crow's effect intensified in many communities with the creation of so-called Negro main streets, where most Black-owned businesses were located or relocated from other parts of town.[39] The intentional undercutting of the Black customer base overlapped the increasing popularity of mainstream barbecue restaurants.

Speaking of location, my search for great Black barbecue often led me to neighborhoods in places that had "East" in its name: East Austin, East Cleveland, East Denver, East Detroit, East St. Louis, East Palo

Alto, and Northeast Washington, D.C., to name a few. I never put two and two together until I heard anthropologist and venture capitalist Stephen DeBerry make this observation: "These are communities that are on 'the other side of the tracks.' It may literally be train tracks that set these areas apart, or it could be a river or highway. But the idea is that these communities are geographically separated from their neighbors. Eastside Economies bear the burden of their demographic and geographic history, often cut off from various core resources."[40] In a captivating TED Talk, DeBerry posits that these communities are located on the east side of town because of "black smoke" of another kind: industrial pollution. In the United States, the prevailing winds generally blow eastward. Elite communities would of course never be situated where they were on the receiving end of such pollution. Powerless, marginalized communities, however, had no say in the matter. It's too early to draw definitive conclusions, and DeBerry is now at Harvard University to research and substantiate his intriguing theory.

The last aspect of government regulation falls under the subcategory "higher scrutiny." Such scrutiny could be initiated by government staffers or by a private citizen's complaint. Though entrepreneurs of all colors must comply with these laws, Black entrepreneurs believe that they have been selectively and disproportionately enforced on their businesses. These could be violations of local, state, and/or federal government laws, particularly regulations dealing with health codes, workplace safety, or business-related taxes.

This kind of scrutiny of Black restaurateurs has not been systematically studied, but there are studies that have examined how a similar dynamic exists with municipal fines. In a 2017 study, researchers Michael W. Sances and Hye Young You examined "city governments' use of fines and court fees for local revenue, a policy that disproportionately affects black voters, and the connections between this policy and black representation." Using data from more than nine thousand cities, they showed that "the use of fines as revenue is common and that it is robustly related to the share of city residents who are black." They also found that "black representation on city councils diminishes the connection between black population and fines revenue."[41] In short, the more that whites control the levers of power, the more that Blacks have borne the financial burden of higher scrutiny.

Air pollution control is a commonly used rationale for increased scrutiny. Barbecue joints were frequent offenders because, as southern barbecue's vanguard, they continued to use wood, which creates smoke. Black barbecuers considered any effort to stop them from cooking with wood an affront to their heritage. Homer Hall, a Black barbecue man who had operated Dixie Pig Bar-B-Q in Maryland's Anne Arundel County since 1946, is one example of someone forced to close. In the early years, no one really complained when he was operating just on the weekends. As he expanded his business to multiple days during the week, his neighbors, his Black neighbors, began a months-long successful campaign to close him down, succeeding in 1984.[42]

In 2010, Snoop Dogg's uncle Reo Varnado constantly battled with his Portland, Oregon, restaurant's neighbors about its smoke. These battles included a temporary closure, a suspicious fire, and a private lawsuit filed against him. Varnado ultimately relocated to Los Angeles, and he has said on multiple occasions that he believes that much of the opposition was racially motivated.[43] In an interview for *Saveur* magazine, the father-and-son team of Robert Adams Sr. and his son Robert Adams Jr. described their struggles with opening and operating Honey 1 BBQ in an affluent white neighborhood in north Chicago:

> 12 years at the location, the business was increasingly subject
> to complaints from neighbors about smoke and smells. Robert
> Adams Jr., who runs the business with his father, said even after
> they spent tens of thousands of dollars to mitigate those issues, the
> city was still regularly issuing tickets prompted by the complaints
> of nearby residents. He knew barbecue restaurants on the South
> Side just weren't experiencing the same level of public scrutiny. The
> implication was clear: "City fees, lawyers—we had major expenses,
> and in the end, the neighborhood still didn't support us," he said.
> "There were a lot of people who didn't want us there." In 2015,
> Honey 1 relocated to Bronzeville, a neighborhood on the South
> Side, where the restaurant has flourished.[44]

I'm grateful that Honey 1 survived because it makes some of the best rib tips in town. These no-win situations were typically small, neighborhood-level squabbles, but the scrutiny sometimes rose to encompass entire communities.

In the 1990s, when the Los Angeles area South Coast Air Quality Management District started citing barbecue joints for polluting, a cultural brush fire was fanned. The *Los Angeles Times* summed up the concerns of barbecuer Robert Thomas this way: "The way he sees it, however, he may be forced to abandon the purity of his ethnic cuisine—this time because of the smog. He and other pit barbecuers say that changing the time-honored way they cook ribs would discriminate against black culture, akin to forcing Japanese cooks to broil sushi, or Italians

IN THE SMOKE WITH ERNESTINE VANDUVALL
AN EXODUSTER LEGACY IN BARBECUE
(FEBRUARY 16, 1921–MAY 25, 2004)

The story of Ernestine VanDuvall is really the tale of two women in two cities. The other woman, in this case, is VanDuvall's niece Angela Bates. The two cities are historic Nicodemus, Kansas, and Pasadena, California. Nicodemus was founded in 1877 by formerly enslaved people who left the South for a chance at a better life in an agricultural colony in western Kansas. A combination of intentional racism from white neighbors to thwart the all-Black town's progress, unfavorable weather patterns, and the Great Depression dealt severe blows to this unique community.

Like many, VanDuvall sought fortunes in other parts of the country, and she eventually settled in Pasadena. There, she and Bates ran a beloved soul food restaurant. Bates does much to keep alive both VanDuvall's legacy and the spirit of Nicodemus. The annual homecoming celebration at the end of July is so inviting that strangers feel completely welcome at the expansive family reunion. You may also get a taste of some good barbecue, served up by Bates in the restaurant that VanDuvall used to run. There's really no better person to tell VanDuvall's story than Bates. What follows is her tribute to her truly impressive aunt.

A professional cook, singer, and entrepreneur, VanDuvall was born Ernestine Caroline Williams in Nicodemus, Kansas, the seventh of thirteen children of Charles and Elizabeth Williams. The members of the Williams family were descendants of Tom Johnson, a former slave of Vice President Richard M. Johnson of Georgetown, Kentucky. In 1877 the Johnson family migrated and settled in the historic all–African American town of Nicodemus. The tradition of cooks in the Johnson and Williams families dates back to the days of slave kitchens, when Vice President Johnson hosted a large barbecue for the French general the Marquis de Lafayette in 1824. His slaves prepared over fifteen hundred pounds of barbecue meat for the event.

Ernestine grew up assisting her mother in the kitchen and learned

to cook pies in a wood-burning stove. Her favorite pie to make (as well as to eat) was lemon meringue. The recipe for her lemon meringue pie and other recipes had been passed down for generations; however, Ernestine learned to add her own twist to these dishes.

At the age of nine Ernestine began working for a local restaurateur named Julia Lee. It was at Julia Lee's Café that Ernestine learned how to cook and to serve the public. Lee taught her how to prepare and fry chickens, make desserts, assist in the preparation of other dishes, clean and iron the linens, set the tables, and dress and decorate the dessert and candy cabinets. Ernestine's favorite job was to sit on an orange crate and peel potatoes. During this time Ernestine became affectionately known as "Chub" because she had always been a chubby girl. However, she once told a customer not to call her Chub while she was working at Julia Lee's Café but to refer to her as Ernestine.

Ernestine was a quick learner and a hard worker, but she did have vices. Lemon drops were her weakness, and she could not resist the urge to suck the sugar off them before they were put in the display cabinet. In Nicodemus, many people, adults and children alike, did not know that lemon drops came coated with sugar until Ernestine finally told them when she was older.

During her late teens and early twenties Ernestine and four of her sisters began a singing group called the Williams Sisters. They sang gospel music and played piano all across the state of Kansas, and they frequently traveled to Nebraska and Colorado. After singing off and on together for over forty years, the sisters finally recorded an album in the 1980s.

In Phillipsburg, Kansas, on December 22, 1947, twenty-six-year-old

Ernestine married Phillip VanDuvall, also of Nicodemus. They never had children; however, Ernestine helped to rear Phillip's four children from a previous marriage. After they were married, Ernestine moved to Phillip's farm and raised chickens and turkeys for sale. In the years that followed she visited family and friends in Denver, Colorado, and occasionally worked as a cook and maid for several prominent Jewish families.

In the early 1950s, after the death of Ernestine VanDuvall's mother, she and Phillip visited one of his sons then living in Los Angeles. This was their first trip to California, and both loved it so much they decided to move to Pasadena. Phillip secured a job with the city of Pasadena as a maintenance worker, and Ernestine began doing what she did best, which was cook. They purchased a modest home with a large kitchen, and she began to prepare meals and deliver them to workers at the local car washes. She also began a catering service, offering her home-cooked food to the general public. During this time, she catered personal parties for the famous Walt Disney, founder and creator of the Walt Disney Company. Her business grew until she finally opened a small restaurant on Fair Oaks Avenue called Ernestine's Bar-B-Q. She sold not only barbecue but offered an entire soul food menu. She hired her two nieces, Cheryl and Angela Bates, whom she trained and employed until they graduated from high school.

In the early 1970s Ernestine and Phillip VanDuvall returned to Nicodemus. They purchased a building and began renovating it for a restaurant. In November 1975 the restaurant was finished, and Phillip returned to California to bring back their remaining furnishings. On the return trip he died in a car accident. Although devastated and grief-stricken, Ernestine was determined to move forward and open the restaurant. In the spring of 1975, she opened Ernestine's Bar-B-Q on Highway 24. She catered parties and special events and served many businesses in the area. People came from all over the state to Ernestine's Bar-B-Q, where they ate her famous barbecue and wiped their hands on signature paper towels instead of napkins. She entertained guests by playing the piano and singing gospel and blues songs. Often, she had the whole restaurant singing and playing along. Senator Robert Dole of Kansas, among other political leaders, ate at Ernestine's Bar-B-Q before she closed the restaurant in 1985. After closing the restaurant, the aging VanDuvall returned to California.

Pasadena had changed since the VanDuvalls had lived there, and things were not the same for Ernestine without Phillip. After two years in California, she was still depressed and yearning for home, so she returned to Nicodemus in 1987. In 1995 many of her family members and former customers convinced VanDuvall to reopen her restaurant. She did just that in a trailer on the land where she had grown up. She took her nephew Terry Jukes under her tutelage, and they worked together serving barbecue meals. She also began catering for her niece and former cook Angela Bates, who had returned to Nicodemus and opened a tour business. After horse-drawn wagon tours around Nicodemus, tourists were fed VanDuvall's barbecue. Once again, her name and demands for her barbecue were echoed across the state. To say "Nicodemus" was to say "Ernestine's Bar-B-Q."

In 2002 Bates opened an Ernestine's Bar-B-Q in Bogue, five miles from Nicodemus, and in 2003 she opened an Ernestine's Bar-B-Q in Nicodemus. VanDuvall's health was failing, and she had to be admitted to a nursing home. Although she had recently returned from a stay in the hospital, she was determined to be at the grand opening of the second Ernestine's Bar-B-Q restaurant. Also around this time, the first annual Nicodemus Jazz and Blues Festival was sponsored by VanDuvall and Bates. Although VanDuvall did make it to the opening, she was confined to a wheelchair and stayed for only a couple of hours. During her brief appearance she greeted customers and sang one of her favorite blues songs, "I Hate to See That Evening Sun Go Down," to a crowd of over four hundred people.

VanDuvall died of kidney failure a year later, leaving a long and proud legacy for the succeeding generation. Before her passing, she saw her barbecue sauce professionally bottled. Ernestine's Bar-B-Q sauce was available for purchase in most stores across Kansas. VanDuvall was buried in the historic Nicodemus cemetery one mile north of the town. With her culinary talents, she left her mark in the pages of Kansas history and in the annals of the western United States.

to microwave their pasta."[45] After an uproar that rallied the Black community, Black politicians, and threats of possibly producing steamed barbecue, the AQMD called a truce, and eventually, some culturally sensitive work-arounds were implemented.

Heightened scrutiny hits Black entrepreneurs hard because many do not have the resources in terms of time, money, and adequate representation to deal with constant inspections, or to fight and resolve disputes about fines. An adequately financed entrepreneur would at least have a chance, which leads to the next component.

Another main, and critical, element of ill will is that African American entrepreneurs often lack access to adequate financial resources. This includes financing as well as the range of advisers needed to comply with applicable financial regulations and implement a profitable business strategy. Jared Weitz, in a 2018 blog post for the Forbes Finance Council, identifies the core problem: access to capital. He observes that "minority-owned firms are much less likely to be approved for small business loans than white-owned firms. And, even if they do get approved, minority-owned firms are more likely to receive lower amounts and higher interest rates. According to findings from the U.S. Department of Commerce Minority Business Development Agency, these discrepancies have made minority business owners more likely to not apply for small business loans, usually out of fear of rejection."[46] Weitz elaborates that minorities are more likely to be denied credit because they tend to have a lower net worth, the business is located in an undesirable area, and the minority applicant has a poor credit history or no credit history at all.[47]Add in that for a long time, especially in the South, a Black barbecuer couldn't get a loan unless a white man vouched for him.

Without access to credit, Black barbecue entrepreneurs must resort to using their own wealth or obtaining private financing from relatives, friends, or extended social networks. A restaurant is a risky proposition anyway, so it really comes down to who you know. Unless a personal relationship exists, much like the olden days, barbecue entrepreneurs need someone to vouch for them, to believe in them, and finance them. Unfortunately, few African American entrepreneurs run in social circles where they meet people of substantial wealth who would extend private equity.

Today, Black barbecue businesses are such a success story that they are the standard for Black entrepreneurship . . . even to the point of derision. When giving examples of different types of Black-owned businesses, the website Blacknews.com writes: "Black-owned businesses of today are no longer typecast to barbecue joints and barber shops."[48] When Detroit-based chef Lester Gouvia told Civil Eats about his struggle to find financing to transition from a food truck to a brick-and-mortar space for a fine dining Trinidadian restaurant, he said, "The reality is that most black men are supposed to own a barber shop or a barbecue spot, so [the banks] don't think that we should own a fine-dining restaurant."[49]

The last key element of ill will concerns the theft of intellectual property. We know that intellectual property adds value to a business, but how does one account for it being stolen by competitors? I have spoken to several restaurateurs who have had people (not all of them white) work for them and learn from them and then go open their own barbecue business. I've learned of three examples where the appropriator has innocently asked to learn from a storied Black pitmaster without sharing his intentions to make a big play in the restaurant industry. I also know of a successful restaurant chain in a western city where the founders worked in a Black restaurant as employees, got the recipes, and learned how to barbecue. They then quit, took that accumulated knowledge, and started their own restaurant with those recipes. Many have gone on to be successful with little or no acknowledgment of the person who trained them. As much as I'd love to call these people out, I honor the requests of Black pitmasters that I refrain from doing so.

Where does one draw the line between apprenticeship, appropriation, and theft? Far too many white barbecue restaurants owe a debt to an African American who trained cooks and permitted the use of his or her personal recipes. Some white barbecuers have acknowledged this influence. In a 1954 interview for the *Raleigh News and Observer*, legendary North Carolina barbecue man Bob Melton "concede[d] that an elderly Negro man actually did most of the cooking along then [when he learned to barbecue during his childhood], but at least he 'got his hand in.'"[50] Unfortunately, when it comes to giving Black barbecuers their due, the Bob Meltons of the world are uncommon.

Are there ways to rectify this situation? An important first step for African American barbecuers is to protect their intellectual property with confidentiality and noncompete agreements or by licensing the use of expertise. This could balance out the power dynamic. What can be done to honor the trainers? The most dramatic would be to give a share of the restaurant's profits to the African American cooks who helped the business. If the cook is dead, give the proceeds to the surviving spouse or heirs. The restaurant should also acknowledge the debt on its menu, in servers' stock answers to customers' questions, and on all promotional materials. If restaurants are taking the time to tell us everything about how and from where they source their meat, the name and personal hobbies of the animals, and so on, they can "culturally source" the inspiration for their menus.

This isn't hard to do. They could just take a page from the world of fast-food hamburgers by adopting the way the Los Angeles–based chain Fatburger acknowledges its founder, Lovie Yancey, an African American woman. Yancey opened the first Fatburger restaurant in Los Angeles in 1947. Since Yancey's sale of her interest in the restaurant to an investment group, hundreds of Fatburgers have opened in the United States and overseas. I don't know if this is the case in every Fatburger, but the Aurora, Colorado, location has a nice picture of Lovie Yancey in a prominent location with the words "Our Founder."

Despite the challenges, Black barbecuers found ways to thrive in a changing competitive environment. Between the 1890s and the 1930s, barbecue stands and restaurants sprouted up all across the country from the Carolinas to California.[51] Just flipping through the classifieds and advertisements in newspapers from that era gives one some idea of the gold rush mentality. Much of this growth was because of the increasing popularity of automobiles. More people in the city were driving to rural areas on excursions. Barbecue was marketed as the perfect food for such excursions, and rural roadside stands multiplied. The boom didn't escape urban areas either, as rural migrants brought a taste for barbecue with them. Not all these restaurants were Black run, but a good number were.

The barbecue restaurant explosion changed the cuisine's landscape and expanded its influence. Now, barbecue restauranteurs were in a position to interpret what barbecue meant to their immediate community by hewing to tradition or innovating or doing a combination of both. Robert F. Moss, who first theorized this point, posits: "The single greatest influence on the regionalization of barbecue styles seems to have been the rise of barbecue restaurants. As they transformed what were once large scale, occasional public gatherings into smaller, more regular businesses, barbecue restaurateurs standardized the meat they served, creating new and different methods of cooking and their own signature sauces. These styles and techniques were passed down from one local pitmaster to another through an informal apprentice system, in the process creating distinct styles in different regions of the country."[52] Whether conscious of it or not, African Americans were certainly a part of this development, but this was a period when white barbecue operations were apt to get as much praise as Black barbecuers.

At that moment in history, I'm sure Black barbecuers felt like Black jazz musicians. Barbecue, like jazz, was something that they felt they had created, but the white guys were getting the most publicity and making the most money. Though many of the white-run restaurants of the era didn't last, enough thrived to create a palpable sense of loss in the Black community. A 1932 editorial in the *Baltimore Afro-American* read like a eulogy: "Even the barbecue stand, the fried pie and the fried fish sandwich, definitely Negro conceptions, are now the basis of large commercial enterprises dominated by others."[53] Unlike the jazz artists, Black barbecuers didn't protest by creating something new that they thought whites couldn't mimic. Barbecuers clung to traditional barbecue preparations and kept doing their thing.

In the 1940s, some commentators refused to sign Black barbecue's death certificate. Rather than weeping and gnashing their teeth, they saw the entrance of white business interests into the field, sometimes on a large scale, as possibly expanding the market for everyone. One industry analysis concluded, "This is the evidence that Negroes might re-enter this kind of business with profit. The modern barbecue stand is a beautiful establishment, often air-conditioned, and providing amusement features and carhop services. Here the lowly sandwich is built into a masterpiece of culinary art by skilled hands."[54]

Chain barbecue started blossoming in 1940s and 1950s. Black entrepreneurs certainly entered the field, and many have flourished at the local level—most notably, Gates Bar-B-Q in Kansas City, Missouri, and environs (six locations strong as I write this). Yet a national Black-owned barbecue chain has yet to materialize. Is it due to a lack of capital, a lack of confidence, or perhaps a lack of imagination? If any Black barbecuer could have started one it was Arthur Bryant in Kansas City, Missouri. In a 1975 interview, he spoke of the numerous offers he got to franchise. He was simply uninterested, and the article underlined the point: "And the thought of a mass-produced Bryant's chain nauseates him worse than store-bought barbecue sauce on undercooked ribs."[55] Maybe Black entrepreneurs felt the same as North Carolina pitmaster Ed Mitchell, who told me that he was hesitant to franchise because he felt that he needed to be present and supervise the cooking to maintain high quality. As we'll see in chapter 10, Mitchell's son Ryan has them on the big-scale barbecue path, and South Carolina whole hog specialist Rodney Scott certainly looks like he's taking the same journey.

Chain barbecue has left a discernible imprint on national barbecue culture. In his essay "The Changing Landscape of Mid-South Barbecue," Edward M. Maclin makes some interesting points about how small barbecue restaurants fare at a time when "increasingly across the South, . . . the top-ranked barbecue restaurants in urban areas are franchises or chain restaurants, according to local newspapers. . . . All of these restaurants offer efficiency, predictability, and control—in short, they have been McDonaldized. . . . While McDonaldization allows for expansion and regularity, it does so at a steep price: increased constraint on creativity and diversity."[56] An annoying trend that I've certainly noticed in chains as well as independent restaurants is a tendency to ignore terroir altogether and present to diners an eclectic menu that samples regional styles across the country. I haven't seen that in too many Black-run places, but it remains to be seen what the next crop of barbecue entrepreneurs will do.

I'll stop for now with the chronic business challenges and pick up the discussion in the final chapter. What's important to note here is that Black barbecuers met every challenge thrown their way, and they've thrived. Though written in 1970, this comment from a *Philadelphia Inquirer* columnist is timeless: "Barbecue restaurants are probably the most popular eating place[s] in the black communities. And a highly appreciated tip to a black newcomer to the city is the whereabouts of the best barbecue in town."[57] You saw just a sliver of Black barbecue business greatness earlier in the profiles of John Hamilton in Seattle, Washington, and Ernestine VanDuvall of Nicodemus, Kansas. More of these stories await discovery.

RECIPES

Angela "the Kitchenista" Davis's Grilled Lemon Pepper Wings

Angela Davis is not a barbecue restaurateur, but she is a food entrepreneur. She's an accountant with a passion for cooking. In 2012, she decided to become a full-time creative and start a blog called *The Kitchenista Diaries*. In September 2019, I participated in a fun annual backyard party hosted by Steve and Kimberly Weatherington Cunningham in Denver. It's called Meatfest, and attendees can bring a dish to compete against others, based on such categories as "land," "air," and "sea." Even though chickens don't fly, I won the "air" category with these wings. The secret is a buttermilk brine, "which tenderizes the chicken, seasons it throughout, and creates golden brown skin on the grill," as Davis indicates in her blog.

Note: You'll need a zester or fine grater and a spice grinder for this recipe.

Makes about 16 whole wings (10–12 servings)

For the lemon pepper
4–5 large lemons, preferably Meyer lemons
2 tablespoons black peppercorns
2 teaspoons white peppercorns (if unavailable, use more black peppercorns)
1 teaspoon coriander seeds
2 teaspoons garlic powder
1 teaspoon onion powder

For the chicken
4 pounds whole chicken wings
2 tablespoons kosher salt
2 cups buttermilk, more as needed (low-fat or whole will work)
3 tablespoons canola oil
1 teaspoon smoked paprika
½ teaspoon cayenne pepper
¼ cup unsalted butter
¼ cup honey
1 tablespoon soy sauce (or tamari, or coconut aminos)
1 tablespoon hot sauce
Juice and zest of 2 lemons
1 tablespoon finely minced fresh parsley (optional)

For the grill
Charcoal briquettes
Applewood or other fruity wood chips and chunks (optional)

TO MAKE THE LEMON PEPPER

1. Use a zester or fine grater to shave off the outer layer of the lemon peel. Four lemons should yield about 3 tablespoons of zest. It's okay if you end up with more, but zest the fifth lemon if you are short.
2. The easiest way to dry lemon zest is to spread it out on a parchment-lined sheet pan and leave it out overnight. The fast way? Put the pan in the oven at 200° for about 20 minutes. Keep an eye on the zest and pull it out when it's dried but not yet starting to brown.
3. For optimum flavor, toast the peppercorns before grinding them. If you already have the oven on, simply add the peppercorns and coriander to the sheet pan for the last 10 minutes of drying the zest. If you didn't oven dry the zest, simply warm the peppercorns and coriander in a dry skillet over low heat for a few minutes, until fragrant.
4. Measure out the garlic powder and onion powder separately; there's no need to toast this.
5. Transfer the dried lemon zest, peppercorns, and coriander to your spice grinder (or grind with a mortar and pestle).
6. Pulse a few times until the mixture is coarsely ground, then add the garlic and onion powder and continue grinding until the lemon pepper blend is as fine as you'd like it. Set aside. *Note*: If you aren't using the lemon pepper right away, transfer it to a container with a lid and use within a couple weeks. The volatile oils that give black peppercorns their flavor lose intensity over time.

TO PREPARE THE WINGS

1. Place the wings in a shallow container, ideally one that accommodates them in a single layer.
2. Season both sides of the wings with the salt. (Yes, it's more salt than you'll think you need, but it won't all be absorbed.) Next, pour over enough buttermilk to cover the chicken. It's okay if the wing tips stick out; just make sure the flats and drumettes are coated in buttermilk.
3. Cover the chicken and let it hang out in the fridge for at least 4 hours, up to overnight.

4. After the wings have been brined, carefully drain the buttermilk. Pat the wings down with paper towels as best you can.

5. Toss the wings in oil, then season with 2 tablespoons of the lemon pepper, the paprika, and the cayenne. Rub the spices into the chicken to make sure they're evenly distributed. You can return the wings to the refrigerator for up to 1 day or cook right away.

6. Prepare a barbecue grill for indirect cooking.

7. Arrange the wings skin side up, in a single layer, on the cool side of the grill. None of the chicken should be directly over any coals.

8. Cover the grill, and let the chicken cook for 20 minutes. If you are using applewood chips, add another round of wood now, and let it burn off for a minute before closing the grill. It's always a good idea to make sure none of the chicken is cooking too fast. If so, rearrange it to be a little farther from the heat source. Check it again in another 20 minutes, adding a final ½ cup or so of wood.

9. Meanwhile, as the chicken finishes cooking, you can whip up an easy glaze to finish. In a small pot over medium heat, melt the butter. Add the honey, soy sauce, hot sauce, lemon juice and zest, and 2 teaspoons of the lemon pepper. Whisk together and cook for 5 minutes, just until the glaze thickens a bit.

10. After an hour, the chicken should be golden brown and just starting to crisp around the edges. Using an instant-read meat thermometer, confirm that the thickest parts of the wings have hit at least 170°. They'll likely go above that, which is fine.

11. Once the chicken is cooked all the way through, you can sear it. To do this, use your tongs to move a few pieces of chicken at a time over to the hotter side of the grill, directly above the coals.

12. Cook for a minute or two, flipping to get both sides crisp. Then return the chicken to the cooler side of the grill. Work in batches until all the chicken is seared. If you have any flare-ups, close the grill briefly until the flames die down.

13. After the chicken is seared, glaze one side with the lemon butter concoction. A thin layer is all that's needed.

14. Flip the chicken and glaze the other side. You can cover the grill for a minute to set the glaze, but it's such a thin layer that it doesn't take long to dry. Carefully transfer the chicken wings to a clean platter for serving.

15. If you have any extra glaze, drizzle it over the chicken on the platter, and dive in. A little extra lemon juice doesn't hurt either.

C. B. Stubb's Bar-B-Q Brisket

C.B. "Stubb" Stubblefield is a legendary barbecuer who first burnished his reputation with a restaurant that he ran in Lubbock, Texas, in the late 1960s. He eventually moved to Austin to operate a well-known combined barbecue restaurant and a live music venue. I've been there for the gospel brunch, and I can tell you from experience that the food is divine . . . especially the smoked chicken. Stubb died in 1996, but his legacy lives on through that restaurant, a posthumously published cookbook, and a very successful line of barbecue sauces and spices sold nationwide. Here's his beef brisket recipe.

Makes 16 servings

1 (6-pound) beef brisket, untrimmed
½ cup Stubb's® BBQ Rub
Soaked wood chips (for smoke flavor, if using charcoal)
1 bottle Stubb's® Original BBQ Sauce

1. Rub the entire brisket with Stubb's Bar-B-Q Rub. Let rest for a minimum of 30 minutes, which allows the rub to penetrate the meat.
2. While the brisket is resting, prepare your smoker for indirect low heat cooking (225°–250°). If using charcoal, layer the soaked wood chips with the charcoal. Place a foil pan under the grates of grill or smoker to catch the drippings.
3. Cook the brisket, fat side up, over indirect heat until the internal temperature of the thickest part of the brisket reaches 180°–185°. This usually takes 8–10 hours depending on your pit. To maintain low heat, check every hour to adjust vents and add more charcoal and soaked wood chips as needed.
4. Remove the brisket and let it rest at least 15 minutes or up to 45 minutes. Slice the brisket against the grain and slather with Bar-B-Q sauce to serve.

Tip: For extra-juicy, tender meat, baste brisket with Stubb's Moppin' Sauce every 30 minutes during cooking.

BLACK BARBEQUE IS BEAUTIFUL
TOWARD AN AFRICAN AMERICAN BARBEQUE AESTHETIC

6

John Grisham (incredulously): "What's the difference between Black barbecue and white barbecue?"
Adrian Miller: "Black barbecue tastes better."

The above exchange happened in late April 2017 at the lovely home of John and Renee Grisham. We, along with some fellow authors, were part of a fundraiser for the University of North Carolina Press. Though I was there to discuss my previous work, John Grisham asked me what my next project would be. I told him that I was working on a book about African American barbecue culture. After the exchange above took place, the audience roared with laughter. Grisham was momentarily nonplussed. I'm not sure how often he gets that feeling. My blithe answer aside, Grisham was curious about a deeper story, one whose punchline had eluded me for a long time. Are there discernible differences that make African American barbecue exceptional? This chapter answers with an enthusiastic "Yassss!"

At first, it seemed like a tricky argument to prove. Bob Garner, a North Carolina barbecue expert, observed that "barbecue customs among North Carolina's African Americans often cross or ignore the established boundaries."[1] When it comes to barbecue, what happens in North Carolina doesn't stay in North Carolina. African American barbecuers across the nation are apt to deviate from as much as they conform to expected norms of a regional style. I'm not saying that, individually, these things are exclusive to African American barbecue culture. Yet if one stands back and surveys the entire barbecue culture, a culinary signature emerges. Unlike the other chapters in this book, I don't profile individual cooks.

Stephen Smith, in his essay "The Rhetoric of Barbecue: A Southern Rite and Ritual," runs down of all the things about barbecue that can lead to fightin' words. "Areas of disagreement include: (1) definition of the South; (2) definition of barbecue; (3) correct spelling of the word;

(4) type of meat; (5) type of cut; (6) ingredients for sauce; (7) type of pit; (8) type of wood; (9) wet versus dry cooking; (10) the highest shaman; (11) the preparation ritual; and (12) the design of the temple."[2] This is a useful framework for exploring the cultural differences between African American barbecue to that prepared by others.

As we've seen, African Americans have long been effective barbecue ambassadors, even as the cooking style was defined, rooted in place, redefined, and transplanted elsewhere. At first, it was heavily associated with Virginia. As barbecue spread to other places, its new geographic home became an adjective that modified what people called barbecue, even though they cooked whole animals the same way as the early Virginians. Restaurants redefined barbecue again by incorporating different smoking techniques and the specialized cooking of individual cuts of meat. Even with all of these changes, the disparate styles still fell under the umbrella of "southern barbecue." Southerners and nonsoutherners see the region as barbecue's birthplace and the area where the most authentic traditions within the cuisine thrive. For these reasons, I embrace the most expansive definition of the South: a region that stretches as far west as eastern Texas and as far north as the upper southern states of Kentucky and Maryland, bordered on the south by the Gulf of Mexico and on the east by the Atlantic Ocean.

As to what "barbecue" is, some cultural fissures develop, but much depends on what period someone is using as a reference point for southern barbecue. Until the late 1800s, barbecue was whole animals cooked directly over burning wood in a pit dug in the ground. In the early 1900s, barbecue increasingly meant smaller cuts of meat cooked directly or indirectly over wood or charcoal in a contained space made of brick, glass, or metal and sauced before serving. Today, the conventional wisdom is that the only true way to make barbecue is to cook indirectly from a heat source for many hours, the well-known mantra of "low and slow." Later in the chapter, we'll see how Black barbecuers continually buck this conventional wisdom.

The language of barbecue unveils interesting cultural differences. Michael Twitty has raised an interesting linguistic possibility for an African origin: "The word barbecue also has roots in West Africa among the Hausa, who used the term 'babbake' to describe a complex of words referring to grilling, toasting, building a large fire, singeing hair or feathers and cooking food over a long period of time over an extravagant fire."[3] Intrigued, I checked Hausa-language dictionaries to find out more about contemporary meanings. *The Hausa-English/English-Hausa Dictionary & Phrasebook* (2018) defines *gasashshe* as "grilled," *gashi* for "roasted," and *kyaffafe* for "smoked" or "toasted," with no entry for *babbake*.[4] Paul Newman's *Hausa-English Dictionary* (2007) defines *babbak* as "to grill or "toast," *gas* as the root word for "roast, bake, toast (bread)," and *kyaf* as the root word meaning to "grill meat or fish on a skewer."[5] Since Newman's book gives the most promising lead, I followed up with him to get his thoughts on the possible link to the word "barbecue." He wasn't convinced. It's likely that "babbake" is the contemporary Hausa speakers' approximation of the word "barbecue": an example of the Indigenous American word traveling westward across the Atlantic Ocean and getting transformed like food.

So much for etymology. But what about pronunciation. Bobby Seale, a former Black Panther turned barbecuer, in a clever bit of self-promotion, mused about the correct pronunciation: "Bobbyque? Yes! To my young ears it always sounded like that, an idiomatic expression I certainly didn't question. For most of my life, when Black folks pronounced *barbeque*, the first two syllables literally sounded like my name."[6] Seale further posits an interesting theory that the pronunciation is an African linguistic survival based on the fieldwork of Lorenzo Dow Turner in *Africanisms in the Gullah Dialect* (1949). "Many Black Americans pronounce such words as *these* 'dese,' *those* 'dose,' *floor* 'flo' and *barbecue* 'bobbyque.' Here the lack of the 'ar' sound produced 'bobby' instead of 'barbe.' The 'th,' 'er,' and 'ar' sounds are in fact absent in West African languages, and Black Americans are largely descendants of West African peoples. The etymological path has been 'ba coa,' barbacoa, barbe*cue*, *barbe*que, and 'bobbyque.'"[7] Turner's analysis may actually lead us back to the Hausa language after all. In the *Hausa-English Dictionary*, *bà* means "the burning and cackling of fire."[8] I've heard many older African Americans, especially those from Texas, pronounce "barbecue" as "bobby-cue."

Then there's how the word "barbecue" is spelled. I had noticed that there were so many ways that barbecue is expressed. Could it be that African Americans like to put the "q" in 'cue? As Seale observes:

> Oddly enough, throughout all my years from Texas to California, I had very seldom seen a pit or restaurant sign that used the dictionary spelling barbecue (especially in the Black community). When I had seen such signs near or outside my community, I didn't feel that familiar mouth-watering effect which my favorite food could provoke instantly. I later began to think perhaps I had an inborn prejudice to such signs because in the Black community the word was always spelled "Bar Be *Que*" or "Bar B Que" or initialed "B Q," and accompanied with that special hickory aroma. I began to feel that the "*cue*" spelling represented something drab, or even "square," as we used to say in the 1950s. My realization was that most restaurants whose signs lacked the suffix -que seemed to be void of that ever-pervasive down-home hickory-smoked aroma which would literally carry for blocks.[9]

Seale's arguing here that a restaurant's sign let diners know who was doing the cooking and signaled how the food was cooked. Now you see why this chapter and chapter 2 include "barbeque" in their titles.

I wondered, is Seale's theory mystical or provable? Barbecue expert John Shelton Reed explored this topic as well and suggests that the linguistic variation may have a native, geographic habitat: "'Barbecue' is the most common spelling... but not in the South. Despite the shortcomings of 'barbeque' (... one dictionary huffily points out that no other word in English has '-que' as a stand-alone last syllable), Google shows it in a statistical dead heat with 'barbecue' in the Carolinas, and over the mountains in Kentucky, Tennessee, Alabama, Mississippi, and Arkansas, it's about twice as common as the authorized spelling."[10] In a way, Reed's research may indicate a word changing as the cuisine moved. Seale's own experience speaks of the word's usage in the western part of the country, outside of the South.

This is not a recent phenomenon. The *Garnett Journal* in Kansas mocked the variant spelling in a 1881 editorial about a barbecue event advertised in a local African American newspaper: "Our *Plaindealer* man announced last week that some of our colored citizens went to Ottawa to attend a 'barbeque.' Well, what in the name of Moses is a 'Barbeque?' One of our colored friends wanted to know, but we couldn't tell him. We have heard of a thing called a 'barbecue,' but that animal mentioned in the *Plaindealer* man has never crossed the horizon of our visual orbs. Wonder if it will bite?"[11] Another possibility is that "barbeque" may be a spelling that was once quite common in English but fell out of use over the years, and African Americans held onto it. My own experience of eating my way through the country doesn't show an African American preponderance for this spelling. My social media poll results on this question back me up. Yet there are partisans. Bob Hayes emphasized the point when he wrote this in his U.S. travel guide for African Americans in the early 1970s: "No town can brag about its soul food unless it includes a top quality Bar-B-Que (that's how *we* spell it) house."[12]

Now that we have a feel for the African American language for barbecue, let's get to the eating. Before we begin, a quick word from the management. I focus on entrées in this chapter. Yes, I know about all the glorious sides and desserts that are so vital to Black culture and the Black barbecue tradition. I could spend an entire chapter on peach cobbler and potato salad debates alone. When people think barbecue, though, they usually think first about the meat.

Using Smith's framework, let's combine and discuss at length the type and cut of the meat barbecued. We've learned that African Americans barbecued almost anything that could be. Yet it's undeniable that pork is the most popular meat, especially spareribs. Full stop. It's the reason why food writer Scotta Tymas wrote in 1968: "Note: In Soul City, when you say simply 'Bar-b-que,' you mean 'Ribs.'"[13] African Americans' love of pork spareribs dates back to enslavement. For centuries, home cooks have tended to barbecue smaller cuts of meat, and whole animal cooking was left to the experts. In the plantation context, the smaller cuts were available at hog killings. In order to manage meat resources for an entire year, people raising pigs would wait for colder weather to arrive to slaughter, process, and preserve hundreds of pigs. Several neighboring farms pooled resources, especially labor, and coordinated their schedules to collectively kill their hogs at the same time.

The reward of such work was free meat that could be cooked and immediately consumed, usually during a celebration of the work being done. The ham and shoulder meat were usually pickled or smoked and stored. The rest was given away. Thomas Cole spoke of this pecking order: "First we would eats all de chitlins den de marster would begins issuing out back bones ter each family til dey was gone and den along comes de spare ribs."[14] Just because the spareribs were last, doesn't mean they weren't cherished, as Morris Sheppard attested. "De hog killing means we gits lots of spare-ribs and chitlings, and somebody always git sick eating too much of dat fat pork."[15] George and Martha Washington also recognized its special status since they gave their enslaved people spareribs as a reward for helping out with hog killings.[16]

When Blacks migrated to urban areas, their love of spareribs didn't abate. Because they weren't raising or killing their own hogs or lacked adequate facilities to do so, sourcing was a challenge. Spareribs varied in popularity with whites, so depending on local market conditions and custom, slaughterhouses and butchers either sold them very cheaply, gave them away for free, or threw them away. Some early barbecue entrepreneurs were hyperlocal with their sourcing, so they just got the spareribs from a butcher's or stockyard's garbage, cleaned them, and cooked them. Barbecue cooks did this until the meat purveyors caught on and start charging. Yet the economics facing Black barbecuers still shows up in home and restaurant barbecue.

The mainstream choice for spareribs is the St. Louis cut, which creates a more rectangular, uniform appearance than a less butchered rack of ribs that African Americans tend to get. In the latter case, the rack of ribs is more ovular in shape, the breastbone and rib tips are not separated (as they would be with the St. Louis cut), a brisket flap remains on the back, and there's a lot more untrimmed fat. In the Black barbecue restaurants where I've dined, barbecuers and their customers clearly prefer the less butchered spareribs. If I saw St. Louis cut ribs, or even baby back ribs, it was at places that opened within the past decade. Perhaps these more recent Black barbecuers are trying to match current consumer expectations of what spareribs should look like.

African Americans are so serious about spareribs that in some parts of the country, you get told exactly where your ribs are located on the rack. I first experienced this at M & D's Barbecue and Fish Palace, a now closed restaurant in Denver, Colorado. Most often, I ordered the magnificently barbecued pork spareribs. I was intrigued by what the menu called "the small end." This was the first time my spareribs had a specific location. When looking at an intact set of spareribs, these were the smaller bones at the opposite end from the larger, meatier bones. M & D's menu described them as "the filet mignon of ribs. Tender, juicy, and definitely a mouth full of goodness." After getting my fill, I saw no lies in what the menu claimed.

Rib geography is a high art form in Cleveland, Ohio. At several restaurants, the menu indicated that the ones from the small end described above were called "short ribs," then the "center ribs" in the middle, then the "long ribs." The short ribs from the smaller end tended to be the priciest.

Another African American barbecue specialty is the somewhat nonsensical "rib sandwich." When the Earl of Sandwich proverbially requested two slices of bread in order to hold some roasted meat while he played cards, he gave birth to an entire category of food. African Americans have wholeheartedly embraced the idea that if you have anything with two slices of bread involved, it's a sandwich. If you think a sandwich cannot have bones, then, honey, you don't understand Black barbecue. A standard menu option is a rib sandwich, which is the polar opposite of the boneless McRib sandwich: a deconstructed pile of two to four bone-in spareribs placed on top of two slices of white bread with sauce ladled—check that—drenching the entire thing.

Ardie Davis, a highly-regarded Kansas City barbecue authority, explored this topic for an article he wrote. "This is a truly vernacular barbecue expression which lacks a well-documented history," he said. One of the few articles I found that discussed rib sandwiches in detail was one in January 3, 1928, in the *Emporia Gazette* titled "For Men Only": "Enter the wayside chef with a new American contribution to international cuisine—the barbecue rib sandwich. The barbecue sandwich is even more thoroughly American than its slightly germanic [sic] forebears, the hot dog and the hamburger." The article went on to declare the rib sandwich "a man's dish" that "never will be domesticated" enough to serve to female diners.[17] Beef rib sandwiches make unexpected cameos on Black barbecue restaurant menus, and I particularly remember one I got at Hillery's Barbecue in Kenosha, Wisconsin. The ribs weren't the enormous kind that would shock Fred Flintstone but instead were four heavily sauced short ribs. Regardless of the meat used, when I confront a rib sandwich, I eat it all separately, usually with sauce-drenched white bread making a nice accompaniment.

The skyrocketing popularity of the St. Louis–cut spareribs created another Black barbecue specialty: rib tips. Leon Finney, one of Chicago's famous rib men, explained its origin in a 1979 interview with the *Chicago Defender*. "The rib tip food industry began in Chicago in the 50's. . . . Before we started buying them, meat wholesalers were throwing the back side of the rib cut away as garbage, and now they're trying to raise the price nearly to the price of prime St. Louis rib."[18] Notice a familiar theme? Elsewhere, Finney describes the creative culinary process:

The ribs are rubbed with seasoning and marinated for up to two days before being barbecued. Finney calls the crew who perform this task the "process men." They come in at 6 in the morning and cut the brisket bone off the back side of the slabs. These short ends, or brisket bones, are Chicago's famous rib tips. "The choice part is the middle to small end," Finney explains. The slabs go into the custom-built smoker, and the rib tips go on a rotisserie over coals. When cooked to melt-in-your-mouth tenderness, each order gets a ladleful of Finney's special sauce.[19]

Finney's invention caught on so extensively that it spawned an underappreciated regional style: South Side Chicago barbecue.

South Side Chicago's barbecue style, at its core, is about rib tips and hot link sausages, nesting on a mound of French fries with everything drowned in spicy, sweet, tomato-based barbecue sauce. When I ate my way through the South Side, the most memorable places were Alice's, Honey 1 BBQ, Lem's, and Sunny's Bar B Que. They all presented their barbecue in pretty much the same way: a Styrofoam container with a layer of white bread, a layer of fries (sometimes on the very top), the selected barbecue, sometimes with wax paper in between, and then the entire thing covered with sauce. Of course, there were differences in how it tasted, but the presentation was rather uniform.

I'm a fan of the South Side style, but its version of "barbecued chicken" is a head-scratcher. When I order that, I'm expecting poultry that's been grilled or smoked and slathered with barbecue sauce. In Chicago, "barbecued chicken" is fried chicken drenched in a thin barbecue sauce. I don't know how on earth this happened, but I'm thinking it's the influence of the highly successful Harold's Fried Chicken chain, which serves its fried chicken with a barbecuelike sauce called "mild sauce," which we'll hear more about in the next chapter.

Ultimately, it may just be a Midwest thing. In the late 1960s, when the soul food craze was most potent, Blacks wondered aloud why so many whites were, as a magazine title said, "Eating Like Soul Brothers": "In Detroit, Charlie Red, owner of a soul-food takeout business who is known locally as the 'King of Wings,' reports that orders from whites for his fried chicken wings in barbecue sauce have nearly quintupled in the past two months."[20] This is one of those things that isn't technically barbecue, but people within and outside the culture associated it with barbecue, and that's mainly because of the sauce.

It does, however, remind me of something in North Carolina called "dipped chicken." In their essential book on North Carolina barbecue,

John Shelton Reed and Dale Volberg Reed expound: "One of the most unusual versions [of fried chicken] is that served at Keaton's Barbecue, a black-owned place near the Rowan-Iredell line since 1953 (the mailing address is Cleveland), which Jane and Michael Stern have proclaimed 'the best chicken on earth.' Keaton's fries the chicken nice and crisp, then dunks it in a pot of boiling sauce. The sauce recipe is secret, of course—all we can tell you is that it's thin, Piedmont-style, with enough sugar to caramelize a bit, and the result is delicious."[21] I trekked to Keaton's in Cleveland, North Carolina, on a bright day in February 2019. I liked the restaurant fine enough, especially its story. The chicken was solid but not spectacular. Dipped chicken seems to thrive only in a few regional spots here and there. Other than some Midwest cities and western North Carolina, I haven't seen much dipped chicken. So, fried chicken drenched in barbecue sauce is a thing, and to twist Steve Wonder's amazing lyrics for the song "As," I'm saying that this is in the barbecue world but not of it.

Chicken isn't the only thing that gets dipped. In southern Kentucky and northern Tennessee, a particular cut called pork steak gets the same treatment. In his fine *Kentucky Barbecue Book*, Wes Berry notes:

> In south-central Kentucky, "shoulder" means thinly sliced pieces of Boston butt grilled over coals (usually cooked-down hickory, but some use charcoal) until done. The meat is often seasoned with pepper and salt and sopped with a thin sauce of vinegar, black and red pepper, and fat (either butter, lard, or a combination of these), akin to the old-fashioned sauces of eastern North Carolina. If you like your barbecue hot, then get it "dipped," which means your slices of peppery pork shoulder will be coated, either by dunking into the sauce pot with tongs or by drizzling on the thin sauce with a ladle.[22]

Also known as "Monroe County Barbecue," or pork steaks, this cut of meat comes from slicing a frozen Boston butt according to the desired thickness of the customer.

Pork steaks are popular throughout the Midwest, including St. Louis, Missouri. This particular barbecue style is centered primarily around Tompkinsville, Kentucky, and several African American restaurants feature the dish. Curiously, this "one-town signature style" is not known as "Kentucky barbecue," but Owensboro's "mutton and black dip" style is. It really shows how arbitrary and artificial the die-hard barbecue classifications are to which so many people cling.

Sausages are another by-product of a hog-killing event—a way to preserve meat for future use. Detailed written accounts of sausage-making in the antebellum period are rare and lack important details: whether the meat was chopped or ground; whether it was free-form patties or stuffed into intestines; how it was seasoned. The slave narratives don't have many mentions of sausage. "Uncle" Hemp Kennedy, who grew up in Mahned, Mississippi, recalled, "We had plen'y to eat—smoke sausage, beef, home made lard, an'—yes sir, possum when we wanted hit."[23] It's hard to nail the geographic distribution of sausage-loving as well. We do know that it seems to be most intense in the Upper Midwest, Kansas City, and Texas. The biggest difference between the hot links that African Americans love compared to others is that the spice level is usually much more intense and the sausages are more coarsely ground.

I write "usually" because I was sorely disappointed with the hot link sausages that I ate on Chicago's South Side. The sausages were tasty, but they were bland, reminding me of flavorful, sage-spiked breakfast sausage. I've teased the native Chicagoans in my life about the bland sausage, and they've assured me that the city's hot links are supposed to be spicy. A possible explanation is a change in manufacturer, and in their defense, I may not have been eating the hot links of their youth. Rather than making their own sausage or dealing with a meat supplier, many Chicago barbecuers got their hot links at a nearby Moo & Oink grocery store. When the Moo & Oink chain closed, restaurateurs went elsewhere, and the sausage was different. I'm shocked that customers didn't revolt, or at least voice complaints. I experienced similar pain when the Gold Star Sausage Company, which made my favorite hot link in Denver, was sold and their transcendent hot link was no longer available. It was the kind of hot link that had a deep red color, a foot long with cut off, rather than rounded, tied ends, coarsely ground meat with red specks from ground cayenne pepper, and even an occasional red chile seed here and there. That's the hot link of my youth. Fortunately, Gold Star's hot links have made a comeback in Denver markets, and they tasted just fine when I gorged on one at my family's Labor Day barbecue meal in 2020.

Speaking of youth, I had an interesting conversation with Chef Jason Alston, who runs Heaven's Table Catering and BBQ at a food hall in Milwaukee, Wisconsin. He serves a tasty sausage, but it was the kind that I'd expect in a white-run barbecue joint. It was finely ground, pale, and bland. He explained that the sausage is house-made using his own recipe. He tried to re-create the Polish sausages served at the corner markets in Black neighborhoods. He said that a lot of the stores had meat markets inside, and they seemed to have their own recipes. Another unusual sausage I experienced is the venison sausage served at Gatlin's BBQ in Houston, Texas. There, Greg Gatlin makes a venison sausage that has a ruddy color, a fine grind, and a nice kick of spice, and it's slightly juicy. Both serve as cautionary tales against overgeneralizing when it comes to barbecue aesthetics.

In eastern Texas, where cattle country meets bayou country and the rice country, there's an interesting regional style that is often overlooked. It's an area where barbecue menus include boudin (also spelled "boudain")—a Cajun sausage made of seasoned beef and pork and rice that is most often boiled but could be baked or smoked—as well as variety meats like smoked pork necks.

Customer demand for a healthier option created a hyperlocal tradition of chicken hot links in Los Angeles. This tradition was new to me until Garrett Snyder reached out to interview me for a *Los Angeles Times* story. I was immediately intrigued because I had seen more turkey links than anything. Snyder wrote that an African American version of chicken sausage appeared in grocery stores that served the city's Black enclaves: "Sometime around 1980 there were two neighboring families, the Holmeses and the Hookses, who sold sausage out of their Crenshaw homes. Darryl Holmes was originally from Texas. He served in the Army before moving to L.A. and, while stationed in Germany, met his wife, Pia. Holmes' sausage fell somewhere between bratwurst and what's often labeled 'country sausage,' heavy with sage and red pepper but also dashed with hints of ginger, nutmeg and cardamom, a dual reflection perhaps of Darryl's Texas roots and Pia's Bavarian heritage."[24] The home-based businesses were eventually shut down by local government, and the chicken thigh–based sausages eventually resurfaced in such local commercial establishments as barbecue joints, corner markets, and the world-famous Roscoe's Chicken and Waffles.

Okay, that's plenty about pork and chicken, but what of beef? In a lot of food media, the African American predilection for pork leads to a conclusion that African Americans don't barbecue beef. From what you've already read we know that this is an absurd conclusion. Beef was frequently barbecued throughout the South, but by the early 1900s, many preferred barbecuing pork. Outside of the South, African Americans, usually with roots in Texas, brought beef barbecuing to other parts of the country. One of the most famous examples is Arthur Bryant, who, for decades, ran his renowned barbecue restaurant in Kansas City, Missouri.

In the 1930s, Bryant, along with his brother Charlie, moved from Texas to Kansas City and soon apprenticed under Henry Perry, whom we met in chapter 5. When Bryant went out on his own, he became famous for his beef brisket, pork shoulder, and spareribs. He became the reference point for what good barbecue was in Kansas City, and his product was flown all over the country to satisfy salivating customers. He was also an innovator, creating one of the trendiest items in contemporary barbecue: "burnt ends." Burnt ends are created during the process of barbecuing brisket. Technically, these are the charred part of the brisket's point section after the fat renders. Many barbecue purveyors simply threw them in the garbage as scraps, but Bryant took a different path. In the grand tradition of lagniappe in New Orleans, the people working the counters at his restaurant collected the bits and put them on a tray for people to snack on—something that would whet their appetite or satisfy their cravings as they waited. Calvin Trillin, probably the biggest booster that Bryant's restaurant had ever seen, famously wrote in *Playboy*, "The main course at Bryant's, as far as I'm concerned, is something that is given away free—the burned edges of the brisket."[25]

The biography of burnt ends is a great parable for what barbecue has now become. As word spread, burnt ends became extremely popular, and with that popularity, restaurateurs thought of "market opportunity" instead of "expanded generosity." They sold them and made gobs of money. The problem was that there are only so many burnt ends that one can get from a brisket. In order to meet demand, Kansas City restaurateurs redefined—some might say gentrified—burnt ends. Kansas City barbecue expert Ardie Davis pointed out the difference to me when he touted the excellent burnt ends at L.C.'s Bar-B-Q. "You don't always hear about this place. The owner is actually from Mississippi, yet his burnt ends remind me of more of an authentic burnt end than some of the others that just cube pieces of brisket. They're tender and packed with flavor, thanks to a little bit of fat and bark. It's closer to the trimmings that Arthur Bryant used to serve."[26] With that change, now almost anything can be a "burnt end"—regardless of the meat used, the amount, or its shape, provided it has some fat, a seasoned crust (a bark), and some smokiness. And, of course, people now pay a lot of money for something that was once given away. The only other place where I've seen truly authentic burnt ends, according to Davis's definition, is Jones Bar-B-Q in Kansas City, Kansas.

Bologna is another clear import from central Europe that African Americans embraced. I certainly enjoyed it during my childhood as an after-school snack. I'd get and heat a cast iron skillet, peel off the outer circle of tubing and put a thin slice of "baloney" in the skillet, watch it puff up, flip it, put a slit in it, top with a slice of cheese, and put it in between two slices of white bread with mustard and mayonnaise. For a lot of people, bologna runs much deeper. As late as 1872, a "German barbecue" in upstate New York in support of U.S. presidential candidate Horace Greeley included "pretzels, Bologna sausages, and lager for the multitude."[27] Judging from newspaper advertisements and mentions, barbecued bologna was most popular in Oklahoma and Texas, though it is known as "Mississippi prime rib."

I first saw barbecued bologna on a TV program featuring Jim Neely of Interstate BBQ. To demonstrate how he made it, he took a good-sized tube of bologna with the casing still on, he stabbed it in select places to allow smoke to penetrate it, and then he put the entire tube on the smoker. After a couple of hours, he took the tube out of the smoker and held it until ready for serving. To serve, a thick slice (a quarter inch to a half inch) was cut, the slice was grilled to give it some char, and then it was placed between two slices of white bread topped with sauce and maybe some coleslaw. I was mesmerized by the account. When I had a chance to finally eat the sandwich, it was in Memphis but not at Interstate BBQ. I took my first bite at Cozy Corner Restaurant, and I became an instant fan.

East Texas is also known for an all-beef link sausage. This sausage finds a nice home at Patillo's Bar-B-Que Restaurant, one of the oldest, continuously run barbecue restaurants not only in Texas but in the United States. According to Texas barbecue expert Daniel Vaughn:

> Founder Jack Pat(t)illo is believed to be a direct descendant of one of the earliest Texas settlers, George Alexander Pattillo. The recipes they still use today came from a woman who traced her ancestry to the McFaddins, a powerful local family who amassed wealth from land and cattle. These family ties aren't simple, and the stories behind them don't figure into Patillo's marketing strategy.
>
> Robert Patillo runs the restaurant now in a wooden structure his forebears built in 1950. He hand-stuffs the same spicy beef links that his great-grandfather Jack Pat(t)illo cooked when he opened the doors in 1912. Robert Patillo says that Jack married into the recipe by way of his second wife, Roxie, in 1907. (She made him drop one of the "t's" to become Patillo.) Five years later, they opened a small restaurant together downtown, cooking with recipes from Roxie's mother, Martha McFaddin. The thin, gravy-like barbecue sauce they still make was hers, says Robert. And "she developed the all-beef link, and that's the way it has always been made."[28]

Made from ground beef that is seasoned with garlic, red chiles, and a lot of fat, these sausages are also known as "garlic bombs" and "grease balls." The beef link is delicious, but it hasn't really caught on outside of East Texas. In January 2019, *Houston Chronicle* food writer J. C. Reid gave me a guided tour of the joints in Beaumont, Texas, the native habitat of these sausages, and we grubbed at Patillo's Bar-B-Que Restaurant. As much as I loved the beef links, I was over the moon with the sizable sandwich piled high with chopped beef served with the rich gravy sauce described above.

Perhaps it's because of my Colorado heritage that I'm a big fan of lamb. Chefs all over the world clamor for Colorado lamb. If you ask a knowledgeable butcher for a "Denver rack," you'll get a rack of lamb ribs. When pairing the words "lamb" and "barbecue," few barbecue fans think about Colorado. I certainly didn't. Most likely, their minds are on the mutton tradition of Owensboro, Kentucky, and the Worcestershire-based black dip that's served with it. However, after reading Wes Berry's book on Kentucky barbecue and consulting with him, it doesn't look as if Black barbecuers in Kentucky have embraced lamb. I had to look elsewhere.

My first taste of lamb barbecue was a rack of lamb ribs that I got at Charlie Vergos's Rendezvous Restaurant in Memphis, Tennessee. The next time was at Taylor's Grocery run by the Reverend Jim Davis in Taylor, Texas, not too far from Austin. The third time was at Fiorella's Jack Stack in Kansas City, Missouri. All three versions had a similar taste. They were all lightly smoked, fatty, and absolutely delicious. I've heard that Gates Bar-B-Q has mutton on its menu, but when I was last in Kansas City at one of the chain's locations, I was told that it would not be available for several months. I tried again a little bit later—not to be annoying, but I've stood in line at Gates before and heard things go in and out of availability within minutes of an announcement; it really seemed to depend on who answered from the back. The second time I asked, I got a clear, and polite, indication that I really shouldn't ask again. My sense is that lamb will never be a big-time barbecue item. Many dislike the gamey taste. For some, it's too greasy. Others, I think, are reluctant to eat lamb because they are so cute. Either way, a lot of carnivores are missing out on some good eating.

Though one of the most widely eaten meats in the world, goat is uncommon in the United States save for Texas and at backyard gatherings in the Deep South. I've never had goat myself, but I've heard stories of it being popular in some parts, namely Mississippi. There is a type of goat called the "Juneteenth goat" that's worth a mention. Writing for a Black genealogical publication, Ophelia Pinkard noted:

Juneteenth is a festive occasion that emphasizes the family coming together. The day is highlighted by the bar-b-q (bar-b-q is the European-American spelling of the word) and the cooking of goat. . . . Preparation of the Juneteenth goat is the black woman's response to the black man's bar-b-q. The goat is selected two weeks to a month in advance of Juneteenth. During the time before the holiday, the goat is slaughtered, dressed, and turned over to the lady of the house. The meat is washed and most fat removed. It is then soaked in a solution containing vinegar, pepper, onions, garlic, and salt. The soaking can take from twelve to thirty-six hours. This is done "to get the goat taste out of the goat." After the soaking the goat meat is boiled with seasoning added to the boiling water. Once the boiling is complete, the meat is removed from the boiling pot and placed in a roasting pan. It is then roasted and as it is roasting, the lady of the house bastes it with a sauce made of honey, lemon, mustard, and other secret ingredients that make the goat so tender and juicy that it is said to "fall off the bone and melt in your mouth."[29]

Pinkard throws an interesting gender curveball here, showing once again that Black women have been in the barbecue game for a long time. I haven't seen goat on many restaurant menus, so I think it's more something that people cook at home. Noted southern foodways authority John T. Edge once told me that the family of famed musician Otha Turner has a long tradition of goat barbecue events. Sadly, I wasn't able to make one before writing this book.

Fish has always been a big part of the African American diet. It makes a lot of sense since so many of us are descended from people of coastal West Africa. Most of the time, Black cooks will fry fish instead of barbecuing it. Fortunately, there's an exception along the Carolina and Florida coasts. John Shelton Reed points out that "historically, smoked mullet was a common lunch for turpentine hands and other working-men, and it still has a special place in the hearts of many Southerners from coastal areas, especially African Americans."[30] As barbecue writer Robert F. Moss noted in a 2016 article for *Saveur*, "Unfortunately, few outside the state of Florida have discovered the virtues of this slow-smoked delicacy. Smoked mullet served over grits is a staple in the Gullah/Geechee community on Sapelo Island off the Georgia coast, but that's about as far north as it goes."[31] Tampa chef Greg Baker sums it up nicely when he emphatically states, it's "kind of our *de facto* barbecue dish."[32]

Ah, but where could one find African American expressions of smoked mullet? In *Roadfood*, Jane and Michael Stern describe a fantastic place in Mt. Dora, Florida, fueled by a Black man's recipes. "Uncle Suggs was a black man who lived in the woods near the Oak Grove Market. Blacks, and a few whites, used to walk through the woods to Uncle Suggs' whenever they could smell the smoke from the bar b que. That meant he was making mullet. Uncle Suggs kept his recipe all to himself, and became a Mt. Dora legend."[33] Ernest Arwood was one of Suggs's few loyal, white customers, and when he opened the Oak Grove Market, he repeatedly failed to recruit Suggs to be his cook. One day in the late 1960s, "One of the colored boys came by and told Ernest to go into the woods. Uncle Suggs wanted to see him. Ernest came back late afternoon and said, 'Uncle Suggs is dying. He told me how he does the mullet.'"[34] Sworn to secrecy, Arwood made and sold the specialty until Oak Grove Market closed in the 1990s. This much we know: "First, the large heavy fish is scaled, split open, eviscerated, and smoked over smoldering wood. It absorbs the barky smoke flavor, but never loses its dense mullet taste."[35]

Smoked mullet remains a hyper-regional specialty for now, waiting for an advocate to take it to other parts of the country. It might not be long as barbecue continues to its postmodern trajectory. One of the current crazes is to find healthier alternatives to traditional barbecue, such as smoked fish, fruit, and vegetables. Whoever figures out how to mass produce such items and maintain great taste and consistency will strike a gold mine. A lot of chefs these days are experimenting with jackfruit, a tropical fruit from Asia. The first time I had jackfruit was at a place (now closed) called Ghost BBQ in Boulder, Colorado. I just happened to pass by it after a meeting had ended. I was going to get my usual standby item (ribs), but I inquired about the jackfruit. The restaurateur then told me a pretty compelling story.

There once was a vegan convention happening down the street from his restaurant. Quite expectedly, the vegans were adamant that they get food without any animal products. Many barbecue jackfruit sandwiches were sold that day. Within a few minutes, several sandwiches were sent back to the kitchen because they were convinced the jackfruit was actually meat. He had to reassure the angry customers that it was in fact fruit. I was sold. I ordered the sandwich, and I must say, the way the chef prepared it really reminded me of North Carolina–style pulled pork. I was completely shocked. I've had jackfruit at other barbecue restaurants, and it's been a mixed bag. It's ranged from being porklike to more like a hearts of palm salad. Jackfruit's future in mainstream barbecue restaurants remains unclear. It doesn't sell well, and for that reason, many places remove it from the menu after a few months or they do serve it as a periodic special. Looks like people really want meat when they go to a barbecue restaurant. Go figure.

Black barbecue restaurateurs tend to have an "if ain't broke, don't fix it" attitude toward traditional barbecue preparations, but there has been innovation in recent years. Turkey is the hottest trend, and the variety of preparations surprises. Many barbecue restaurants have turkey breasts on their menu in order to provide a lighter option. Here's where barbecue has more in common with the current trends in soul food. In part for healthier alternatives, in part because of cheaper prices, Black-run joints have long featured turkey legs rather than turkey breast. Now I'm observing more iterations of turkey barbecue.

The most prominent are hot link sausages made with turkey meat. I had a great version at a place called Q's Tips & Wings on Chicago's South Side. Quincy Jones (yes, that's his name—but, no, it's not THAT Quincy Jones), the proprietor, opened this place up in 2015 after making barbecue as a side hustle. Almost everything on Q's menu can be substituted with turkey. Another innovation is turkey tips. One taste of the succulent, smoky meat let me know that this cut of meat had nothing to do with a cartilage-filled turkey wing tip. Tips are made by smoking turkey tenderloin (some places use breast meat), cutting it into smaller pieces, and then smothering the pieces in sauce. These were a revelation. I was expecting dried-out nubs like one would find at closing time in a buffet line, but these tips were moist and addictive.

I had my first taste of turkey ribs in 2019. Shawn Filer, a St. Louis native and Stanford student who spent that previous summer at a Denver-based internship, told me about them. On a visit to his hometown, he stopped by the Gobble Stop restaurant and shipped them to Jill Folwell, who hosted him over the summer. Calling it a "rib" is a misnomer. This cut of meat is really from the area around a turkey's shoulder blade. It's roughly the same size of a baby back rib, but it looks like the flat part of a chicken wing. The ribs had a light smoked flavor and were moist, but I think the sauce really makes this dish. At first, I thought these ribs were limited to the St. Louis area, but I've seen them on barbecue menus throughout the Upper Midwest, especially Cleveland. In 2013, a restaurant trade magazine indicated that turkey ribs "represent a crossover product that's been popular at carnivals and fairs and is slowly making a move from the midway to the mainstream."[36] I definitely see them catching on elsewhere given how inexpensive they are.

In parts of the country where chopped or pulled pork are fashionable, a turkey version is being served up. A memorable place where I first had chopped turkey was at the Backyard BBQ Pit, one of the few remaining African American-run barbecue joints in Durham, North Carolina. If you hadn't told me, I would have sworn I was eating chopped pork, given the meat's appearance and the balanced vinegar flavor. I had a similar dish of pulled turkey when I visited Boogie's Turkey Barbecue in Elm City, North Carolina, to film an episode on barbecue for Chef Vivian Howard's *Somewhere South*. I had pulled turkey when I ate at Ball Hoggerz BBQ in Memphis, Tennessee. This joint was started by a young couple who had some success on the local competition scene. I knew that I was eating turkey, but it was a good approximation of what the pulled pork version would look and taste like. My experience got me thinking about the city in a larger context as a barbecue incubator and innovation lab.

Black barbecue's most innovative town is undoubtedly Memphis. I wonder what it is about Memphis that inspires so much creativity. The answer lies in its status as a magnetic regional hub. A place that over generations attracted people from the small towns and rural sections of the Mississippi Delta, as well as steamboat traffic from New Orleans and St. Louis. The rich mix of class, culture, and race created a diverse barbecue scene. That city gave birth to dry-seasoned ribs (spareribs dusted with Greek spices, thanks to Charlie Vergos's Rendezvous Restaurant), the pulled pork sandwich topped with coleslaw (Leonard's Pit Barbecue), and barbecue pizza (Coletta's). That's just a sample of what was invented in white-owned barbecue joints.

Perhaps my favorite dish created by a Black barbecuer is barbecue spaghetti. The place to get the original version is the Bar-B-Q Shop run by the father and son team of Frank and Eric Vernon. Hazel Vernon, the matriarch, handles the online barbecue sauce business. The Vernons didn't invent it, though. They inherited the recipe when they purchased Brady and Lil's, a decades-old barbecue business.[36] Barbecue spaghetti consists of pasta mixed with a barbecue sauce base that can have smoked meat either mixed in or placed on top. The key is the base, and it goes far beyond just barbecue sauce, almost approaching a light gravy. It takes twelve hours to make, and it's incredible.

"Snoots" are the *nom d'oeuvre* for pig snouts. This item is most associated with St. Louis, but it was also well known in Memphis as late as the 1950s. There's even a place selling snoots in Kansas City, Missouri. Snoots can be given to you whole, but I've always had them cut into smaller pieces. Maybe it's hard for people to get over looking at a pair of nostrils before taking a bite. Snoots are pretty much like fried pork rinds in taste, texture, and consistency in restaurants. Snoots are often presented as a sandwich, slathered in sauce, between two pieces of white bread. I was lucky enough to get home-cooked snoots from Zach McNeil, a St. Louis native and a successful concessionaire at Denver International Airport. He fried them on the spot, and these were sweeter and slightly chewier than what I got in a restaurant.

Returning to Smith's barbecue framework discussed earlier in this chapter, a big dividing line that's occurred is the way African Americans traditionally prepare barbecue. The look, smell, and taste imparted by charcoal cooking is unmistakable. Here's a great description written by a white *New York Times* reporter who took the "A" Train to Harlem in the late 1930s:

> Whether Harlem barbecues meats on a rotisserie spit or over a pit, the visitor is struck with the elaborateness of the preparations. If the restaurant uses the pit method the procedure is reminiscent of the Southern Negro's traditional mass barbecue for an occasion like the Emancipation Day picnic, when long trenches are dug to receive a whole cow and a fire burns all night to provide charcoal for the feast day. In Harlem the meat is cooked on a grate over a pit filled with charcoal so that the grease falls onto the coals, vaporizes and is wafted back to the meat. Meantime the meat is basted with barbecue sauce.[38]

The charcoal vapors infusing the meat seems in stark contrast to how whites expected, or described, how barbecue was cooked. Take this example from the late 1880s of how a man named "Uncle Moses" barbecued: "With what infinite care he has selected his young pigs, and dressed them properly! It is a high art by itself to know how to secure them to the wooden spits. A little too hot a place would scorch or would smoke them."[39]

Regardless of what meat is cooked and where the restaurant is located, a definite signature of Black barbecue is having a charcoal-grilled flavor. At Grady's Barbecue in Dudley, North Carolina, Steve and Gerri Grady make superlative eastern North Carolina barbecue. If you're familiar with that regional style at all, you know that the meat is infused with a vinegar sauce. I think eastern North Carolina barbecue gets a bad rap because most people outside the state are probably getting served a really bad version of it. If only you could have it at Grady's. The succulent, chopped pork shoulder has a sweet, subtle, vinegary taste, immediately followed by a light charcoal taste that truly surprises. I write that because North Carolina barbecue usually isn't that smoky. It may be because the Gradys are cooking cuts of meat instead of a whole hog protected by a layer of skin and fat. By the time this book is published, there's a real question whether Grady's will still be open. The Gradys are well within retirement age, and the relative who's in training may not be game for such labor-intensive work. Please do an internet search, call to make sure they're open, and get thee to Gradys with haste.

Barbecuing with charcoal affects the meat's appearance. Quite simply, for many Black folks, if it doesn't look slightly charred, it's not true barbecue. My father, Hyman Miller Sr., had the opposite reaction because he didn't (perplexingly to me) have any barbecue while growing up outside of Helena, Arkansas, in the 1940s and 50s. When his large family had a special meal, fried chicken was the featured entrée. He didn't first see barbecue until he went to Memphis in the late 1950s as a young man. He told me he didn't order the barbecue displayed in a restaurant's window because it looked "burnt up" to him.

That distinctive charcoal look and taste comes only from cooking directly over coals, usually at high temperatures for a shorter time. That's why the "low and slow" mantra doesn't ring true for so many Black barbecuers. "Hot and fast, then slow" is more typical, and I've seen two famous Black barbecuers demonstrate as much on television. The first was Ed Mitchell, a North Carolina pitmaster, whom I profile at the end of this book. On a Food Network program, Mitchell talked about cooking a whole pig at an excess of 400° for a few hours before lowering the heat. I was gobsmacked because I had uncritically gulped down the gospel of low and slow cooking. Legendary Kansas City pitmaster Ollie Gates did the same during a guest spot on *Martha Stewart's Kitchen*. Gates prepared a slab of pork ribs, starting over high heat, flipping frequently to prevent scorching, and then moving the ribs to a cooler side of the grill to finish cooking. Some Black barbecuers certainly embrace the low and slow method, but it's not the way most Black barbecuers that I've observed cook.

With all my talk about charcoal cooking, a quite maddening thing is that there seems to be a whole lot of baking going on in restaurants. When I see barbecue on a restaurant menu, I always ask if the barbecue is truly smoked or is baked in the oven. Soul food cookbook author Bob Jeffries aptly described the phenomenon in the late 1960s, and it still holds true today: "North of the nation's capital (a little less than north of Baltimore), there is still some confusion as to what barbecue actually is." Many people think it is roasted meat with a hot sauce, the hot sauce itself, or even chicken cooked on one of those infrared-ray contraptions you see in the delicatessens around town. Actually, true barbecue is none of these things. Instead, it is simply a method of cooking over woodsmoke so that the smoke penetrates and flavors what you are cooking.[40] As for what restaurant servers tell me about how their barbecue is cooked, the answer overwhelmingly is "baked." This holds true in some Black-owned restaurants as well. For many, it's the sauce, not the cooking process, that makes something barbecue.

Alas, the Black barbecue aesthetic has some regrettable aspects that are deeply engrained for the moment. The first is white bread. I know that white bread was once thought of as a superlative. There's a reason why people say, "That's the best thing since sliced bread." The magic of white bread was really strong for African Americans. Cornbread was the staff of life, and wheat flour–based bread was reserved for special meals, so much so that some enslaved people nicknamed cornbread "Johnny Constant" and wheat bread "Johnny Seldom."[41] Few enslaved African American cooks had unfettered access to wheat because whites considered it to be more prestigious than corn. It makes sense that if some restaurateurs wanted to seem a little classier, they would feature wheat bread on the menu. Functionally, white bread is piled high in barbecue restaurants because grease and sauce are so ubiquitous in African American barbecue. Something is needed to soak up all of that liquid.

Some early commercial barbecuers wrapped their barbecue in newspaper, as Henry Perry did in Kansas City. That became somewhat problematic if newspaper ink began to run onto to the food served, but that didn't stop some restaurateurs. White bread was another alternative because it worked much better than cornbread, which would just disintegrate and require more eating with one's fingers. Again, white bread's soaking ability, lack of crumbling, and ability to still taste kind of good after that absorption made it a go-to addition to most meals. For this reason, white bread is plentiful with barbecue meals. When ordering to go, white bread is usually laid on top of everything so that it's the first thing that you see when opening the container. I have a slight attitude toward white bread mainly for health reasons. It is usually less nutritious than bread made with whole grains.[42] I also noticed that I started packing on more pounds when I made white bread a regular part of my barbecue research.

In the Midwest, though, French fries have supplanted white bread as a favorite to sop up grease and sauce. French fry devotees are quite serious about what constitutes fry legitimacy: questions of the kind of cut, freshness, length, and width have all been intensely debated on my social media platforms. Evidently, crinkle-cut fries draw the most ire because they can't be fresh cut, so they are always frozen. No one

169

crinkle cuts their own fries. Despite the extensive territory of frydom, from Cleveland in the east to Kansas City in the west, Chicago to the north, and the Gulf of Mexico to the south, white bread is the dominant accompaniment to African American barbecue across the country.

Now a little bit more about containers. As glorious as African American barbecue is, the tradition floats on a sea of "extruded polystyrene foam," better known as Styrofoam. This is the Black barbecuer's equivalent to the tin plate so prevalent in today's trendy barbecue joints. It's used as both a dine-in and a to-go container. It can have a deep well or be compartmentalized. I completely understand why restaurateurs use it. It's incredibly cheap, and it does a decent job of holding heat. Then it's usually bagged in some very cheap plastic. On the user end, it's bound for some landfill or, even worse, any old place in the environment. Biodegradable and compostable packaging has been developed and is available on the market. Yet for entrepreneurs barely making ends meet, it's too costly, especially if they can't pass that cost along to consumers. Switching to sustainable packaging will not be easy because I've heard Black customers being highly critical of barbecue prices that were quite affordable, nowhere near what other places charge in white neighborhoods. But, it's a matter of perspective and purchasing power. Maybe some brave souls, for the sake of our planet, will give it a try.

Returning to Smith's framework on the rhetoric of barbecue, the only things I'm not exploring more closely are the "shamans" and "preparation rituals." I mention a lot of shamans throughout the book, and I list my top twenty barbecue joints toward the end. This chapter was a look at how barbecue plays out when African Americans make barbecue on their own terms. If I had to rank the element that most distinguishes African American barbecue from contemporary barbecue culture, it'd have to be sauce. In the next chapter, we're not just dipping our toes into barbecue sauce culture. We're doing to do a deep dive.

RECIPES

Otis P. Boyd's Famous Hot Link Sausage

Otis P. Boyd was a famous Kansas City barbecue man, often mentioned in the same sentence as the city's other greats, including Arthur Bryant, Ollie Gates, and Henry Perry. This recipe is adapted from the one in Lolis Eric Elie's *Smokestack Lightning: Adventures in the Heart of Barbecue Country.* For the best sausage, you need a certain amount of fat. Use meat that has at least 20 percent fat.

Makes 5 pounds of sausage

2½ pounds ground pork (shoulder cut, also known as pork butt or Boston butt)
2½ pounds ground beef (brisket, chuck, round, or sirloin)
2 teaspoons dried sage
2 teaspoons crushed red pepper
2 teaspoons paprika
2 teaspoons ground cumin
2 teaspoons dried sweet basil
2 teaspoons anise seed
2 teaspoons dried oregano
Salt and ground black pepper, to taste

1. Mix the meat with the spices.
2. For sausage links, attach 2¼-inch sausage casings to the stuffer nozzle on a hand meat grinder.
3. Stuff the casings to the desired length, cut the links, and secure the ends with string.
4. Prepare a barbecue grill or smoker. Barbecue at 225° for 2 hours, or slow smoke at 185° for 4 hours.
5. For sausage patties, form the meat mixture into a roll and cover it with wax paper.
6. Slice the roll into patties and peel off the wax paper.
7. The patties can be fried or grilled.

Chef Ricky Moore's Smoked Mullet with Cider-Sorghum Syrup Glaze

Chef Ricky Moore is a strong believer that mullet is most delicious when it's smoked. If you ever get the chance to dine at one of his Saltbox Seafood Joint locations in Durham, North Carolina, you'll learn to trust his opinion. The use of sorghum is interesting here, and it will remind you of molasses, but with a cleaner finish on your palate. Use 6 ounces of wood chips for each pound of fish.

Makes 6–8 servings

2 gallons water, divided, plus more for soaking the wood chips
1¼ cups salt
½ cup packed light brown sugar
2 tablespoons plus ¾ teaspoon freshly cracked black pepper, divided
2 tablespoons dried thyme
8 bay leaves
¼ cup hot sauce (preferably Texas Pete brand)
4 (1-pound) mullets, scaled, gutted, heads removed, and butterflied
1 large yellow onion, coarsely chopped
1 tablespoon whole black peppercorns
¼ cup apple cider vinegar
¾ cup sorghum
3 tablespoons finely chopped shallots
3 sprigs of fresh thyme
¾ teaspoon freshly cracked black pepper
1–2 teaspoons vegetable oil

1. In a large container, combine 1 gallon of the water with the salt, brown sugar, 2 tablespoons of the cracked black pepper, dried thyme, bay leaves, and hot sauce.
2. Stir to dissolve the salt and sugar.
3. Add the fish, cover the container with plastic wrap, and chill for 48 hours.
4. Soak the wood chips in a bucket of water for 2–3 hours, then drain.
5. Prepare a home smoker according to the wood chip manufacturer's directions and place the soaked chips in the bottom tray.
6. In the upper container of the smoker, combine the remaining gallon of water with the onion and the peppercorns.
7. Cover the smoker and let the fire burn for 30 minutes.
8. In a small saucepan, make a glaze by combining the vinegar, sorghum, shallots, thyme, and the remaining cracked black pepper.

9. Simmer the glaze to reduce the volume by a fourth.
10. Remove the pan from the heat, let cool, and set aside.
11. Lightly coat the grill with the vegetable oil.
12. Remove the fish from the brine and pat them dry inside and out.
13. Gently brush both sides of each fish with the glaze.
14. Place the fish on the grill above the water and cook, covered, turning once, until crisp and the skin is dry, about 1–1¼ hours.
15. Remove the fish from the smoker and server either hot or chilled.

LIQUID BLACK SMOKE
THE PRIMACY OF SAUCE

Willie Powe lived a full life. The one-time Harlem Renaissance-era "hoofer" (tap dancer) and renowned community barbecue man from the Carolinas and Mobile, Alabama, spent the last few months of his incredible life with family in Mobile. Though their marriage had dissolved years before, Willie's former wife, Marcella, believed that it was important for a man to keep his dignity. She demonstrated that lesson to her children in many ways. Willie was welcomed to join her and their children for Sunday dinner, which he did regularly, often sitting at the head of the table.

Over the years, Willie "showed" Marcella and his children how to make his family's century-old barbecue sauce. The exact recipe was known only to Willie and his brother Leo. The sauce was so famous that he regularly filled requests to mail the sauce in dry ice containers from Mobile to people around the country. He was often paid with high-quality cigars that he cherished. Eventually, that passion for cigars took

Arthur Bryant and St. Peter at the Pearly Gates. Illustration courtesy of Lee Judge.

a toll on his larynx, and he lost much of his ability to speak. Later in life, he taught others how to make his sauce by pointing and nodding. Yet these lessons always involved a "lesser-pe," a recipe with a key ingredient that Willie left out. I'm sure you know the type. Those benefiting from Willie's culinary knowledge knew two things: something was missing, and Willie was probably never going to tell them. Every once and a while, someone would ask what the missing ingredient was. Those who made the sauce speculated that the unicorn-type ingredient might be Worcestershire sauce or liquid smoke, but Willie would never confirm or deny when directly asked. He would just smile.

Now that Willie's death was imminent, the family gathered. Not solely for Willie's final arrangements but for one last attempt to coax the complete barbecue sauce recipe out of him. Marcella was a woman who took pride in her appearance—so much so that she never, ever, let Willie see her without makeup. At the appointed time, she dressed "to the nines" and set the scene for the final ask. "Now, Willie," she said as she stroked his hair, "We want you to be comfortable." Willie was now fading in and out of coherent consciousness. "Now that barbecue sauce. Tell me what that ingredient was that you and Leo used to put in it." Willie couldn't talk at all at this point, and he just looked at her and smiled. Marcella persisted, "C'mon, Willie. I'm going to get a pen and pad, and you can write down what it was. Even if you can't spell it, I think I know it. Was it this or this?" She wrote something down on the pad. "Was it this?" As he had done years before, he just smiled in response to her queries and didn't say a word. Marcella tried again, and before it was over, he smiled one last time, rolled over, and peacefully transitioned to the afterlife. One more heavenly barbecue sauce was added to the celestial cupboard.

Varion Walton, Willie Powe's granddaughter and a successful, award-winning television news journalist who resides in Mobile, Alabama, told me that story in 2016. The moment I heard it, I knew it had to be in this book because it brings so many aspects of barbecue culture together: secrecy, pride, deliciousness, family, church, commerce, and, ultimately, death. Death has a way of lingering around barbecue sauce lore. I don't mean that eating the sauce will kill you. It's more about stories like Willie Powe's. How people, usually relatives, are always in pursuit of an honored barbecue sauce recipe before the soulful saucier dies. On the rare chance that one gains access to a recipe, it's usually on pain of death and cannot be revealed until one knows that one's own death is imminent. The latter circumstance presents quite the conundrum. For the highly regarded barbecue cook, the sauce is often as much a testament to a lifetime of good works as the meat he or she prepared. It's why St. Peter asked Arthur Bryant that vital question in this chapter's opening cartoon.

Johnnie Brown, an African American barbecuer from Willis Point, Texas, grappled with the weighty questions of life, death, and sauce when a legendary barbecue man named Lank Robinson bequeathed to him a "devil's sauce recipe." Described as "cheerful" by famed Texas folklorist Frank X. Tolbert, Brown felt "heavily burdened." He told Tolbert, "About fifteen years ago, Lank Robinson give me the receipt for his barbecue sauce, and it is the best devil's sauce they is. Lank Robinson was a real barbecuing man. He could cook sweeter over red oak than anyone else can over hickory. He made me swear not to tell what's in that sauce until I'm just about to die. What worries me is how am I going to know when I'm just about to die?"[1]

Sauce is sharpening the dividing line between Black and white barbecue aesthetics. I use the word "sharpening" because, for centuries, Blacks and whites in the South agreed on what barbecue sauce should be and what its role is in the cooking process. As barbecue has changed, notions for the proper role of sauce have changed as well. Now the emerging conventional wisdom is that proper barbecue should not be sauced so that the diner may experience the true taste of the meat. Otherwise, the cook is hiding something. I must admit, I bought into this thinking myself because I was seduced by the skyrocketing popularity of central Texas–style barbecue. Yet, my love for barbecue sauce was always there. It's why I nod in agreement when legendary Memphis barbecue restaurateur Jim Neeley said: "When I was a kid, the barbecue sauce was so good that you didn't need meat."[2]

Sauce has a very special place in African American barbecue culture. I offer as Exhibit 1 a conversation that I had with Andre, an African American Uber driver, while on a barbecue research trip to Washington, D.C. I had recently conducted a highly unscientific Twitter poll, asking my followers what they thought was most important to good barbecue: meat, sauce, or both? The "meat" or "both" answers were clearly in the lead until Derek Kirk, also known on social media as "soulphoodie," retweeted my poll. I love it when he does that because he has a significant African American following. I noticed that the percentage answering "sauce" had a marked increase. By the end, the split was more even. With those unscientific results in mind, I sought validation by asking Andre the same question. Without missing a beat, he answered, "Oh, it's definitely the sauce. Anyone can cook the meat." I was a little stunned that he said it with such confidence, but it reinforced what I had been feeling.

For many Black people, though, in life and death, barbecue isn't the real deal unless it has sauce, and it's long been that way. As historian Ophelia Pinkard quipped, "The bar-b-q sauce for the meat is a 'work of art.' Each Juneteenth an effort is made to foster the bar-b-q sauce as the talk of the day. When word is passed on about so-and-so's bar-b-q sauce, people come from 'miles around' just to taste that sauce. Tradition has it that no maker of a good bar-b-q sauce will give a family recipe to outsiders. It has been noted that marriages are arranged so that the recipe can be passed on to a family seeking it."[3] Barbecue sauce also inspired love marriages. In a memorable 2010 interview, Reggie Turner discussed why he married Helen Turner, the dynamo running Helen's Bar-B-Que, a whole hog restaurant, in Brownsville, Tennessee: "'That's why I married her, for the sauce,' Helen's husband Reggie smiles. 'I thought it was for love?,' Helen shy fully [sic] smiles. Reggie: 'Well yeah, but the sauce comes with that!' They both shake their heads in laughter."[4]

The many importance-of-barbecue-sauce conversations that I've had with African Americans got me wondering if sauce is an African culinary survival. Is there a "mother sauce" when it comes to barbecue? Better yet, in terms of lineage, is there a "mother barbecue sauce" from West Africa? The short answer is "no." The sauce story begins elsewhere. According to Jessica B. Harris, an early account of sauced barbecue comes from Father Jean-Baptiste Labat, a French priest living on Martinique in the 1690s. Harris writes, "Labat . . . say[s] that the cavity of the pig was filled with lemon juice, salt, and hot chiles. When cooked, the pig was served with a dipping sauce in two strengths, mild or hot, along with the condiments that seemed to have consisted of a calabash of the sauce from the stomach of the pig and another of lemon juice, salt, pepper, and chile, from which the diners could prepare their own sauce."[5] This sauce is credited to Indigenous cooks. Immigrant cooks built on that formula to create a wide variety of sauces. Indigenous food expert Gary Nabhan adds that in addition to chiles, "The immigrants and refugees [to the Americas]—Europeans, Africans, and Asians—also introduced another ingredient for flavoring and saving meats from spoilage: vinegar."[6] Europeans had been using vinegar-based sauces since the Middle Ages, and the mixture of vinegar and chiles eventually became the "mother sauce" of southern barbecue. It wasn't considered just a condiment; it was integral to the barbecuing process.[7]

West African cooks traditionally incorporated sauces into a meal, and, as a result of colonization, later adapted to the European notion of sauce as a condiment. Well into the 1900s, southern barbecue's mother sauce was commonly called "soption." The earliest soption used could have a variety of ingredients. Barbecue historian John Shelton Reed notes, "[In 1732], one of the earliest printed recipes for a sauce specifically designed for barbecuing appeared, in Richard Bradley's *Country House-wife*. To prepare 'an Hog barbecued, or broil'd whole,' Bradley says, season the hog with salt and pepper and cook it on a gridiron, skinside up. After turning it, fill the cavity with water, white wine, lemon peels, sage, and cloves. Later, serve this liquid as a table sauce."[8] The key was that the basting sauce, or sop, and the finishing sauce, or condiment, were one and the same. Food writers Bob, Cora, and Rose Brown add, "The 'soption,' as the basting sauce is called, is ready, consisting of a couple of quarts of hot vinegar, well seasoned with salt and red pepper pods, floating with melted butter. The skin side of the pig is greased, before it is turn over, and the soption goes on the flesh side, with its own natural container for the basting. After the soption is enriched with pig juice, some of it is taken out to be used as sauce for serving with the meat, and basting continues until all is done."[9] Culinary historian Ken Albala points out that, from the Middle Ages on, vinegar became increasingly popular as a "go-to" ingredient for such sauces. "Sauces were an integral and essential part of the art of cookery in the past. Sometimes they were poured over a dish before service but often were presented in several little bowls scattered around the table that the diner could choose from to suit their taste. Unlike today, sauces were rarely based on butter or cream. More often they were sour vinegar- or verjuice-based, thickened with bread crumbs and intended to contrast in flavor with the main dish. They were almost always heavily spiced as well, or laden with garlic and herbs."[10]

Early descriptions of barbecue sauces don't give much detail except for containing vinegar and pepper. Yet some examples from Black barbecuers show surprising complexity. One such barbecuer, in the 1850s, was Wesley Jones of Union County, South Carolina. According to one account, Jones "was a youthful pitmaster for big barbecues that were held regularly at Sardis Store, with fiddling and political speeches. He cooked 'whole goats, whole hogs, sheep and de side of a cow.' He mopped the meat all night with a 'sass' of vinegar, black and red pepper, salt, butter, a little sage, coriander, basil, onion, and garlic—a process he called 'anointing' it. 'Some folks drop a little sugar in it,' he said, implying that this was a common sauce recipe for that time and place."[11] Here, "sass"

WHO'S ★ WHO IN AMERICAN BARBECUE

NEW RECIPES FOR MAIN COURSES AND SIDE DISHES FROM EXPERTS AROUND THE COUNTRY

"Who's Who in American Barbecue," Bon Appetit, *July 2003. Illustration by Tom Bachtell.*

Lady of Q competition barbecue team logo. Image courtesy of Sylvie Curry.

Helen Turner managing the pit at Helen's Bar BQ, Brownsville, Tennessee.
Photo by Andrew Thomas Lee.

Chopped pork shoulder sandwich with mustard slaw, Payne's Bar-B-Q, Memphis, Tennessee. Author's photograph.

Ed Mitchell's ball cap displaying an enduring message. Author's photograph.

Outdoor sign, Backyard BBQ, Durham, North Carolina. Photograph by Jai Williams.

Steve Grady,
Grady's Bar-B-Q,
Dudley, North
Carolina. Author's
photograph.

Savoring the moment at Bon Gout BBQ, Miami, Florida. Photograph by Angel Valentin.

was an analogue for sauce. Still, the vinegar and pepper, specifically red pepper, formula dominates.

Ultimately, sopping was so connected with Blackness that descriptions of the cooking process would include Black men. As one newspaper article noted, "But most exclusively Texan of all these various entertainments, and it is by no means entirely exclusive, is the rodeo. . . . There is usually a barbecue in conjunction, a few slaughtered beeves and sheep and pigs roasting on an open fire, being mopped with 'sop' by a colored man."[12] In these situations, the "mop" was usually a stick with rags wrapped around it at one end.

Soption descriptions from the nineteenth century are plentiful, and the most consistent description is that soption was spicy, sometimes intensely so, because of the liberal addition of red pepper. Given the medicinal reputations of red pepper and vinegar, I wonder if the early sauce was conceived of as an antiseptic agent. This may not seem like such a big deal today since American palates have been warming quite considerably in the past couple of decades. We're at the point now where some cooks wear gas masks when they prepare spicy barbecue sauces using incredibly piquant chiles. Back then, using a spicy sauce ran counter to European sensibilities about how sauces, and food in general, should be subtle and balanced. Eating aggressively seasoned food was considered lower class, but it was a hallmark of African American sauce alchemy.

The addition of copious amounts of red pepper is a definite culinary signature of African-heritage people in the Americas. The Atlantic Slave Trade introduced chiles, botanically identified as from the genus *Capsicum*, from the Americas to West Africans, who immediately embraced them. Various types of red peppers were introduced into West Africa by the 1670s, and they were used as provisions on slave ships in the 1700s.[13] Enslaved Africans removed to the Americas would have been familiar with this plant. Since African Americans were doing most of the cooking, and they were given latitude as to how they were spiced, these cooks clearly bent barbecue to their own tastes.

By the nineteenth century, the essential ingredients for barbecue sauce in the American South were vinegar and red pepper. "Your veritable gourmand never fails to regale himself on his favorite *barbecue*— which is a fine fat pig called 'shoat,' cooked on the coals, and highly seasoned with cayenne," wrote one unnamed newspaper reporter.[14] "Red pepper," wrote Sarah Hicks Williams to her parents in New York in 1853, "is much used to flavor meat with the famous 'barbecue' of the South & which I believe they esteem above all dishes is roasted pig dressed with

IN THE SAUCE WITH
ARGIA B. COLLINS
MUMBO'S THE WORD

Many whites say they can tell when they're in a black neighborhood, even blindfolded, especially on Friday and Saturday nights, when the aroma of smoke-flavored ribs permeates from rib joints which seem to be on every major street. — Argia B. Collins

Rather than fitting an existing category, some barbecue sauce entrepreneurs create their own tradition. Sometimes writers get signs. Before I drafted this profile, I took a quick break and turned on the television. No joke, the magnificent musical *West Side Story* was on. Moments later, the high school dance scene began, and what did the Jets and Sharks and their dates shout? "Mambo!" I took it as a sign that I was right to explore mambo sauce, mumbo sauce, mild sauce, and Argia Collins.

I don't know who first coined the term, but no surprise, there are fierce debates over its origins, ingredients, and application. Before it was applied to sauce, "mambo" referred, according to the *Oxford English Dictionary*, to a voodoo priestess in Haitian Creole and a type of Latin American dance in Spanish. Those versions of mambo were popular in the 1930s and the 1940s, respectively, but mambo—the sauce—didn't show up until the 1950s. Though an early advertisement called it mambo sauce, it soon became mumbo sauce. Much of this is owed to one man: Argia B. Collins of Chicago, Illinois.

While growing up in Indianola, Mississippi, Argia B. Collins watched his father, a reputed (you guessed it) barbecue king, do his thing. Collins "would watch his father prepare meat in the huge pit at the Collins home and he would ask questions. 'It's not the meat that makes the barbecue,' the elder Collins would tell the boy, 'it's the sauce.'"[1] That important lesson shaped Collins's life in immeasurable ways that he may not have appreciated at the time. He left home around age fifteen to pursue his dreams in the big city of Chicago.

After serving in the United States Navy, Collins moved to Chicago's West Side in the mid-1940s, where he worked for his eldest brother,

1. Johnnie A. Moore, "Personality Spotlight," *Chicago Defender*, Sept. 26, 1959, 7.

180

Argia B. Collins, creator of MUMBO Sauce, Chicago, Illinois. Photograph courtesy of Allison Collins.

who owned a local grocery store. All six of the Collins brothers lived in the Windy City, and they were spirited entrepreneurs who opened rib joints across the city heralded for world-class barbecue. In 1948, Collins learned more intentionally about the barbecue business by working in a restaurant operated by his brother Ernest.

By 1950, Collins was ready to go out on his own. He staked his claim on Chicago's South Side, opening his first restaurant in the historic Bronzeville neighborhood. He eventually opened two more locations, including one in Gary, Indiana. A culinary perfectionist, Collins wasn't impressed with the ho-hum national brands available to restaurants at the time. So, inspired by his southern roots, he perfected a family barbecue sauce recipe, something they called mumbo sauce. The Collins brothers claimed that it was "a Spanish 'Mumbo' sauce, first brought to Florida by Ponce de Leon nearly 400 years ago and now held by them as a family secret."[2] The earliest flavors were "hickory," "mild," and "tangy." His restaurant soon became the test kitchen for the delectable recipes he would concoct, experimenting with exotic spice and seasoning blends. Collins took steps to protect his intellectual property by patenting the process, proving that he was miles ahead of other barbecue entrepreneurs.

Before long, restaurant customers began asking for extra dollops of this delicious sauce with their meals. Next, they brought in jars to take the robust sauce home! Collins realized he had a winning sauce and an incredible opportunity. Collins was quite brilliant in his business plan. He opened a manufacturing plant and began selling Mumbo Sauce in his South Side Chicago restaurants. He then moved

2. "Opens Fifth Barbecue Shack"; *Jet*, Nov. 1, 1951, 24.

on up and had some success with independent retailers, but he ran into a dead end with the major grocery stores in the city. As he shared in a 1971 interview:

> "And then I ran into the brick wall of a closed consumer market that wouldn't let me into the stores," he explained. Collins said he took samples to various stores, and they approved them but told him he had to wait until next season "because by the time the buyers had their meetings and completed all the red tape procedures, they said it was too late for my seasonal product." He said he didn't let up in his attempts to get into the warehouses, but the stores "played seasonal football" with his product for more than six years until Operation Breadbasket put pressure on them.[3]

Operation Breadbasket revealed an interesting circle-of-life moment, repaying the kindness that Collins had shown others when they were down and out.

When civil rights leader the Reverend Jesse L. Jackson arrived in Chicago to start Operation Breadbasket, he took to Collins's barbecue the same way his mentor took to barbecue in Atlanta. Hazel Thomas, a longtime volunteer for the organization, remembered: "When Rev. Jackson first came to town, he was very poor. Because Argia B. was just so free, we'd call over there and say, 'Rev. Jackson wants to know if it's OK if we can get some food.' Somebody would get in the car and go get it. Whoever needed to be fed, we'd tell them to go to the barbecue house. It was phenomenal. Argia was well-loved. He was a kind, generous person. We ate a lot of barbecue."[4] Through direct action techniques and negotiation, Collins got his product placed in local groceries, most notably Jewel. It was one of Collins's biggest accomplishments.

Collins embarked on a major advertising campaign to promote his popular and now widely distributed barbecue sauce. He made a strong play for the white consumer market. He advertised in Chicago newspapers with a white readership, used white models in advertising images, and emphasized Mumbo Sauce as an all-purpose sauce of which barbecue was just one application. The pinnacle of attention for Mumbo Sauce came when it was featured in a 1970 *Life* magazine article. Today, Mumbo Sauce is widely distributed throughout the United States, one of the few Black-owned foods to earn that status.

Mumbo Sauce put me in a state of confusion. There's a sauce by the same name in Washington, D.C., and then Black Chicago has another popular condiment called "mild sauce." I reached out to Charla Draper,

3. Angela Parker, "Black Business Scores in Barbecue Sauce Trade," *Chicago Tribune*, Nov. 14, 1971, W A14.

4. Brad Webber, "Restaurateur Created Mumbo Barbecue Sauce," *Chicago Tribune*, Feb. 6, 2003, 3–11.

a longtime Chicago resident and food authority to help me sort it out. Draper explained, "Now comparing the two is an interesting proposition. Mumbo Sauce was created in 1950 by Argia B. Collins, Chicago entrepreneur and local pit master. This Chicago area barbecue sauce infused with spices is slightly thicker than mild sauce with a whisper of smoke undertones." Draper further explained that the sauce is not as readily available as it was the 1950s and 1960s, but you can find it in Chicago area stores and online.

Somehow the sauce migrated to Washington, D.C., where it became the condiment of choice for the D.C. subculture. A lot of confusion and arguments have flowed from this migration. Draper described the difference between the two. "Mild Sauce is another tomato-based condiment, yet the flavor is lighter. The texture is not quite as thick as Mumbo Sauce and sweeter. It is a sweet, well-balanced blend of ketchup and mildly flavored barbecue sauce with a shot of hot sauce. Mind you the heat component is a mild spice and not the POW punch of spiciness linked to Nashville's hot chicken; the spice however will hit you in the back of the throat." Draper consulted Percy Billings, owner of Harold's Chicken Shack Express, rated by *Chicago* magazine as one of the top five Harold's sites in the metro area. He said, "Our mild sauce is not a recipe we created. We sourced it via a food broker and our customers like it."[5] To add to the confusion, the D.C. version of mumbo sauce is used as an all-purpose condiment, not specifically for barbecue. The Chicago version of mumbo sauce was definitely a barbecue sauce suggested for a variety of purposes.

Collins was an entrepreneur's entrepreneur, full of ideas and pursuing many of them. My personal favorite is that he started a music production company, June 1 Records, in the early 1970s. He did manage to create some labels, sign acts (the Velvet Hammer group, Artie "Blues Boy" White, and Garland Green), and release music. Collins retired from the business in 1992, but his daughter, Allison E. Collins, keeps the legacy alive. Collins died on February 1, 2003, of heart and kidney failure, but it's certain that he did his father proud. By 1959, the *Chicago Defender* newspaper was already calling him a barbecue sauce king. That title suits him well, but let's add visionary entrepreneur and barbecue sauce pioneer to the list.

5. Charla Draper, email message to author, Dec. 27, 2019.

red pepper and vinegar."[15] The fiery taste was synonymous with barbecue, and like so many aspects of southern cooking, it was just accepted that African American cooks made barbecue sauce that way.

Remember the horrifying story of "Old Ford's Hell" in chapter 2? The combination of vinegar and red pepper was also a similar gateway to a nefarious, and hidden, horrifying aspect of barbecue history. Annie Tate of Raleigh, North Carolina, shared this story from her enslaved grandmother: "One day while the master was away, her grandfather got into a dispute with, and ultimately severely injured, the overseer. The master's son severely punished the grandfather, imprisoned him in a barn, and eventually sold him. The grandmother was devastated at the news that her husband was sold, and the master's son told her 'dat if'en she whimpers 'bout him sellin' de Black bastard dat he will whup her, den wash her down wid vinegar, red pepper an' salt.'"[16] If the threat didn't suffice, some slaveholders completed the inhumane act. One historian noted that "Elizabeth Sparks witnessed her owner 'Beat women naked an' wash 'em down in brine.' On backs that were so lacerated that they looked like raw meat, owners, drivers, or overseers poured salt, red pepper, vinegar, or turpentine to increase the pain, [to] stop the bleeding, and to act as an antiseptic."[17]

Torture via barbecue sauce inflicted maximum pain, but the victims usually survived. Yet there were tragic cases where even that line was crossed. Analiza Foster recalled a story her mother told her about an enslaved pregnant woman who fainted while working the field. The overseer believed that the woman was faking it, and he secured permission from the slaveholder to beat the woman, as long as he didn't kill her unborn baby.

> The driver then dug a hole in the ground into which he put the woman "'bout ter her arm pits, den he kivers her up an' straps her han's over her haid." He then took "de long bull whup an he cuts long gashes all over her shoulders an' raised arms, den he walks off an' leaves her dar fer a hour in de hot sun." During the hour, "de flies an' de gnats day worry her, an' de sun hurts too an' she cries a little, den de driver comes out wid a pan full of vinegar, salt an' red pepper an' he washes de gashes. De 'oman faints an' he digs her up, but in a few minutes she am stone dead." Analiza Foster considered the case the worst she had ever heard of, but reckoned "dar wuz plenty more of dem."[18]

This wasn't called "negro barbecue" as lynching was, but the terrorizing effect was the same. The evils of American slavery may never be fully accounted for and appreciated, but these are just a few examples of how slaveholders kept barbecue's supposed barbarous aspects alive and well.

In the latter half of the nineteenth century, barbecue sauce diversified. One of the new sauces that caught on was called "dipney," and it was popular in the Upper South, especially in Tennessee. An 1888 newspaper reference tells of an African American man named "Uncle Sprig" who prepared a July 4th barbecue in Kentucky. He cooked the "lambs, shoats, and kids" for twelve hours. The first ten hours, Sprig "basted every 10 minutes alternately with salt water and strong pepper tea." Then came a change of pace. "At the eleventh [hour] came 'dipney' compounded of sweet lard, strong vinegar and black pepper in about equal quantity, stewed in a great pot beside the fire and mopped over the barbecue till outside was half a pepper crust. Hot was no word for it."[19] Dipney's distinguishing feature was the addition of fat.

Southern food expert Martha McCulloch-Williams used dipney as an example of how white barbecuers' talent fell short of Black barbecuers'. "For one thing, they never found the exact secret of 'dipney,' the sauce that savored the meat when it was crisply tender, brown all over, but free from the least scorching."[20] Dipney's association with Black cooks lasted for decades. In a syndicated newspaper column that appeared in the late 1950s and was reprinted for a decade, Hoyt Alden refers to dipney as "a mixture of country lard, salt, strong vinegar, and a lot of red and black pepper." He then praises it as "the grand-daddy of all barbecue sauces."[21] Allen Flossie, an African American barbecue man, was Alden's interlocutor in the earliest, full-length version of the column, which showcased dipney and possibly it introduced to a national audience. The asymmetric power dynamic was readily apparent as Alden coaxed Flossie to give up the recipe, one he promised his daddy to keep secret, and published it for anyone to see.[22] By the time the article was widely reprinted in the late 1960s, Flossie no longer got explicit credit and was solely identified as "a native Tennessean."[23] He was erased from barbecue sauce history.

Soption and dipney were definitely part of the African American barbecue cook's repertoire, as were, to a lesser extent, the butter-based sauces that also emerged during this time period. An early recipe appeared in *Mrs. Hill's New Cook Book* listing "butter, mustard, red and black pepper, vinegar" as ingredients without indicated proportions.[24] In terms of African American cookbooks, the earliest recipe that I've found for a butter-based barbecue sauce is in a 1923 church cookbook. In a special section titled "Choice Recipes by the Ladies of the 25th U.S. Infantry, Nogales, Arizona," one "Buffalo Soldier" housewife listed:

SPANISH BARBECUE SAUCE (FINE) —One half-pound butter, one-fourth cup vinegar, one quart of water, one teaspoonful mustard, one teaspoonful red pepper, one ounce of sugar, one ounce of salt, one teaspoonful thyme, one ounce of Worcestershire sauce, one clove garlic, one onion, two bay leaves, serve with pork or lamb or beef.[25]

This recipe is much more elaborate than Mrs. Hill's and indicates a chef's touch with its use of herbs for seasoning.

Though vinegary sauces had long been in use, barbecue sauce changed significantly with the introduction of tomatoes, and African-heritage cooks welcomed the addition. John Mason, a Yoruba culture expert who wrote about West African culinary survivals in the Americas, noted: "More tomatoe [sic] sauce and paste began to be used to give food the red coloring that palm oil of traditional cooking gave. The slaves of the Caribbean continued to make the food hot and spicy because they knew that red pepper, for example, is a natural blood cleanser, is good for purging the digestive tract and helps regulate the system. Spices continued to be used because they were also good for controlling and killing bacteria in foods."[26]

Just like the liberal use of red pepper, a Black cook's comfort with tomatoes would have shocked some European-heritage diners in the seventeenth century. Because tomatoes, botanically speaking, are a part of the nightshade (a well-known poison) family, it was commonly held that tomatoes must be poisonous and fatal if consumed. A widely circulated story in the 1800s discusses how Robert Gibbon Johnson of Salem, New Jersey, set out to prove everyone wrong. I'm going to re-imagine the scene, just a little, through an African American lens. On September 26, 1820, Gibbon climbed the steps of the Old Salem County Courthouse with a basketful of ripe tomatoes. History hasn't recorded what the crowd yelled at him as he took his first bite. In my Black re-imagining of that scene, perhaps Messrs. Ricky Bell, Michael Bivens, and Ronnie Devoe were in attendance and yelled, "That fruit is poison!" The Johnson anecdote drove culinary historian Andrew F. Smith to go on a truth-seeking mission, and it was hard for him to find corroborating facts. Smith ultimately concludes that the story unlikely happened as told. It is a great story, though, and the main takeaway point is that tomatoes were widely accepted, particularly in condiments, well before Gibbon's very public taste test.

It's hard to imagine ketchup as anything other than tomato based, but its earliest versions were tomatoless. The same transition happened with barbecue sauces. As people moved westward, one can actually track when tomatoes were accepted in various communities. A great example of this is western North Carolina, where a little bit of tomato and a lot of vinegar is the traditional sauce. Generally, as people headed west, the amount of tomato increased until Kansas City, where you get the really goopy stuff that locals love. (By the way, I love it too.)

Again, culinary historian Andrew F. Smith helpfully sheds light on this aspect of tomato history. "The first Anglo-American recipe for tomato sauce had been published in Great Britain in 1804 by Alexander Hunter. Hunter's recipe was purloined by Maria Eliza Rundell and included in many of her variously titled cookbooks published both in Britain and in America."[27] Here's a recipe for "Tomata Sauce, for hot or cold Meats" that appeared in the 1814 edition of Rundell's *New System of Domestic Cookery*: "Put tomatas, when perfectly ripe, into an earthen jar; and set it in an oven, when the bread is drawn, till they are quite soft; then separate the skin from the pulp; and mix this with capsicum vinegar, and a few cloves of garlic pounded, which must both be proportioned to the quantity of fruit. Add powdered ginger, and salt to your taste. (Some white-wine vinegar and Cayenne) may be used instead of capsicum vinegar. Keep the mixture in small wide-mouthed bottles, well corked, and in a dry, cool place."[28] Tomato-based sauces were also used in the antebellum South. In 1857, a South Carolina newspaper printed a recipe for "tomato catsup" with the following ingredients: tomatoes, black pepper, red pepper, mustard, allspice, and "vinegar to your taste." Hmmm, reads a lot like a barbecue sauce. To underscore that point, the recipe ended with, "You have a condiment that will provoke the most sluggish appetite to seize with aridity upon the turkeys, the spare-ribs, and even the possums, of winter."[29] The latter two were definitely associated with barbecue.

Three years later, one newspaper similarly reported in a defense of "plantation barbecues" against abolitionists: "Could one of these whining fanatics attend an occasion of the sort, and see the smoking viands then and there profusely spread out, the piles of loaf bread, the bowls of Irish potatoes, the dishes of tomato sauce, the tubs of savory hash, and various other kinds of good cheer; and could he see our honest darkey laying hold of the welcome feast with unaffected gusto, while his ivory shiners give unmistakable proof of his freedom from care."[30] In a report on a Fourth of July barbecue in the late 1880s, a tomato-based sauce makes another cameo. "What more exciting than the rush of the crowd when the signal is given—the scramble for places—the crunching of toothsome bones full of marrow—the tearing of tender flesh—the splash and splatter of the red gravy? A fourth of July barbecue is an education—its enjoyment is one of the finer arts that are not taught in the schools."[31]

Vinegar-as-the-main-ingredient-sauces had a long, good run, but tomato sauces now dominate the barbecue sauce market. This likely coincided with a growing ketchup craze. As Malcolm Gladwell wrote in a 2004 *New Yorker* article, the early preservatives in commercially available ketchups were believed to be a human health risk. Food scientists struggled with how to give ketchup a good consistency (not too thin or thick), a great taste (not too tomatoey), and a better shelf life. The persuasive scientists "argued that by greatly increasing the amount of vinegar, in effect protecting the tomatoes by pickling them, they were making a superior ketchup: safer, purer, and better tasting. They offered a money-back guarantee in the event of spoilage. They charged more for their product, convinced that the public would pay more for a better ketchup, and they were right."[32] In essence, the "solution" was to make ketchup more like a vinegar-based barbecue sauce.[33]

But why did tomato-based sauces become so popular in the Black community when vinegar-based sauces dominated for so long? I never really knew why until Bob Miller, "The Younger," profiled in chapter 1, proposed an interesting theory. In an interview, he posited: "In the 1940s . . . because of the shortage of imported spices, people bought 'C' ration cans of catsup by the cases. Soldier cooks sold them. They were using catsup, tomato puree and their tomato product in barbecue sauces. There was no refrigeration being used in those sauces. That is where KC barbecue sauce came in. Jazz and barbecue. World War II and making the fast dollar bill is what happened to old fashioned Southern style barbecue."[34] To connect the dots a little, the big difference for Miller was the departure from an old-school, vinegar-based sauce. Since these tomato sauces were plentiful and cheap, they spread in popularity with a number of Black barbecuers. In time, food companies chose to mass produce and market the sweet tomato-based sauces of Kansas City to millions of people. It became the nation's default barbecue sauce.

Other than tomatoes, the second biggest change in the barbecue sauce condiment category was the addition of sugar. It made sense that the sop recipes didn't include much sugar because it would have caramelized during the barbecuing process, most likely burning. The increased use of tomatoes, a vegetable with an appreciable amount of sugar, opened the door to adding more sweeteners. As with the use of tomatoes, it's hard to pinpoint when sugar became a mainstay ingredient for barbecue sauce. Sugar is scarcely used in print media recipes until the late 1920s and appears more regularly in the 1940s. African Americans already blurred the lines between savory and sweet in other aspects of southern cooking (such as putting sugar in cornbread and vegetable preparations), so adding sugar was readily accepted. The contemporary regional barbecue styles strongly associated with African Americans—Deep South, Kansas City, Memphis, South Side Chicago, and southeastern Texas—all feature barbecue sauces that are spicy, sweet, or a combination. In mainstream supermarkets, though, the oceans of sweet barbecue sauces for sale show that it's an important aspect of Black barbecue culture but not exclusive to it.

Black barbecue culture thrives on competition, and a lot of energy is put into convincing others that your sauce is the best. "Comeback sauce" was a marketing ploy as ubiquitous as "barbecue king." By the early 1900s, barbecue purveyors of all types used this moniker to entice customers. A man named R. W. Alexander sold a popular comeback sauce in the Fort Scott, Kansas area. When a local newspaper reporter asked Alexander's wife about the name of the sauce after unsuccessfully trying to get the recipe, she gave an answer with the best spirit of the name: "Because of the fine flavor and the alluring taste—everyone that ever tasted it comes back for more. Its spicy taste goes well with not only barbecued meat, but soups, roasts and meats of any kind."[35] Feeling pity on the reporter, she gave that person a recipe for vegetable salad. Comeback sauce is purely a marketing slogan that relies on word of mouth to make it stick. As a side note, this is not to be confused with the comeback sauces of the Mississippi Delta that Susan Puckett describes as a "creamy sauce—akin to a spicy Thousand Island dressing."[36]

One historical example of a comeback sauce advertisement certainly sent a mixed message. The Reverend J. W. Hurse of St. Stephen's Baptist Church in Kansas City announced on the front page of the *Kansas City Sun* that he would preach a sermon titled "Hell" on a Sunday night in March 1914. Hurse was also a noted barbecuer, and those reading the advertisement were notified that "the Café will be opened with a genuine Southern barbecue and Hurse's famous 'Comeback sauce,' and on Sunday, March 8th, they'll serve an elegant Sunday dinner with the following: Roast Turkey, Roast Chicken, Roast Beef, Roast Pork, Stewed Chicken and Dumplings, Cream Potatoes, Tomatoes, Corn, Spinach, Green Onions, and Lettuce."[37] Not all churches took this approach. My home church, Campbell Chapel AME Church, in Denver, Colorado, hosted a "grand barbecue" in 1909 that touted "Edward Johnson, Chief Barbecuer, with his famous Come-back Sauce, if you get a taste you will come back for more."[38] The advertisement for Campbell's event mentions an excursion, but lacked indication of a final destination that would be warmer than Denver's lovely streets during July.

African American barbecuers have long valued variety when it comes to barbecue sauce. A newspaper account of a 1909 Juneteenth celebration in Brazos County, Texas reported: "Well done barbecued meats, breads, pickles, and all kinds of barbecue sauces constituted the menu and no one could doubt that the large crowd enjoyed the feast."[39] However, it's not all ketchup, chiles, vinegar, and sugar in the Black barbecue tradition. Mustard-based sauces show up in a lot of places. In my experience, mustard hot spots are northern Florida (especially the Jacksonville area) and South Carolina. The most memorable mustard sauce in my experience is the golden elixir sold at Jenkins Quality Barbecue in Jacksonville, Florida. When you order a full rack of ribs, they come with several pieces of white bread underneath and a generous serving of their orangish addictive sauce on top.

Sometimes that "long-held secret family recipe" for barbecue sauce is no secret at all. It's just a commercial sauce doctored up by a Black barbecue cook. I've fond memories of seeing my late mother putting spices and halved lemons in a pot filled with Open Pit barbecue sauce. For a long time, I thought "legit" barbecue sauce must have lemon seeds floating in it. Anecdotally, many of the home cooks I know tweak K.C. Masterpiece, Kraft, or Sweet Baby Ray's, some of the nation's top-selling barbecue sauces. In the times that I've had a chance to tour the kitchen of a barbecue joint, I've seen more jugs of commercial barbecue sauces than I thought I ever would. You may be curious about what places and what sauces, but I ain't no snitch.

Barbecue sauce etiquette, so to speak, exists for those who continually pose nosy questions to the cook. The first rule of engagement is that one should never, ever ask for a barbecue sauce recipe. As one observer in 1930s Harlem noted:

> Requesting a recipe for barbecue sauce is one of the unpardonable breaches of Harlem etiquette that the uninitiated may commit. The restaurant keepers are as generous in giving information on most points of the cuisine as they are with portions of the food itself, but the secret of barbecue sauce is something else. The only certain way of obtaining such a recipe is to wheedle it from a private cook untroubled by thoughts of it reaching a competitor's kitchen. . . .
> For the Negro cook has an understandable distrust of recipes which reduce the rights of the kitchen to a scientific formula. Cooking

is an art, mysterious and undefinable, that the white man may discuss in terms of half-cups and other fractions just as he speaks of strange things like calories in vitamins.[40]

You've probably noticed that when you ask a barbecuer for tips on the cooking process, he or she is somewhat forthcoming. It's when you ask for recipes that everyone becomes tight-lipped. Why? Because a barbecue sauce recipe is easy to replicate, but when it comes to cooking, a pitmaster counts on you being too lazy to actually prepare traditional barbecue.

A barbecue restaurant's entire reputation and fortunes may hinge on its sauce. One Harlem barbecue joint in 1944 touted its barbecue sauce maker as a French restaurant would tout its saucier: "J. R. Hinch, proprietor of the new barbecue heaven known as Jerry's Barbecue, 151st St. and Amsterdam Ave., made a personal research to find the right sauce chef. Sauce being the final touch to barbecue and its fans. Milford Daniels answers to the title of 'Perfect Sauce Chef.'"[41] Before the rise of sweet sauces, many restaurateurs made a spicy sauce their calling card. Look at the firsthand accounts of sauces made by barbecue greats like Henry Perry of Kansas City, Missouri, and Adam Scott of Goldsboro, North Carolina, and you hear the same thing: the sauce was much too hot, and they loved it! M & D's Barbecue and Fish Palace, mentioned in chapter 6, served a tomato-based sauce with three spice levels: mild, medium, and hot. When I asked for hot sauce, it was the first time that a server has ever discouraged me from ordering something I wanted (this was before I started going to Thai restaurants). I persisted, and my spareribs soon arrived covered in that infernal sauce. It was quite hot, and I should have heeded the warning. Medium for me from now on!

This is one distinction of the Black barbecue tradition that has lost its punch because American palates have warmed overall. Now one can get an incendiary sauce at any restaurant. In fact, it's quite expected. A number of barbecue sauce makers are hell-bent on creating the hottest sauce on the market. It's an interesting trend, but I wonder how much things are out of whack when people sign a legal release, have lots of dairy products on hand (to quench the fire), and wear gloves and goggles before eating. Annoyingly, a lot of barbecue restaurants urge you to "customize" your barbecue experience by pouring on your meat any one of various regional sauces assembled on your table. This is most egregious with Carolina sauces because, as we've learned, that sauce has been applied throughout the cooking process, giving the meat a depth of flavor that won't come from a quick splash right before eating. Sigh.

IN THE SAUCE WITH
DEBORAH AND MARY JONES
KEEPING UP WITH THE JONES
BARBECUE SISTERS

got my first taste of Jones Bar-B-Q on a very cold day in Kansas City, Kansas. It was so cold (21°) that I had to wear my Denver Broncos ski cap. This is very risky behavior in the heart of Kansas City Chiefs country, but I wasn't scared. Jones Bar-B-Q is a carryout-only place with limited outside seating. Something was going on with Deborah and she wasn't there, but Mary Jones was on the move, hustling from the kitchen of the black-and-red cinderblock structure to the large vertical grill just next to the restaurant. Business was bustling, even on such a cold day. They run out of food quickly here, but I managed to get some burnt ends, rib tips, and an unbelievable coarsely ground sausage.

In addition to their tasty barbecue, they are well known for their barbecue sauce. The Jones Sisters were already selling their barbecue sauce when they got a wonderful break in March 2019. They were featured on an episode of *Queer Eye*—a Netflix show that was born on NBC as *Queer Eye for the Straight Guy*. They were a smash hit. Their social media numbers skyrocketed, and their business has taken off. On March 29, their Instagram feed showed a picture of a warehouse filled with boxes of their barbecue sauce ready to be shipped around the world. I love it when great things happen to nice people!

Jill Silva, a fellow alum of Smoky Hill High School in Aurora, Colorado, and someone who is deeply knowledgeable about Kansas City's barbecue scene, wrote the following essay about the Jones Sisters. She was there when I first visited the restaurant, a few weeks before they became famous. At that point, it was hard for me to get an interview, so I asked Jill for help because she knew the sisters well. She wrote the following:

> For more than thirty years, Deborah Jones and her sister Mary Jones Mosley have built their reputation on old-school sausage, rib tips, burnt ends, and sliced beef, turkey, and ham suffused with smoke from Missouri white oak and hickory.

Deborah and Mary Jones, Jones Bar-B-Q, Kansas City, Kansas. Photograph courtesy of Jill Silva.

Jones Bar-B-Q operates out of a former gas-station-turned-taco-stand located in a heavily industrial section of Kansas City, Kansas. Freight trains from the tracks running parallel to Kansas 32 whistle loud enough to drown out conversations midsentence. Deborah is the designated pit master. Mary, the more outgoing of the two women, chops meat on the block and holds court at the order window.

"She does no cooking in the kitchen," says Mary, who has a deep, throaty, and infectious laugh. "But now isn't that funny!" she shakes her head as if in disbelief, "Take this right here—with more work and more heat—and she's good at it. I love it, too, don't get me wrong. But she is *obsessed* with it."

When I first met Deborah in 2016, she watched over the fire starting at dawn while seated on her "throne." Like her upright pit smoker, the throne was a flea-market find from A-Lotta-Stuff located a few yards across the asphalt parking lot. The wrought-iron bench had a padded seat and ash-encrusted tassels harking back to a more glamorous life as a vanity set.

Deborah's throne disappeared after the sisters' makeover on an episode of Netflix's *Queer Eye*, which aired in March 2019. Designer Bobby Berk spiffed up the barbecue joint by repainting the red-brick building black, adding more eye-catching signage, reorganizing the tiny kitchen for maximum efficiency, and adding a patio and picnic tables for al fresco dining. (Previously, whenever I paid a visit, I brought my own lawn chair!)

Queer Eye catapulted the smoke sisters into a world that has offered them fame and a host of new business opportunities but also put a strain on the capacity of their humble barbecue stand.

In an effort to keep up with increased demand, Deborah arrives at midnight or 1 a.m. to start the fire.

She dresses in layers—a smart strategy for an outdoor pit where she is exposed to scorching heat or the bone-chilling cold, depending on the time of year. But Mary says she rarely peels any of the layers off, regardless of the weather. Mary arrives around 8 a.m. and gets things in the cramped "we-be-bumpin'-booties!" kitchen quarters ready for a steady stream of customers. Jones Bar-B-Q is open 11 a.m. to 3 p.m., Tuesday through Saturday, but the sisters often run out of smoked meats before noon.

"Some people come directly from the airport," Deborah says, her softer, steadier voice registering tones of amazement as she shakes her head in disbelief. "With their suitcases!" Mary chimes in. "We've always had a big family, but our family is really BIG now!" So big, in fact, a public relations firm handles the sisters' social media accounts, posting selfies of the sisters posing with their customers like presidential hopefuls on the campaign trail.

While women pitmasters are fairly uncommon across the nation, a prominent Black woman–owned barbecue business in Kansas City remains a rarity even in 2020. One of the earliest mentions of Jones Bar-B-Q appears in *Grand Barbecue*, by Doug Worgul. A striking sepia-hued portrait on the last page shows Deborah sitting on a woodpile and Mary gazing up at photographer from a sunken barbecue pit.

"It was the jointiest joint I've ever been in," Worgul, a former *Kansas City Star* editor who went on to become director of marketing at the vastly popular Joe's Kansas City, told me after a lunch visit to reunite with the sisters. "There were a couple of folding tables like you'd find in a church fellowship hall. It was definitely the most handmade dining room you could ever imagine, but the food was good."

Worgul's first visit to Jones Bar-B-Q was at its original location at 1805 North Tenth Street. The sisters ran the restaurant from 1987 to 2003, then moved to 609 North Sixth Street from 2005 to 2009, reopening in their current location in 2015.

Deborah, nicknamed "Little," and her younger sister, Mary "Shorty," grew up as two of eight siblings born to Juanita and Leavy Jones Sr. The couple raised their children in Kansas City, Kansas, and Leavy, who left school in the seventh grade, was adamant about teaching his children practical trades, from laying carpet to changing the oil or fixing a flat tire on a car.

"Daddy always said, 'Nothing is for free.' If you ever get unemployed, you have to have other skills," Deborah recalled when I interviewed her for a *Kansas City Star* profile published in 2016. "We've always worked, because nothing is free," Mary echoes. "And if it is, you better question it."

Leavy was an electrician by trade. He moonlighted at an establishment owned by a legendary if somewhat shadowy barbecue figure Hezekiah French. Mary and Deborah grew up around that pit and remember helping out at the restaurant as soon as they were old enough to stand on milk crates and help crank out the family's unwritten sausage recipe.

As adults, Deborah worked for the postal service while Mary earned a degree in nursing. They always looked at barbecue as a side hustle, something to fall back on. But after their father was in an accident and severely injured and their brother Daniel received a terminal medical diagnosis, Deborah began training to take over the pit duties.

Jones Bar-B-Q continued on under female leadership until, as Mary puts it, "Deborah's ticker almost went down." When Deborah protests at the characterization, Mary says, "I said *almost*." After recovering from heart surgery, Deborah got the itch to get back to barbecue. Mary, who had retired and moved to Topeka, Kansas, recalls, "She called me one day and she said, 'I've got a building and I'm not done. Are you in?' I said, 'I'm on my way!'"

Ardie Davis, renowned barbecue folklorist and a charter member of the Kansas City Barbeque Society, describes Jones Bar-B-Q as "old school, not fancy." The ribs are untrimmed by today's barbecue competition standards. The coarse-grind, all-pork sausages are chopped, hand cranked, and stuffed into natural casings that snap with each bite. The burnt ends, a Kansas City specialty that gained fame when Kansas City–born and bred writer Calvin Trillin made famous in the 1970s, are singed by fire and tend to be fatty, charred, and chewy.

Deborah removed the built-in thermometer from her pit smoker. "You should be able to look at the meat and know that it is done," she insists. Until recently, she could mostly keep up with the volume of sales coming from blue-collar workers who stopped by for lunch and a loyal clientele from the African American community who followed Jones Bar-B-Q to each new location.

When they reopened in their present location, Deborah typically bought a dozen rib tips, four racks of ribs, and a few pork butts to put on the fire each day. If they sold out, she'd put more meat on the fire and tell the customers to come back in an hour or two. Mary's mantra: "We have got this thing about freshness. You have to sit on the throne and play with this [fire] all day. It takes time if you want to do it right. We were never about the dollar bill. It was about pleasing the customers. My customers are everything."

After my 2016 profile was published, the Jones sisters' story attracted national media attention. The sisters appeared on the *Steve Harvey Show* and National Public Radio. They were declared "The Most Influential Women in Southern Barbecue Now" by *Southern Living* magazine.

Deborah's adult daughter, Izora Thompson, nominated her mother and aunt for a *Queer Eye* makeover. The sisters were the first double makeover coupled with the show's first restaurant makeover. Deborah's stubborn refusal to share the family sauce recipe and Mary's new smile, the result of extensive dental work, coupled with good-natured ribbing of one another, made them an instant fan favorite.

But only days before the episode was set to air, I found Deborah sitting on an overturned food-safe plastic bucket. Berk had replaced her throne with a pair of red vintage-reproduction Griffith metal patio chairs, and although Deborah counts herself a fan of the reality makeover show experience and its hosts, she quietly pulled up what she considers a more comfortable seat by the fire.

"We gained a lot of customers and interest from the media," Deborah told me during an interview for KCPT's digital magazine *Flatland KC*. "I never rode in so many limos in my life. Aww, it was just too much! I see why people have bodyguards and stuff. Heck, I'm just a simple barbecue girl."

But life is suddenly more complicated, requiring lawyers, contracts, and nutrition labels.

A dream of bottling the family's sweet and tangy barbecue sauce recipe has become a reality, selling eleven thousand bottles in thirty-six hours. The lineup has since expanded to include a seasoning rub and an unusual coconut and pineapple sauce. On the weekends, the sisters can be found sampling their sauces at Williams-Sonoma, Hy-Vee, Price Chopper supermarkets, and a temporary holiday kiosk at a suburban mall. The sisters are also in negotiations to lend their name to a filling station in Kearney, Missouri. Carhartt, a rugged outerwear company, has offered clothing in exchange for a photo shoot. And they've been interviewed for an upcoming exhibit at the Museum of Food and Drink.

Meanwhile, Deborah has started working on supervising the construction of a new pit in the style of the sunken pit at their original location. As they work on increasing volume, they have tried to involve more of their family in the business but have found few members who have the patience for the long, tedious hours required to tame a fiery pit.

"It'll make you or break you, especially when that heat flares up and it's 100 degrees outside. It's a real job. It's not something you just jump into," Deborah says during a *Chew Diligence* podcast. Recently a young from Japan woman shadowed the sisters as they worked. Her interest in barbecue got the sisters thinking about offering cooking classes to make it easier for women to carry on a culinary art form dominated by male pitmasters.

"This is worse than a drug. It's an addiction. It's in your blood, and she's really the junkie," Mary says as she reflects on the primal lure of barbecue. She cocks her head toward Deborah, who is staring intently at the fire. "She breathes this and loves it. She goes to sleep to get up for this. She doesn't care about the money. This is her No. 1 spot."

Samuel A. Flagg, aka "Po' Sam," bucked the trend toward homogenization by creating a sauce that defined a hyperlocal regional style. In the early 1950s, he opened an eponymous barbecue restaurant in Colbert, Oklahoma, off U.S. 69. I'd never heard of Po' Sam until I met Tammy Abramovitz through a mutual friend. Her distinctive beehive 'do, colored glasses, infectious laugh, big heart, and personality to match help make her one of the most party-havingest people I know. It's not my sole opinion. In 2018, she made the "Salonnière 100" list for her "exceptional ability to leverage the power of parties to enhance the lives of others."[42] I was at one of her classic southern-vibe parties, and somehow Flagg came up in conversation. She waxed nostalgically and rhapsodically about Flagg's brown gravy, which she had enjoyed growing up, and it was completely new to me.

Abramovitz grew up in the 1960s on the Texas side of the Red River, but her family crossed over into Oklahoma almost every weekend to Calera, where her grandmother lived. If they were lucky, her dad had a little spending money, and they'd veer off east of Interstate 75 at the Colbert exit and head down the river road to get a BBQ sandwich at Po' Sam's. "We'd pull up under the pole barn–style corrugated tin roof and honk the horn," Abramovitz remembered. "Someone would come out and we'd order brisket sandwiches either 'sliced or chopped.'" Abramovitz wasn't that impressed with Flagg's meat, but it's that sauce that brought memories. "Po' Sam didn't have a BBQ 'sauce,' Po' Sam smothered his smoked brisket in gravy. Thick, spicy, hot, pungent gravy. The kind of stuff that makes your mouth sting and your eyes sweat but keeps you going back for more and more and more." I guess that's another way of saying that Flagg had a "comeback sauce." Abramovitz said that Flagg's sauce was so highly regarded that Heinz supposedly offered him a lot of money for the recipe, but he turned it down. Based on her description of it as a brown gravy, as Flagg's sauce was called, I thought it might have inspired its A-1 Brand steak sauce. Abramovitz assured me that it was nowhere close to that.

Not surprisingly, there seem to be several restaurateurs in the vicinity of Colbert that sell a brown gravy with their barbecue, and some claim that it's Flagg's recipe. I've looked at some of the recipes, and they don't square up with the high heat index that rests in Abramovitz's memories:

> I've often tried to describe the gravy as a delivery vehicle for all the spices used in traditional BBQ sauces and rubs that he served up in a brisket dripping–fueled roux. The spices come through stronger than when they're delivered in a tomato-based sauce, and

the amount of cayenne he used made the gravy an ethereal color. Some would say brown, but the eyes of my childhood recall an almost reddish-orange hue, a dark peach. The sauce was thickened with flour and thinned with a bit of chicken broth, but the gravy was translucent, and you could see the specks of peppers that were equal parts pain and pleasure. I can still taste that gravy, and I haven't had the real deal in close to fifty years. Po' Sam had a good thing and a great sense of humor. His motto was, "Not the best . . . but hard to beat."

Flagg died in the 1980s, and though his signature sauce recipe may have died with him, its fabled status lives on.

Barbecue sauce followed a similar arc as barbecue: variety, convergence, then fragmentation. Yet in all its forms, barbecue sauce is still beloved in African American barbecue circles. It's why Freda DeKnight spilled a lot of ink on the subject in her groundbreaking cookbook, *A Date with a Dish*, the first comprehensive, nationwide collection of African American recipes. In her preface to the recipes, she wrote:

> In my travels about the country, I have come across many tasty seasoning tricks for preparing meats. . . . Each person I met insisted that his or her barbecue sauce was the perfect recipe. But the variations were almost endless. After weeks of testing barbecue sauces, each one a little different, I was at a loss as to know how to select the best of them for your approval. I developed barbecue jitters. Out of the dozens of barbecue sauces I tested, all good, I was finally able to choose a few which you will want to try many times over. . . . The spicy, pungent sauce will literally make your mouth water and the aroma will fascinate you. You will never forget the flavor of good barbecue, a dish you will repeat for any occasion to treat your friends as well as show off your culinary talents. Of course, you can serve barbecue sauce with any of your favorite meat[s], or as a dressing for cool, crisp summer salad, or as a sauce for spaghetti. And don't forget the crunchy garlic bread that gets the last bit of savory sauce from your plate.[43]

DeKnight not only argues for barbecue sauce as an essential aspect of Black barbecue culture but shows its versatility for other unexpected culinary applications. As you read in the previous chapter, I'm definitely an advocate for barbecue spaghetti. I first had an attitude about using barbecue sauce as a salad dressing, but couldn't a North Carolina sauce be reinterpreted as a vinaigrette?

So, the sauce flows in home kitchens and restaurants, and in most cases, it's very good. I've been to restaurants where the barbecue plate presented to me was a sea of sauce with islands of smoked meat poking through. The sauce is so good at some places, like Dreamland Bar-B-Que, in Tuscaloosa, Alabama, that they'll sell you a bowl all by itself with some white bread to sop it up. Many restaurants also sell private label bottles to customers. The love of sauce is widespread among Black people, but I can't say it's universal. I'm sure there are some "Black unicorns" out there who request their sauce "on the side," or snub it altogether, but I have yet to witness this.

If you've read the profiles in this chapter of two influential barbecue sauce entrepreneurs, Argia B. Collins, who sells his spicy Mumbo Sauce in Chicago, Illinois, and the Jones sisters, who hawk a spicy tomato-based sauce in Kansas City, Kansas, you may feel the same way I do: When someone authoritatively claims that barbecue should be unsauced, I immediately think, "Says who?"

MUMBO®-Glazed Shrimp Salad

This light summer recipe was developed by Chef Karrie Snow and Jasmine Glean for Select Brands, LLC, the parent company for MUMBO Sauce. If you can't get MUMBO Sauce in your area, you may substitute any tangy, tomato-based barbecue sauce.

Makes 4 servings

28 (16/20-count) shrimp
8 ounces (1 cup) MUMBO Sauce, or any tangy, tomato-based barbecue sauce, divided
4 ounces olive oil
2 tablespoons Dijon mustard
Juice of 1 lemon
½ teaspoon salt
1 teaspoon black pepper
4 cups mixed greens
12 strawberries, sliced

1. Marinate the shrimp in ½ cup of the MUMBO Sauce for 30 minutes.
2. Make the vinaigrette. In a blender, combine the remaining ½ cup MUMBO Sauce, olive oil, mustard, and lemon juice. Blend to form an emulsion and set aside.
3. Preheat the grill to medium-high heat.
4. Wipe any excess sauce from the shrimp, and season them with salt and pepper.
6. Grill the shrimp, flipping them over when they turn pink. Remove to a clean platter.
7. Toss the mixed salad greens with the MUMBO vinaigrette, garnish the salad with the sliced strawberries and grilled shrimp, and serve.

LIQUID BLACK SMOKE

"Daddy" Bruce's Barbecue Sauce

This is the sauce of "Daddy" Bruce Randolph Sr., a legendary barbecue man in Denver, Colorado, who is profiled in chapter 7. This barbecue sauce (adapted from Linda Ruth Harvey, Jenny Von Hohenstraeten, and Mary Jo Fostina's *Colorado's Gourmet Gold: Cookbook of Recipes from Popular Colorado Restaurants*, published in 1980) is a hybrid between a standard eastern North Carolina sauce and a Deep South barbecue sauce.

Makes 4 cups

1 cup ketchup
½ cup Louisiana-style hot sauce
¾ cup Worcestershire sauce
2 cups vinegar (apple cider or white)
4 cloves garlic, chopped
1 cup packed brown sugar
1 tablespoon salt
½ tablespoon black pepper
½ cup lemon juice, freshly squeezed

1. Heat all ingredients in a medium saucepan, stirring, to dissolve the sugar.
2. Transfer to jars and refrigerate. This sauce improves with time and shaking.

SHORT-CIRCUITED
AFRICAN AMERICANS AND
COMPETITION BARBECUE

8

"Nah, I can't afford it," he scoffs, but he doubts he would win [the Houston Rodeo Cookoff] anyway. "Black people know how to cook brisket, but the rules for judging are not really about how it tastes. It's all about how pretty it looks. I've eaten brisket cooked by a team that won, and it was nothin' special." — William Little, roadside barbecuer, Dickinson, Texas, 2011

In late 1927, Ed Hodges, a reputable African American barbecuer in Dallas, Texas, had a bone to pick. Actually, because we're dealing with Texas barbecue, it's best to call this a "beef." Hodges believed that he could make better barbecue than another African American barbecuer living in Waco, Texas. He publicly called out one man in Waco and set the stage for their "barbecue contest" to coincide with the annual meeting of the Texas Managing Editors Association.

Though some newspaper reports framed the contest as "Dallas v. Waco," the Blackness of the mano-a-mano contest was undeniable. Two Black men of barbecue renown would cook at Paul Quinn College, a historically Black college affiliated with the all-Black African Methodist Episcopal Church, in Waco. Funds raised by the contest would benefit the Rescue Home for Negroes in East Waco. Hodges was described as an "after the war" negro, and the other man as a "before the war" negro, which loaded expectations of how they viewed their place in society and supposedly their barbecue expertise. Oh, yeah, in every single report, including the final report of the contest ending in "a draw," the formerly enslaved person from Waco remained anonymous.[1]

The competitive spirit is a raging fire in contemporary barbecue, and competition barbecue has done much to shape restaurant culture and media coverage of this cuisine. Some people live for barbecue, and some live to prove that their barbecue is superior. For years, barbecue challenges have been parochial, taking place in someone's backyard, at a private event, or at a county or state fair. Now barbecue competitions are big in every way (statewide, regional, national, and global in scope), with some of the larger contests featuring hundreds of teams and thousands of dollars in prize money. Kind of like professional boxing, there are now hundreds of contests each year under the jurisdiction of multiple sanctioning bodies. The rise and expansion of competitive barbecue has remarkably reshaped America's barbecue culture. Success on the barbecue circuit has translated to success in the restaurant business, television appearances, and public notoriety. Yet African Americans don't significantly participate in competition barbecue as either contestants or judges. The reasons why have to do more with class and culture than race.

I haphazardly entered the world of competition barbecue as a certified judge, rather than as a competitor. Before embarking on this project. I was working on my first book, *Soul Food: The Surprising Story of an American Cuisine, One Plate at a Time*. I had noticed while researching and writing that book that many soul food joints had a barbecue option (though usually oven baked) on the menu and that many Black-owned barbecue joints had soul food options, especially the side dishes. I thought that, to better understand soul food, I needed to better understand barbecue.

Lo and behold, in July 2004, I'm reading the *Rocky Mountain News*, and I see an advertisement about becoming a barbecue judge with the Kansas City Barbeque Society (KCBS). "A dream come true," I thought. A few weeks later, I made my way to the Adams County Fairgrounds. When I strolled into the room where the judging class took place, I immediately discerned my future. I was the only person in the room under "two fiddy" (two hundred and fifty pounds), and I was okay with that being my possible future. Besides becoming a "Master Certified Barbecue Judge," I aspire to have a "Unified Elastic Barbecue Belt" establishing my credentials in every existing barbecue association. I've got some work to do.

I thought the class would teach me how to barbecue, but it was really about the logistics of a KCBS-sanctioned competition. We learned about entry categories (beef brisket, chicken, pork shoulder, and pork spareribs), the competition sequence, scoring criteria (appearance, taste, and texture), and additional rules (some pretty arbitrary). Then we simulated scoring a barbecue entry during a competition. Usually something was placed before us that violated some rule, just to see if we'd catch it. If we didn't, a supervisor gently instructed us on what we missed. After that, we stood and took a "barbecue oath." I'm not going to repeat it here because it is a sacred thing, and I can already tell that some of you will mock it. A few weeks later, I got my KCBS badge in the mail, and I was now free to judge as many KCBS contests as I liked. I've been asked more than once, so in case you're wondering, I DO NOT use my badge to try to skip the line or get free food at a trendy barbecue spot.

After judging a few contests, it was evident that being an African American barbecue judge is a lonely existence. I met only one other African American doing the same thing while I was heavily involved in judging. Before and after I finished judging, I would walk around the venue and observe who was competing and who was vending barbecue. African Americans were noticeably few in number among those groups as well. Certainly, being in Colorado, a state with a lower African American population than most other states, doesn't help. I began to wonder why. In my experience, the KCBS event organizers and the attendees are certainly hospitable, and the judging class and annual membership dues are affordable. It was only when I helped a competing team that I got a better feel for the economics and logistics of being in a contest.

Ronald and Louella Brooks were longtime members of my church (mentioned more extensively in the church barbecue chapter) who operated Brooks' Smokehouse in Denver. Brooks is from Opelousas, Louisiana, and he's the first (and only) self-described "Black Cajun" I've ever met. Their restaurant was a memorable place because it reminded you of being in someone's home. Ronald is a carpenter by trade, and he moved to Colorado for contracting work. A few years after he arrived, and as a proud barbecue man, Ronald decided to enter a few organized barbecue contests. In seven years of competition, the Brooks' Smokehouse team finished well in several categories but never took an overall championship. Their highest achievement was winning a "People's Choice" award for their overall selection of alligator (he's Cajun, remember?), brisket, chicken, pulled pork, and potato salad dishes.

The competition scene in Colorado is challenging because most of the contests happen in the mountain towns. Contestants are cooking at altitude, and even during the summer, it can get cold at night. In 2014, the Brookses competed in the Frisco BBQ Challenge—the largest barbecue contest in Colorado, usually held the second weekend in June. I had judged that competition a couple of times, but I was curious about what it was like to compete. I asked Ronald if I could join his crew that year, and he said yes. I persuaded my friend Gretchen Geary to join me because I thought she would like to hang out and see the festival. Nope! She wanted to help compete.

With this competition, as with most, I think, the team shows up on either Thursday or Friday, depending on how many categories it will enter, to set up and start cooking. Contestants have to time things just right so that they can turn in their entries at the right time during the judging sequence, usually starting at noon that Saturday. It was quite the production and certainly required "all hands on deck." I volunteered to help at the last minute, and I seriously wondered how Ronald would make the deadlines without me and Gretchen. He barely did, even with our help. If a team competes in all four KCBS categories, all entries are submitted by 1:30 or 2:00 p.m. The next, and most stressful, part of the day begins as the contestants clean up and wait for the judging results. Depending on the number of contestants, this could be several hours. After the results are announced, the contestants may have another day or two of travel ahead of them, depending on their starting point, and some teams do travel great distances to compete. Many employees only have two weeks of vacation a year. If one gets really serious about competition, it takes up a lot of that time. I'm guessing that only people who have very flexible jobs or are retired can compete.

Another factor may be cultural. Black competitors can feel unwelcome by the overall vibe created by the contestants, not the organizers:

> Jim Auchmutey of the *Atlanta Journal-Constitution* attended a Georgia cook-off called the Big Pig Jig in 1994. "Only a few black teams registered, an imbalance that's typical of the cook-off circuit," he wrote. Although organizers would like to see more black teams, the Caucasian block-party atmosphere drives them away, Auchmutey reported. One sign he saw read, "Redneck Mardi Gras." And that sums up the cook-off atmosphere pretty well, he tells me on the phone. Confederate flags were much in evidence at the Georgia event. "The flag is a big issue at these things," he says. "If you fly even one, that puts out a signal to black people that this isn't our scene."[2]

This scene is by no means universal. Sylvie Curry, a decorated barbecue competitor based in California whom I profile in this chapter, told me that in her experience it was uncommon to see a Confederate flag displayed at a barbecue contest outside of the South.

Time commitment and culture are significant factors, but the real barrier to greater African American participation in competition is something else: "'The main reason Blacks don't enter barbecue cook-offs is money,' says [Louis] Archendaux, who runs his own chemical company in Sugarland [Texas]. 'You've got to know somebody. We don't have any sponsors—except for friends and relatives who help us out with a few bucks here and there. We have one of the little booths out here. We are barely getting by with $5,000 or $6,000.'"[3] It's hard to imagine having thousands of dollars as just managing, but Archendaux's statement gives you an idea of how this amateur sport has become a money game.

Let's calculate the typical costs of barbecue competing. A basic, entry-level grill set-up is going to cost about $1,500 dollars. Some custom-made barbecue grills can cost as much as $15,000.[4] Aside from that sunk cost, let's consider the cost of entering a single contest with an expected arrival on Friday and departure the following Sunday. These amounts will vary, but here's my best guess at an average total cost: entry fee (typically around $250), meat that's going to be cooked ($200, more if one is going to vend to event attendees), hotel stay ($250 for two nights), supplies ($200), food and drink ($100), charcoal ($50), gas ($50), and seasoning and sauce ($20). So, each contest, a competitor is in for at least $1,000. And that's not including the vacation time used to travel to a contest. To win big prize money, a competitor often has to win several qualifying competitions. One can see how taking this sport seriously can quickly become costly. I surmise that few African Americans have the means to compete on the barbecue circuit unless they've got a nice nest egg or someone in their life who is subsidizing their competition.

One obvious question to the outside observer is, "Why would someone do this to themselves?" There are several answers, but the most persuasive is that it's a lucrative endeavor with big cash prizes, thanks to funds generated by team entry fees and corporate sponsors. The biggest and most prestigious competitions in the United States right now are the American Royal (Kansas City, Missouri), the Houston Livestock Show and Rodeo Bar-B-Que Contest, the Jack Daniels World Championship Invitational Barbecue (Lynchburg, Tennessee), and the world's largest barbecue competition, the Memphis in May World Championship Barbecue Cooking Contest. At some of these contests, it's now possible to win $25,000 to $50,000 . . . *in one weekend.* The biggest prize to date is the $100,000 that Shad Kirton of Grimes, Iowa, won on *BBQ Pitmasters* in 2010.[5] One can also win big bucks at the annual World Food Championship (which rotates cities), if one wins a number of qualifying barbecue competitions. Thus, for the serious competitor, it's worth the investment. Even if one doesn't win all the time, currying enough sponsorships from local businesses can help cover one's costs.

Let me take you back to another time when bragging rights, not huge sums of money, were the coin of the barbecue competition realm. A fantastic example is the Memphis in May contest. Carolyn Wells, a longtime executive director of the KCBS, describes the early days of

IN THE SMOKE WITH SYLVIE CURRY, THE BARBECUE COMPETITION CIRCUIT'S LADY OF Q

I got the name from someone who wrote an article in a barbecue journal about the ladies of barbecue, and I was one of them. And I went "OK. I'm a Lady of Q." And that's where I came up with the name. — Sylvie Curry, 2015

"I grew up in South Central L.A. I don't ever remember my parents having a grill or doing barbecue in the backyard. If we had barbecue, it would have been going to a relative's house, and it would have been hamburgers and hot dogs. . . . I really didn't even get into barbecue, or doing anything on a grill, until we moved to a house in L.A. [to Ladera Heights as an adult in the early 1980s] that already had a grill in the backyard." Not exactly what I expected to hear when I interviewed Sylvie Curry, one of the most accomplished African American women on the barbecue competition circuit. I thought she would tell me some tale of teething on a rib tip. Curry's family, though not poor, didn't really go out to eat that much. When they did go out for barbecue, it was a neighborhood Black joint, and she only got ribs.

Her foray into the competitive barbecue world was accidental. She started cooking when she got married, and she loved watching cooking shows. A personal favorite was Nathalie Dupree because she was a good cook and "so down to earth." Curry started her *Soul Fusion Kitchen* blog in 2005, and it features posts on food from various cuisines. Neil "Big Mista" Strawder was a fan of Curry's blog, and they often exchanged email messages back and forth when Curry posted about barbecue. Without ever having met face to face, Strawder talked Curry into competing with him.

Along with Shuji Sakai and Luis Ramirez, they formed the Four Q barbecue team, which competed from 2006 to 2009. They were successful, but in time, the other team members went on to do other things, including Strawder, who opened a restaurant. Strawder was so confident in Curry's barbecue skills that he encouraged her to

Sylvie "Lady of Q" Curry, Los Angeles, California. Photograph by Wally Skalij. Copyright © 2015. Los Angeles Times. Used with permission.

keep competing. Curry made a strategic decision and spent a couple of years honing her barbecue judging skills. That way, she'd know how judges evaluated competition barbecue. After that journey was completed, Curry took a barbecue cooking class taught by Melissa Cookston, a seven-time world barbecue champion who is oft called the Winningest Woman in Barbecue. After her class, Curry firmly believed, "I can do this, too." She changed the team name from Four Q to Lady of Q. I love her logo: a female pig with enough bling to make Miss Piggy green with envy.

Curry is a double oddity on the barbecue circuit world because she's a Black woman who *cooks by herself.* Most teams have several people with each handling different aspects of food preparation. I'm stunned that in her first couple of years of competing, she solo performed for ten to fifteen contests a year. As she shared in a *Los Angeles Times* interview:

> I compete the same way as the guys do, but it took awhile for them to get respect for me—there are a lot of them that couldn't believe I can do all this by myself. A lot of the male teams are three, four, five or even more players competing. So the mere fact that I do this by myself, I think I get more respect from the guys. I think it's more that they like to say I'm a role model. Other competitors bring their kids—they'll bring their little girls a lot of times to take pictures with me. And they'll say, "Look, women can do this."[1]

1. Noelle Carter, "As Lady of Q, Sylvie Curry's Competitive Barbecue Spirit Flares," *Los Angeles Times*, May 22, 2015.

Her husband, Greg, helps with a lot of background things, and that's pretty much all the help she needs. When it comes to the cooking, Sylvie is on her own. It's not that she doesn't like people, she's just very focused. She had helpers at one time, but they kept asking her questions when she was trying to do her thing. Never again. When she's in competition mode, as she put it, "People know not to bother Sylvie." You know it's serious when someone refers to herself in the third person.

I asked Curry about her game plan for a competition. When she started describing it, I felt as if I was talking to one of those brilliant NASA mathematicians, or human calculators, portrayed in the movie *Hidden Figures*. Quite naturally, she didn't give me all her secrets, but just keep in mind that she starts prepping for a competition two weeks in advance. Her chicken entry is already trimmed and in the freezer a week before the competition. All her dedication and hard work has paid off. She's had four grand championships since 2012, and she consistently places in the top-ten overall spots in most contests.

In terms of African Americans, Curry didn't have much company in the judges' booth or under the competitor's tent. The earliest all-Black team that she could think of was Hayward Jr. and Eva Harris from Riverside, California, who competed as the Rib Doctor in the early 1990s. Other than that, on a good day, maybe 10 percent of the teams will be African American. Curry speculates that there are a lot of reasons why African Americans don't participate in competition barbecue, which echoes the collective wisdom given earlier in this chapter. "Depending on how far that I have to travel, I'm spending $1,000 to $1,500 per contest." This includes entry fees, costs of the meat, sauces, rubs, and so on. Not everyone can spend that amount of money multiple times a year just to compete.

Other barriers are cultural. Curry believes that African Americans don't bother because they think it's a "white sport because most of the judges and the competitors are white." Also, the way that African Americans barbecue may not score well with white judges. Curry points out that African American barbecue tends to be darker because of charcoal cooking. That char probably won't score well when the judges assess points for appearance.

Even if one does compete, the way one makes barbecue at home is vastly different than what one does in a competition. In the same interview for the *Los Angeles Times*, Curry explained the difference between competitive barbecue and barbecuing at home: "The biggest difference between competition and regular is that we have to be able to wow a judge with just one bite—the judges can't eat a whole lot of it. When the judges bite into your entry, that one bite represents your whole barbecue. At a competition, you have to cook chicken, ribs, pork and brisket. You want to be good in all four. Even when you may have one you consider a specialty, you have to be good at all four."[2] To emphasize the point, she told me, "You don't inject meat when you cook at home."

Gender role assumptions have given Curry more heartburn on the competition circuit than race matters. When people visit her trailer, some will first talk to Greg, as if he was the barbecuer-in-chief. Race hasn't been an issue for Curry on the local competition circuit, but a recent snub for a national barbecue competition makes Curry wonder. Since 2016, the annual World Food Championship (WFC) has hosted a "no boys allowed" barbecue competition called the Cowboy Charcoal Fire & Ice Women's Championship Barbeque Series. This is a lovely contrast to what happened with competitive barbecue in the 1960s.

Ending that series in 2018, the WFC announced the 2019 Fire Woman Challenge—a one-off competition of five women to see who is "America's best lady pitmaster." The organizers had an open nomination process, and Curry's husband submitted her name. Curry liked her chances since she had previously qualified at the Fire & Ice competitions in 2016 and 2018. In 2018, she finished as the reserve grand champion (second place). The very next year, for unexplained reasons, Curry was not selected for any of the five contestant spots. Like a wisp of dissipating smoke, the most accomplished African American woman barbecuer is gradually becoming invisible.

Despite the egregious slight, Curry endeavors because she's really doing this for fun. The accolades are certainly appreciated, but they're gravy. "Look, I'm retired, and I don't need to work again. If this ever starts feeling like work, then I'll call it quits." Don't think for a second that Curry isn't motivated to undo the invisibility. "Why would I drive all the way to Orange Beach, Alabama for [the 2018 World Food Championship]? Because I wanted to be on that stage, and I wanted folks to see a Black woman on that stage." Curry's stage is getting larger, thanks to her star turn on the Netflix special *The American Barbecue Showdown*, which debuted in spring 2020. We definitely see you now, Lady of Q!

2. Carter.

the famous contest in her book *Barbecue Greats, Memphis Style: Great Restaurants, Great Recipes, Great Personalities*: "The founders scraped together a few thousand dollars to produce the first contest on May 5, 1978. Twenty teams competed that first year for $1,000 in prize money. The winner, Bessie Mae Cathey, attributed her success to 'ribs that come from high on the hog.' When asked how she knew she cooked good barbecue, she said, 'because everybody who eats it says it is.'"[6] Cathey is African American, and she won the entire thing with a very minimalist barbecue set-up. That's right, a Black woman won the very first Memphis in May competition. Wells and her husband, Gary, have been on record about their astonishment with the KCBS's growth. "The original rule of the KCBS was that none of it would be taken seriously. The organization was founded on the premise of promoting barbeque and having fun."[7] Well, they ended up being half right because the competition is taken very seriously these days.

Some of the African Americans restaurateurs that I interviewed greeted competitive barbecue with deep ambivalence, bordering on a collective yawn. Desiree Robinson of the Cozy Corner Restaurant in Memphis, Tennessee, told me that, without fail, someone in town for the Memphis in May competition will stop by her restaurant. After tasting her barbecue, they tell her how good it is and that she should enter the contest because it's better than much of what they ate there. She serenely told me that she doesn't compete because "I have nothing to prove." If you try her crispy-seared barbecue bologna or her impossibly tender Cornish hens, you'd agree.

George Gerard of Gerard's Barbeque Diner in Beaumont, Texas, gave me another angle that I hadn't considered—it's bad business. "Why give away for free something that I sell for my livelihood?" I had always framed participating in a barbecue contest as a type of advertising, but I'm now more aware of the downside. These barbecue chefs don't get compensated. They often have to prepare a significant amount of food and take staff away from their restaurants. It's a strain on their businesses that doesn't necessarily pay off because festival attendees don't necessarily translate into customers. Some recoup their expenses by vending at the festival, but that invites another set of headaches.

Barbecue competitions have long been with us in some form or fashion. In the twentieth century, especially with the popularity of backyard barbecue, lots of people threw small-scale, intensely local, barbecue competitions: 4-H clubs, local businesses looking for publicity, state fairs, television stations, nonprofit fundraisers, and so on. Curiously, a number of "for men only" barbecue competitions emerged. The most prominent was the America's Cookout Championship (ACC), started in 1959. I think this competition was a response to the Pillsbury Bake-Off Contest, started in the late 1940s, which was open to everyone but garnered a lot of attention and money for women. The ACC brought twenty-five finalists to Hawaii in April 1964 for a barbecue contest. The finalists' wives could "go along with their husbands for the 7-day treatment, all-expense paid trip to Hawaii. The grand prize is $10,000 cash."[8] That prize amount was significant for its time. Four other contestants were offered a station wagon as a consolation prize.

The contest, sponsored by Kaiser Foil (now Kaiser Aluminum) at an annual cost of $400,000, wasn't about barbecue in the traditional sense.[9] "Of the 25 male chefs in the finals of this national barbecue competition, seven will pin their hopes for fame and cash on beef concoctions, while eight others, evenly divided at four each, will [take] the lamb or chicken route. Three men will develop recipes for fish. The remaining seven in the cook-off will prepare, respectively, pork, Cornish Hen, duck, rabbit, wiener, ham, and veal."[10] In 1965, one Jerome D. Ivice represented Illinois to the ACC with his "Pizza wiener roll" recipe.[11] Based on the happenstance nature of how the contest was reported, it's difficult to tell if any African Americans participated or won, but it was the kind of contest that was more inviting. Why? Because it was cheap to enter.

As community barbecue contests proliferated beginning in the 1970s, African Americans noticeably participated. That certainly was the case with Cleveland's National Rib Cook-Off, which began in the 1980s. One of the city's Black newspapers, the *Call and Post*, informed its readers: "The barbecue contest will include some of Cleveland's best Black cooks, both professional and amateur, many of whom were not able to participate in some of the larger barbecue contests in the past months because of prohibitively expensive entry fees."[12] Black barbecue entrepreneurs like Eugene "Hot Sauce" Williams regularly competed in the annual contest, and that made a lot of sense. Even if he didn't win, he was getting plenty of advertising. A 1986 newspaper advertisement for the event declared, "If you're not in Cleveland come August, You're not in Barbecue."[13]

As was the case in many other cities, the popularity of this contest spawned others. Cleveland was soon host to the Rib Burn-Off, which seems to have a stronger African American vibe. A 1983 newspaper recap of the contest gives insight to its structure: "'Never mind the bibs, bring the ribs!' shouted one of the celebrity judges [at] the start of the Rib Burn-Off Contest, July 17. Celebrity judges sampled 35 rib entries apiece and scored them on appearance, the tenderness and taste of the meat, and the sauce. . . . At one point during the contest a great cloud covered the festival, and a gust of wind ripped apart the judges['] tent. The judges grabbed that which was most precious to them — the ribs."[14] Among the celebrity judges that year was a local weatherman for WKYC-TV named Al Roker, who was reportedly pleased with the results.[15]

It's fitting that a newspaper columnist initiated a local barbecue contest that became beloved by African Americans. After all, newspapers have a huge role in barbecue culture. Local reporters paid more attention to their community's barbecue traditions and its practitioners. In the early days of restaurants, barbecue to-go orders were wrapped in newspaper, and many a barbecue fire has been started with it. Mike Royko, a white man and a legendary and longtime Chicago newspaper columnist, wrote in late June 1982 that he could make ribs better than anybody. He challenged anyone who thought better to join him in Grant Park in early September. The response was overwhelming. Letters flooded into the *Chicago Tribune*'s mail department pleading to be a part of the contest by laying out their barbecue credentials. Others responded with bravado about their skills.

Four hundred or so competitors showed up on the appointed day. After a vigorous competition refereed by a panel of judges, Charles Robinson, an African American ice cream distributor who grew up in Lambert, Mississippi, before moving to Chicago, emerged victorious. Robinson credited his success to a two-hundred-year-old family recipe passed along to him by his grandfather. This recipe was reportedly enjoyed by "fourteen generations of Robinsons." Robinson eventually parlayed the tremendous publicity from his win into a couple of restaurants, a catering business, a food truck, and a book, *The Charlie Robinson Story: From the Son of a Mississippi Delta Sharecropper to the Top of the Chicago Barbecue Charts.*[16]

Another interesting historical footnote: The annual competition took place in 1985, which left Royko quite dismayed. As he wrote in a column recapping the event, "The 1985 grand champion is a white yuppie. Even worse, he doesn't know a damn thing about ribs. This is the first time he ever cooked them. Let us begin with his name. Steve Crane. What kind of ribmaster's name is that? Charlie Robinson. Cleo Williams. Rufus. Bubba. Willie Mae. Now, those are rib-cooking names."[17] What was "bad news" for Royko would become good news for American consumers. That same year, a chef named Larry Raymond placed second with a barbecue sauce that he gave the same nickname as his little brother David. Today, "Sweet Baby Ray's" is one of the best-selling barbecue sauces in the country.

Competitive barbecue's biggest game-changer since the Memphis in May competition's founding was the 2009 debut of *BBQ Pitmasters*. This extremely popular television show about competitive barbecue had a seven-year run on the Destination America cable channel. The show's first season followed selected teams to various barbecue competitions around the country. The format was changed for the second season, and several barbecue teams competed for a large cash prize based on the evaluation of three judges: Myron Mixon, a barbecue competition circuit legend and Season 1 contestant; Chef Art Smith, often known as "Oprah's Chef," and Warren Sapp, a former professional football player.

During the rest of its run, the format remained the same and Mixon anchored the show, and the other judges rotated—most notably, George "Tuffy" Stone, another competition circuit legend, and Aaron Franklin of Austin, Texas, a rising star (at that time) restaurateur. His Franklin Barbecue is now, arguably, the most famous barbecue restaurant in the world. Other than Sapp, the only other African American who regularly judged was Moe Cason (profiled later in this chapter), who, like Mixon, competed on the show before becoming a judge. There were several African Americans contestants, notably including Michael Character (owner of Character's Famous BBQ), Neil Strawder (pitmaster at Bigmista's BBQ), and Solomon Williams (the "Carolina Rib King"), but most of the competitors are white.

Barbecue industry experts acknowledge the profound influence that *BBQ Pitmasters* has had on its viewers in the years since its launch. In 2016, Dedra Berg, the senior director of marketing at Smithfield Foods, observed, "Smithfield expects to see continued growth of consumer interest in not only barbecue consumption but also preparation. 'Cooking shows in general continue to grow in popularity, specifically grilling focused shows like 'BBQ Pitmasters' as consumer interest in barbecue and grilling are at an all-time high.'"[18] Home cooks eagerly replicate the competition cooking experience in their own backyards. Meat industry analysts note that the sale of "competition cuts" of meat like brisket, pork shoulder, and pork spareribs have increased noticeably in recent years.[19] More home cooks have taken to the leap and actually compete. In the past decade, the number of barbecue competition teams has doubled.[20]

Competition barbecue has also influenced restaurant culture. As I ate my way through barbecue America, I saw what success on the competi-

IN THE SMOKE
WITH MOE CASON
BRAND BARBECUE!

Texas barbecue, in general, has really pushed, nationally, barbecue.
People are trying to emulate that Texas flavor. Because, I'm telling
you, that barbecue, it will change you.—Moe Cason

I n 2018, Moe Cason sat down for an interview on *Traditions
with Marty Smith* at La Barbecue in Austin, Texas—one
of his favorite spots and mine. Cason credits his paternal
grandmother Margaret Cason with getting him interested in
food while he grew up in Des Moines, Iowa. After all, she had
seventeen children (yes, that's right, seventeen!), so Moe had plenty
of opportunities to eat at numerous family gatherings. Later in the
interview he talked about the first thing he did after finishing a stint
in the U.S. Navy, serving aboard the USS *Missouri*. Dig this, that ship
is an Iowa class battleship nicknamed "Big Mo." "When I got out, the
first thing I bought was a little Brinkman, little grill, a little grill I
bought, and I just started cooking it up in my neighborhood. At the
time, I didn't see, uh, TV shows about barbecue. Up to that point, it
was just us in the neighborhood, battling against neighbors, you know,
who had the best ribs, who had the best this and that, you know. And,
uh, for me, I did my first cook-off in 2006, and I was hooked. One-man
team, I did like twenty something contests that year, and I was just
like, this is where I need to be."[1] Could this all be a function of fate?

According to his website, Cason is an accomplished competitive
barbecuer: "Multiple Grand and Reserve Grand Championships;
Multiple 1st & 2nd place awards in chicken, ribs, pork, and
brisket; Competed and won awards in 35 states; Competed in the
following BBQ sanctions KCBS (Kansas City Barbeque Society),
IBCA (International Barbecue Cooker), GBA (Georgia Barbecue
Association), and MBN (Memphis BBQ Network), Memphis in May;
3 perfect "180" scores in chicken, ribs, & pork shoulder; 2nd Place
Sauce at the 2012 Jack Daniel's World Championship Invitational."[2]
Thus, he was poised to take full advantage of any opportunities.

Cason's big break came when appeared on the *BBQ Pitmasters*

1. "SEC Traditions."
2. Moe Cason BBQ.

Moe Cason, Des Moines, Iowa.
Photograph by Nick Thake.

show's second season on the Destination America channel in 2010. His one-person Ponderosa BBQ won the first round of competition, but he was eliminated in the final competition. He became a fan favorite and got a recurring role on the show as a competitor (Season 3) and a judge (Season 6) alongside legendary barbecue competitors Myron Mixon and Tuffy Stone.

Cason has nailed the art of self-promotion. I remember showing a literary agent the picture of Cason that I used for this book, and he said, "Now, that's what a pitmaster should look like!" He's had promotional deals with B&B Charcoal, Big Red soda (love the red drink tie-in), and Smithfield. In addition to his denim overalls, ball caps, and jackets emblazoned with his logo, Cason has a designer line of high-end cutlery along with a line of spice rubs and sauces to sell. The spice rubs are used for a variety of meats, and they are inspired by his grandmother Margaret.

He's also been around the world to spread the gospel of barbecue. According the Armed Forces Entertainment website, Cason "shares his knowledge by holding BBQ pitmaster classes all over the world— United States, Germany, Sweden, Australia, New Zealand, and soon to be Brazil." Alas, the COVID-19 pandemic sacked the 2020 Moe Cason's Pro Blitz BBQ Bash that included planned stops in Guam, Singapore, and Diego Garcia, a British military base in the middle of the Indian Ocean.[3]

I don't know how in the world that I missed this, but in 2019, Cason was selected as Reynold's Wrap's Chief Grilling Officer. Cason beat out twenty-six thousand applicants . . . and I was one of them. At the company's expense, he went on a two-week, four-stop tour of the

3. "Moe Cason's Pro Blitz BBQ Bash."

United States, visiting Chicago, Nashville, Charleston, and Miami. All right, not exactly the tour that I would have put together, but it's good that Cason gave these places some love. Cason blogged about his trip, giving us insight on each city's barbecue scene.

Regrettably, Cason didn't make it to a lot of African American joints, or if he did, they weren't noteworthy enough to mention. He missed Chicago's South Side during his stay in the Windy City. The only Black-run joint that made the final cut was Rodney Scott's Whole Hog BBQ in Charleston. Cason was impressed, writing:

> Whole hog reigns supreme in this establishment, and his signature menu item is succulent, flavorful, and cooked perfectly. The spare ribs had a beautiful, sticky sheen that I know were properly mopped with Scott's original BBQ sauce. The sauce tasted so good that I wanted to drink it! The simplicity of the seasoning complimented the sauce for a pleasant balance of tangy and savory. But my favorite aspect of these lip-smacking ribs was the flame kissed grill flavor which can only be achieved cooking directly over hot coals. James Beard would have had a pile of clean bones, sticky napkins, and smile on his face; just like I did.[4]

During his time in Charleston, Cason also went to John Lewis Barbecue. It was in Lewis's Austin, Texas, restaurant that Cason uttered the words that open this profile. It was a beef rib that Lewis prepared that was so life-changing for Cason. He's a Lewis fan, and even though Lewis got a change of venue from Texas to South Carolina, it was still his overall favorite.

I can't end this profile without gleaning some of Cason's barbecue wisdom. From the evidence of several quotations and interviews, Cason gives pretty consistent advice. When Marty Smith asked him, "What's the secret to being great at barbecue?" Cason demonstrably said, "Low and slow, taking your time, giving great seasoning, smoke, cooking great tender barbecue. That is what is most important. Your flavor is your flavor." For Cason, texture is paramount: "Once you master the texture, everything else you can build on later on." He often tells knowledge-seeking barbecuers to grill "naked." Not without clothes, but without a lot of seasoning. Just use salt and pepper, and work on cooking it well. Get fussy later.

Cason is a great example of what someone can do to leverage his or her barbecue skill into global notoriety. His example inspires me, too. Like Cason and Snoop Dogg, I endeavor to be "internationally known, and locally respected."

4. Cason, "Moe Cason."

tion circuit has wrought. Award-winning barbecue competition teams are now opening restaurants, displaying their trophies, and hoping that their competition success will translate into a steady flow of customers. Menus track competition categories by offering brisket, chicken, pork shoulder, and pork spareribs. I understand the impulse to be all things to all people, but I have a soft spot for the barbecuers who cling to local tradition or stick to cooking the few things that they do well. Memories arise of highly specialized menus like the chopped pork sandwich at Jones Bar-B-Q Diner in Marianna, Arkansas, or the pork spareribs and slices of white bread at Dreamland Bar-B-Que in Tuscaloosa, Alabama. Another indication that the current restaurant ethos isn't "less is more": one industry observer indicated that "barbecue restaurants are also promoting bigger platters featuring several varieties of smoked beef brisket, pork, and meats for dining parties to share."[21]

Restaurant diners' passion for competition barbecue has put pressure on Black barbecuers that didn't previously exist. Beef brisket is the poster child for this phenomenon. In my experience, this trendy cut of meat was an uncommon sight on the menus of Black-run barbecue restaurants, except in places like Kansas City, Missouri, the states of Oklahoma and Texas, and a smattering of locations in the West. Even in those parts, brisket was often something that was served chopped or thinly sliced, lightly smoked, and drowned in sauce. Thanks to the influence of competition barbecue and the central Texas regional barbecue style, brisket is in high demand. By June 2019, brisket soared to record prices and became the third priciest cut of beef, trailing only prime rib and loin (from where T-bone steaks are cut) as the most expensive cuts of meat.[22]

As a result, Black barbecuers have more customers who are walking into their restaurants and asking, "Where's the brisket?" Seeing none, they are likely to leave and dine elsewhere. Black barbecuers who are virtuosos at cooking pork now consider whether to add brisket to the menu. If they do, they then have to consider making it in a way that is more consistent with an African American aesthetic or a central Texas aesthetic featuring thicker-cut slices that are well-smoked, glistening with fat, and nicely manicured with a seasoned crust (bark). As this development unfolds, I think of Black-run barbecue restaurants that have opened in the past few years and serve central Texas–style brisket in unexpected places–places like Heaven's Table Catering and BBQ in Milwaukee, Wisconsin, where Jason Alston dons his chef's whites and serves tasty brisket on a metal tray in the corner of a hip food hall.

For African Americans, less visibility in the barbecue competition world has meant increased invisibility in the other aspects of contemporary barbecue culture. They consistently lack the high-end sponsorships, book deals, lines of accessories, television appearances, and trips around the world that successful competitors secure. As you've seen, several talented African American competitors, such as Sylvie Curry and Moe Cason, have proven their mettle.

RECIPES

Sylvie Curry's Grilled Rack of Lamb Marinated in Rosemary-Garlic Infused Olive Oil with Mint-Parsley Chimichurri Sauce

When I meet someone who loves to cook, I often ask them what their show-off dish is—something they would make for someone special. This is what Sylvie Curry told me. A rack of lamb, which will be cooked by a hot and fast technique, may not be what you expected, but the results here are marvelous.

Makes 4 servings

For the chimichurri sauce
2 garlic cloves, minced
2 tablespoons red wine vinegar
½ teaspoon salt
¼ teaspoon black pepper
¼ teaspoon red pepper flakes
½ teaspoon dried oregano
¼ teaspoon dried rosemary
6 tablespoons olive oil
1 cup fresh mint
1 cup fresh parsley

For the lamb
2 racks of lamb (7–8 bones each)
Salt, to taste
Black pepper, to taste
2–3 cloves garlic, minced
¼ teaspoon fresh rosemary leaves, or ⅛ teaspoon dried
¼ cup olive oil

For the grill
Charcoal
Pecan wood chunks
Rosemary sprig

TO MAKE THE CHIMICHURRI SAUCE

1. Put the garlic, vinegar, salt, black pepper, red pepper flakes, oregano, rosemary, and olive oil in a food processor or blender and blend to mix well.

2. Add the mint and parsley. Blend again until the sauce reaches the desired consistency. Set aside.

TO PREPARE THE LAMB

1. Prepare the grill for indirect cooking with a reverse sear.
2. French trim each rack of lamb (or have the butcher do it when you purchase them). Remove the silver skin and excess fat.
3. Sprinkle a moderate amount of salt and pepper on the front and back of each rack.
4. Whisk together the garlic, rosemary, and olive oil, then coat the ribs with the mixture, and set the lamb aside for 20–30 minutes.
5. Place the lamb on top of a cooling rack in a roasting pan.
6. A temperature probe may be inserted in the meaty section of the racks. Set it for 118°.
7. Add the pecan wood chunks and the rosemary sprig to the charcoal.
8. Place the lamb racks on the grate for indirect cooking.
9. Once the lamb reaches 118° (15–20 minutes), move the racks from the indirect grate to sear over direct heat for 2–3 minutes on each side, or until an internal temperature of 125° for rare or 135° for medium rare is reached.
10. Let the lamb rest before slicing between the bones.
11. Serve with the chimichurri sauce.

Big Moe's Memphis-Style Chicken

One thing that I've noticed in my short stint as a barbecue judge is that most competitors cook chicken the same way, and it's always thighs. That makes sense because the chances of drying out breasts are too high. Getting a significant markdown is the difference between a top-ten finish and being toward the bottom of all competitors. Here's a good recipe adapted from Moe Cason that will allow you to create competition-level chicken in your home. *Note:* For this recipe you'll need a needle tenderizer, hickory chips or chunks, and a smoker or a gas grill with a smoke box or foil pan for the wood chips.

8 servings

For the barbecue chicken rub
1 cup sugar
½ cup paprika
¼ cup pink sea salt
¼ cup celery salt
3 tablespoons granulated onion
3 tablespoons chili powder
2 tablespoons dried mustard
1 teaspoon cayenne pepper

For the barbecue sauce
12 ounces ketchup
¾ cup white vinegar
½ cup sugar
1 tablespoon Worcestershire sauce
1 tablespoon coarsely ground black pepper
1½ teaspoons dried mustard
1 teaspoon hickory liquid smoke
1 teaspoon chili powder
1 teaspoon ground white pepper
½ teaspoon ground coriander
½ teaspoon cayenne pepper
½ cup water
¼ cup Cognac

For the chicken
8 bone-in chicken thighs with skin
⅔ cup packed dark brown sugar
½ cup coarse kosher salt

8 cups water

¼ cup canola oil

TO MAKE THE RUB

1. In a bowl, combine the sugar, paprika, pink sea salt, celery salt, granulated onion, chili powder, mustard, and cayenne and whisk until combined. Set ¼ cup aside for this recipe; store the rest in an airtight container.

TO MAKE THE SAUCE

1. Mix the ketchup, vinegar, sugar, Worcestershire, black pepper, mustard, liquid smoke, chili powder, white pepper, coriander, cayenne, and water in a saucepot.
2. Bring to a simmer and cook for 15–20 minutes, stirring continuously.
3. Turn off the heat, add the Cognac, and stir to combine. Set aside.

TO MAKE THE CHICKEN

1. Trim the chicken thighs to make them more uniform, then use a needle tenderizer to perforate the skin to aid in achieving bite through the skin.
2. In a large pot, combine the brown sugar, kosher salt, and water. Heat until the sugar and salt dissolve in the water.
3. Remove the brine from the heat, let it cool at room temperature, and place it in the refrigerator to chill. When the brine has chilled, add the chicken and brine it in the refrigerator for 2–3 hours.
4. Set up a smoker or a gas grill for indirect heat at a pit temperature of 300°. Use hickory chips or chunks for the smoker. If using a gas grill, put the chips in a smoke box or foil pan under the grates on the burners.
5. Remove the chicken from the brine and pat it dry.
6. Coat the chicken with the canola oil, then sprinkle it with ¼ cup of the chicken rub on both sides. Place the chicken in a mesh grill basket or on a wire rack.
7. Cook until the chicken reaches 185°, about 35–45 minutes. It's technically done at 165°, but take it to a higher internal temperature to achieve a better mouth feel.
8. Remove the chicken, coat it with 1 cup of the barbecue sauce, and put it back on the grill for a few minutes to set the sauce. Serve with the remaining sauce on the side.

BLOWING SMOKE
THE FADING MEDIA REPRESENTATION OF AFRICAN AMERICAN BARBECUERS

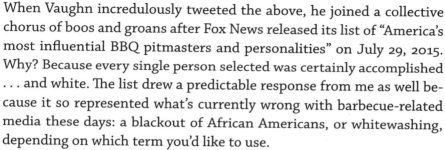

"America's most influential [white] BBQ pitmasters. . . ."
I'm on the list, but not Henry Perry? Child Please.
—Daniel Vaughn tweeting as @BBQsnob

When Vaughn incredulously tweeted the above, he joined a collective chorus of boos and groans after Fox News released its list of "America's most influential BBQ pitmasters and personalities" on July 29, 2015. Why? Because every single person selected was certainly accomplished . . . and white. The list drew a predictable response from me as well because it so represented what's currently wrong with barbecue-related media these days: a blackout of African Americans, or whitewashing, depending on which term you'd like to use.

Many of my friends have often heard me gripe—after I've consumed big helpings of barbecue-related media—"Come on! 42 million Black people in the U.S., and y'all couldn't find ONE brother or sister who barbecues?" Now that we've glimpsed the glory that is African American barbecue, you can see why I reacted as strongly as I did to Paula Deen's southern barbecue show. As I started paying more attention to barbecue-related media, I realized that her Food Network show was far from an isolated example. The lack of African American representation in barbecue was glaring.

How did we get to such a sad place where Black barbecuers have been pushed to the margins? I see the interplay of six separate developments that fed off one another to form perfect conditions in the 1990s for a media blackout of African American barbecuers: the rise of foodies; the explosion of media catering to foodies; the skyrocketing of competitive barbecue; a growing involvement in barbecue by professionally trained chefs; the reframing of barbecue as a craft; and the increasing economic potential of barbecue as it became more and more commodified and accessible to a wider eatership. I discussed competitive barbecue in the last chapter, so I won't rehash it here.

Everyone has to eat, but each person gives that act of survival different meaning. If there was an eating spectrum, on one end there'd be food as fuel and, on the other end, food as recreation. What's fascinating about this moment in history is that there seem to be a lot more people who are so deeply interested in food that it has become part of their identity—another way to distinguish themselves from others. For our purposes, I'll define a "foodie" as "a person who devotes considerable time and energy to eating and learning about good food, however 'good food' is defined."[1] These are people who consume inordinate amounts of food media and will work and travel for good food. I should know. I'm one of them. By no means should you consider the United States as the foodies' native habitat. This is a global phenomenon.

Sustained economic growth experienced in some countries greatly expanded the number of middle-class people who could spend their leisure time exploring food. One distinction with this new class of foodies is that they wanted to disrupt the snobbery previously displayed by the old guard of food tastemakers. They weren't interested in high cuisine and low-class food distinctions. They searched for experiences where they could get authentic food from other cultures, and they, not anyone else, could decide what was good. Most important, they now had sufficient means to make those experiences happen.

Barbecue is the perfect example of how the distinction between high and low cuisine has eroded. Some eaters are ready to travel near and far across the United States in order to experience regional styles for themselves. They want the truest authentic experience, and barbecue as presented in their hometowns may not, they suspect, be authentic. These authenticity seekers created a surge of food tourism and a demand for curators—informed and trusted people who could tell foodies where to go. This is where things started to get off track.

Print media has been a home to food tourism curators. From the 1930s to the 1950s, a traveling salesman named Duncan Hines wrote books telling people where to eat affordable and delicious meals in various cities. Newspapers, though, held the strongest sway. Local food columnists and restaurant critics interpreted the local food scene for their readers and did much to drive business to certain food establishments.

During the 1980s, high-end food media, such as *Food and Wine* and *Gourmet*, saw the tremendous potential in foodie markets. They got in on the act previously dominated by local media by shifting the focus away from luxury and sophistication to providing more accessible content. As vernacular forms of cooking got more play, barbecue benefited from all of these trends. Print media, especially magazines, featured more barbecue articles and recipes. In time, annual issues, timed for the summer months, were completely dedicated to barbecue. Media heard the call from their foodie readers, and they responded.

One of the best examples of an effective curator is Calvin Trillin and his U.S. Journal, which ran in the *New Yorker* from 1967 to 1982 and explored Americana. Reflecting on his time as a columnist, Trillin wrote, "I realized that a series about America could accommodate a light story now and then about Americans eating—a sort of change up that rested the arm, even at risk to the midsection. . . . I wrote about eating rather than food, and I wrote as a reporter who was enjoying his work rather than as an expert. If there was a unifying proposition in what I wrote on the subject, it was that Americans should celebrate rather than apologize for the local specialties that they actually enjoyed."[2]

Trillin's love for America's vernacular food is so evident in his writing, and he was certainly passionate about barbecue—and about one African American-run restaurant in particular. In 1972, he emphatically wrote, "It has long been acknowledged the single best restaurant in the world is Arthur Bryant's Barbeque at 18th and Brooklyn in Kansas City."[3] Though somewhat facetiously presented, Trillin's advocacy for Arthur Bryant's should not be downplayed. It had been nearly two decades since a Black barbecue cook had been so publicly celebrated. Trillin endeavored to bring local barbecue legends to national notice.

During the same period, however, other writers were doing the opposite by pushing notable Black barbecuers to the margins—including those who had helped create the beloved regional style the writers were boosting. This regrettable wave of storytelling was particularly acute in Texas, where from an early time it began to split apart what had once been a shared cuisine. Over time, Texas barbecue became divided into subregions with the central Texas style dominated by a white narrative and East Texas driven by a Black narrative. Famed Texas folklorist Frank X. Tolbert, in his 1953 book *A Bowl of Red*, was one of the earliest to articulate this geographic split. He began a chapter titled "A Land of Hot Sausage and Barbecue" with a lengthy exposition of the meat-smoking traditions of the German, Polish, and Czech immigrants who were present from the days when Texas was a republic. Then, opining that "East Texas' most memorable barbecue artists are (or were) blacks," he wrote about a few African American barbecuers, including King Solomon, Johnny Brown, Lank Robinson, and R. O. Shoemaker.[4]

Some twenty years later, Griffin Smith Jr., with some help from Paul Burka, picked up where Tolbert left off with *Texas Monthly*'s first full-length feature on barbecue. Smith identified twenty barbecue places while pushing the idea that the State of Texas barbecue was crisscrossed by geographic dividing lines. "Smith delineated the traditional Central-versus-East Texas barbecue styles," said J. C. Reid of the *Houston Chronicle*, "noting the sauceless, beef-centric smoked meats associated with Austin versus the sauced and chopped pork traditions of joints around Houston."[5] And, according to Smith, the latter style was more closely associated with African Americans. Closing the article with his list of the twenty best barbecue places, Smith included three African American restaurants—Howard's Bar-B-Q in Austin, Matt Garner's in Houston (employee Beulah Mouton was pictured in the article), and Swan's Country House Barbecue in Hempstead.

It seems harmless enough to show subregional differences in the cuisine, but a few years later in the *Atlantic Monthly*'s special issue on Texas, Smith went a step further:

> That is not to say pork cannot be had in Texas; little restaurants in the eastern counties sell it often, usually on a bun with spicy hot sauce, and occasionally topped with cole slaw, a desecration in the eyes of the true barbecue devotee. But barbecued pork is more southern than Texan, and the tradition of spicy sandwiches has been left in the custody of inspired black barbecuers whose forebears relied on slow cooking and hot sauce to tenderize and mask the flavor of meat deemed unworthy at the Big House. Authentic Texas barbecue grew up in the resolutely German farming communities of Central Texas. Small-town meat markets satisfied the hunger of Saturday shoppers who converged from the surrounding countryside.... And to this day the best barbecue in Texas can be found at noontime on Saturdays in small-town meat markets.[6]

This was media whitewashing in action. By defining the indirect meat smoking process practiced by white central European immigrants as the "authentic" type of barbecue, Smith dissed at best, and erased at worst, a century-plus of African American barbecue tradition and influence in Texas. The same applies to Latino-heritage cooks who made barbacoa well before Texas existed as a state.

Seeing that passage reminded me of what Neil Foley, a historian who has deeply studied race relations in Texas, explained in an interview with the *Houston Press*'s Robb Walsh. Just like with barbecue, some Texans had whitewashed Texas history itself. "African Americans have been completely erased from the meta-narrative of Texas history," Foley said. Foley further stressed that some Texans didn't want a continued association with the state's slaveholding past and all of its associated cultural baggage. African Americans were a constant reminder of that past. Foley emphasized in the interview that "Texas had something no other Southern state had—the Alamo. Texans were the men who won the West, the men who defeated the Mexicans. . . . There are no African Americans in the Alamo scene."[7]

Unfortunately, what played out in 1970s in Texas food media is now more commonplace across the country, especially in restaurant criticism. Barbecue is being whitewashed by food media content creators who either ignore, downplay, denigrate, or completely write off African American contributions to a community's barbecue scene. Whether the story is local, regional, national, or global, the dissing persists. I've noticed such a familiar pattern to this kind of writing that I can formulate a tried-and-true recipe easily enough:

Disappearing Black Barbecue

Serving size: From hundreds to millions of people
1 cup laziness
Media platform of any type
4 cups of a nondiverse professional network
2 cups of a nondiverse social network
1 cup public relations press releases
White barbecuers, especially hipsters, to taste
2 cups lack of imagination
½ cup complacency

1. Display laziness by refusing to research previous stories on your, or another, media platform about the barbecue in your area. This is especially important if you work for a print publication that's been operating for more than twenty years. Otherwise, you'll probably find stories about African American barbecuers.
2. Consult nondiverse professional and social networks and press releases for suggestions on whom to profile.
3. Once the desired amount of white barbecuers are assembled, exercise a lack of imagination to keep from expanding the list to include diverse barbecuers.
4. Begin barbecue feature by describing an area as a "barbecue wasteland" or by declaring that no "real" or "good" barbecue existed in that area before a white person started doing it.
5. Once your white barbecuer profile is completed, bask in your false

confidence that you've thoroughly covered the topic for, and done a disservice to, those who consume the media you create.

More often than it should happen, relatively unknown or unproven barbecuers get a spotlight shown on them. These finds are sometimes so obscure that I really think the food writer should get an award for investigative journalism. As much as the coverage of Black barbecuers has diminished, print media (especially local media) usually fares better than television.

What about cookbooks? In the United States, the big publishing houses have published only a handful of barbecue books written by African Americans. *Smokestack Lightning: Adventures in the Heart of Barbecue Country*, by Lolis Eric Elie, is my favorite, but it is not solely a cookbook. In fact, the current roster of Black barbecue cookbook authors by major publishers includes Al Roker (a television weatherman) and Bobby Seale (a former Black Panther). Only one cookbook that I'm aware of was directly attributed to a restaurateur, and that is a posthumously published cookbook in honor of Texas barbecue legend C. B. "Stubb" Stubblefield. Just think of all the great African American–owned barbecue restaurants out there. Then think of all the barbecue books published every year. Think about the authors of those books and how those books confer authority on barbecue. Chef Bobby Flay has written three barbecue cookbooks, and Steven Raichlen has written eleven barbecue cookbooks in the span of two decades. These are fine books, but why aren't more of these cookbooks, or books about barbecue history, written by African American authors who are barbecue experts?

Television has had a giant impact on the obscuring of the African American barbecue story and really any Black food story. Aside from guest spots on local television, barbecue in general didn't really get that much attention in national programming until the late 1980s on public broadcasting and cable television. In 1987, *Great Chefs, Great Bar-B-Q*, narrated by country singer Tennessee Ernie Ford, was broadcast on public television stations across the country. The show got off to a good start by opening at Arthur Bryant's Barbeque in Kansas City, Missouri. Though most of the on-air talent was white, several African American–owned places, or white-run establishments featuring a Black cook, were profiled beyond just a mere cameo. The show then took an odd turn from travelogue to fine dining and cooking demonstrations by classically trained chefs and career cooks. Before the credits rolled, an African American woman named Gracie Carruthers of Leonard's Pit Barbecue in Memphis, demonstrated how to make onion rings—not what I think of as part of the barbecue canon. More representation would have been great, but the show put forth a solid effort.

In 1991, *Great Southern Barbecue* broadcast nationally on public broadcasting stations and cable systems. Narrated by country singer Tom T. Hall, it was billed as "a grand tour" that started out in Kansas City, like Ford's show did. But *Great Southern Barbecue* focused on the American Royal barbecue contest, not on local restaurants. The scene moved to Colonial Williamsburg, where Rich Davis, purveyor of the hugely popular K.C. Masterpiece barbecue sauce, oversaw an "eighteenth-century barbecue." Davis points out the authenticity of the event based on diaries uncovered at the historical site. I'm not sure if this is historically accurate, but one sees Blacks and whites, men and women, working side by side to cook half a pig over a fire using a spit. Referring to the antebellum period, Hall says, "When [Fort] Sumter [in South Carolina] was fired upon, a remarkable society also blew up. Already the South had developed a distinctive regional cuisine supported by big, rich plantations and a slave-based economy. It made almost any culinary magic possible. Incidentally, Black cooks have profoundly affected southern food, from the very beginning." Yes, you read that correctly.

For the rest of the hourlong special, Black cooks got only cameos making barbecue, most notably, "Daddy" John Bishop of Dreamland Bar-B-Que in Tuscaloosa, Alabama. Not one had a speaking part. The special ends with Bishop smiling with his trademark pipe jutting out from his mouth, but the overall silence in the episode is deafening.

The Food Network, which launched in 1993, just a couple of years after *Great Southern Barbecue* aired, was the biggest game changer in food media—and it became an influential force in the growing interest in barbecue. Similar to print media, television producers catered to the desires of foodies, and the Food Network greatly multiplied the availability of food programming.

In May 2004, newspapers carried the following press release.

Chef and grilling specialist Bobby Flay is the host of two weeks of Food Network programming dedicated to everything you need to know about grilling and barbecue, between Memorial Day and Father's Day. Flay stars in the premiere of his new series, *BBQ with Bobby Flay*, which takes him throughout the country in search of known and unknown barbecue delights. Two other new series will have their premieres during this time. In addition, current series, including *Emeril Live!, Unwrapped, Roker on the Road,* and

Alton Brown's Good Eats, will focus on grilling and cook-offs, as will specials such as *The BBQ Circuit*, *Paula's Southern BBQ*, *Big Pig Jim*, and *American Royal BBQ*.[8]

From this push, *BBQ with Bobby Flay* emerged, and the series ran from 2004 to 2007. According to the Food Network website: "Chef and grilling star Bobby Flay travels the country in search of all that is grilled, smoked, barbecued and enjoyed. Join him as he meets colorful characters, visits undiscovered BBQ joints and tries every grilling gadget imaginable. From ribs in Memphis and salmon in Alaska to the world's biggest BBQ cook-off, he'll discover all the foods and flavors that make BBQ one of America's favorite cooking styles and backyard pastimes."[9] I've only seen a few episodes of this show, so I asked some hardcore fans of Flay's if they recall seeing an appreciable number of African Americans on his show. Most said "no," but they did qualify that Flay didn't often have guest cooks on this particular show.

The Food Network's power to bestow authority, and thus shape its viewers' opinions, affected Americans' views on barbecue during a critical time in barbecue's increased popularity, and viewers rarely saw Black barbecuers. If so, it was usually a quick cameo on a travelogue-type show. As we saw in the last chapter, even in barbecue-specific competitions, the lack of African American representation is woeful.

There are some bright signs. Food television has of late been paying more attention to issues of diversity, equity, and inclusion. There's a long way to go, and I hope that the trend continues. Yet much damage has been done. At the very moment that foodies were looking for more content about barbecue, they saw few African American experts, which has left the food world—and legions of barbecue lovers—with a horribly skewed view of the barbecue scene in the United States. The problem goes beyond the media outlets I've identified here. Next time you watch a barbecue television show on any network, pay closer attention to who gets the most screen time, how the host relates to that person, and who gets treated like a barbecue expert.

Either the Food Network was prescient or it kickstarted the trend, but a wave of classically trained chefs got into the barbecue game during the 1990s and 2000s. These chefs either began featuring barbecue on their fine-dining restaurant menus or opened up casual barbecue restaurants. As industry observers note, that trend has not abated a couple of decades later. "'The increase in flavors demonstrates that, across the board, barbecue, which is a very traditional food, is currently experiencing a creative moment across foodservice segments, with chefs blurring the lines of regionalism, international inspiration playing a stronger role and innovation blending with tradition,' says Diana Kelter, a foodservice analyst at Mintel International, in Chicago."[10]

Perhaps inadvertently, chefs have helped disrupt a key part of barbecue's historical narrative. Once barbecue transitioned from cooking whole animals to cooking lesser cuts of meat, it became mostly about the artistry of cooking those cuts. This has had mixed results. Chefs are now on the forefront of advocating for more ethically raised, antibiotic- and hormone-free meat, which, I think, would be good for everyone. But does a brisket have to be cooked with Kobe or Wagyu beef in order to be the best barbecue? Is that realistic for a lot of Black barbecuers who still buy their meat at the local grocery store because of unreliable or unscrupulous suppliers? We may find more balance since a growing number of chefs are reconnecting barbecue to whole-animal cooking and are being less bullish on barbecuing high-grade meat.

I'm tempted to write that comparing chef-driven barbecue to traditional barbecue is comparing apples and oranges, but I'm not so sure. Chefs have changed barbecue expectations of what great barbecue is. Smoked meat is now presented in a well-manicured and social media–ready way. Salt and pepper are supposedly all the seasoning that's needed. Oh, and you can charge higher prices for it! Pork spareribs are regularly twenty-five dollars for a rack, and I've seen brisket go as high as thirty-six dollars a pound. Black barbecuers could certainly follow suit and charge more for their food, but they have a customer base that's very price sensitive.

Another critical development is the reframing of barbecue as a craft. This is the third, and last, redefinition of barbecue. Language played an important role. We've seen barbecue cooks called many things, and pitmaster is the favored title these days. Daniel Vaughn, *Texas Monthly*'s barbecue editor, has deftly examined the question, "What should we call the barbecue greats?" Though there are scant references to the word before, he suggests that the term gained currency in the late 1970s and the 1980s.[11] In its most favorable light, the word "pitmaster" implies that a person not only makes barbecue but makes it at a skill level not possessed by most human beings. That is, the person is practicing a craft, something beyond a profession or doing a job. He, or she, is a "master" who has conquered something! Unfortunately, the term has become so overused that it no longer holds special meaning. As R. L. Reeves aptly noted in Vaughn's article, "If you can butt a Bic lighter up against a Kingsford briquette these days, you've earned the sobriquet 'pitmaster.'"[12] Still, the wide application of the term "pitmaster" facilitated the reframing of barbecuing as a craft. But what does one mean by "craft," and should it apply to making barbecue?

In 1990, Janet Kardon, director of the American Craft Museum, defined "craft" as objects "created by trained professionals or individuals who are carrying on traditions transmitted from their elders. The artist is aware of the historical continuum of craft, either within the ethnic or national community or from the larger mainstream, and is often committed to extending and expanding that continuum in inventive ways."[13] Though Kardon wrote in terms better suited for material objects, the definition works well for food and how some barbecue cooks are currently perceived.

If craft represents the professionalized production of material, then the work of supposedly untrained people falls into a catchall category called "folk art." Influential art curator Holger Cahill expanded the definition. He describes folk art as "the expression of the common people, made by them and intended for their use and enjoyment. It is not the expression of professional artists made for a small cultured class, and it has little to do with the fashionable art of its period. It does not come out of an academic tradition passed on by schools but out of craft tradition, plus the personal quality of the rare craftsman who is an artist."[14] Kardon then poignantly concludes, "Rarely are folk artists formally trained, and most remain anonymous. Modestly, they make objects for others like themselves and probably do not consider themselves artists in origin, intent, or execution. Craft, even with its democratic aspirations, is not quite as humble."[15] Now that the comparison has been laid bare, which one sounds more like an African American barbecuer to you?

When African Americans dominated barbecue, it was highly appreciated, menial work that led to delicious results. It had the trappings of craft, but few talked about it that way. Barbecue as craft opened up a new space that a wider spectrum of people, who wouldn't have otherwise, gleefully entered because it is cool. Though not specifically writing about barbecue, Richard E. Ocejo, a leading scholar on contemporary craft culture, deftly describes the convergence of several factors that in turn allowed this aspect of craft culture to explode. In an online interview, Ocejo opines on this new generation of craftspeople:

> Primarily, they pursue the elite versions of these jobs because they allow them to use their heads, hands, and social skills. Like much knowledge-based work, these jobs require workers to use cultural information to be creative. Unlike it, however, they get to do so

by using their bodies to perform craft-based tasks and provide tangible products and services. Finally, they also get to share this knowledge with consumers. Thus, these attributes give these jobs greater status than they normally have. They become knowledge workers who get to learn a craft and directly serve the public.[16]

Like the barbers, bartenders, and butchers that Ocejo chronicles in his book, barbecue is something that fits into this template. Using Ocejo's conceptual framework, making barbecue become cool wonderfully combines a preference for work that relies on intellectual capability as much as one's hands.

Cultural critic Lauren Michele Jackson gives a penetrating critique of the emerging, reframed "white craft culture" and applies it to barbecue thusly:

> Even though its roots in pit-style cooking on plantations are well known, its transmutation from a staple to a product of true craft is a feat largely attributed to the exceptional taste and unique skill of the white pitmasters who have claimed it as their own. In the process, the people and cultures most instrumental to the development of barbecue are effectively barred from participating in the genre at its highest and most exalted levels. Instead, they're left to continue developing it in their own communities and establishments—waiting for their innovations to inevitably be taken and elevated so that they can be distributed to a wider, whiter audience always hungry for the next carefully packaged piece of another culture's cuisine.[17]

Craft culture is more prestigious than folk art. It's an effective marketing term that has generated notoriety and prosperity for a cadre of savvy barbecuers.

The people who decide which barbecue stories will get told crave some sort of hook to get the attention of whoever is consuming that medium. A craft culture focused on artisans created that hook. "The national press would have you believe barbecue is dominated by white hipster males," food writer Robb Walsh has noted, pointing to coverage that leaves out or diminishes the work and visibility of Black pitmasters.[18] Given the sheer number and types of people who make barbecue, it's puzzling and disheartening that the same white dudes get highlighted over and over again while others, especially women and African Americans, are consistently overlooked.

The craft-oriented redefinition of barbecue is notable because, now, the last factor comes into play, the one that keeps feeding this beast. As a craftsperson, one can potentially make a lot more money than as a folk artist: charge higher prices on one's menu, franchise restaurants, write books, get on the professional speaking circuit, market barbecue-related accessories, get investors, monetize one's online presence, and so on. Apart from former heavyweight boxing champ George Foreman and his grilling machines (I'm definitely not calling that authentic barbecue equipment), no African American has had marked success capitalizing in these spaces . . . yet. Influential food media got certain people noticed and boosted the market for what, where, and to whom, barbecue entrepreneurs sold their goods.

The sense of loss has been palpable even in academic circles. At a 1994 gathering of food academes and enthusiasts in Oxford, England, food writer Josephine Bacon presented a paper titled "The Great American Art of Pit Barbecue Is Fast Disappearing." Bacon's paper relies on three newspaper clippings lamenting the dying or dead barbecue scenes in Baltimore, Maryland, and Memphis, Tennessee. Eight of the twelve barbecue joints mentioned had Black pitmasters. Invoking the language of craft without explicitly saying so, Bacon concludes:

> Pit barbecuing is a very slow and delicate process, as well as something of an art, so it is hardly surprising that the land that invented fast food should apparently be trying to deal it a death blow. However, its aficionados are many and with enough support from its fans, it might tenuously survive, though not quite in the robust, traditional manner of old, thanks to new-fangled fads and bureaucracy such as food hygiene regulations. Let us pray that automation and electronics never rear their ugly heads in barbecue, or we shall have to resort to "virtual pit" to experience what pit barbecue used to taste like![19]

It didn't quite work out the way Bacon predicted. The twenty-first century's first decade saw an intensifying interest in barbecue, in part because southern food was also trending. Barbecue is so closely associated with that cuisine that Charles F. Kovacik wrote: "The eating place with the strongest Southern identity is the barbecue restaurant."[20]

Aside from media, I pondered other ways that African Americans could be fairly represented for their contributions to barbecue. I found out that the American Royal Barbecue Hall of Fame ("the Hall"), was based in Kansas City, Missouri! Surely, there would be some well-deserved recognition for African American barbecuers there. I was in for a surprise.

The Hall was founded in 2011. Of the twenty-seven inductees chosen by 2018, only one African American and another person of color were in the Hall. The African American inductee is Henry Perry—the acknowledged father of Kansas City's now-famous barbecue scene. The other inductee of color is Dave Anderson, whom I mentioned earlier. Anderson is a Native American with Choctaw and Ojibwe tribal heritage. Both deserve the recognition. Guess who's in the Hall's very first induction class? Henry Ford. Why? For popularizing charcoal briquettes.[21] That means Ford is in the Hall for something he didn't actually do. The other notable inductee is Guy Fieri, a Food Network megastar. Before you completely lose it, Fieri does have some barbecue bona fides. He was part of the Motley Que Crew that won the 2012 Houston Livestock Show and Rodeo Bar-B-Que Contest.[22] The other inductee was Johnny Trigg, a more orthodox choice, given that he's won "more than 60 grand championships and countless category wins to his name, [and he] has cooked more than 600 events during his storied career."[23]

Perhaps sensing a public relations problem, the Hall's selection committee sought nominations from the general public for its 2018 induction class. When I found this out, I went on social media repeatedly to encourage people to submit diverse nominees so that there could be a diverse pool of candidates for consideration. People enthusiastically responded, and as a result, four of the nine finalists nominated for the Hall were African Americans. Despite an 88 percent chance that at least one of these diverse candidates would be one of the three selected, none were. The deserving people who were selected: Tuffy Stone of Lynchburg, Virginia, and longtime restaurateurs Tootsie Tomanetz of Lexington, Texas, and Charlie Vergos of Memphis, Tennessee. I asked myself, "What gives?"

Several African Americans that I know wrote off the Hall as totally useless and even mused about creating another hall of fame that would be more diverse and representative. I chose the path of reforming the existing institution. I was so dismayed that I reached out to the Hall to express my disappointment and urge more inclusion. The Hall responded, but I sensed no urgency about addressing the lack of African American representation. So, I penned an op-ed that ran in the *Kansas City Star* on July 8, 2018, titled "It's Time to Diversify Kansas City's Barbecue Hall of Fame." I made the similar arguments for inclusion that you've read in *Black Smoke*. In addition to highlighting the historical absurdity of having only one African American in the Hall, I made some process suggestions that could help. Ultimately, I concluded that "a hall of fame recognizes people who have excelled in a particular field, and it tells a story. We can learn a lot about barbecue—its history, its present popularity and the possible future it inspires—through the lives of the people who are inducted. An honorific body for barbecue that's overwhelmingly white just looks bad, and it doesn't reflect reality."[24] As we'll see in the next chapter, my experience with the Hall has a happier ending.

The next month, I began working on *Black Smoke*. In the early stages of my research, I came across a regrettable July 2003 *Bon Appetit* article that was a perfect metaphor for the frustration that I'd been feeling. Titled "Who's Who in American Barbecue: New Recipes for Main Courses and Side Dishes from Experts Around the Country," the article features illustrations of an idyllic scene where the experts are having a grand old time at a barbecue cookout. Some are cooking, some are grubbing, some are sipping wine while others play badminton and croquet. Other than two women and one guy who is apparently Asian American, everyone in the illustration is a white dude (see the color photo section).

Even when I tried to "Netflix and chill," the barbecue-related slights continued. First up was the series *Ugly Delicious*, produced by Chef David Chang and Peter Meehan. I didn't watch the episodes in order, and I started with the one on fried chicken. It wasn't perfect, but I was extremely pleased with how deftly and honestly they talked about food and race. Next, I watched the barbecue episode. After watching the show, I only remembered seeing some African Americans relishing barbecue in a cameo during the opening credits. The narrative, after visually feasting on some barbecue traditions around the globe, featured few Black people in the United States.[25]

I had a similar reaction watching *Barbecue*, a 2018 James Beard Award–winning film that explores barbecue traditions around the world. The visually stunning film opens with scenes of Black South Africans and white South Africans having a *braii* in separate venues—a nice balance in storytelling. Much later in the film, Texas is designated as the representative place to tell the U.S. barbecue story. The film's segment is deeply immersed in white, rural Texan culture to create context for the story. Viewers see people shooting firearms, then attending a rodeo where the announcer speaks of God, military service, and patriotism. Of the ten or so people who get on-air speaking time, the only African American is Robert Patillo, mentioned in chapter 6.[26]

I'm not going to lie. Once I started paying attention, consuming barbecue-related media since 2000 has left me with a bad case of heartburn. It has been as if I was looking lovingly at a salivating platter full of the very best barbecue from every corner of the nation, and someone came in and drowned everything by pouring a bucket of Alabama white sauce all over it.

So, what's the big deal, you may ask? Why can't I just eat some barbecue without getting so hung up on race? My reasons are twofold, and conveniently, Charlie Vergos, the Greek American owner of the legendary Rendezvous Restaurant in Memphis, Tennessee, summed them up during an interview for a 2004 barbecue documentary called *Smokestack Lightning*:

> I knew as a kid that I'd see them cook it, but it never entered my mind that later on in life that I would get into that type of thing. When I used to go home, I used to go by a certain area, and there was a fellow that had a drum. That's where I learned to be honest with you. A Black feller had a drum. I would bring a six pack with me, I'd bring something from the package store. It's 2 o'clock in the morning. I'd stop there, I'd eat barbecue, and he showed me. He taught me as much and more than anybody I know. . . . To be honest with you, it don't belong to the white folks. It belongs to the Black folks. It's their way of life, it was their way of cooking. They put it together, it was their way, they created it, they done it, we took it and we made more money out of it than they did. I hate to say it, but that's a true story. All we done was pick somebody's ideas up, and put it to work, and we made money out of it. I'm proud of the fact, and I appreciate those fellas, you know, whoever they were, wherever they are now, for showing me those things and helping me do what I did.[27]

Quite simply, while barbecue remains extremely popular and profitable, I want African American barbecuers properly acknowledged, celebrated for their contributions, and sharing in the barbecue prosperity. It's not something that has to happen at the expense of others who enjoy making barbecue. Just like those barbecues described in the nineteenth century, there's plenty of room at the long tables for everyone.

To round out the collective barbecue meal presented in this book, let me offer a couple of essential, barbecue-meal-ending-the-right-way-kind-of-dessert recipes. The banana pudding comes from my late mother, Johnetta Miller, and the peach cobbler recipe belongs to a rising baking celebrity named Vallery Lomas who is a recovering attorney just like me.

RECIPES

Johnetta Miller's Banana Pudding

This is the dessert that my late mother, Johnetta Miller, made. She liked to chill her mixer beaters in the freezer before using them to whip the pudding's topping; she said it helped create a stiffer meringue. And she liked to bake the pudding in a clear dish, to show off the layers. The custard is pretty sweet when you use a full cup of sugar, less so when you use ¾ cup. *Make ahead*: If you're making this more than a few hours in advance, assemble the banana pudding without its meringue, cover, and refrigerate for up to one day. Bring it to a cool room temperature while the oven is preheating and you're making the meringue.

Makes 12 servings

For the pudding
¾–1 cup sugar
½ cup all-purpose flour
½ teaspoon salt
4 cups whole milk
4 large egg yolks
2 teaspoons vanilla extract
1 (11-ounce) box vanilla wafers
Flesh of 8 fairly firm bananas, peeled and cut crosswise into slices
    (your choice of thickness)

For the topping
4 large egg whites
½ teaspoon cream of tartar
½ cup sugar

TO MAKE THE PUDDING

1. Heat a few inches of water in a medium saucepan over medium-high heat.
2. Fill a heatproof bowl with the sugar (to taste), flour, and salt, then place it on top of the saucepan so that it fits snugly. Reduce the heat to medium, and pour in the milk. Cook, whisking constantly, so that the mixture becomes well combined and smooth.
3. Lightly beat the egg yolks in a liquid measuring cup. Whisk a few tablespoons of the hot milk mixture into them (to temper them), then whisk that egg mixture into the heated bowl. Cook for a

few minutes, whisking, until slightly thickened, then remove the bowl from the heat. Stir in the vanilla extract. This is your custard, which will thicken further as it cools yet will still be pourable.

4. Preheat the oven to 350°. Have a 9 × 13-inch baking dish at hand; make sure it's at least 2 inches deep.

TO MAKE THE TOPPING

1. Combine the egg whites and the cream of tartar in the bowl of a stand mixer or handheld mixer; beat on low, then medium-high speed, until frothy.
2. On medium-high speed, gradually add the sugar to form a meringue that holds stiff peaks.

TO ASSEMBLE

1. Create a single layer of vanilla wafers in the bottom of the baking dish. Use half of the sliced bananas to create a layer covering the wafers. Spread half of the custard over the bananas. Repeat those three layers, ending with the custard.
2. Spread the meringue topping so that it covers the custard entirely; swirl it decoratively to make it look nice. Bake on a rack in the center of the oven for 15 minutes or until the meringue is lightly browned in spots.
3. Let cool completely, then refrigerate (with a tent of foil over the top that does not touch the meringue) for at least 2 hours or until well chilled. Serve.

Vallery Lomas's Peach Cobbler

If you love to bake and you haven't heard about Vallery Lomas, you need to correct that situation as soon as possible. Lomas won Season 3 of ABC's *Great American Baking Show*. Unfortunately, after a few episodes aired, the remainder of the season was canceled because sexual harassment allegations surfaced against one of the show's celebrity judges. Lomas didn't get her time to shine before a worldwide audience, but she's turning lemons into lemon curd. She graciously gave me this elegant peach cobbler recipe that you'll surely enjoy.

Makes one 9 × 13-inch cobbler (12 servings)

For the crust
3¾ cups all-purpose flour
4 teaspoons sugar
1½ teaspoons kosher salt
3 sticks (1½ cups) cold unsalted butter, cut into 1-inch pieces
¾ cup plus 1–2 tablespoons cold water

For the filling
3 (29-ounce) cans sliced or halved peaches in heavy syrup
⅓ cup sugar
¼ cup all-purpose flour
3 tablespoons lemon juice (juice from 1 large lemon)
1 tablespoon grated lemon zest (zest from 1 large lemon)
2 teaspoons vanilla extract
½ teaspoon ground nutmeg
½ teaspoon kosher salt

For assembly
2 tablespoons all-purpose flour
2 tablespoons sugar, divided
3 tablespoons unsalted butter, cut into ½-inch pieces
½ teaspoon ground cinnamon
1 egg, any size

TO PREPARE THE CRUST

1. Whisk the flour, sugar, and salt together in a large bowl. Add the butter and use a pastry cutter or a food processor to cut the butter into the flour, until the mixture resembles split peas and no large clumps of butter remain.
2. Add ¾ cup of the water and stir or pulse until most of the flour is moistened and the mixture resembles cottage cheese; add the rest of the water as needed.

3. Tip the contents onto a clean work surface, knead a few times, and then gather into a large disk.

4. Wrap the disk in plastic and refrigerate for at least 2 hours. (The dough can be prepared up to 3 days in advance, stored in the refrigerator.)

TO PREPARE THE FILLING

1. Drain the canned peaches and place them in a large bowl.

2. Stir in the sugar, flour, lemon juice, lemon zest, vanilla, nutmeg, and salt.

TO ASSEMBLE

1. Preheat the oven to 400° and place a rack in the center of the oven. Remove the dough from the refrigerator. Use a knife to cut the disk into 2 pieces—one about ⅔ of the mass, the other ⅓ of the mass. Working swiftly, roll the larger piece of dough ¼ inch thick and fit it in a 9 × 13-inch baking pan, pressing it in the bottom and up the sides (you may have some dough left over). Roll the second piece of dough to a 10 × 14-inch rectangle. Place that dough on a parchment-lined baking sheet (this will become the top layer of the cobbler), and refrigerate it while assembling the rest of the cobbler.

2. Sprinkle the flour and 1 tablespoon of the sugar in the bottom of the cobbler crust. Pour in the peach filling (and any accumulated syrup) into the bottom of the dough-lined baking pan. Arrange the pieces of butter on top of the peaches in an even layer.

3. Remove the top layer of pie dough from the refrigerator. Place it on top of the peaches and crimp the edges of the dough by folding them over and pinching them together. Whisk the egg with a teaspoon of water and brush the egg wash evenly over the crust. Cut 4 slits in each quadrant of the cobbler and an "X" in the middle so that the steam can vent (this will keep the cobbler from becoming too liquidy).

4. Combine the remaining tablespoon of sugar with the ground cinnamon and sprinkle over the crust. Bake for 40–50 minutes, until the crust is browned all over and juices from the cobbler are bubbling up through the vents.

5. Remove the cobbler from the oven and let it cool slightly before serving. (The longer the cobbler cools, the more the filling will thicken.)

10

GLOWING EMBERS
THE FUTURE OF AFRICAN AMERICAN BARBECUE

[I have a] whole lot of hope in barbecue. It's not going anywhere. I'm starting to see things like Barbecue Nation, Barbecue Season, you know, Barbecue Remixes on Underground CDs, you know, you see this kind of thing and—and people are saying more and more about barbecue. And if you go to your local hardware store, chances are there's a barbecue grill somewhere out front for sale. And it's all over the place. You can't—can't live without it.
—Rodney Scott, 2012 oral history interview

I started thinking about the appropriate theme music for this concluding chapter. In the 1980s, former Dallas Cowboys football player–cum–sports announcer "Dandy" Don Meredith serenaded me and others watching the end of a *Monday Night Football* broadcast with the lyrics, "Turn out the lights, the party's over. They say, all good things must come to an end." That's too corny. Perhaps a medley of Boyz II Men's "End of the Road" and their remake of "It's So Hard, to Say Goodbye." Those are too sad.

This send-off is with an eye toward the future or, at least, possible futures for African American barbecue culture. Fortunately, the brother or sister making backyard, parking lot, roadside, or sidewalk barbecue isn't going away. The culture's too strong. What we need up in here is a D.J. to mix songs like Montell Jordan's "This Is How We Do It" and Sister Sledge's disco anthem "We Are Family."

What are the options? Those who choose barbecue as a profession must navigate a stratified barbecue market. John Shelton Reed lays out a great roadmap of the current state and the commercial contours of barbecue. The three prominent forms are folk barbecue, haute barbecue, and mass barbecue. Reed further defines: "*Folk barbecue* is tradition-driven, geographically specific, and diverse. Different locales have different menus, each with few choices. *Haute barbecue* is chef-driven, reflecting the tastes and interests of individual cooks. Some choose to adhere to local traditions and (as they see it) perfect them; others express themselves with innovative departures from tradition. Different establishments have different menus, perhaps changing often. *Mass barbecue* is market-driven, seeking the broadest possible appeal and geographical uniformity. Ideally, in this model, there will be one menu with many choices, the same everywhere."[1] At this point, most African American barbecuers fall into the folk barbecue category and will probably remain there by being unapologetically Black by clinging to their traditional aesthetic.

Brent and Juan Reaves, co-owners of Smokey John's Bar-B-Que in Dallas, Texas, seemingly agree with this, but they gave a scintillating spin in a *Racist Sandwich* podcast interview:

> In the Black communities, they're not worried about Pecan Lodge [a white-run barbecue establishment] because their customer base, they're not the ones going to Pecan Lodge ... that's not their market. I do think that it's affected their ability to get recognized in magazines and countdown lists ... but the core of their community is not driven by that. What we've learned is that, if you're built off a PR machine, if you're not staying on the absolute top of your game, you're gonna be gone, you're not going to make it. Whereas, we've figured out kind of what our niche is. I think a lot of the Dallas, old-school barbecue places, they know who their market is. They don't care about those other people. Their price point is different, their market's different, their approach is different. They may not get the recognition, but I don't think that it's affected their business.[2]

It does raise an interesting question that possibly undercuts the entire rationale of this book: If Black barbecue restaurateurs and their customers don't care about the lack of recognition, why should I? First, I know that many care because a bevy of Black barbecue people have griped to me about it and they're thrilled that I'm writing this book. Second, white barbecuers, with a combination of hustle and privilege, have shown new possibilities in the world of barbecue, so why be complacent?

There's tremendous opportunity for entrepreneurs should they pursue any type of barbecue vibe they want—mom and pop, streetside, church, haute, or even mass barbecue. Yet barbecue people must learn from the past to be poised for future success. They can do this by: protecting their intellectual property, getting adequate capital, networking to build relationships that could pay dividends in the future (for example, joining a chamber of commerce and going to its events), creating and implementing a profitable business model, forming a team of

IN THE SMOKE WITH RODNEY SCOTT
CHANGING THE BARBECUE GAME

To me barbecue is a calling of a reunion, a party for everybody to come and join in and enjoy each other's company and — and just a laid-back event, as well as a business. — Rodney Scott, 2012

"Quiet cooks."[1] That's how Rodney Scott once described people in Hemingway, South Carolina, who were good cooks but unknown outside of that community. For a time, that label might have been applied to Scott himself, but no more. He's one of the hottest names in barbecue, and he's been on an extended winning streak that includes winning the James Beard Foundation Award for Best Chef of the Southeast in 2018. This made him only the second barbecue specialist, besides Aaron Franklin, to win a coveted regional chef award. Scott models what it's likely going to take for an ambitious African American barbecuer to excel: he's good at what he does, he's networked, and he's got people who believe in him and they have deep pockets.

In 1972, his father, Roosevelt "Rosie" Scott, opened a combination convenience store and gas station in Hemingway when Scott was a year old. Whole hog barbecue was eventually added to the menu, and Scott's Bar-B-Que was born. Scott barbecued his first pig when he was eleven. His first cooking performance portended a bright future: "Well, my dad gave me an option: if I wanted to go to this basketball game that was that day that I had to cook the hog first. And he had the hog set up for me and he left, not — not knowing that somebody was actually, you know, watching over what I was doing. And he told me what to do and I kept everything going all day. And when they flipped the hog over it was just where it needed to be — perfect."[2] Clearly, all those years of watching and working with his dad, and his mom, Ella, had paid off. By the time he was seventeen, Scott felt that he could run the family business on his own.

Everything on the production side of the family's roadside stand in Hemingway screams "local." The hogs are from a farmer an hour

1. Fertel, "Interview: Rodney Scott," 7.

2. Fertel, 7.

246

Rodney Scott, Charleston, South Carolina.
Photograph by Andrew Thomas Lee.

away. Much of the hickory, oak, and pecan wood used is donated by neighbors. It's a different case when it comes to customers. Thanks to some favorable press in national media, people from around the world descend on the place seeking great barbecue. In fact, Scott said that the family restaurant was the kind of place "where a lot of people just stop by even when there was no barbecue available, they'd stop by and talk. Tell me about that. It seems to be this kind of meeting place, this rallying point."[3] So many people from different walks of life are showing an interest in whole hog barbecue that Scott's wondered aloud if "pork is the new beef."[4]

In July 2016, he started a new chapter and opened Rodney Scott's Whole Hog BBQ, his own venture in Charleston, South Carolina. It's certainly a leap to venture out on one's own, but this was a calculated game. For years, people had trekked from Charleston to his family's restaurant in Hemingway. I should know. I was one of them in 2015 when I was in town for a retreat. I had previously had Scott's barbecue at a Southern Foodways Alliance symposium, and this time I brought some professional colleagues along. We were very fortunate that we got the last of the whole hog barbecue while standing in line: a mix of all parts of the pig—the belly, hams, and shoulder—doused in a spicy barbecue sauce. Scott once described it by saying, "The sauce is vinegar and pepper based which is pretty common here in the South Carolina Pee Dee region and we use ground red pepper in it, vinegar, love, lemons, some more love, and we put it on the stove and stir the love."[5]

Speaking of love, Scott certainly has it for whole hog cooking. To hear him speak of his craft, his virtuosity is apparent: where to place and level the burning wood, why one checks the color of the belly

3. Fertel, 56.
4. Fertel, 27.
5. Fertel, 53.

and spareribs, the tenderest part of the hog, to make sure the hog is cooking correctly, and how vinegar is the best fire extinguisher a pitmaster could have. I really respect the old-school vibe he brings, even if in an urban context. He's also in the rarified air where he travels internationally to demonstrate barbecue. In recent years, his itinerary has included stops in Australia, Belize, France, St. Lucia, and Uruguay. But let's get back to matters of home.

Scott's Charleston restaurant differs from the Hemingway restaurant in many respects. It's fancier and hipper with lots of varnished wood, bright colors, and wall-length photographs of Scott in action. The menu is expansive. In Hemingway, barbecue was either sold as sandwiches or sold by the pound. On the Charleston restaurant menu, the whole hog keeps company with other items such as catfish, chicken, pork spareribs, salads, and turkey. There are also soul food side dishes and banana pudding for dessert. There are even pork cracklings sold by the bag at the counter. The day I interviewed Scott and dined there, it bustled more than usual due to a surprise guest. Senator Kamala Harris of California included the restaurant on her presidential campaign trail stop in South Carolina. As a former White House staffer, I know good campaign staff work when I see it.

As I savored the fantastic food, I glimpsed a possible future for Black barbecuers. "This must be what it's like when an entrepreneur has adequate capital and mentoring," I thought. Through events at the Charleston Food and Wine Festival, the Southern Foodways Alliance, and beyond, Scott ran in the right circles and forged a strong relationship with Nick Pihakis. Pihakis owns a restaurant group that includes the thriving Jim 'n' Nick's Community Barbecue restaurant chain. With Pihakis's help, Scott eyes expansion. He's already got a second location in Birmingham, Alabama, and another in the works for Atlanta, Georgia.

In addition to the restaurants and the accolades, Scott's legacy may be somewhat intangible. As he put it, "Getting the James Beard Award was an inspiration to others. African American entrepreneurs look at [my example] and think 'I can do this.'" Of course, rising to the top brings out the haters and other adversities, but I have no doubt that Scott will persevere. It reminds me of what he said about barbecue pit fires—proof that you have to go through something in order to know your true purpose: "We have had pit fires. . . . You can't—you can't get past it until you've had a fire. It's like riding a motorcycle. Once you fall, you know you can ride. Once you burn a building down, you know you can cook a hog."[6]

6. Fertel, 45–46.

business advisers to navigate what it takes to operate a business, being active on social media, being good at running a business, and most important, making next-level barbecue. In the twenty-first century, being good at cooking gets you far, but it's not always enough to thrive.

I think of places like Gatlin's BBQ in Houston, where Greg Gatlin hired Chef Michelle Wallace, someone with fine dining experience, to join his staff. They have a section of the kitchen that they call the "innovation lab" where each comes up with mad-scientist-like barbecue creations. I can personally vouch for the smoked oxtail menudo: velvety pieces of meat in a spicy broth. Whew, chile! Cozy Corner Restaurant and Payne's Bar-B-Q in Memphis come to mind as examples of intergenerational staff, usually all family, holding barbecue to a high standard. I think about places like Everett and Jones in Oakland, California, and Hecky's in Evanston, Illinois, which have been in the barbecue game for decades. I was tremendously saddened to hear of Hecky Powell's death from a COVID-19-related illness as I was finishing this book. I also think of Bryan Furman in Atlanta and Savannah, Georgia, and Matt Horn in Oakland (whose barbecue I didn't get a chance to taste), but they portend a promising barbecue future.

It's also a time of innovation for barbecuers, just as their forebears have done in other centuries. Could barbecue's future be one like in *2001: A Space Odyssey*, where "barbecue" is a flavored paste scooped up with a small spoon? I sure hope not, but modernist chefs are certainly headed in that direction. I won't even go there with the "meat" shown in the movie *Soylent Green*. Barbecue technology has created an interesting present and near future. One can now print "meat" using a 3-D printer that combines chemicals and amino acids in the right proportions. Meat can be grown in a test tube that, aside from questions of taste, is the nutritional equivalent of the real thing. Meat substitutes and alternatives are more prevalent. Toriano Gordon of Vegan Mob in the Bay Area has people lined up for his plant-based barbecue. The Seasoned Vegan in Harlem cuts and cook lotus root to resemble rib tips dipped in a sweet sauce. All of this makes me wonder: Will Black folks one day munch on "Impossible" ribs? I just don't know.

I began this book with a plea for more recognition of African American barbecuers. Will this plea go unanswered? I think things are improving. In print media, more and more people writing about barbecue are consciously shining a spotlight on African Americans. As I was wrapping up this manuscript, *BBQ Brawl*, the Food Network's latest competition show (surprise!), featured two African American contestants (Kevin Bludso and Phil Johnson). I've been to their wonderful,

IN THE SMOKE WITH CHEF KENNY GILBERT
BARBECUE INNOVATOR

"I'm a beast in the kitchen."

I had never heard anyone describe themselves that way until I heard Chef Kenny Gilbert confidently say it during an interview on *Top Chef*, Season 7: *Washington*. Gilbert didn't win the competition, but he had an impressive run. The second surprising thing he said a few years later was that he was going to create a new Florida regional barbecue style. At first, I thought this was contrary to the hip-hop group TLC's advice, "Don't go chasing waterfalls, please stick to the rivers, lakes, and swamps that you're used to" kind of stuff. Then I thought, "Why not?" With all the artifice permeating barbecue these days, a brother should do what he's gotta do. I've been thinking of doing the same for Denver, something based on bison or lamb. Unlike me, when Gilbert thinks of barbecue proteins, he's got his mind on the sea, not the land. This new style would be anchored by fish and alligator. Yes, that's right, alligator. More on that later.

Florida is Gilbert's adopted home. He grew up in the suburbs of Cleveland, Ohio, where his dad was an accomplished barbecuer. Gilbert's website biography shows his father's influence. "Kenny's father, an avid BBQ man, schooled him in the ways of the grill, including homemade sauces and rubs, presenting him with his very own small Weber at the age of seven."[1] Rather than barbecue in the backyard, Gilbert says, "My dad would leave the house and go to one of our city parks. He would cook pork shoulder blade and ribs." On the holidays, the park's grills were first-come-first-served. The cooking progressed in sequence with hot dogs, hamburgers, chicken, ribs, and then steaks. Their sides were baked beans, a mayonnaise-based coleslaw, potato salad, collard greens, butter beans, and field peas. In fact, Gilbert endeared himself to Oprah Winfrey when he made some crowder peas. Those were favored by Winfrey's father. Gilbert has cooked several private meals for Winfrey, including Thanksgiving.

After graduating from the Pennsylvania Culinary Institute, Gilbert began his career in Jacksonville, Florida. By the age of twenty-

1. Chef Kenny Gilbert website.

Chef Kenny Gilbert, Jacksonville, Florida.
Photograph by Agnes Lopez.

three, he became the chef de cuisine at the Ritz-Carlton Hotel on Amelia Island, Florida. He left that position to pursue other fine dining opportunities around the country, and he returned to Fernandina Beach in northern Florida in 2015 to open a concept called Gilbert's Underground Kitchen. Barbecue wasn't on the menu when the restaurant first opened, but Gilbert tested market demand with some barbecue pop-ups in the restaurant's parking lot when festivals happened nearby. Gilbert was thinking about giving up on barbecue when another chef in the area encouraged him to try again. It was well-timed encouragement. At the next pop-up, Gilbert sold three thousand dollars' worth of product in three hours.

Since there was no other barbecue restaurant on the island, the Underground Kitchen became his testing ground for Florida barbecue. Gilbert tells me that he doesn't think Florida has ever had a distinct identity for barbecue. "So many people don't even think that Florida is part of the South anymore. That may be true for the southern points like Fort Lauderdale and Miami, but it's different in the panhandle." In 2018, Gilbert elaborated on his vision in a local magazine article:

"I wanted to take the idea of BBQ and make it my own." Tailoring his offerings to the unique micro-cultures immediately surrounding each restaurant, Chef Gilbert takes the connection between BBQ and its sense of place to another level. "Smoking seafood is BBQ," Kenny argues. "You're smoking mullet, amberjack, smoked shrimp, smoked oysters, scallops. Smoked seafood is really Florida." And why stop at smoking seafood? How about reptiles? That's right, Chef Gilbert has been known to smoke entire 40 to 50-pound alligators for eight hours until the meat falls apart like pulled pork. . . . Kenny admits that this idea isn't new. Native Timucua and Seminole tribes were roasting whole alligators over wood fires long before the first cows and pigs ever even touched their hooves on American soil.[2]

This certainly begs the question, "What would an inclusive Florida barbecue menu look like?"

Gilbert did his best to answer that question when I dined at his restaurant in late February 2019. The meat selection was alligator ribs, andouille sausage, beef brisket, burnt ends, jerk chicken, pork spareribs, pulled pork, and a turkey drumstick. The side dishes were baked beans, Brussels sprouts, collard greens, field peas, potato salad, and slightly sweet rolls. Though it wasn't served to me that day, Gilbert would certainly add frog legs to the larder. All of it was excellent, and the alligator ribs were a standout. Gilbert was spot on when he rhetorically asked me, "What if a chicken and a grouper [fish] had a baby?" I don't think much about interspecies sex, but the results in this case were good. The meat was moist and dusted with some Cajun seasoning. Gilbert's mustard sauce really gave the gator some zip, probably because it included bits of charred jalapeño. As for the sides, I could see why Oprah loved those crowder peas. Braised until there was just a little bite, the earthy peas really hit the spot.

Another thing that I loved about the Underground Kitchen was its strong embrace of Kool-Aid culture. While growing up in the Cleveland area, Gilbert's family always had Kool-Aid in the kitchen. His mom let the kids pick the flavor. Gilbert strongly feels that there's nothing more southern than eating fried chicken and a biscuit and washing it all down with Kool-Aid. Gilbert showed his entrepreneurial skills as a child by selling "chilly cups," a Dixie cup that was filled with Kool-Aid, frozen, and then sold on warm-weather days for anywhere from twenty-five cents to a dollar based on the cup's size. In the restaurant, one employee gets the privilege of deciding the Kool-Aid flavor of the day, and they are encouraged to experiment by mixing flavors. It's a real mixed bag in terms of what one gets. The grape-lemonade mix that I got was just okay.

When I think of what it takes to create a regional barbecue style, it seems that Gilbert has created a functional set of building blocks. The local meats are alligator sourced from farms in Florida, Georgia, and South Carolina, as well as plentiful seafood from the ocean and the region's waterways. Those meats are smoked with native oak and

2. Twachtman, "Bold Bites."

pecan wood. He's developed distinctive barbecue mops and sauces using local fruit and chiles like the datil pepper. I don't think side dishes are as much of a requirement as they were years ago, and Gilbert hasn't created anything truly distinctive. I could see the sides I mentioned being served in any contemporary barbecue restaurant, which leads to the pivotal point: it can only become a regional style if other restaurants and perhaps home cooks in the area follow his lead. That hasn't happened yet.

Gilbert had planned to open a wood-fired-fare restaurant in Raleigh, North Carolina, in the spring of 2020, but the COVID-19 pandemic ended that pursuit, as well as the Underground Kitchen. He remains in the Jacksonville, Florida, area working on a cookbook, a new restaurant concept tied to the forthcoming cookbook, a line of seasoning products, and a barbecue sauce line. Despite the curveballs that he's been thrown, Gilbert offers an inspiring blueprint for how other Black barbecue entrepreneurs can innovate and prosper.

IN THE SMOKE WITH ED AND RYAN MITCHELL
NORTH CAROLINA BARBECUE'S DYNAMIC DUO

The work, the effort, the culture, the history, and the love is where the skills are. You can hide behind the recipes. People ask me about recipes all the time. My recipe is the love of the game.
—Ryan Mitchell, November 2019

Ed Mitchell has been barbecuing since he was fourteen years old, when his father made him help with some whole hog cooking in rural North Carolina. This basic training came in handy years later when he visited his mother, who ran a grocery store in Wilson, North Carolina. She was sad because her husband, Ed's father, had recently died and the business wasn't doing too well. He shared this moment in an oral history interview:

> So anyway, I was trying to cheer her up so I says, "Hmm, Mother, what are you cooking?" And what she was cooking was back there — she was — back there she was cooking some greens that, basically, was part of their dinner because they got there in the mornings and they stayed there all day, and so she was like preparing this lunch. And — and she was still in the same routine as if he were still living. And so I said, "Mother, what are you cooking?" And she says, "I'm cooking some greens." So I said, "Okay, what — what do you want to eat?" She said, "I don't know. I've got a taste for some old-fashioned barbecue." Well I knew what that meant because, as I said earlier, growing up all our lives on any celebration — it didn't make any difference what the celebration was — if it — if it was significant enough to be recognized, it had to be accompanied by barbecue. And that was the way things were — good times were synonymous with — with family gathering and cooking of barbecue and just having a good time.[1]

That simple request reignited a barbecue life previously interrupted by military service in Vietnam, a regional manager position at the

1. Evans, "Ed Mitchell," 5.

254

Ford Motor Company, a fledgling real estate practice, and a manager's position in North Carolina state government.

What turned out to be a special treat for his mother caught the attention of some of the grocery store's customers. Eventually, the grocery store stopped selling groceries and focused exclusively on barbecue. Mitchell did a decent job of cooking a pig, but he knew that he needed more knowledge to take his barbecuing to the next level. As a twist of fate, Mitchell's kindness to a notable barbecue cook named Jim Kirby, after several bad hands of poker, was repaid with Kirby's commitment to mentor Mitchell. Thanks to Kirby's tutelage, word of Mitchell's whole hog cooking prowess spread. He became one of the most recognizable barbecue cooks, not only in North Carolina, but across the country.

I first had Ed Mitchell's food at the 2002 Southern Foodways Alliance symposium on barbecue in Oxford, Mississippi. It was extraordinary, and unlike anything that I had experienced before. I'd heard much about whole hog cooking, but I expected it to be a vinegary mess. That wasn't the case. The meat was tender, slightly sweet, slightly smoky, and plentiful. It made me wonder how many people would forgo an experience like this because they had eaten so many bad representations of North Carolina barbecue.

Mitchell has done a lot of high-profile barbecues, especially multiyear stints at the Big Apple Barbecue Block Party, which New

York City hosted from 2002 to 2018. One year, Mitchell astonished the other barbecue cooks by cooking thirty whole hogs in one weekend! As they watched Mitchell doing his thing, many were terrified that the entire set-up would be engulfed in flames. Fortunately for them, Mitchell knew what he was doing. Mitchell even beat the Food Network's Bobby Flay in a 2009 throwdown. He's also been involved in a number of business ventures with varying degrees of success. Mitchell remains undaunted, and he may finally have the big break that he's been awaiting. His son Ryan is now actively engaged in his father's barbecue endeavors.

Getting Ryan involved took some convincing. Like many of his generation, Ryan didn't see much return on investment for all the hard work involved with making good barbecue. Ryan already earned some business chops with Credit Suisse working on retail transactions, commercial loans, and credit default swaps. His interest piqued when he noticed the good press his dad got and that what his dad did was "cool."

When I jointly interviewed the father-and-son team in their unfinished Raleigh restaurant, Ed Mitchell described how one conversation went after a particularly good article ran in a local publication:

> Ryan: "Dad, did you see that article?"
> Ed: "Yeah, I saw it."
> Ryan: "Daggone, man, we need to do something about that."
> Ed: "Okay, what are *you* going to do?"
> Ryan: "I'd like to be the guy who owns several of these restaurants."

This was music to his father's ears. Ed Mitchell had previously thought about expanding his operations, but he didn't think that he could duplicate this process anyplace else unless he was physically there to oversee everything. Ryan is helping his dad think about replication and expansion.

I was impressed with Ryan's keen sense of where he fits into his family's entrepreneurial legacy:

> My grandfather didn't care if he only made a dollar. He didn't care about winning or losing. He just wanted to wake up in the morning saying I don't have to answer to a white man. I don't have to hear "N word do this" or "N word to that." I can call my own shots.
> My father comes along and my uncles come along, and they are a little more motivated. For them, it was about the pride of being

an entrepreneur. Then I come along, and I wonder about how to take it to the next level. I had to combine the pride of being an entrepreneur and see the disconnect with my generation. We need to understand that these dudes are getting major coins in this industry off things that we created. It just doesn't happen in music. It doesn't just happen in entertainment and film. It also happens in food and beverage.

Ryan went on to describe how many his age have only negative opinions of the food and beverage industry. They think of the "Colored Only" signs and the years of menial labor they performed without making much money and getting much credit. The African American success stories in this sector of the economy are unknown to them. Ryan and his father hope that by putting more positive information out about what can be accomplished, more African Americans may enter the barbecue field and dream big.

Though nothing is ever certain, the Mitchells have a real chance to pull this off. They have a big money investor who's all in for the next restaurant in Raleigh. The COVID-19 pandemic delayed the initial opening, but the restaurant is scheduled to open in summer 2021. They hope to source the restaurant with heritage-breed pigs raised by local farmers, so that today's diners may get an idea of what barbecue was like a century ago. Everything else about their business plans are forward looking, including selling barbecue online through a company called Potbelly.com. They're looking into a line of barbecue sauces that will target the health and wellness market rather than fighting for a sliver of the crowded space on your typical grocery store shelves. A school to teach whole hog cooking the old-fashioned way is in the works. Ed Mitchell is even thinking about an apparel line that trades off his rural denim-overalls-and-dark-blue-ball-cap vibe. Ed Mitchell wore a ball cap the morning I interviewed him that pretty much summed up his back to the future approach: "PITMASTER: Return BBQ to Its Roots."

respective restaurants in Los Angeles, California (Bludso's Bar & Que), and Phoenix, Arizona (Trapp Haus BBQ). I'm also grateful that Howard Conyers, based in New Orleans, and Michael Twitty, based in Washington, D.C., continue their demonstrations to educate people about respective African American barbecue traditions in the Carolinas and in the antebellum South. Rodney Scott, a prominent whole hog barbecue artist, has a cookbook on the way, ending a embarrassingly long publishing drought for Black barbecue experts.

I am personally involved in making the Barbecue Hall of Fame more inclusive. To the Hall's credit, they invited me to join its board in 2019 after I wrote that critical opinion piece in the *Kansas City Star*. Many of the members shared my concerns, and they realized that it was time for reform. I certainly can't take credit for the diverse induction classes of recent years, but I am glad to be a part of it now. The Hall also acted on my idea of releasing the names of all the final nominees so that, even if they weren't inducted, they could still be recognized for their achievement in the world of barbecue. I'm also working with my fellow board members to create a diverse Hall in a very short time frame, especially by honoring barbecuers who practiced their art generations ago.

The burning question is whether African American barbecuers can adapt to the shifting terrain that's pushing them to the margins, the huge curveball thrown by the COVID-19 pandemic, and the cascading rejuvenation of the Black Lives Matter movement triggered by another string of murders of unarmed African Americans by the police and private citizens. Fortunately, several African American barbecuers are changing the game just as the rules are being rewritten: Ed and Ryan Mitchell (making "back to the future" barbecue), Chef Kenny Gilbert (creating a new regional style), and Rodney Scott (visionary expansion).

RECIPES

Chef Kenny Gilbert's Alligator Ribs

"Alligator tastes like a free-range chicken and a fish had a baby. There's a slight poultry flavor and texture with a hint of a meaty grouper taste.

"Growing up in Florida, I heard stories of my uncle Frank, my mom's brother, wrestling gators for a show as a teen. Fried gator tail was a delicacy in that household, and for a period of time, my grandma kept a pet alligator in the shed. When I was older, there was even a small gator in the pond at the center of my condo's development. He didn't bother anybody. You'd see him sunbathing or sometimes his head would pop up while he was wading around.

"I started preparing alligator ribs several years ago when I was the chef of the Grill Room at the Ritz-Carlton, Amelia Island in Florida because I wanted to serve something that was local and distinctive to the region. So I called my vendor at the time, Gary's Seafood out of Orlando, and I asked if they had anything different. When he told me they had alligator ribs, I was like, 'I'll take 20 pounds!'

"Now I buy my alligator ribs from Cypress Creek Farms, out of Starke, Florida, where they've been raising alligators indoors since 1988. They harvest the gators at 6 feet long, and their ribs are 14–16 ounces per slab. (They barely shrink when they cook.) It's a combination smoking and braising approach, and the results are magical—tender and full of flavor."

Makes 4–6 servings

1 cup yellow mustard
1 cup brown mustard
1 cup Creole mustard
½ cup Dijon mustard
2 cups packed brown sugar
2 cups apple cider vinegar
½ cup lemon juice
½ cup lime juice
1 cup Worcestershire sauce (preferably Lea & Perrins)
¼ cup Chef Kenny's Fried Chicken Seasoning, or your favorite
    poultry seasoning
1 tablespoon crushed red pepper flakes
1 tablespoon ground cinnamon

4 (13–14-ounce) slabs alligator ribs, preferably from
    Cypress Creek Farms
Chef Kenny's Raging Cajun Spice mix, or your favorite Cajun
    seasoning
1 cup water

For the smoker
Charcoal
Pecan and oak wood

1. In a large bowl, combine the mustards, brown sugar, vinegar, lemon and lime juices, Worcestershire, chicken seasoning, red pepper flakes, and cinnamon. Mix well and set aside 1 cup for this recipe; store the rest in an airtight container in the refrigerator.
2. Preheat the smoker with charcoal and pecan and oak wood and bring it to approximately 300°.
3. Season the ribs with Raging Cajun Spice mix, then place them on the smoker and smoke for 2 hours. Add additional wood to keep the smoker at around 300°.
4. Preheat your oven to 400°.
5. Remove the ribs from the smoker and place them in a roasting pan. Mix 1 cup of the mustard barbecue sauce with the water and pour the mixture over the ribs. Cover the ribs with parchment paper and then with aluminum foil.
6. Bake at 400° for 1 hour and 15 minutes, or until a meat thermometer inserted in the thickest part of the ribs registers 165°. Remove and serve!

Variation: Add 1 pound of charred jalapeño chiles puréed with 1 cup of water to the combined mustard mixture.

Ed Mitchell's Mother's Whole Turkey Barbecue— Eastern North Carolina Style

Who better to make the transition from cooking whole hogs to whole turkeys than Ed Mitchell? It turns out that Mother knows best! In a 2011 blog post, meterologist Don Schwenneker featured Ed Mitchell's mother's whole turkey barbecue. Mitchell told him, "My mother developed this recipe for whole turkey barbecue many years ago so that our family members who did not eat pork could still enjoy great barbecue. It became so popular in our family that I started serving turkey barbecue in my restaurants and at events as well." Be mindful to adjust the amount of seasoning and cooking time if your turkey differs from the suggested size.

Makes 20 servings

1 (18–20-pound) turkey
1 cup apple cider vinegar
¼ cup crushed red pepper flakes
1 tablespoon salt
1 tablespoon black pepper
2 tablespoons sugar
¼ teaspoon cayenne pepper (optional)

For the grill
Charcoal or wood pieces

1. If you are using a direct-heat grill, place the charcoal or wood pieces in a rectangular pattern on the bottom of the grill that is large enough that the turkey can sit above the space in the rectangle.
2. Bring the temperature of your grill up to 250°–275°.
3. Split or butterfly the turkey, but keep it attached at the breastbone.
4. Lay the turkey out, skin side up, on the grill over the rectangle of charcoal or wood pieces.
5. Cover the grill and roast for 2 hours, then flip so that it sits skin side down, and roast for another 45–60 minutes.
6. While the turkey is cooking, combine the remaining ingredients in a bowl and set the spicy vinegar mixture aside.
7. Once the turkey is cooked to your preference, take it off the grill and remove the skin and bones, making sure to remove all the small bones.
8. Chop or pull the turkey, according to your preference.
9. Add the spicy vinegar mixture to the meat and mix by hand.
10. Once the ingredients are well blended, serve in potato buns with coleslaw.

TENDING THE FIRE

This celebration is finished, and it's time to push back from this generous feast of African American barbecue history. I am blessed to be able to recover the stories laid out in this book—but I could do that only because, at some point, someone else thought it was important to tell these stories in the first place. I believe that many more stories about barbecue—barbecue and more—will be told.

We're an enslaved woman buying her freedom with barbecue,
We're an enslaved man running a takeout barbecue business from
    his cabin,
We barbecued to resist oppression,
We're barbecue's best ambassadors,
We're a Chris Rock character asking, "How much for one rib?"
We're champions when the barbecue playing field is leveled,
We're barbecue's mad scientists, making a smoker out of a file
    cabinet or even a toilet,
We're offering a free foot massage with your takeout barbecue
    order,
We're craftspeople,
We're folk artists,
We're barbecue royalty,
We're *Black Smoke*.

MY FAVORITE AFRICAN AMERICAN BARBECUE RESTAURANTS

I know that everyone is going to ask, so I figure that I might as well name them!

MID-ATLANTIC
Texas 202 Barbeque of Maryland, Brandywine, Maryland

MIDWEST
Ashley's Bar-B-Que, Milwaukee, Wisconsin
Gates Bar-B-Q, multiple locations in the Kansas City, Missouri, area
LC's Bar-B-Q, Kansas City, Missouri
Q's Tips & Wings, Chicago, Illinois (my twin sister, April, seconds this choice!)

SOUTH
Backyard BBQ Pit, Durham, North Carolina
The Bar-B-Q Shop, Memphis, Tennessee
Cozy Corner Restaurant, Memphis, Tennessee
Dreamland Bar-B-Que, multiple locations in Alabama
Grady's Bar-B-Q, Dudley, North Carolina
Jenkins Quality Barbecue, multiple locations in Jacksonville, Florida
Payne's Bar-B-Q, Memphis, Tennessee
Rodney Scott's Whole Hog BBQ, Charleston, South Carolina

TEXAS
Burns Original BBQ, Houston, Texas
Fargo's Pit BBQ, Bryan, Texas
Patillo's Bar-B-Que Restaurant, Beaumont, Texas
Ray's BBQ Shack, Houston, Texas

WEST
Bludso's Bar & Que, Los Angeles, California
Lil' Red Jamaican BBQ and Soul Cuisine, Seattle, Washington
West Alley BBQ & Smokehouse, Chandler, Arizona

Before you head to one of these places, please check to see if they're open . . . and tell them that I sent you!

ACKNOWLEDGMENTS

I have so many to thank for helping with this process. Foremost are all of my "barbecue research assistants," who helped me eat my way through the country: Lynn Bell, Jennifer Biggs, Richard Booth and Lauren Byrne, Tim Carman, Katy and Josh Carpman, Bill Chaney, Ardie Davis (for an epic KC barbecue tour as well!), Kathy Dixon, Laura Chi Hood and her daughter Piper, Ashley Dior-Thomas, Charla Draper, Chef Valerie Erwin, Fitz and Deb Freeman, Dwight Fryer, Eddie Gehman Koman, Peter Gibbons and family (Kate and Andrew), Matt and Karissa Gottlieb, Gary Guesnier, Eden Hagos, Peter Hairston, David and Rebecca Harris, Tara Holeman, her husband, Eric, and son, Adam, Chef Raymond Jackson, Leina Johannsen and her daughter Liora, Kirk Johnson and Chase Deforest, Marcus Jones, Prof. Betcy Jose, Ahsahn Kahn, Angie King Keesee, Leslie Kelly, Prof. Chris Laurent, Carroll Leggett, Jeff Mazique, Dave Mekeel, Rev. Russell Meyers, Michael Miller, my twin sister, April Miller-Cook, and brother-in-law Stanley Cook, Maneesha Mithal, Jennifer Montague and her family, Jennifer Marie Moore, Chef Lamar Moore, Jeremy, Kevin, and Rosy Murphy, Robin Nagel and her family (Jan, Cole, and Willow), Andrew Newman, Terri Ngyuen, Chef Paul Osher and friends, Talisha Padgett-Matthews, Hanna and Kenny Raskin, Naben Ruthnum, Kevin Schuyler, Jarice Shaw, Jonathan Shaw, Joyce Shaw, Jill Silva, Jeff and Rachel Sopha, Rev. Dr. Jack Sullivan, Kyle Sutton, Jim Vitol, Dylan and Sophia Walker, Anthony Wood, Kendee Yamaguchi, and Joe York.

Thanks to all who gave me shelter: Eric Ames, Don Graves and Melissa Tessmer Graves, and April Miller-Cook and my brother-in-law, Stanley.

I heavily relied on the resources and staff of several institutions, especially the Denver Public Library, Johnson and Wales University–Denver Campus (Merrie Valliant and Victoria Westpawl), and the University of Denver's Special Collections Department staff.

For helping improve and pull together this manuscript, much thanks to the late Kelly Bates for her heroic amount of help, Mary Caviness of UNC Press for doing far more than she should have had to, as well as Suzanne Fass, Jason Gelender, Carrie Hale, Ernest House, Kirk Johnson, Patrick Malloy, Debra Meyer, Miriam Rubin, Merv Tano, and my anonymous reviewers.

Thanks to my interns Clarke Jackson (Spelman College) and Miles Francisco (University of Oklahoma) for research help.

Thanks to the following people for letting me bend their ears: Jim Auchmutey, Howard Conyers, John T. Edge, Jessica B. Harris, Joseph Haynes, Mike Johnston (Savory Spice Company), Carroll Leggett, Wayne Lohman, Angie Mosier, Robert F. Moss, John Shelton Reed, J. C. Reid, Chef Todd Richards, Melvin Simmons, Michael Twitty, Daniel Vaughn, and Eric Vernor.

Thanks to Elaine Maisner and the University of North Carolina Press for believing in me and for being so enthusiastic about this project. I am happy to acknowledge the support of the funders who created the Marcie Cohen Ferris and William R. Ferris Imprint at UNC Press.

As always, I thank God for the gift of writing and the opportunity to share and savor the history of my people with others.

NOTES

CHAPTER 1

1. Warnes, *Savage Barbecue*, 15.

2. Warnes, 15.

3. Essig, *Lesser Beasts*, 126–27.

4. Warnes, *Savage Barbecue*, 25.

5. Haynes, *Virginia Barbecue*, 54.

6. Warnes, *Savage Barbecue*, 78; Haynes also notes that the English also called these cooking frames "hurdles." *Virginia Barbecue*, 44.

7. Swanton, *The Indians*, 369.

8. Swanton, 369.

9. Haynes, *Virginia Barbecue*, 67.

10. Milanich, "Devil in the Details," 30–31.

11. Algren, *America Eats*, 7–8.

12. Quoted in Milanich, "Devil in the Details," 30–31.

13. Gibbons, *Indian Recipes*, n.p.

14. Black and Thorn, "Hunter-Gatherer Earth Ovens," 205.

15. Deutsch and Elias, *Barbecue*, 57.

16. Haynes, *Virginia Barbecue*, 78.

17. Haynes, 80.

18. Haynes, 80.

19. Stavely and Fitzgerald, *America's Founding Food*, 78.

20. *Indian Cook Book*, 9.

21. Hendrix, *Traditional Cherokee Food*, 36.

22. Rountree, "Uses of Domesticated Animals."

23. Swanton, *The Indians*, 374.

24. Haynes, *Virginia Barbecue*, 57.

25. Haynes, 124–25.

26. McClusky, "Grilling over Gas."

27. *Oxford English Dictionary*, s.v. "gridiron."

28. Warnes, *Savage Barbecue*, 86.

29. Day, "Over a Red-Hot Stove," 55–56.

30. Day, 64.

31. John L. Heaton, "John Bull's Xmas Roast," *Topeka State Journal*, Dec. 25, 1890, 7.

32. "England."

33. "Colonial Policy, British."

34. Dippie, "American Indians."

35. Klein, *Anglicanism*, 299.

36. Klein, 313.

37. Klein, 314.

38. Shefveland, "Indian Enslavement."

39. Haynes, *Virginia Barbecue*, 143.

40. Shefveland, "Indian Enslavement."

41. Workers of the Writers Program, *The Negro in Virginia*, 10.

42. Walsh, *Barbecue Crossroads*, 117.

43. Albala, "What Does Barbecue Tell Us About Race?"

44. Koch et al., "Earth Systems Impact," 16–17, 21.

45. Coward, *Indians Illustrated*, 182.

46. Phippen, "Kill Every Buffalo You Can!"

47. Phippen.

48. "Ribs on Stakes," *New York Times*, July 23, 1886, 2.

49. "American Indian Records in the National Archives."

50. *New York Sun*, June 13, 1894, 6.

51. *New York Times*, Nov. 17, 1907, 8.

52. Everett, "Indian Territory."

53. Reese, "Freedmen."

54. "Afro-American Cullings," *Pittsburgh Courier*, Nov. 11, 1911, 7.

55. John B. Foresman, "Oklahoma Indians Mark 100-Year Progress of Five Civilized Tribes," *Christian Science Monitor*, Oct. 29, 1948, 9.

56. Zobel, "Hog Heaven," 59–60.

57. Haynes, *Virginia Barbecue*, 91–92.

58. "The Indian Territory," *Boulder County Courier*, Sept. 27, 1878, 2.

CHAPTER 2

1. A term for false information coined by culinary historian Andrew F. Smith.

2. Berlin, *Making of African America*, 73.

3. Osseo-Asare, *Food Culture*, 28.

4. Harris, *Beyond Gumbo*, 11.

5. Opie, *Hog and Hominy*, 24; Opie, *Zora Neale Hurston on Florida Food*.

6. Twitty, "Colonial Roots of Southern Barbecue."

7. Osseo-Asare, *Food Culture*, 28; Bascom, "Yoruba Cooking," 126.

8. Brace, *Evolution in an Anthropological View*, 195.

9. Lewicki, *West African Food*, 7.

10. Lewicki, 79–104.

11. Lewicki, 205.

12. Lewicki, 208.

13. Lewicki, 208.

14. Lewicki, 209.

15. Ayensu, *West African Cooking*, 58.

16. Osseo-Asare, *Food Culture*, 27.

17. Kemble, *Journal of a Residence*, 235.

18. Kemble, 237.

19. Baëta, *Ghana Cookbook*, 74.

20. Thiam, *Yolele!*, 24.

21. Osseo-Asare, *Food Culture*, xv.

22. Harris, *Beyond Gumbo*, 9.

23. Adrian Miller, *Soul Food*, 12.

24. Opie, *Hog and Hominy*, 23.

25. Haynes, *Virginia Barbecue*, 108–12.

26. Berlin, *Making of African America*, 104.

27. Audubon, "Kentucky Barbecue."

28. Editor and McTyeire, "Plantation Life," 360.

29. Wiggins, *O Freedom!*, 28; "Uncle Willis Anderson," 22.

30. Editor and McTyeire, "Plantation Life," 360.

31. Abrahams, *Singing the Master*, 259.

32. "Negro Barbecues," *Weekly Standard*, Aug. 25, 1858, 4.

33. Jones, "Miss Effie Cowan," 2132–33.

34. Osburn, "Ellen Bettis," 272.

35. Alexander, *Reminiscences*, 235.

36. McCulloch-Williams, *Dishes and Beverages*, 273–74.

37. Jordan, *White over Black*, 116.

38. Bowden, "Lewis Johnson," 350.

39. "Burning of Negroes," *Boston Weekly Messenger*, July 29, 1830, 3.

40. "Nat Turner's Insurrection," 173.

41. "Slave Insurrection in Southampton County," *Workingman's Advocate* (New York), Oct. 15, 1831, 1.

42. *Negro in Virginia*, 198–201.

43. "Slave Insurrection."

44. "Slave Troubles in Tennessee," *Buffalo (N.Y.) Daily Republic*, Dec. 26, 1856, 2.

45. Holmes and Montgomery, "Ex-Slave, Amite County," 1556–57.

46. Shelby, "Jeff Davis," 420.

47. Creel, "Joseph William Carter," 47–48.

48. "A Celebration," *National Era* (Washington, D.C.), Aug. 5, 1852.

49. Wiggins, *O Freedom!*, xx.

50. "New Year's Day in Port Royal, South Carolina," *Christian Recorder*, Jan. 17, 1863, n.p.

51. "Juneteenth" (Waymarking .com).

52. "Juneteenth."

53. Wiggins, *O Freedom!*, 81.

54. "The Barbecue," *Macon (Ga.) Telegraph and Messenger*, Oct. 4, 1884, 2.

55. *Daily Phoenix* (Columbia, S.C.), June 17, 1869.

56. "The Beard of an Oyster," *Atlanta Constitution*, July 7, 1888, 4.

57. "Colored Conservatism," *Brownlow's Knoxville Whig*, Sept. 2, 1868, 1.

58. "African Democracy," *Chicago Tribune*, Aug. 15, 1868, 2.

59. "The Debt Repudiators Beaten," *New York Times*, Nov. 5, 1879, 5.

60. Berger, "How They Killed Civil Rights."

61. Blight, *Race and Reunion*, 108.

62. Equal Justice Initiative, *Lynching in America*.

63. Equal Justice Initiative.

64. Watkins, *On the Real Side*, 82–83.

65. Tipton-Martin, *Jemima Code*, 2.

66. "Barbecue Man Known Here Invents Lightning Device," *Daily Chronicle* (Columbia, S.C.), June 15, 1931, 1.

67. "News of the Cafes," *Los Angeles Times*, July 20, 1928, A10.

68. "Living: Regional Food."

CHAPTER 3

1. Micah 6:6–8, *New International Version Holy Bible*.

2. "Actress-Evangelist Returns," *Cleveland Call and Post*, Feb. 9, 1939, 1.

3. "Evangelist," *Chicago Defender*, July 4, 1936, 19.

4. Ken Jessamy, "Baptist Ministers Would Oust Rev. Settle: Use of Actress-Evangelist Scorned by Local Minsters," *Cleveland Call and Post*, Mar. 2, 1939, 1.

5. "Easter Reed," 505.

6. Ferry, "Boar's Head," 253–54.

7. Olsen Faulkner et al., *When I Was Comin' Up*, 65.

8. Wiggins, *O Freedom!*, 28.

9. Daris E. Saunders, "Heritage of Cooking Series: Country Recipes from the Carolinas," *Oakland (Calif.) Post*, Sept. 19, 1978, 6.

10. McCune, "Slave Narrative of Jasper Battle."

11. Foreman, "Walter Leggett," 2320.

12. "Robert Shepherd," 253.

13. Loguen, *Rev. J. W. Loguen*, 105.

14. Pratt, *Radical Hospitality*, x.

15. Du Bois, "The Negro Church," 201.

16. "Examining the Role of the Black Preacher."

17. Garner, *North Carolina Barbecue*, 5–6.

18. Stubb's Legendary Kitchen, *Stubb's Bar-B-Q Cookbook*, ix.

19. Stubb's Legendary Kitchen, ix.

20. Doris Funnye Innis, "The Church Dinner: A Harlem Tradition," *New York Times*, Aug. 26, 1981, C1.

21. Lawrence, "Chapter 57."

22. "Barbecue," *News and Observer* (Raleigh, N.C.), Apr. 12, 1959, 20.

23. Beverly Beyette, "The Struggle to Save Harriet Tubman's Church," *Los Angeles Times*, Sept. 22, 1983, G1.

24. Kathleen Hendrix, "Ministering on the Front Line: In Watts, the New Beginning Storefront Church Offers Hope, Comfort to Those Facing Hard Times," *Los Angeles Times*, Mar. 11, 1992, E1.

25. "Colored Christian Church," *Hopkinsville Kentuckian*, July 7, 1899, 5.

26. "Church Barbecue," *Washington Times*, Nov. 9, 1898, 6.

27. "Barbecue for a Church," *New York Times*, Oct. 1, 1896, 9.

28. "Young Films King Spot at Aleck's Barbecue Heaven," *Atlanta Daily World*, Dec. 19, 1985.

29. "Young Films King Spot."

30. Charles Perry, "Mt. Hermon's Ribs Take the Hungry and Make 'Em Believers," *Los Angeles Times*, Apr. 2, 1989, FW114.

31. Perry, FW114.

32. Engelhardt, *Republic of Barbecue*, 32.

33. Williams, "Black-Owned Businesses."

CHAPTER 4

1. "The Union Party in Kentucky," *Cincinnati Daily Gazette*, Aug. 3, 1868.

2. "Barbecues and Burgoo-Making," *Louisville Courier Journal*, Nov. 15, 1896.

3. "Taft to Deny All Cabinet Stories," *St. Louis Globe-Democrat*, Jan. 10, 1909.

4. Pierson, *In the Brush*, 93.

5. Pierson, 95.

6. "Down in Old Virginia," *Chicago Tribune*, Oct. 19, 1889.

7. Schlichting and Noel, "Ill Smelling Bones," 13.

8. Jane Eddington, "'New' Barbecue Is Really Old as the Hills," *Chicago Tribune*, June 23, 1928.

9. J. Frank Dobie, "Barbecue's a Natural for Political Races," *Austin American-Statesman*, Feb. 3, 1952.

10. Vaughn, "What Should We Call the Barbecue Greats?"

11. *Testimony Taken by the Joint Select Committee*, 403–7.

12. "KKK Is Near Fizzle When Negro Chef Balks," *Port Arthur (Tex.) News*, Aug. 12, 1922, 1.

13. "Aged Negro Pays No Poll Tax," *Richmond (Va.) Times-Dispatch*, Apr. 22, 1906, E8.

14. A. C. Kinard, "The Barbecue Feature," *Columbia (S.C.) Record*, July 30, 1912, 3.

15. A. W. Parke, "Arkansas Moves to Aid Politicians; No Longer Will Candidates Have to Pay for Unlimited Barbecues," *New York Times*, July 22, 1934, E7.

16. Parke, E7.

17. "Telegraphic Summary, Etc.," *Baltimore Sun*, July 28, 1882, 1.

18. "Barbecue Artist Is Here," *Charleston News*, June 30, 1909, 9.

19. "Barbecue Artist Is Here," 9.

20. "At Stone Mountain," *Atlanta Constitution*, June 12, 1890, 4.

21. Moss, *History of Barbecue*, 56.

22. Daniel Hayes Bomar, "Kentucky Barbecues," *Louisville Courier-Journal*, Oct. 31, 1897, 3:1.

23. Andrew Hamilton, "He's the Kingpin of Barbecue Men," *Saturday Evening Post*, Apr. 21, 1956, 49, 84.

24. Zanger, "African American Food," 10–11.

25. Jones and Vaughn, *Whole Hog BBQ*, 2.

26. Reed and Reed, *Holy Smoke*, 32–33.

27. Tolbert, *Bowl of Red*, 156.

28. "The Cozy Corner," *Roswell (N.Mex.) Daily Record*, Jan. 15, 1930, 2.

CHAPTER 5

1. Egypt, "Cornelia," 285–86.

2. "To the Military and Citizens of Alexandria and Its Vicinity," *Alexandria (Va.) Times*, June 30, 1798, n.p.

3. Jones and Vaughan, *Whole Hog BBQ*, 22–23.

4. Work, "The Negro in Business Enterprise," 304.

5. Work, 306.

6. Pillsbury, *Geography*, 13; Tim Miller, *Barbecue: A History*, 80.

7. *Texas: A Guide to the Lone Star State*, 98.

8. Pickering, "Green, Harry S."

9. Olson, "Harry Green."

10. Worgul, *Grand Barbecue*, 17.

11. Worgul, 17.

12. "In King Barbecue's Court," *Kansas City (Mo.) Star*, Jan. 17, 1911, 14.

13. "In King Barbecue's Court," 14.

14. Green, "Brief History."

15. History.com editors, "Great Migration."

16. Walker, "Jones Bar-B-Q Diner."

17. "Life in the 'Promised Land,'" 2.

18. "Life in the 'Promised Land,'" 2.

19. "Life in the 'Promised Land,'" 2–3.

20. "Life in the 'Promised Land,'" 3.

21. "Barbecue Invades Baltimore, Called Breach States Rights," *Baltimore Afro-American*, Nov. 26, 1927, 10.

22. "Barbecue Invades Baltimore," 10.

23. "Germ Dealers Imperil Health on South Side," *Chicago Defender*, June 3, 1922, 3.

24. "Place Dixie Eat Shops in Main Streets," *Chicago Defender*, Oct. 22, 1921, 1.

25. "Germ Dealers Imperil Health."

26. Dorothy Beaver, "Food along the Highroad," *New York Times*, July 14, 1935, SM14.

27. McGill, "What's Wrong," 102.

28. Joffe, *Some Food Patterns of Negroes*, 18.

29. Joffe, 14.

30. Fondevila, "Goodwill."

31. Pierce, *Negro Business*, 186.

32. *Topeka Plaindealer*, May 2, 1919, 2.

33. "Pickets Call Negro Cafe Segregated," *Sacramento Bee*, Aug. 21, 1962, 10.

34. Johnson, *Patterns of Negro Segregation*, 9–10.

35. Johnson, 11.

36. Lee, "A Vast Wealth Gap," 83.

37. Tracy Jan, "Redlining Was Banned 50 Years Ago; It's Still Hurting Minorities Today," *Washington Post*, Mar. 28, 2018.

38. Gatlin, communication with author.

39. Carter, "Negro Main Street," 236.

40. DeBerry, "Rise of Entrepreneurial Hotbeds."

41. Sances and You, "Who Pays for Government?"

42. Michael J. Clark, "Arundel Orders Dixie Pig to Shut Down," *Baltimore Sun*, Apr. 12, 1984, D5.

43. Korfhage, "Snoop Dogg's Uncle Blames Racism."

44. Pang, "Chicago Is a City Divided by Barbecue."

45. Judy Pasternak, "It's the Pits, Say Barbecue Owners of AQMD Action," *Los Angeles Times*, Feb. 18, 1992, A1.

46. Weitz, "Why Minorities Have So Much Trouble."

47. Weitz.

48. Williams, "Black-Owned Businesses."

49. Perkins, "Does Detroit's Food Revival Leave the City's Black Residents Behind?"

50. "Tar Heel of the Week," *News and Observer* (Raleigh, N.C.), Aug. 1, 1954, 3.

51. Staten and Johnson, *Real Barbecue*, 45.

52. Moss, *History of Barbecue*, 34.

53. "Africans Started Beauty Business," *Baltimore Afro-American*, Sept. 17, 1932, 19.

54. Pierce, *Negro Business*, 185–86.

55. Glassner, "Where Is the World's Best Barbecue?," 19.

56. Maclin, "Changing Landscape of Mid-South Barbecue," 110.

57. Sandra Haggerty, "Avoid Old Stereotypes? Some Are Fun," *Philadelphia Inquirer*, Feb. 1, 1970, 107.

CHAPTER 6

1. Reed and Reed, *Holy Smoke*, 57.

2. Smith, "Rhetoric of Barbecue," 61.

3. Twitty, "Colonial Roots of Southern Barbecue."

4. John and Mawadza, *Hausa-English/English-Hausa Dictionary*, 110.

5. Newman, *Hausa-English Dictionary*, 12, 71, 135.

6. Seale, *Barbeque'n*, 2.

7. Seale, 4–5.

8. Newman, *Hausa-English Dictionary*, 12.

9. Seale, *Barbeque'n*, 1.

10. Reed and Reed, *Holy Smoke*, 19.

11. *Garnett (Kans.) Journal*, June 25, 1881, 3.

12. Hayes, *Black American Travel Guide*, 253.

13. Tymas, *Soul Cooking*, 7.

14. Smith, "Thomas Cole," 788.

15. Halliburton, *Red over Black*, 176–77.

16. Katherine Calos, "Tours Recall Mount Vernon's Other Residents," *Tampa Tribune*, Apr. 23, 1995, Travel-9.

17. "For Men Only," *Emporia (Kans.) Gazette*, Jan. 3, 1928, 2.

18. Roy Harvey, "Price of Rib Tips Causing a Crisis," *Chicago Defender*, Mar. 31, 1979.

19. Cusick, "Chicago Style," 41–42.

20. "Eating Like Soul Brothers."

21. Reed and Reed, *Holy Smoke*, 118.

22. Berry, *Kentucky Barbecue Book*, 175.

23. "Uncle Hemp," 87.

24. Snyder, "How Chicken Sausage Links Became a Centerpiece."

25. Blaise and Bender, *Burnt Legend*.

26. Bolois, "Most Underrated BBQ in Kansas City."

27. "The Cue of Success for Greeley—Lager and a German Barbecue," *New York Herald*, June 18, 1872, 6.

28. Vaughn, "Grease Balls of Southeast Texas."

29. Pinkard, "Juneteenth."

30. Reed, *Barbecue*, 45.

31. Moss, "Now's the Time."

32. Reed, *Barbecue*, 45.

33. Stern and Stern, *Roadfood*, 127.

34. Stern and Stern, 127.

35. Stern and Stern, 127.

36. Kruse, "Chains Talk Turkey to Consumers."

37. Fertel, "Interview: Frank and Eric Vernon."

38. August Loeb, "In Harlem New Frontiers Await the Gourmet," *New York Times*, Jan. 8, 1939, 110.

39. "A Southern Barbecue," *Streator (Ill.) Free Press*, Aug. 26, 1887, 4.

40. Jeffries, *Soul Food Cook Book*, 51.

41. Boyer, "Interview with Alex Bufford."

42. Zeratsky, "How Can Bread Be Labeled."

CHAPTER 7

1. Tolbert, *Bowl of Red*, 158.

2. *Southern Barbecued Everything.*

3. Pinkard, "Juneteenth," 12.

4. Kail, *Meat, Fire, Wood*, n.p.

5. Harris, *Beyond Gumbo*, 16–17.

6. Nabhan, "From Coa to Barbacoa to Barbecue," viii.

7. Albala, *Cooking in Europe*, 14.

8. Reed and Reed, *Holy Smoke*, 25.

9. The Browns, *Outdoor Cooking*, 200–201.

10. Albala, *Cooking in Europe*, 14.

11. Reed and Reed, *Holy Smoke*, 31–32.

12. Perry, *Texas*, 116.

13. Alpern, "European Introduction," 27.

14. "The Richmond Barbecue Club," *Torch Light and Public Advertiser* (Hagerstown, Md.), Oct. 1, 1829, 1.

15. Genovese, *Roll, Jordan, Roll*, 542.

16. Tate, *American Slave*, 334.

17. Diouf, *Slavery's Exiles*, 302.

18. Fox-Genovese, *Within the Plantation Household*, 190.

19. "Dining with Uncle Sprig," *Hartford Courant*, July 12, 1888, 7.

20. McCulloch-Williams, *Dishes and Beverages*, 274.

21. Hoyt Alden, "No Off-Season in Outdoor Cooking," *St. Louis Post-Dispatch*, Sept. 5, 1968, 5F.

22. Hoyt Alden, "'Dipney'—

Ancestor of Barbecue Sauce," *Morning Call* (Allentown, Pa.), June 14, 1957, 8.

23. Alden, "No Off-Season in Outdoor Cooking."

24. Hill, *Mrs. Hill's New Cook Book*, 140.

25. *Mission Cook Book*, 32.

26. Mason, *Onje Fun Orisa*, 17.

27. Smith, *Pure Ketchup*, 19.

28. Smith, *Tomato in America*, 178.

29. "Tomato Catsup," *Edgefield (S.C.) Advertiser*, Oct. 21, 1857, 2.

30. "The Plantation Barbecues," *Charleston Mercury*, July 12, 1860, 4.

31. "An Old Fashioned Barbecue," *Atlanta Constitution*, July 1, 1888, 14.

32. Gladwell, "Ketchup Conundrum."

33. Perry, "A Mystery Begins."

34. Worgul, *Grand Barbecue*, 20.

35. "Alexander's Sauce," *Fort Scott (Kans.) Tribune and Daily Monitor*, June 10, 1921, 4.

36. Puckett, *Eat Drink Delta*.

37. *Kansas City (Mo.) Sun*, Mar. 7, 1914, 1.

38. *Franklin's Paper the Statesman* (Denver, Colo.), July 3, 1909, 5.

39. "Big Emancipation Celebration," *Bryan (Tex.) Daily Eagle and Pilot*, June 19, 1909, 3.

40. Loeb, "In Harlem."

41. George Palmer, "Tavern Topic," *New York Amsterdam News*, June 17, 1944, 9B.

42. McDonald, "Salonnière 100."

43. DeKnight, *Date with a Dish*, 139.

CHAPTER 8

1. "Texas Editors Meet in Waco," *Fort Worth Record-Telegram*, Dec. 11, 1927, 9; "Hoffmanettes to Add Dance Party to Editors' Fete," *Waco (Tex.) News-Tribune*, Dec. 11, 1927, 1; "Texas Newspaper Men Will Participate in Barbecue Contest Exhibits," *Waco (Tex.) News-Tribune*, Dec. 4, 1927, 8; "Editors Elect '28 Officers Monday," *Waco (Tex.) News-Tribune*, Dec. 13, 1927, 8.

2. Walsh, "Texas Barbecue in Black and White," 49.

3. Walsh, 48.

4. Goldwyn, "Don't Try to Cook."

5. Patt Johnson, "Texas-Style Barbecue Eatery Opens in Waukee," *Des Moines Register*, Mar. 31, 2016.

6. Wells, *Barbecue Greats, Memphis Style*, xv.

7. Wells, 150.

8. "Only Men Can Compete in This Contest," *Washington Post*, Sept. 19, 1963, D5.

9. Knauth, "Roast That Got the Judges Off the Hook."

10. "Cookout Chefs Compete for Big Cash Awards," *Chicago Defender*, Apr. 14, 1965, 23.

11. "Illinois Cookout Champion Named," *Chicago Defender*, Apr. 1, 1965, 22.

12. "Vote for Best Ribs," *Cleveland Call and Post*, Sept. 13, 1984, 1A.

13. *Cleveland Plain Dealer*, Aug. 8, 1986, 26.

14. William R. Wood, "Barbecue Madness Prevails at Annual Rib Burn-Off," *Cleveland Call and Post*, July 28, 1983, 4B.

15. Wood, 4B.

16. "The History."

17. Mike Royko, "A Painful Report on Ribfest 1985," *Chicago Tribune*, Sept. 24, 1985.

18. Fuhrman, "Barbecue Bonanza."

19. Fuhrman, "A New Spin on Barbecue," 43.

20. Fuhrman, 44.

21. Fuhrman, 40–41.

22. Min, "Brisket Prices Soar."

CHAPTER 9

1. Johnston and Baumann, *Foodies*, x.

2. Trillin, *Tummy Trilogy*, ix–x.

3. Trillin, "No!," 208.

4. Tolbert, *Bowl of Red*, 158–59.

5. Reid, "Barbecue Lists Are Wildly Popular."

6. Smith, "Barbecue."

7. Walsh, "Texas Barbecue," 55–56.

8. "Food Network Heats Up Grill."

9. Metzger and Recht, *BBQ with Bobby Flay*.

10. Fuhrman, "Barbecue Trends."

11. Vaughn, "What Should We Call the Barbecue Greats?"

12. Vaughn.

13. Kardon, "Within Our Shores," 24.

14. Kardon, 24.

15. Kardon, 24.

16. Ocejo, "On His Book."

17. Lauren Michele Jackson, "White Lies of Craft Culture."

18. Jackson.

19. Bacon, "Great American Art of Pit Barbecue," 29.

20. Kovacik, "Eating Out."

21. "Henry Ford."

22. "Guy Fieri."

23. "Johnny Trigg."

24. Adrian Miller, "It's Time to Diversify Kansas City's Barbecue Hall of Fame," *Kansas City (Mo.) Star*, July 8, 2018.

25. Zeldes, *Ugly Delicious*.

26. Salleh, *Barbecue*.

27. Bransten, *Smokestack Lightning*.

CHAPTER 10

1. Reed, "Mass Barbecue Is the Invasive Species."

2. "Episode 58: Erasing Black Barbecue."

BIBLIOGRAPHY

AUDIOVISUAL MATERIALS

"Best in Smoke—Full Cast & Crew." IMDb.com. n.d. https://www.imdb.com/title/tt1927244/fullcredits?ref_=tt_cl_sm#cast.

Blaise, Cole, and Jonathan Bender, dirs. *Burnt Legend: The Story of Burnt Ends.* KCPT in partnership with Recommend Daily, 2016. 30 mins.

Bransten, David, dir. *Smokestack Lightning: A Day in the Life of Barbecue.* Produced by Lolis Eric Elie, 2001. 49 mins.

Brown, James. "It's a Man's, Man's, Man's World." Comp. James Brown and Betty Jean Newsome, 1966.

"Episode 58: Erasing Black Barbecue (w/ Johnny Walker, Adrian Miller, Daniel Vaughn, and Brent & Juan Reaves)." *Racist Sandwich*, podcast, Sept. 26, 2018. www.racistsandwich.com/episodes/2018/9/11/e58-erasing-black-barbecue-w-johnny-walker-adrian-miller-daniel-vaughn-and-brent-juan-reaves.

Metzger, Lauren, and Gordon Recht, dirs. *BBQ with Bobby Flay.* 55 episodes. Aired on Food Network, June 2, 2004–Oct. 29, 2007. https://www.foodnetwork.com/shows/bbq-with-bobby-flay.

Salleh, Matthew, dir. *Barbecue.* Gravitas Ventures, 2017. DVD, 121 min.

"SEC Traditions: Texas Barbecue with Big Moe Cason and Marty Smith." Academy Sports + Outdoors, Nov. 29, 2018. https://youtu.be/Fg6r8pUs7yU.

Southern Barbecued Everything. Season 1, episode 5, "Barbecue Time." Aired on Great American Country, 2014. https://www.greatamericancountry.com/shows/southern-barbecued-everything/episodes/100/barbecue-time.

Zeldes, Jason, dir. *Ugly Delicious.* 11 episodes. Netflix, 2018.

GOVERNMENT PUBLICATIONS

Bureau of Labor Statistics. "CPI Inflation Calculator." n.d. https://data.bls.gov/cgi-bin/cpicalc.pl.

Swanton, John R. *The Indians of the Southeastern United States.* Smithsonian Institution, Bureau of American Ethnology, Bulletin 137. Washington, D.C.: Government Printing Office, 1946.

U.S. House of Representatives. *Testimony Taken by the Joint Select Committee to Inquire into the Condition of Affairs in the Late Insurrectionary States.* Washington, D.C.: Government Printing Office, 1872.

NEWSPAPERS

Alexandria (Va.) Times

Morning Call (Allentown, Pa.)

Arkansas Gazette (Little Rock)

Atlanta Constitution

Atlanta Daily World

Atlanta Journal Constitution

Atlantic Monthly

Austin American-Statesman

Baltimore Afro-American

Baltimore Sun

Boston Globe

Boston Herald

Boston Journal

Boston Post

Boston Weekly Messenger

Boulder County (Colo.) Courier

Brooklyn Eagle

Brownlow's Knoxville Whig

Bryan (Tex.) Daily Eagle and Pilot

Buffalo (N.Y.) Daily Republic

Charleston Mercury

Charleston News

Chicago Defender

Chicago Tribune

Christian Recorder

Christian Science Monitor

Cincinnati Daily Gazette

Cleveland Call and Post

Cleveland Plain Dealer

Columbia Missourian (Columbia S.C.)

Council Grove (Kans.) Republican

Daily Chronicle (Columbia, S.C.)

Daily Oklahoman (Oklahoma City)

Daily Phoenix

Dallas Morning News

Denver Post

Denver Republican

Des Moines Register

Edgefield (S.C.) Advertiser

Emporia (Kans.) Gazette

Evansville Daily Journal

Evening Telegraph (Philadelphia)

Fort Scott (Kans.) Tribune and Daily
    Monitor

Fort Worth Record-Telegram

Frank Leslie's Illustrated Newspaper

Franklin's Paper the Statesman
    (Denver, Colo.)

Garnett (Kans.) Journal

Greeley (Colo.) Tribune

Hartford Courant

High Point (N.C.) Enterprise

Hopkinsville Kentuckian

Kansas City (Mo.) Star

Kansas City (Mo.) Sun

Leavenworth (Kans.) Post

Leavenworth (Kans.) Times

Littleton (Colo.) Independent

Los Angeles Times

Louisville Courier-Journal

Louisville Courier Journal Magazine

Macon (Ga.) Telegraph and Messenger

Montpelier (Vt.) Evening Argus

National Anti-Slavery Standard

National Era (Washington, D.C.)

National Town Courier

New Amsterdam News

New Journal and Guide

New York Amsterdam News

New York Herald

New York Sun

New York Times

New York Tribune

News and Observer (Raleigh, N.C.)

Oakland (Calif.) Post

Pacific Commercial Advertiser

Paducah (Ky.) Sun

Pensacola News

Philadelphia Inquirer

Pittsburgh Courier

Pittsburgh Press

Port Arthur (Tex.) News

Richmond (Va.) Times-Dispatch

Rocky Mountain Business Journal

Rocky Mountain News (Denver)

Roswell (N.Mex.) Daily Record

Sacramento Bee

Saturday Evening Post

Savannah Tribune

Seattle Times

St. Louis Globe-Democrat

St. Louis Post-Dispatch

Streator (Ill.) Free Press

Tacoma Times

Tampa Tribune

Topeka Plaindealer

Topeka State Journal

Torch Light and Public Advertiser
    (Hagerstown, Md.)

Waco (Tex.) News-Tribune

Washington Post
Washington Times
Weekly Arkansas Gazette (Little Rock)

Weekly Standard
Workingman's Advocate (New York)

ORAL HISTORY INTERVIEWS

Bowden, Bernice. "Ella Pittman." In *The American Slave: Arkansas Narratives*. Series 2, Vol. 10, Part 5, edited by George P. Rawick, 347–50. Westport, Conn.: Greenwood, 1972.

———. "Louis Johnson." In *The American Slave: Arkansas Narratives*. Vol. 2, Part 4, edited by George P. Rawick, 100–101. Westport, Conn.: Greenwood, 1972.

Boyer, Carl B. "Slave & Negro Lore." Vol. 10, Missouri Narratives. In *Slave Narratives: A Folk History of Slavery in the United States from Interviews with Former Slaves*, 70–72. Washington, D.C.: Library of Congress, 1941.

Cook, Iris. "The Story of Alex Woodson." In *The American Slave: The Indiana Narratives*. Vol. 6, edited by George P. Rawick, 214–17. Westport, Conn.: Greenwood, 1972.

Creel, Luana. "Joseph William Carter." In *The American Slave: Indiana Narratives*, edited by George P. Rawick, 43–49. Westport, Conn.: Greenwood, 1972.

Davis, Annie Ruth. "Sylvia Cannon." In *The American Slave: South Carolina Narratives*. Vol. 2, Part 1, edited by George P. Rawick, 187–95. Westport, Conn.: Greenwood, 1972.

Diard, Francois Ludgere. "Clara Davis." In *The American Slave: A Composite Autobiography*, edited by George P. Rawick, Ken Lawrence, and Jan Hillegas, 121. Westport, Conn.: Greenwood, 1977.

"Easter Reed." In *The American Slave: Georgia Narratives*. Supp. Ser., Vol. 4, Part 2, edited by George P. Rawick, 502–9. Westport, Conn.: Greenwood, 1972.

Egypt, Ophelia Settle. "Cornelia." In *Unwritten History of Slavery; Autobiographical Accounts of Negro Ex-Slaves*, edited by Ophelia Settle Egypt, J. Masouka, and Charles S. Johnson, Social Science Documents No. 1, 284–91. Nashville: Fisk University, Social Sciences Institute, 1945.

Evans, Amy. "Ed Mitchell." Sept. 5, 2007. https://www.southernfoodways.org/interview/mitchells-ribs-bar-b-q-chicken.

Fertel, Rien T. "Interview: Frank and Eric Vernon, The Bar-B-Q Shop, Memphis, Tenn., July 31, 2008." https://www.southernfoodways.org/interview/the-bar-b-q-shop/.

———. "Interview: Rodney Scott, Scott's Bar-B-Que, Hemingway, S.C., June 21, 2012." https://www.southernfoodways.org/interview/scotts-bar-b-que/.

Foreman, Heloise M. "Walter Leggett." *The American Slave: A Composite Autobiography*. Vol. 6, Part 5, edited by George P. Rawick, 2319–24. Westport, Conn.: Greenwood, 1974.

"George Fisher." In *The American Slave: Mississippi Narratives*. Supp. Series, Vol. 7, edited by George P. Rawick, 731. Westport, Conn.: Greenwood, 1977.

Graham, Charles. "Samuel S. Taylor." In *The American Slave: Arkansas Narratives*, edited by George P. Rawick, 67–69. Westport, Conn.: Greenwood, 1972.

Holmes, Mrs. Wm. F., and Laura Montgomery. "Ex-Slave, Amite County." In *The American Slave: Mississippi Narratives*. Supp. Ser. 1, Vol. 9, Part 4, edited by George P. Rawick, Jan Hillegas, and Ken Lawrence, 1550–59. Westport, Conn.: Greenwood, 1977.

———. "The Autobiography of Ann Drake, Pike County." In *The American Slave: Mississippi Narratives*. Supp. Ser. 1, Vol. 7, edited by George P. Rawick, Jan Hillegas, and Ken Lawrence, 642–52. Westport, Conn.: Greenwood, 1977.

"Jerry Boykins." In *The American Slave: Texas Narratives*. Vol. 16, Part 1, edited by George P. Rawick, 1121–24. Westport, Conn.: Greenwood, 1972.

Jones, P. W. Martha. "Miss Effie Cowan." *The American Slave: A Composite Biography*. Vol. 6, edited by George P. Rawick, 2130–34. Westport, Conn.: Greenwood, 1979.

McCune, Grace. "The Slave Narrative of Jasper Battle." n.d. https://access genealogy.com/georgia/slave-narrative-jasper-battle.htm.

Moore, Edith Wyatt. "Charlie Davenport, Ex-Slave." *The American Slave: Mississippi Narratives*. Vol. 7, edited by George P. Rawick, 558–72. Westport, Conn.: Greenwood, 1977.

"My Mother Was the Smartest Black Woman in Eden." In *The American Slave: Unwritten History of Slavery*. Vol. 18, edited by George P. Rawick, 283–303. Westport, Conn.: Greenwood, 1972.

Osburn, Lois. "Ellen Bettis." In *The American Slave: Texas Narratives*. Supp. Ser. 2, Vol. 2, Part 1, edited by George P. Rawick, 265–80. Westport, Conn.: Greenwood, 1941.

"Robert Shepherd." In *The American Slave: Georgia Narratives*. Vol. 13, Part 3, edited by George P. Rawick, 246–63. Westport, Conn.: Greenwood, 1979.

Shelby, Levi D., Jr. "Jeff Davis Used to Camouflage His Horse." In *The American Slave: Alabama Narratives*. Vol. 6, edited by George P. Rawick, 413–22. Westport, Conn.: Greenwood, 1972.

Smith, William E. "Thomas Cole." In *The American Slave: Texas Narratives*. Supp. Ser. 2, Vol. 3, Part 2, edited by George P. Rawick, 783–86. Westport, Conn.: Greenwood, 1941.

"Uncle Hemp." In *The American Slave: Mississippi Narratives*. Vol. 7, edited by George P. Rawick, 84–90. Westport, Conn.: Greenwood 1972.

"Uncle Willis Anderson." In *The American Slave: Texas Narratives*. Vol. 4, Part 1, edited by George P. Rawick, 21–24. Westport, Conn.: Greenwood, 1941.

SECONDARY SOURCES

Abrahams, Roger D. *Singing the Master: The Emergence of African-American Culture in the Plantation South*. New York: Penguin Books, 1994.

Adkins, Courtney. "Juneteenth in Louisiana: 'If I Found Out It Was a Holiday, I'd Try to Celebrate It.'" *Southern Folklore* 56, no. 3 (1999): 195–207.

Albala, Ken. *Cooking in Europe, 1250–1650*. Westport, Conn.: Greenwood, 2006.

Alexander, Dr. John Brevard. *Reminiscences of the Past Sixty Years*. Charlotte, N.C.: Ray Printing, 1908.

Algren, Nelson. *America Eats*. Iowa City: University of Iowa Press, 1992.

Alpern, Stanley B. "The European Introduction of Crops into West Africa in Precolonial Times." *History in Africa* 19 (1992): 13–43.

Anderson, A. A. *Experiences and Impressions: The Autobiography of Colonel A. A. Anderson.* New York: Macmillan, 1933.

Armbruster, Kurt E. *Before Seattle Rocked: A City and Its Music.* Seattle: University of Washington Press, 2011.

Auchmutey, Jim, and Susan Puckett. *The Ultimate Barbecue Sauce Cookbook.* Atlanta, Ga.: Longstreet Press, 1995.

Audubon, [James]. "Kentucky Barbecue on the Fourth of July." *Family Magazine,* June 1, 1837, 117.

Ayensu, Dinah Ameley. *The Art of West African Cooking.* New York: Doubleday, 1972.

Bacon, Josephine. "The Great American Art of Pit Barbecue Is Fast Disappearing." In *Disappearing Foods: Studies in Foods and Dishes at Risk: Proceedings of the Oxford Symposium on Food and Cookery, 1994,* edited by Harlan Walker, 24–29. Devon, U.K.: Prospect Books, 1995.

Baëta, Barbara, and Fran Osseo-Asare. *The Ghana Cookbook.* New York: Hippocrene Books, 2015.

Bascom, William. "Yoruba Cooking." *Africa: Journal of the International African Institute* 21, no. 2 (Apr. 1951): 125–37.

Bates-Tompkins, Angela. *Ernestine's Bar-B-Que Cook Book and Autobiography.* Bogue, Kans.: Nicodemus, 2001.

Bendele, Marvin C. "Barbacoa? The Curious Case of a Word." In *Republic of Barbecue,* edited by Elizabeth S. D. Englehardt, 88–90. Austin: University of Texas Press, 2009.

Berger, Morroe. "How They Killed Civil Rights." *New Leader* 32, no. 46 (1972): 7.

Bergman, Jolie Dawn. *Seattle's Music Venues.* Charleston, S.C.: Arcadia, 2013.

Berlin, Ira. *The Making of African America: The Four Great Migrations.* New York: Viking, 2010.

Berry, Wes. *The Kentucky Barbecue Book.* Lexington: University of Kentucky Press, 2015.

Bettridge, Jack, and Rick Browne. *Barbecue America: A Pilgrimage in Search of America's Best Barbecue.* Alexandria, Va.: Time-Life Books, 1999.

Black, Stephen L., and Alston V. Thorns. "Hunter-Gatherer Earth Ovens in the Archaeological Record: Fundamental Concepts." *American Antiquity* 79, no. 2 (April 2014): 204–26.

Blight, David W. *Race and Reunion: The Civil War in American Memory.* Cambridge, Mass.: Belknap Press of Harvard University Press, 2002.

Brace, C. Loring. *Evolution in an Anthropological View.* Walnut Creek, Calif.: AltaMira, 2000.

The Browns. *Outdoor Cooking.* New York: Greystone, 1940.

Bryan, Mrs. Lettice. *The Kentucky Housewife.* 1839. Facsimile ed. Bedford, Mass.: Applewood Books, 2001.

Carter, Wilmoth A. "Negro Main Street as a Symbol of Discrimination." *Phylon* 21, no. 3 (1960): 234–42.

Clemons, Bernice. "Marriages from 1764–1858 from the Myra McAlmont Vaucin Collection." *Grand Prairie Historical Society Bulletin*, Oct. 2001, 32–37.

Cody, William F. *Buffalo Bill's Life Story: An Autobiography*. 1879. Reprint. New York: SkyHorse, 2010.

Conrad, Horace. "The Health of the Negroes in the South: The Great Mortality among Them; The Causes and Remedies." *Sanitarian* 18 (June 1887): 502–10.

"Cooking Cattle Whole." *Savannah Tribune*, Oct. 24, 1908, 6.

Core, Dorothy J. "Mary John, a Remarkable Woman of Arkansas." *Grand Prairie Historical Society Bulletin* 12 (Oct. 1978): 16–19.

Cover, John W. "Arkansas County Census 1850." *Grand Prairie Historical Society Bulletin* 44 (April 2001): 46–52.

Covey, Eric. "Keep Your Eye on the Boll." In *Republic of Barbecue*, edited by Elizabeth S. D. Englehardt, 82–85. Austin: University of Texas Press, 2009.

Coward, John M. *Indians Illustrated: The Image of Native Americans in the Pictorial Press*. Urbana: University of Illinois Press, 2016.

"Culinary Novelty for Radio Stars." *Evening Telegraph* (Philadelphia), Oct. 21, 1948, 8B.

Cusick, Heidi Haughy. "Chicago Style: A Tale of Two Barbecues." *American Visions*, Aug./Sept. 1994, 40–42.

Dant, Sara. *Losing Eden: An Environmental History of the American West*. Malden, Mass.: John Wiley and Sons, 2016.

Day, Ivan P. *Cooking in Europe, 1650–1850*. Westport, Conn.: Greenwood, 2009.

———. "Ox Roasts: From Frost Friars to Mops." *Over a Red-Hot Stove: Essays in Early Cooking Technology*, edited by Ivan P. Day, 55–82. Blackawton, Totnes, Devon, England: Prospect Books, 2009.

DeKnight, Freda. *A Date with a Dish: A Cook Book of American Negro Recipes*. New York: Stratford, 1948.

Deutsch, Jonathan, and Megan J. Elias. *Barbecue: A Global History*. London: Reaktion Books, 2014.

Diouf, Sylviane A. *Slavery's Exiles: The Story of the American Maroons*. New York: New York University Press, 2014.

"Doc Hamilton." *Town Crier*, Mar. 26, 1932, 4.

Douelson, Barbara. "Dig-In, Missouri, to a . . . ." *Columbia Missourian*, Jan. 28, 1976, 16.

Dove, Laura. "Southern Barbecue." *On the Grill*, Aug./Sept. 1998, 32–35, 52–53.

Du Bois, W. E. B. *The Negro Church: Report of a Social Study Made under the Direction of Atlanta University; Together with the Proceedings of the Eighth Conference for the Study of the Negro Problems, Held at Atlanta University, May 26th, 1903*. Atlanta, Ga.: Atlanta University Press, 1903.

Dull, Henrietta Stanley. *Southern Cooking*. New York: Grosset and Dunlap, 1928.

"Eating Like Soul Brothers." *Time*, Jan. 24, 1969, 57.

Eaton, Dr. Rachel Caroline. "Social Economy among the American Indians." In *The Indian Cook Book*, 3–4. Tulsa: Indian Women's Club of Tulsa, Oklahoma, 1933.

Editor and H. N. McTyeire of Tennessee. "Art. XXIII.—Plantation Life—Duties and Responsibilities." *De Bow's Review and Industrial Resources, Statistics, Etc.* 29 (Sept. 1860): 357–68.

The 1887 Denver Directory. Vol. 3. Edited by Charles O. Brantigan and Nathan Zeschin. Denver: Canzona, 2002.

Elie, Lolis Eric. *Smokestack Lightning: Adventures in the Heart of Barbecue Country*. Berkeley, Calif.: Ten Speed Press, 2005.

Engelhardt, Elizabeth S. D. "Stories from the Archie Family." In *Republic of Barbecue*, edited by Elizabeth S. D. Engelhardt, 30–33. Austin: University of Texas, 2009.

Essig, Mark. *Lesser Beasts: A Snout-to-Tail History of the Humble Pig*. New York: Basic Books, 2015.

Evans, Albert Gallatin. "Frontier Cookery." *New England Kitchen*, Aug. 1895, 217–18.

Faulkner, Audrey, et al. *When I Was Comin' Up: An Oral History of Aged Blacks*. Hamden, Conn.: Archon Books, 1982.

Ferguson, Sheila. *Soul Food: Classic Cuisine from the Deep South*. New York: Grove, 1994.

Ferry, R. H. "The Boar's Head, or Pig-Eating at Christmas." *Wine and Food*, Winter 1954, 252–54.

Fine, Barbara E. "Publisher's Letter." *On the Grill*, July/Aug. 1996, 4.

Fisher, Mrs. Abby. *What Mrs. Fisher Knows about Old Southern Cooking: Soups, Pickles, Preserves, Etc.* 1881. Facsimile ed. Bedford, Mass.: Applewood Books, 1995.

Fox-Genovese, Elizabeth. *Within the Plantation Household: Black and White Women of the Old South*. Chapel Hill: University of North Carolina Press, 1988.

Fulk, Marion. "It's His Birthday, but Daddy Bruce Does the Giving at a Barbecue for Thousands." *Arkansas Gazette* (Little Rock), Feb. 13, 1984, 1B.

Garner, Bob. *North Carolina Barbecue: Flavored by Time*. Winston Salem, N.C.: John F. Blair, 1996.

Genovese, Eugene D. *Roll, Jordan, Roll: The World the Slaves Made*. New York: Pantheon, 1974.

Gibbons, Lulu. *Indian Recipes from Cherokee Indians of Eastern Oklahoma*. Muskogee, Okla.: Hoffman, [1966].

Glassner, Barry. "Where Is the World's Best Barbecue?" *Sepia*, Aug. 1975, 17–22.

Grant, Billie Arlene. *Daddy Bruce Randolph: The Pied Piper of Denver*. Aurora, Colo.: Accent Advantage, 1986.

Grisham, Cindy. *A Savory History of Arkansas Delta Food*. Charleston, S.C.: American Palate, 2013.

Guillen, Dina, Michelle Lowrey, Maria Everly, and Gretchen Bernsdoff. *The Plank Grilling Cookbook*. Seattle, Wash.: Sasquatch Books, 2006.

Halliburton, R., Jr. *Red over Black: Black Slavery among the Cherokee Indians*. Westport, Conn.: Greenwood, 1977.

Harris, Jessica B. *Beyond Gumbo: Creole Fusion Food from the Atlantic Rim*. New York: Simon and Schuster, 2003.

———. "Caribbean Connection." In *Cornbread Nation 2: The United States of Barbecue*, edited by Lolis Eric Elie, 16–18. Chapel Hill: University of North Carolina Press, 2004.

———. *The Welcome Table: African American Heritage Cooking*. New York: Fireside Books, 1995.

Harvey, Linda Ruth, Jenny Von Hohenstraeten, and Mary Jo Fostina. *Colorado's Gourmet Gold: Cookbook of Recipes from Popular Colorado Restaurants*. Denver: Laika, 1980.

Hayes, Bob. *The Black American Travel Guide*. San Francisco: Straight Arrow Books, 1971.

Haynes, Joseph. *Virginia Barbecue: A History*. Charleston, S.C.: American Palate, 2016.

Hendrix, Janey B. *Traditional Cherokee Food*. Park Hill, Okla.: Cross-Cultural Education Center, 1982.

High, Lake E., Jr. *A History of South Carolina Barbecue*. Charleston, S.C.: American Palate, 2013.

Hill, Mrs. Annabella P. *Mrs. Hill's New Cook Book*. New York: G. W. Carleton, 1872.

The Indian Cook Book. Tulsa: Indian Women's Club of Tulsa, Oklahoma, 1933.

Jackson, James. "Do Racketeers Really Rule America?" *Baltimore Afro-American*, May 3, 1930, 11.

Jarmon, Rufus. "Dixie's Most Disputed Dish." In *Cornbread Nation 2: The United States of Barbecue*, edited by Lolis Eric Elie, 37–47. Chapel Hill: University of North Carolina Press, 2004.

Jeffries, Bob. *Soul Food Cook Book*. Indianapolis, Ind.: Bobbs-Merrill, 1969.

Jehlen, Myra, and Michael Warner, eds. *The English Literatures of America, 1500–1800*. New York: Routledge, 1997.

Joffe, Natalie F., Ph.D., and Tomannie Thompson Walker, M.S. *Some Food Patterns of Negroes in the United States of America and Their Relationship to Wartime Problems of Food and Nutrition*. Prepared for the Committee on Food Habits. Washington, D.C.: National Research Council, n.d.

John, Philip Hayab, and Aquilina Mawadza. *Hausa-English/English-Hausa Dictionary & Phrasebook*. New York: Hippocrene Books, 2018.

Johnson, Charles Spurgeon. *Patterns of Negro Segregation*. London: Victor Gollancz, 1944.

Johnston, Josée, and Shyon Baumann. *Foodies: Democracy and Distinction in the Gourmet Foodscape*. 2nd ed. New York: Routledge, 2015.

Jones, Sam, and Daniel Vaughn. *Whole Hog BBQ: The Gospel of Carolina Barbecue with Recipes from Skylight Inn and Sam Jones BBQ*. Berkeley: Ten Speed Press, 2019.

Jordan, Winthrop D. *White Over Black: American Attitudes Toward the Negro 1550–1812*. Baltimore: Penguin Books, 1973.

"Juneteenth." *Ebony*, June 1951, 30.

Kail, Tony. *Meat, Fire, Wood: The Survival of West Tennessee BBQ*. Published by the author, 2011.

Kardon, Janet. "Within Our Shores: Diverse Craft Revivals and Survivals." In *Revivals! Diverse Traditions, 1920–1945: The History of Twentieth-Century American Craft*, edited by Janet Kardon, 22–30. New York: Harry N. Abrams, 1994.

Keeble, John Bell. *Proceedings of the American Institute of Architects*. Nashville, Tenn.: AIA, 1919.

Kemble, Frances Anne. *Journal of a Residence on a Georgian Plantation in 1838–1839*. Athens: University of Georgia Press, 1984.

Klein, Herbert, S. "Anglicanism, Catholicism, and the Negro Slave." *Comparative Studies in Society and History* 8, no. 3 (1966): 295–327.

Knauth, Percy. "The Roast That Got the Judges Off the Hook." *Sports Illustrated*, July 20, 1964.

Koch, Alexander, et al. "Earth System Impacts of the European Arrival and Great Dying in the Americas after 1492." *Quaternary Science Reviews* 207 (Mar. 2019): 13–36.

Kocurek, Carly A. "Drinking Texas History." In *Republic of Barbecue*, edited by Elizabeth S. D. Engelhardt, 22–29. Austin: University of Texas, 2009.

Kovacik, Charles F. "Eating Out in South Carolina's Cities: The Last Fifty Years." *North American Culture* 4, no. 1 (1988): 53–64.

Kreck, Carol. "Daddy Loves His Barbecue." *Denver Post*, Sept. 20, 1978, AA10.

Kruse, Nancy. "Chains Talk Turkey to Consumers." *Nation's Restaurant News*, Oct. 15, 2013.

Lee, Trymaine. "A Vast Wealth Gap, Driven by Segregation, Redlining, Evictions and Exclusion, Separates Black and White America." *New York Times Magazine*, Aug. 14, 2019. https://www.nytimes.com/interactive/2019/08/14/magazine/racial-wealth-gap.html.

Levy, Walter. "Some Like It Raw: Buffalo Cookery and Foodways in America." In *Wild Food: Proceedings of the Oxford Symposium on Food and Cookery, 2004*, edited by Richard Hosking, 202–8. Devon, U.K.: Prospect Books, 2006.

Lewicki, Tadeusz. *West African Food in the Middle Ages: According to Arabic Sources*. London: Cambridge University Press, 1974.

"Life in the 'Promised Land': African-American Migrants in Northern Cities, 1916–1940." *Art to Zoo* (Smithsonian Institution, Office of Elementary and Secondary Education), Dec. 1990.

Linderman, Frank B. *American: The Life Story of a Great Indian*. New York: John Day, 1931.

Littlefield, Daniel F., Jr. *The Cherokee Freedmen: From Emancipation to American Citizenship*. Westport, Conn.: Greenwood, 1978.

"Living: Regional Food." *Vogue*, Aug. 1, 1947, 144.

Loeb, August. "In Harlem New Frontiers Await the Gourmet." *New York Times*, Jan. 8, 1939, 110.

Loguen, Jermain W. *The Rev. J. W. Loguen, as a Slave and as a Freeman; A Narrative of Real Life*. Syracuse, N.Y.: J. G. K. Truair, 1859.

Maclin, Edward M. "The Changing Landscape of Mid-South Barbecue." In *The Slaw and the Slow Cooked: Culture and Barbecue in the Mid-South*, edited by James R. Veteto and Edward M. Maclin, 107–16. Nashville, Tenn.: Vanderbilt University Press, 2012.

Major, Clarence, ed. *Juba to Jive*. New York: Penguin Books, 1994.

Marshall, John. "Traditional Barbecue Methodology in Hickman County Kentucky: Woody and Will Smith." *Mid-America Folklore* 11, no. 1 (Spring 1983): 21–28.

Mason, John. *Onje Fun Orisa (Food for the Gods)*. 3rd ed. New York: Yoruba Theological Archministry, 1981.

McCulloch-Williams, Martha. *Dishes and Beverages of the Old South*. New York: McBride, Nast, 1913.

McGill, Ralph. "What's Wrong with Southern Cooking?" *Saturday Evening Post*, Mar. 26, 1949, 38–39, 102–3, 105.

Milanich, Jerald T. "The Devil in the Details." *Archaeology* 58, no. 3 (May/June 2005): 26–31.

Miller, Adrian, *Soul Food: The Surprising Story of an American Cuisine, One Plate at a Time*. Chapel Hill: University of North Carolina Press, 2013.

Miller, Tim. *Barbecue: A History*. Lanham, Md.: Rowman and Littlefield, 2014.

The Mission Cook Book. Los Angeles: Woman's Mite Missionary Society of the West Side AME Mission, 1923.

Moss, Robert F. *Barbecue: The History of an American Institution*. Tuscaloosa: University of Alabama Press, 2010.

———. "The History of Barbecue in the Mid-South Region." In *The Slaw and the Slow Cooked: Culture and Barbecue in the Mid-South*, edited by James R. Veteto and Edward M. Maclin, 25–42. Nashville, Tenn.: Vanderbilt University Press, 2012.

Mullen, Frank. "Daddy Bruce, Denver's Rib Royalty." *Rocky Mountain Business Journal*, Sept. 13, 1982, 10–11.

Nabhan, Gary. "From Coa to Barbacoa to Barbecue." In *The Slaw and the Slow Cooked: Culture and Barbecue in the Mid-South*, edited by James R. Veteto and Edward M. Maclin, vii–x. Nashville, Tenn.: Vanderbilt University Press, 2012.

"Nat Turner's Insurrection." *Atlantic Monthly*, Aug. 1861, 173–87.

"New Open Pit Barbecue Sauce Is Versatile; Can Play Many Roles." *Chicago Defender*, Oct. 22, 1957, 16.

Newman, Paul. *A Hausa-English Dictionary*. New Haven, Conn.: Yale University Press, 2007.

"North Carolina." *Philadelphia Inquirer*, Aug. 8, 1963, 5.

"Opens Fifth Barbecue Shack." *Jet*, Nov. 1, 1951, 24.

Opie, Frederick Douglass. *Hog and Hominy: Soul Food from Africa to America*. New York: Columbia University Press, 2008.

———. *Zora Neale Hurston on Florida Food: Recipes, Remedies, and Simple Pleasures*. Charleston, S.C.: American Palate, 2015.

Osofsky, Gilbert. *Harlem: The Making of a Ghetto: Negro New York, 1890–1930*. New York: Harper and Row, 1966.

Osseo-Asare, Fran. *Food Culture in Sub-Saharan Africa*. Westport, CT: Greenwood, 2005.

Perry, Charles. "A Mystery Begins in the Backyard." *Los Angeles Times*, July 31, 2002, H1.

Perry, George Sessions. *Texas: A World in Itself*. New York: Whittlesey House, 1942.

Pickering, Stephen. "Green, Harry S." In *The Kentucky African American Encyclopedia*, edited by Karen Cotton McDaniel, John A. Hardin, and Gerald L. Smith, 214. Lexington: University of Kentucky Press, 2015.

Pierce, Joseph A. *Negro Business and Business Education: Their Present and Prospective Development*. 1947. Reprint. New York: Plenum, 1995.

Pierson, Rev. Hamilton W., D.D. *In the Brush: Old-Time Social, Political, and Religious Life in the Southwest*. New York: D. Appleton, 1881.

Pillsbury, Richard, ed. *Geography*. Vol. 2 of *The New Encyclopedia of Southern Culture*, edited by Charles Reagan Wilson. Chapel Hill: University of North Carolina Press, 2006.

Pinkard, Ophelia Taylor. "Juneteenth." *Journal of the Afro-American Historical and Genealogical Society*, Spring 1984, 11–12.

Poston, T. R. "Harlem Shadows." *Pittsburgh Courier*, Oct. 11, 1930, A1.

Pratt, Lonni Collins, with Father Daniel Homan, OSB. *Radical Hospitality: Benedict's Way of Love*. Brewster, Mass.: Paraclete, 2011.

Puckett, Susan. *Eat Drink Delta: A Hungry Traveler's Journey through the Soul of the South*. Athens: University of Georgia Press, 2013.

Raine, Carolyn. *A Woodland Feast: Native American Foodways of the 17th and 18th Centuries*. Camden, Me.: Penobscot Press, 1997.

Randolph, Mary. *The Virginia House-wife*. Washington, D.C.: Davis and Force, 1824.

Reed, John Shelton. *Barbecue*. Chapel Hill: University of North Carolina Press, 2016.

Reed, John Shelton, and Dale Volberg Reed. *Holy Smoke: The Big Book of North Carolina Barbecue*. Chapel Hill: University of North Carolina Press, 2008.

Reidy, Joseph P. *From Slavery to Agrarian Capitalism in the Cotton Plantation South: Central Georgia, 1800–1880*. Chapel Hill: University of North Carolina Press, 1992.

Ryan, Ed. "Spitting Mad." *Louisville Courier Journal*, July 15, 1977, B3.

Savela, Martin. "The Neck Bone's Connected to the Backbone." *Chicago Tribune*, Nov. 22, 1970, J34.

Schlichting, Darcy Cooper, and Thomas J. Noel. "Ill Smelling Bones and a Bad Reputation." *Colorado Heritage*, Autumn 2004, 32–46.

Seale, Bobby. *Barbeque'n with Bobby*. Berkeley, Calif.: Ten Speed Press, 1988.

Seattle Indian Services Commission. *Going Native: American Indian Cookery*. Seattle, Wash.: Seattle Indian Services Commission, 1991.

Sharpe, Bill. "Culinary Genius Is Imported to Concoct Barbecue for YDC Convention in Winston Salem." *High Point (N.C.) Enterprise*, Sept. 7, 1941, 3.

Silva, Jill Wendholt. "True Pitmasters: The Jones Sisters Are Rare Gems in a Man's World." *Kansas City (Mo.) Star*, Aug. 30, 2016.

Smith, Andrew F. *Pure Ketchup: A History of America's National Condiment*. Washington, D.C.: Smithsonian Institution Press, 2001.

———. *The Tomato in America: Early History, Culture, and Cookery*. Urbana: University of Illinois Press, 1994.

Smith, Griffin, Jr. "Barbecue." *Atlantic Monthly*, Mar. 1975, 37.

———. "The World's Best Barbecue Is in Taylor, Texas; Or, Is It Lockhart?" *Texas Monthly*, Apr. 1973, 38–43.

Smith, Stephen. "The Rhetoric of Barbecue: A Southern Rite and Ritual." In *Cornbread Nation 2: The United States of Barbecue*, edited by Lolis Eric Elie, 61–68. Chapel Hill: University of North Carolina Press, 2004.

South Carolina: A Guide to the Palmetto State. New York: Oxford University Press, n.d.

Staten, Vince, and Greg Johnson. *Real Barbecue: The Classic Barbecue Guide to the Best Joints across the USA*. Guilford, Conn.: Globe Pequot, 2007.

Stavely, Keith, and Kathleen Fitzgerald. *America's Founding Food: The Story of New England Cooking*. Chapel Hill: University of North Carolina Press, 2004.

Steingarten, Jeffrey. *The Man Who Ate Everything*. New York: Vintage Books, 1998.

Stern, Jane and Michael. *Roadfood*. New York: Random House, 1978.

Stimson, Kate. "The Three Harlems and What Is Happening to Them." *Harper's Magazine*, Mar. 1968, 63.

Stovall, Tyler. *Paris Noir: African Americans in the City of Light*. Boston: Houghton Mifflin, 1996.

Stubb's Legendary Kitchen with Kate Heyhoe. *The Stubb's Bar-B-Q Cookbook*. Hoboken, N.J.: John Wiley and Sons, 2007.

Stullken, Gerhard. *My Experiences on the Plains*. Wichita, Kans.: Grit Printery, 1913.

Tartan, Beth. *North Carolina and Old Salem Cookery*. New 4th ed. Kingsport, Tenn.: Kingsport Press, 1974.

Taylor, Joe Gray. "The Food of the New South." *Georgia Review*, Spring 1966, 9–28.

Texas: A Guide to the Lone Star State. Compiled by the Workers of the Writers' Program of the Works Progress Administration in the State of Texas. 2nd printing. Texas State Highway Commission, 1940.

Thiam, Pierre. *Yolele! Recipes from the Heart of Senegal*. New York: Lake Isle Press, 2008.

Tipton-Martin, Toni. *The Jemima Code: Two Centuries of African American Cookbooks*. Austin: University of Texas Press, 2015.

Tolbert, Frank X. *A Bowl of Red*. Dallas: Taylor, 1988.

———. "Indians' Big Chief Is a Barbecue Artist, Too." *Dallas Morning News*, Sept. 2, 1971, 23.

Trillin, Calvin. "No! One of the World's Foremost Authorities on Ribs, Cheeseburgers, French Fries, and Frosty Malts Takes a Gourmet Tour of Kansas City." *Playboy*, Apr. 1972, 107–8, 110, 208–9.

———. *The Tummy Trilogy*. New York: Farrar, Straus and Giroux, 1994.

Tymas, Scotta. *Soul Cooking*. New York: Criscot, 1968.

Ulmer, Mary, and Samuel E. Beck, eds. *Cherokee Cooklore*. N.p.: Stephens Press, 1951.

Vaughn, Daniel. "What Should We Call the Barbecue Greats?" *Texas Monthly*, Aug. 2018.

Villas, James. "Big on Pig." *Bon Appetit*, July 2003, 74–78.

Waddles, Rev. Charleszetta. *The Mother Waddles Soul Food Cookbook*. 2nd ed. Detroit, Mich.: Perpetual Soul Saving Mission for All Nations, 1970.

Walsh, Robb. *Barbecue Crossroads: Notes and Recipes from a Southern Odyssey*. Austin: University of Texas, 2013.

———. "Texas Barbecue in Black and White." In *Cornbread Nation 2: The United States of Barbecue*, edited by Lolis Eric Elie, 48–60. Chapel Hill: University of North Carolina Press, 2004.

Warnes, Andrew. *Savage Barbecue: Race, Culture, and the Invention of America's First Food*. Athens: University of Georgia Press, 2008.

Watkins, Mel. *On the Real Side: Laughing, Lying and Signifying—The Underground Tradition of African-American Humor That Transformed American Culture, from Slavery to Richard Pryor*. New York: Touchstone Books, 1995.

Watriss, Wendy. "Celebrate Freedom: Juneteenth." *Southern Exposure* 5, no. 1 (1977): 80–81.

Wells, Carolyn. *Barbecue Greats, Memphis Style: Great Restaurants, Great Recipes, Great Personalities*. Kansas City, Mo.: Pig Out Publications, 1989.

West, Richard. "Happy Trails to You." *Texas Monthly*, June 1978, 103–11.

Wheeler, Colonel Homer W. *The Frontier Trail; or, From Cowboy to Colonel*. Los Angeles: Times-Mirror Press, 1923.

Wiggins, William H., Jr. "From Galveston to Washington: Charting Juneteenth's Freedom Trail." In *Jubilation! African American Celebrations in the Southeast*, edited by William H. Wiggins Jr. and Douglas DeNatale. Columbia: McKissick Museum, University of South Carolina, [1993].

———. "Juneteenth: A Red Spot Day on the Texas Calendar." In *Juneteenth Texas: Essays in African American Folklore*, edited by Francis E. Abernethy, Patrick B. Mullen, and Alan B. Govenar. Publications of the Texas Folklore Society, 54, 1996.

———. *O Freedom! Afro-American Emancipation Celebrations*. Knoxville: University of Tennessee Press, 1990.

Worgul, Doug. *The Grand Barbecue: A Celebration of the History, Places, Personalities, and Techniques of Kansas City Barbecue*. Kansas City, Mo.: Kansas City Star Books, 2001.

Work, Monroe, N. "The Negro in Business Enterprise." *Southern Workman* 47, no. 5 (May 1917): 304–9.

Workers of the Writers' Program of the Work Projects Administration in the State of Virginia. *The Negro in Virginia*. Winston-Salem: John F. Blair, 1994.

Zanger, Mark H. "African American Food: Since Emancipation." In *The Oxford Encyclopedia of Food and Drink in America*, edited by Andrew F. Smith, 10–11. New York: Oxford University Press, 2007.

Zobel, Kathleen. "Hog Heaven: Barbecue in the South." *Southern Exposure* 5 (Summer and Fall 1977): 58–61.

WEBSITES

Abernathy, Jessie. "Native Sun News: Famous Dave Reflects on Career of Success." *Indianz*, Feb. 17, 2012. http://www.indianz.com/News/2012/004652.asp.

Albala, Ken. "What Does Barbecue Tell Us About Race?" Review of *Savage Barbecue: Race, Culture, and the Invention of America's First Food*, by Andrew Warnes. *Commonplace* 11, no. 3 (Apr. 2011). http://commonplace.online/article/barbecue-tell-us-race.

"American Indian Records in the National Archives." National Archives. n.d. https://www.archives.gov/research/native-americans.

Armstein, Sylvia. "Visual Arts." *Oxford African American Studies Center*. n.d.

http://www.oxfordaasc.com.dclibrary.idm.oclc.org/article/opr/t0003/e0448
?hi=8&highlight=1&from=quick&pos=1#match.

"Barbeque." Jan. 18, 2007. https://www.urbandictionary.com/define.php?term
=Barbeque.

Bates, Angela. "Ernestine Caroline VanDuvall." *Oxford African American Studies
Center*. n.d. http://www.oxfordaasc.com.dclibrary.idm.oclc.org/article/opr
/t0001/e3962?hi=3&highlight=1&from=quick&pos=25#match.

Biblica, Inc. *The New International Version Holy Bible*. 2011. https://www.theniv
bible.com.

Bohnert, Dyan. "Mary John." *CALS Encyclopedia of Arkansas*. n.d. https://
encyclopediaofarkansas.net/entries/mary-john-4367/.

Bolois, Justin. "The Most Underrated BBQ in Kansas City." *First We Feast*, Apr. 1,
2015. https://firstwefeast.com/eat/2015/04/the-most-underrated-bbq-in
-kansas-city.

Bos, Mecca. "Dave Anderson Says Going Public 'Was the Worst Decision I Ever
Made.'" *Citypages*, Aug. 21, 2015. http://www.citypages.com/restaurants
/dave-anderson-says-selling-famous-daves-was-the-worst-decision-i-ever
-made-7584585.

Butterfly, Kitchen. "Nigerian Beef Suya." *Food52*, June 7, 2011. https://food52.com
/recipes/12359-nigerian-beef-suya.

Camacho, Michelle Madsen. "Mother Waddles." *Oxford African American Studies
Center*. n.d. http://www.oxfordaasc.com.dclibrary.idm.oclc.org/article/opr
/t0001/e3969?hi=5&highlight=1&from=quick&pos=1#match.

Carriker, Bob. "Southern Boudin Trail." *Southern Foodways*, Apr. 13, 2006. https://
www.southernfoodways.org/oral-history/southern-boudin-trail.

Carter, Kent. "Dawes Commission." *The Encyclopedia of Oklahoma History and
Culture*. n.d. https://www.okhistory.org/publications/enc/entry.php?entry
=DA018.

Cason, Moe. "Moe Cason: Delicious Charleston BBQ Ribs." *Reynold's Kitchens*.
n.d. https://www.reynoldskitchens.com/moe-cason-delicious-charleston
-bbq-ribs.

Chef Kenny Gilbert. "About." https://www.chefkennygilbert.com/about.

Clancy, Michael. "It's a Woman's World." *Village Voice*, Dec. 18, 2007. https://www
.villagevoice.com/2007/12/18/its-a-womans-world.

"Colonial Policy, British." *Encyclopedia.com*, updated Sept. 12, 2020. https://www
.encyclopedia.com/history/dictionaries-thesauruses-pictures-and-press
-releases/colonial-policy-british.

Davies, James Giago. "A Brilliant Idea Helped Make Chickasaw Man a
Billionaire." *Native Sun News Today*, May 22, 2019. https://www.nativesunnews
.today/articles/a-brilliant-idea-helped-make-chickasaw-man-a-billionaire.

DeBerry, Stephen. "The Rise of Entrepreneurial Hotbeds on 'the Other Side
of the Tracks.'" *Medium*, Nov. 2, 2015. https://medium.com/@TheCenter
/the-rise-of-entrepreneurial-hotbeds-on-the-other-side-of-the-tracks
-9651e1bde120.

"Dibi." *Eat Your World*. n.d. https://eatyourworld.com/destinations/africa
/senegal/dakar/what_to_eat/dibi.

Dippie, Brian W. "American Indians: The Image of the Indian." *TeacherServe, National Humanities Center*. http://nationalhumanitiescenter.org/tserve /nattrans/ntecoindian/essays/indimage.htm.

Dougan, Michael B. "Food and Foodways." *CALS Encyclopedia of Arkansas*. n.d. https://encyclopediaofarkansas.net/entries/food-and-foodways-4032/.

Dunn, Elizabeth Gunnison. "How to Make Some Really Famous Ribs (Without a Smoker)." *Esquire*, July 26, 2011. https://www.esquire.com/food-drink/food /recipes/a10621/famous-daves-ribs-recipe-072611.

"England." *Encyclopaedia Britannica*, n.d. https://www.britannica.com/topic /democracy/England.

Equal Justice Initiative. *Lynching in America: Confronting the Legacy of Racial Terror*. 3rd ed. n.d. https://lynchinginamerica.eji.org/report.

Everett, Dianna. "Indian Territory." *The Encyclopedia of Oklahoma History and Culture*. https://www.okhistory.org/publications/enc/entry.php?entry =IN018.

"Examining the Role of the Black Preacher." *News & Notes, National Public Radio*, July 9, 2007. https://www.npr.org/templates/story/story.php?storyId =11828359.

Fondevila, Javi. "Goodwill: Meaning, Features and Types." *Holded*, Oct. 9, 2018. https://www.holded.com/blog/goodwill-meaning-features-types.

"Food Network Heats Up Grill for This Holiday." *Orlando Sentinel*, May 26, 2004. https://www.orlandosentinel.com/news/os-xpm-2004-05-26-0405260133 -story.html.

Fuhrman, Elizabeth. "A New Spin on Barbecue." *National Provisioner/Independent Processor*, Mar. 15, 2019. https://www.provisioneronline.com/articles/107698 -a-new-spin-on-barbecue.

———. "Barbecue Bonanza." *National Provisioner/Independent Processor*, Mar. 17, 2016. https://www.provisioneronline.com/articles/103025-barbecue-bonanza.

———. "Barbecue Trends: Low-and-Slow Flies High." *National Provisioner/ Independent Processor*, Mar. 13, 2018. https://www.provisioneronline.com /articles/105986-barbecue-trends-low-and-slow-flies-high.

Gladwell, Malcolm. "The Ketchup Conundrum." *New Yorker*, Sept. 6, 2004. https:// www.newyorker.com/magazine/2004/09/06/the-ketchup-conundrum.

Goldwyn, Meathead. "Don't Try to Cook the Way They Cook in BBQ Competitions at Home!" *AmazingRibs.com*, n.d. https://amazingribs.com/bbq -and-grilling-competitions/dont-try-cook-way-they-cook-bbq-competitions.

Green, Amanda. "A Brief History of the BBQ Grill." *Popular Mechanics*, Aug. 29, 2012. https://www.popularmechanics.com/technology/gadgets/a7855 /a-brief-history-of-the-bbq-grill-11000790.

"Guy Fieri." American Royal Barbecue Hall of Fame, 2012. http://www.american royal.com/wp-content/uploads/2019/05/BBQ-HOF-Fieri-Bio.pdf.

Harriot, Michael. "@michaelharriot." *Twitter*, Dec. 13, 2019. https://twitter.com /michaelharriot/status/1205695846391721986.

"Henry Ford." American Royal Barbecue Hall of Fame, 2012. http://www .americanroyal.com/wp-content/uploads/2019/05/BBQ-HOF-Ford-Bio.pdf.

"The History." *Robinson's No. 1 Ribs*. http://www.rib1.com/about.html.

History.com editors. "The Great Migration." *History.com*, updated Jan. 16, 2020. https://www.history.com/topics/black-history/great-migration.

Jackson, Lauren Michele. "The White Lies of Craft Culture." *Eater*, Aug. 17, 2017. https://www.eater.com/2017/8/17/16146164/the-whiteness-of-artisanal -food-craft-culture.

"Johnny Trigg." American Royal Barbecue Hall of Fame, 2012. http://www .americanroyal.com/wp-content/uploads/2019/05/BBQ-HOF-Trigg-Bio.pdf.

Johnson, Myles E. "To Kill the White Gaze." *Afropunk*, May 17, 2019. https:// afropunk.com/2019/05/to-kill-a-mockingbird-white-gaze-broadway-revival.

"Juneteenth." *Waymarking.com*, n.d. http://www.waymarking.com/waymarks /WMT25C_Juneteenth.

Komolafe, Yewande. "Yewande Komolafe's 10 Essential Nigerian Recipes." *New York Times*, June 26, 2019. https://www.nytimes.com/2019/06/24/dining /nigerian-food-yewande-komolafe.html.

Korfhage, Matthew. "Snoop Dogg's Uncle Blames Racism for Fire That Closed His Portland Rib Shack." *Willamette Week*, May 8, 2017. https://www.wweek.com /restaurants/2017/05/08/snoop-doggs-uncle-blames-racism-for-fire-that -closed-his-rib-shack.

Lawrence, Philip, OSB. "Chapter 57: The Artisans of the Monastery." Monastery of Christ in the Desert, n.d. https://christdesert.org/prayer/rule-of-st -benedict/chapter-57-the-artisans-of-the-monastery/.

Lee, Trymaine. "A Vast Wealth Gap, Driven by Segregation, Redlining, Evictions and Exclusion, Separates Black and White America." *New York Times Magazine*, Aug. 14, 2019. https://www.nytimes.com/interactive/2019/08/14/magazine /racial-wealth-gap.html.

McClusky, Mark. "Grilling over Gas Is Objectively, Scientifically Better Than Grilling over Charcoal." *Wired*, May 24, 2019, https://www.wired.com/2013 /07/gas-grilling-is-objectively-scientifically-better-than-charcoal.

McDonald, Carla. "The Salonnière 100: 2018." *Timothy Corrigan*, 2018. http:// www.timothy-corrigan.com/blogs/2018/03/20/490-the-salonniere.

McKay, Brett and Kate. "Are You Hep to the Jive? The Cab Calloway Hepster Dictionary." *Art of Manliness*, Sept. 25, 2008. https://www.artofmanliness .com/articles/are-you-hep-to-the-jive-the-cab-calloway-hepster-dictionary.

"Meet Dave." *Famous Dave's*, n.d. https://www.famousdaves.com/our-barbeque /meet-dave.

Min, Sarah. "Brisket Prices Soaring on Barbecue Popularity." *CBS News*, Aug. 2, 2019. https://www.cbsnews.com/news/brisket-prices-soar-on-growing -appetite-for-barbecue.

Moe Cason BBQ. n.d. https://moecasonbbq.com.

Moss, Robert F. "15 Most Influential People in Barbecue History." *Southern Living*, n.d. https://www.southernliving.com/bbq/15-most-influential-people-in -barbecue-history.

———. "Now's the Time to Eat Smoked Mullet, a.k.a. Southern Lox." *Saveur*, Nov. 2, 2016. https://www.saveur.com/southern-florida-smoked-mullet-fish.

Ocejo, Richard E. "On His Book *Masters of Craft: Old Jobs in the New Urban*

Economy." *Rorotoko*, July 18, 2017. http://rorotoko.com/interview/20170719
_ocejo_richard_on_book_masters_craft_old_jobs_new_urban_economy.

Olson, Kathy Heflin. "Harry Green: Daviess County's Original Pit Master," Feb.
24, 2019. https://www.owensborotimes.com/life/food/2019/02/harry-green
-daviess-countys-original-pit-master.

Pang, Kevin. "Chicago Is a City Divided by Barbecue." *Saveur*, Feb. 8, 2018.
https://www.saveur.com/chicago-barbecue.

Perkins, Tom. "Does Detroit's Food Revival Leave the City's Black Residents
Behind?" *Civil Eats*, Aug. 29, 2017. https://civileats.com/2017/08/29/does
-detroits-food-revival-leave-the-citys-black-residents-behind.

Phippen, Weston, J. "Kill Every Buffalo You Can! Every Buffalo Dead Is an Indian
Gone." *Atlantic*, May 13, 2016. https://www.theatlantic.com/national/archive
/2016/05/the-buffalo-killers/482349.

Raichlen, Steven. "Southern Barbecue with a Fiery Dip and a Deep History." *New
York Times*, Oct. 23, 2018. https://www.nytimes.com/2018/10/23/dining
/monroe-county-pork-steaks-bbq.html.

Reed, John Shelton. "Mass Barbecue Is the Invasive Species of Our Culinary
Times." *American Conservative*, Sept. 3, 2019. https://www.theamerican
conservative.com/articles/mass-barbecue-is-the-invasive-species-of-our
-culinary-times.

Reese, Linda. "Freedmen." *The Encyclopedia of Oklahoma History and Culture*,
https://www.okhistory.org/publications/enc/entry.php?entry=FR016.

Reid, J. C. "Barbecue Lists Are Wildly Popular — and Hard to Get Right." *Houston
Chronicle*, May 19, 2017. https://www.houstonchronicle.com/entertainment
/restaurants-bars/bbq/article/Barbecue-lists-are-wildly-popular-and-hard
-to-11160014.php.

Richman, Alan. "Searching for BBQ Bliss, the Pickings Are Easy." *People*, Aug. 28,
1989. https://people.com/archive/searching-for-bbq-bliss-the-pickings-are
-easy-vol-32-no-9.

Rountree, Helen C. "Uses of Domesticated Animals by Early Virginia
Indians." *Encyclopedia Virginia*. n.d. https://www.encyclopediavirginia.org
/domesticated_animals_during_the_pre-colonial_era.

Rupersburg, Nicole. "America's Most Influential BBQ Pitmasters and
Personalities." *Fox News*, July 28, 2015. https://www.foxnews.com/food
-drink/americas-most-influential-bbq-pitmasters-and-personalities.

Russo, Carla Herreria. "Woman Calls Police on Black Family for BBQing at a Lake
in Oakland." *Huffington Post*, May 11, 2018. https://www.huffpost.com/entry
/woman-calls-police-oakland-barbecue_n_5af50125e4b00d7e4c18f741.

Sances, Michael W., and Hye Young You. "Who Pays for Government? Descriptive
Representation and Exploitative Revenue Sources." *Journal of Politics* 79, no. 3
(July 2017): 1090–94. https://doi.org/10.1086/691354.

Schwenneker, Don. "Ed 'The Pitmaster' Mitchell's Eastern NC Turkey." *Big Recipes
by Don Schwenneker* (blog), Nov. 10, 2011. https://abc11.typepad.com/big
_recipes_by_don_schwen/2011/11/ed-the-pitmaster-mitchells-turkey-spices
.html.

"Scott's Barbecue Sauce." n.d. https://www.scottsbarbecuesauce.com/recipes.

Shefveland, Kristalyn. "Indian Enslavement in Virginia." *Encyclopedia Virginia*. n.d. https://www.encyclopediavirginia.org/Indian_Enslavement_in_Virginia.

Sietsema, Robert. "New York Barbecue: A Thumbnail History." *Eater New York*, June 13, 2016. https://ny.eater.com/2016/6/13/11893476/nyc-barbecue-history.

Smith, Ben. "An Unlikely Echo." *Politico*, Jan. 27, 2008. https://www.politico.com/blogs/ben-smith/2008/01/an-unlikely-echo-005624.

Snyder, Garrett. "How Chicken Sausage Links Became a Centerpiece to South L.A.'s Black Food Culture." *Los Angeles Times*, May 27, 2019. https://www.latimes.com/food/story/2019-08-27/chicken-sausage-south-los-angeles.

Twachtman, Jack. "Bold Bites: Finding Florida BBQ." *Void*, June 12, 2018. https://voidlive.com/finding-florida-bbq.

Twitty, Michael. "The Colonial Roots of Southern Barbecue: Re-Creating the Birth of an American Culinary Staple." *Afroculinaria*, July 14, 2012. https://afroculinaria.com/2012/07/14/the-colonial-roots-of-southern-barbecue-re-creating-the-birth-of-an-american-culinary-staple.

Vaughn, Daniel. "Grease Balls of Southeast Texas." *Southern Foodways*, Fall 2015. https://www.southernfoodways.org/grease-balls-of-southeast-texas.

———. "Interview: Robert Patillo of Patillo's Bar-B-Q." *Texas Monthly*, Apr. 8, 2015. https://www.texasmonthly.com/bbq/interview-robert-patillo-of-patillos-bar-b-q.

Walker, Daniel. "Jones Bar-B-Q Diner." *CALS Encyclopedia of Arkansas History and Culture*. n.d. https://encyclopediaofarkansas.net/entries/jones-bar-b-q-diner-8032/.

Weitz, Jared. "Why Minorities Have So Much Trouble Accessing Small Business Loans." *Forbes*, Jan. 22, 2018. https://www.forbes.com/sites/forbesfinancecouncil/2018/01/22/why-minorities-have-so-much-trouble-accessing-small-business-loans.

Williams, Aubrey. "Black-Owned Businesses on a Path to Domination." *BlackNews.com*, Feb. 12, 2019. https://www.blacknews.com/news/black-owned-businesses-on-a-path-to-domination.

Zeratsky, Katherine, R.D., L.D. "How Can Bread Be Labeled as Both White and Whole Wheat? Is White Whole-Wheat Bread a Healthy Choice?" *Mayo Clinic: Nutrition and Healthy Eating*, Jan. 18, 2020. https://www.mayoclinic.org/healthy-lifestyle/nutrition-and-healthy-eating/expert-answers/whole-wheat-bread/faq-20057999.

INDEX

Page numbers in italics refer to illustrations.